THE ARTHURIAN LEGENDS

THE ARTHURIAN LEGENDS

AN ILLUSTRATED ANTHOLOGY

SELECTED AND INTRODUCED BY RICHARD BARBER

BARNES & NOBLE
BOOKS
NEW YORK

This edition published by
Barnes & Noble, Inc., by arrangement with
Boydell & Brewer Ltd.

1993 Barnes & Noble Books

ISBN 0-88029-050-1

Printed in Slovenia

CONTENTS

ACKNOWLEDGEMENTS

I am grateful to all those who have helped to provide text or illustrations for this anthology. In particular, I should like to thank Dr David Dumville for permission to use the translation from his forthcoming edition and translation of the *Historia Brittonum* (p. 7) and Dr Michael Lapidge for his invaluable help with *The Death of Arthur*, for which he had edited the text and provided a literal translation. Any errors in the free version which appears on p. 31 are my own. The translation of Yvain is also my own; permission for the other translations has been given as follows:

Professor Gwyn Jones, C.B.E. and Mrs Mair Jones for the excerpt from *The Mabinogion*, translated by Gwyn Jones and Thomas Jones (London, J. M. Dent and Sons, 1974), pp. 109–36.

Penguin Books Ltd for the following excerpts:
Geoffrey of Monmouth, *The History of the Kings of Britain*, tr. Lewis Thorpe (1966), pp. 212–61.

Gottfried von Strassburg, *Tristan*, tr. A. T. Hatto (1960), pp. 234–68.

Sir Gawain and the Green Knight, tr. B. Stone (1959), lines 1126–2531.

David Higham Associates Ltd and the estate of T. H. White for the excerpt from *The Once and Future King* (London, Collins, 1958), pp. 52–68.

The estate of Miss M. F. Richey for the excerpt from *The Story of Parzival and the Graal* (Oxford, Basil Blackwell, 1935), pp. 128–49.

Oxford University Press and the estate of Charles Williams for 'The Crowning of Arthur' and 'Taliessin at Lancelot's Mass' from *Taliessin through Logres* (Oxford, 1938).

Acknowledgements for illustrations will be found on p. 223.

RICHARD BARBER

INTRODUCTION

The Adventures of Gawain and Lancelot.
This fourteenth century ivory casket from Paris is decorated with a mixture of scenes from two of Chrétien's romances. On the extreme left and on the right, three scenes show Gawain at the Castle of Marvels from Perceval*: he overcomes the lion which guards the entrance, and survives the test of the perilous bed, to be congratulated by three girls (right). In the second scene from left, Lancelot is shown crossing the Sword bridge (compare p. 53).*
(Metropolitan Museum, New York)

THE REAL ARTHUR · ARTHUR IN LITERATURE · THE GREAT MEDIEVAL TALES · THE NINETEENTH- AND TWENTIETH-CENTURY REVIVAL & & &

For more than eight centuries, poets and writers have been telling stories about King Arthur. From lost legends and scraps of history, from facts and folklore, they have fashioned one of the greatest epics in all literature, full of the world's splendours, heroic loves and spiritual quests. This magical and mysterious world is founded on the figure of an obscure Welsh princeling, about whom we know nothing for certain. Arthur may have been the last Roman general of Britain, the first of those Welsh guerrilla fighters who defied the English until well into the Middle Ages, or a northern prince from Scotland who was later adopted by the Welsh living in Wales. If there was a real Arthur, he lived in the sixth or seventh centuries AD; he may not even have been of royal blood, but he was acclaimed as a hero or leader. That is all that we can say with any confidence about the historical grain of sand in the poetic oyster.

But this book is not about the quest for a 'real' Arthur. It is a celebration of the 'unreal' king, of his exploits in literature, of his far-famed knights and their ladies, of all the high trappings of romance. Arthurian literature tempts one to write in purple prose; yet it is much more than an escape from reality, much more than the lines on my mother's bookplate in the first version of Arthur's story that I read, with its haunting Walter Crane plates:

Here do I sit reading old Things
of knights and Lorn Damsels while the wind sings,
O drearily sings . . .

Arthur's magic is that he is a shape-shifter; but he does so subtly and slowly, changing his form to suit the needs of each new age. It is arguable that the earliest apparently historical references to his career, in the anonymous ninth-century chronicle called *The History of the Britons*, correspond to a revival of Welsh national feeling and power, and were written to meet a demand for a hero from the past who would be an example for the present. Arthur's real fortunes were founded by a much bolder stroke of invention, however: Geoffrey of Monmouth's great imitation of history, *The History of the Kings of Britain*, written in the third decade of the twelfth century. History, for long neglected or reduced to mere chronicle, was being practised once again by English writers, taking the great classical historians of Rome as their models; and Geoffrey, seeing that there was no version of the history of Britain before and immediately after the Roman invasion, took it upon himself to make good this want. His sources are obscure; in places he used scraps of Welsh history and legend, but much of his work was pure imagination, romance in the guise of history, and nowhere more so than in his portrait of Arthur. Arthur emerges from his obscurity to become ruler of the western world, waging a series of wars which carry him, like Charlemagne, towards Rome itself, though he never reaches Rome or becomes emperor, because news of treachery at home reaches him in his hour of triumph, and he returns to meet his death in civil war.

Geoffrey's history was written in Latin, but a French version soon appeared, written for Henry II and Eleanor of Aquitaine by the Anglo-Norman poet Wace. Towards the end of the twelfth century, the English poet Layamon made his version, and many of the less sceptical historians of the period introduced Geoffrey's tales into their works, if only because they neatly filled a gap in their story. Geoffrey's success with historians, however, was nothing to his success in the literary world. The brilliant yet unknown court of King Arthur became the setting for all kinds of romances, many of them drawing on the same stock of Welsh stories, perhaps gathered from passing minstrels, that Geoffrey himself had used. Chrétien de Troyes, who worked for Eleanor of Aquitaine's daughter Marie de Champagne in the mid-twelfth century, was the first and one of the greatest of these writers: from his hand we have the first version of Lancelot's love for Arthur's queen, Guinevere, and the first mention of the Holy Grail. The Grail poem was never finished, leaving us without a clear idea of what Chrétien meant by the Grail, a mystery which was turned to good advantage by later writers.

Chrétien's poems are loosely linked by 'the court of king Arthur'. This was not enough for the writers of the thirteenth and fourteenth centuries, who now set out to tell the whole story of Arthur's career in a great series of romances which have come down to us in several versions. Already Arthur had changed his shape, from pseudo-historical king to lord of a court of heroes and lovers; now he became one of the greatest rulers the world had seen, the peer of Charlemagne and Alexander, and with his own triumph and tragedy as the heart of the cycle of stories. Geoffrey of Monmouth's version of Arthur's history contained all the necessary ingredients, hinting at Guinevere's infidelity and Arthur's mysterious end, all told in little more than bare outline. The romance writers elaborated endlessly on this, and when they had exhausted the possibilities of Arthur's own history, whole new stories were woven in. The Grail romance quickly became a central part of the cycle of tales, providing a high spiritual theme hitherto lacking; and separate romances, such as that of Tristan and Iseult, were incorporated into the cycle. Instead of taking in the new material bodily, like a patch on a cloak, the old and the new were interwoven almost inseparably, so that the storyteller could move easily from one theme to another, bringing them together like the brilliant colours of a tapestry.

For English readers, the culmination of the medieval versions of Arthur's story is Sir Thomas Malory's work, generally known as *Le Morte Darthur* from the title which William Caxton gave it when he printed it in 1485. Malory, like his contemporaries in France and Italy, edited the French manuscripts which he used as his source; but both his editing and the striking flow of his prose style were the work of a writer of genius, and it is his version that has become the Authorised Version of Arthurian legend. Throughout the sixteenth century, the romances remained popular, but the seventeenth century, pious and rational at the same time, frowned on such fripperies and fables, and Arthur's very existence, queried by a handful of doubting Thomases ever since Geoffrey of Monmouth's book first appeared, was now generally regarded as unproven. The taste for romances declined, and Arthur scarcely put in an appearance between the Restoration in 1660 and the end of the eighteenth century.

When he did reappear, it was due to the influence of the fashion for all things Gothick and medieval, and to the romantic writers such as Sir Walter Scott and Wordsworth. Yet it was only after the high tide of romanticism had passed, in the more sober atmosphere of Victoria's reign, that Arthur found his first true modern champion in Alfred Tennyson. Tennyson's *Idylls of the King* made the legends a household word in Victorian England, and a host of lesser versions followed. In Germany, a master in a different artistic field, Richard Wagner, took the stories of Tristan and Parsifal and put them into modern guise as operas. In the wake of these great works, there followed an insatiable demand for popular retellings of the original stories.

The last seventy years have seen continuing intense activity in the reworking of the Arthurian stories. In many ways they have taken the place of the classical myths which once dominated European literature, and to which poets and writers constantly referred or returned. A germ of an idea from the Grail stories gave T. S. Eliot's *The Waste Land* its title; and Arthur, Guinevere, Lancelot, Merlin and Galahad are as familiar in our literature as the gods of ancient Greece.

What follows is an attempt to give a reader new to the Arthurian legends some idea of their scope and range within the covers of a single volume. The extracts have been set out in approximate chronological order so that their development can be seen as well. Of necessity, some of the extracts are artistically unsatisfactory, bleeding chunks from a coherent, carefully planned work; but by and large romances lend themselves easily to such use, because they are made of many individual adventures linked by a theme or a personality. In the introductions, I have tried to set each piece in its context, both historical and literary – the artistic context can be seen in the largely contemporary illustrations – so that anyone who enjoys all or indeed part of this anthology can make his own exploration of the many and glittering treasures of Arthurian legend.

King Arthur as one of the Nine Worthies.
The 'Nine Worthies' were a group of heroes much portrayed in medieval art, three classical, three from the Old Testament and three from romance: Charlemagne, Arthur and Godfrey of Bouillon. This magnificent tapestry was probably made by Nicholas Bataille in Paris about 1400.
(Cloisters Collection, Metropolitan Museum, New York)

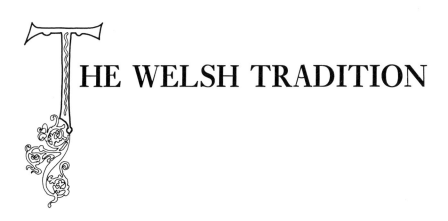

THE WELSH TRADITION

The Annals of Wales
The History of the Britons
The Life of St Carannog

ARTHUR IN HISTORY · EARLY WELSH LITERATURE · HIS GRAVE · THE SAINTS' LIVES

We know very little about the history of Britain between AD 400 and AD 600, between the ending of Roman rule and the emergence of the Saxon kingdoms. We have no contemporary histories, only traditions and rumours and the occasional voice crying in the wilderness of a writer whose works happen to survive in this or that fragment of a manuscript. Archaeology has helped us to uncover something of everyday life, even something of the broad outline of the story of the Saxon invasions; but if we want an account of people and dates, the names of the Saxon and Welsh commanders who fought a long drawn-out succession of campaigns, there is nowhere to turn. To look for a historical Arthur in such a period is a hopeless task: the scraps of evidence are few and far between, and there is no context into which we can fit them. For instance, Gildas, a British preacher who was mainly concerned with castigating the sins of his fellow-countrymen, mentions a few names of kings or kinglets, and tells of one victory, 'the siege of Mons Badonicus' in his sixth-century book on the ruin of Britain. Because these are our only pieces of information, it is easy to overvalue them: Gildas himself implies that there were other engagements as important as 'mons Badonicus' ('mount Badon') but even three hundred years later it had become one great moment in which the tide of the Saxon invasion was stemmed.

In fact, the only thing that is generally agreed about the historical Arthur is that if he did exist, it was in the period between AD 450 and AD 650. Who he was, what he did, where he lived, are questions which can only be answered with guesses. It was perhaps only guesswork that led two unknown writers in the eighth and ninth centuries to name the hero of the 'siege of mons Badonicus' (a siege duly transformed into a battle) as Arthur. The name Arthur is very rare in Welsh sources; the fact that, like many Welsh names, it may derive from a Roman family name, Artorius, has led to all kinds of speculation; all that is indisputable is that, by the ninth century, there was a traditional hero called Arthur. The brief *Annals of Wales* tell us two things about him: he fought at Badon, something which historians have remembered but which the romancers have forgotten, and he was killed at Camlann in the same battle as a certain Medraut, the seed from which the whole 'tragedy of Arthur' was to spring in the romances, but which rarely appears in the historians. The equally anonymous author of *The History of the Britons* (usually attributed to a mythical Nennius) has a great deal more to say about Arthur's career, but he improves the history of the victor of Badon by adding a catalogue of battles, which may well have originally belonged to someone else, as a kind of prelude. An early Welsh poem has survived which lists in very similar style the battles of Cadwallawn, 'fourteen chief battles for fair Britain, and sixty encounters'. Even here the list of Arthur's battles exists in two very different versions, both of which are given below.

The real origins of Arthur as we know him lie not in fifth- or sixth-century history, but in early Welsh literature. Even here he is an enigmatic figure, partly because all that survives of much Welsh literature is rather like a newspaper where only the headlines can be read. We have a whole series of aids to memory used by the poets when they recited their stories: heroes and events are grouped in threes, for example, 'Three Generous Men of the Island of Britain'. The original versions of these occasionally mention Arthur, though many were later adapted to include him. There are other references to him in Welsh verse, including a verse about his grave:

There is a grave for March, a grave for Gwythur,
A grave for Gwgawn Red-sword;
the world's wonder a grave for Arthur.

The implication is that no grave is known for Arthur, and it would be a marvel if it were to be found. Elsewhere Arthur appears as leader of an expedition to the Celtic otherworld, Annwn, in a poem whose obscurity has baffled the best scholars. Something of this side of his character is reflected in the two *Marvels* from *The History of the Britons*.

After the ninth century, Arthur begins to acquire his best-known characteristic: he is a great ruler whose court attracts the bravest warriors of his age. The first evidence that we have of him as a great ruler rather than a great warrior comes in an amusing way. The Welsh Church, like the Irish, venerated almost all its holy men as saints, and vast numbers of saints' lives were turned out in little monasteries or cells up and down Wales, often the product of intense local patriotism. In order to emphasise the greatness of such a saint, he would be shown as superior to a great ruler, and Arthur was often cast in the role of stooge. This is what lies behind the episode from the *Life of St Carannog*, though there is a more devious motive as well, the establishment of a claim by St Carannog's monastery to the lands mentioned in the story. Such stories often contain references to stories about Arthur which have now been lost, but in this case the whole episode seems to have been invented.

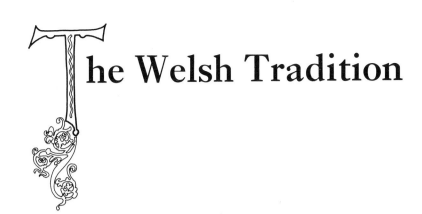

The Welsh Tradition

THE ANNALS OF WALES

Year 72 (=AD 518?) The battle of Badon in which Arthur bore the cross of our Lord Jesus Christ on his shoulders for three days and three nights, and the Britons were the victors.
Year 93 (=AD 539?) Gueith (Battle of) Camlann in which Arthur and Medraut perished; and there was plague in Britain and Ireland.

THE HISTORY OF THE BRITONS

The chronology of the 'History' proceeds by a stepping-stone method, rather than by absolute dates, so that it is often unclear to what precise period the author is assigning any series of events. The following 'Arthurian' section, from the original version in the Harleian MS, is a case in point.

Then in those days Arthur fought against them[1] with the kings of the Britons, but he was a commander in the battles. The first battle was at the mouth of the river called *Glein*; the second, third, fourth, and fifth on another river, which is called *Dubglas* as is in the region of *Linnuis*;[2] the sixth battle on the river called *Bassas*. The seventh battle was in the forest of Celyddon, that is the battle of Coed Celyddon.[3] The eight battle was at *Castellum Guinnion*, where Arthur carried the portrait of Saint Mary, ever Virgin, on his shoulders; and the pagans were routed on that day, and there was a great slaughter of them through the power of our Lord Jesus Christ and the strength of the holy Virgin Mary, his mother. The ninth battle was fought in the *Urbs Legionis*.[4] The tenth battle was fought on the shore of the river called *Tribruit*. The eleventh battle was fought on the mountain called *Agned*.[5] The twelfth battle was on *Mons Badonis*, where in one day nine hundred and sixty men were killed by one attack of Arthur, and no one save himself laid them low. And he appeared as victor in all the battles. And while they[1] were being overthrown in all the battles, they were seeking help from Germany; and they were being reinforced many times over without interruption. And they brought kings from Germany to rule over them in Britain, up to the time when Ida ruled who was son of Eoppa; he was the first king in Bernicia, that is in *Berneich*.

[1]The English [2]Lindsey

[3]A forest area in southern Scotland, often referred to in Mediaeval Welsh literature [4]Chester, or just possibly Caerleon

[5]Some manuscripts of a lightly revised twelfth-century version add here *Cat Bregoion*, 'the battle of *Bregimion*'

In A.D. 944 an English revisor produced a new version of the 'History' in a much less inelegant Latin style. This recension is known, again from its principal manuscript, as the 'Vatican' version. The redactor can be shown not to have worked from a copy of the original, 'Harleian', text, but from an augmented version written in Wales between ca 875 and ca 925; its new matter included some additions to the story of Arthur and his battles.

Then the warrior Arthur, with the soldiers and kings of Britain, used to fight against them.[1] And though there were many of more noble birth than he, he was twelve times leader in war and victor of the battles. He fought the first battle against them at the mouth of the river which is called *Glein*; the second, third, fourth, and fifth on another river, called *Duglas* in Welsh, which is in the district of

Linnuis; the sixth battle was on the river which is called *Bassas*. He fought the seventh battle against them in the wood of *Celidon*: in Welsh that is called the battle of Coed Celyddon. He fought the eight battle against the barbarians near *Castellum Guinnion*; in it Arthur carried on his shoulders a portrait of Saint Mary, mother of God and ever virgin; and all that day, through the power of our Lord Jesus Christ and of Saint Mary his mother, the Saxons were put to flight and many of them perished in a great slaughter. He fought the tenth battle on the river-strand which we call *Traht Treuriot*, and the eleventh on the mountain called *Breguoin* where he put them to flight; we call that the battle of *Bregion*. The twelfth he prosecuted harshly against the Saxons, on *Mons Badonis*: in it there fell in one day nine hundred and forty men before his onslaught – his alone, with God's aid, without assistance from any of the Britons. Men say that he was always victor, in all the aforementioned battles, just as many other British soldiers were too. But no courage or counsel avails against God's will: as often as the Saxons were laid low in the battles, they were unremittingly reinforced from Germany and elsewhere; and they summoned to them kings and leaders with many warriors from almost every province, and they did this up to the time when Ida reigned who was son of Eobba; he was the first king, in Bernicia and in *Cair Affrauc*[2] of the Saxon race.

[1]The English [2]York?

The 'History' closes with accounts of natural marvels of the British Isles, principally of Wales and the border. Among these are two which refer to 'the warrior Arthur'. Neither site can be identified today.

In the district which is called Buellt there is another marvel. There is a pile of stones there, and one stone with the footprint of a dog on it placed on top of the heap. When he hunted the boar Trwyd, Cafall[1] – who was the dog of the warrior Arthur – imprinted the mark of his foot on it; and Arthur afterwards assembled a heap of stones under the stone on which was the footprint of his dog, and it is called Carn Gafall. And people come and carry away the stone in their hands for a period of a day and a night, and on the following day it is found on top of its heap.

In the district which is called Archenfield there is another marvel. There is a tomb there, next to a spring which is called Llygad Amr.[2] And the name of the man who was buried in the tomb was called thus, Amr; he was son of the warrior Arthur, and the latter killed him in that place and buried him. And people come to measure the tomb – it is now six feet, now nine, now twelve, now fifteen in length. At whatever size you will measure it on one occasion, you will not again find it of the same size. And I myself have tested it.

[1]The name means 'horse' [2]'The Spring of Amr'

THE LIFE OF SAINT CARANNOG

And afterwards he (St Carannog) returned to his own country of Cardigan, to his cave, with many clergy, and there did many good deeds which cannot be related. And Christ gave him from on high a marvellous altar, whose colour no one could describe. And after that he came to the River Severn to set sail, and put the altar in the sea, so that it would lead him wherever God wished him to come. In those days Cato and Arthur ruled in that country, living at Dindraithov; and Arthur came searching for a very fierce, huge and terrible serpent which had laid waste twelve parts of the fields of Carrum. And Carannog came and greeted Arthur, who accepted his blessing joyfully. And Carannog asked Arthur whether he had heard where his altar had landed, and Arthur replied: 'If you reward me, I will tell you.' And he said, 'What reward do you want?' He answered: 'Bring me the serpent which is near you, so that we can see if you are the servant of God.' Then saint Carannog continued on his way and prayed to the Lord, and the serpent came there with a great noise, like a calf running to its mother; it bowed its head before the servant of God, like a servant obeying his lord with a humble heart and downcast eyes. And he put his stole around its neck and led it away like a lamb; it did not ruffle up its feathers or its spines, and its neck was like the neck of a seven-year-old bull, so that the stole scarcely went round it. Then they arrived together at the castle, and greeted Cato, and were welcomed by him. And he led that serpent into the middle of the hall and fed him in the presence of the people; and they tried to kill it. But he did not let them kill it because he said it came by God's command to wipe out the sinners who were in Carrum and to show God's power to them. And then he went outside the castle gate, and Carannog let it go, ordering it not to hurt anyone as it left, and not to come back again. And the serpent left and held to what the man of God had commanded. And Carannog took the altar, which Arthur had thought of making into a table; but whatever was put on it was hurled a long way off it. And the king begged him to accept Carrum to hold it by charter for ever, and afterwards he built a church there.

GEOFFREY OF MONMOUTH

The History of the Kings of Britain

Coronation of Arthur.
From the fifteenth century Chronicle of St Albans. (*Lambeth Palace Library MS 6, f.54v*)

HISTORY AND FICTION · GEOFFREY'S SOURCES · ARTHUR AS SEEN BY GEOFFREY · THE CHRONICLERS AND GEOFFREY ❧ ❧ ❧

The matter-of-fact title of Geoffrey of Monmouth's work seems to promise the truth about the historical Arthur. Instead, we are given one of the greatest medieval works of fiction, which was nonetheless taken as history by many generations of later writers. Until now, the stories of Arthur had largely circulated by word of mouth: Geoffrey's work was the gateway through which he entered the world of literature.

We know little about Geoffrey himself. Probably born about 1100, he seems to have lived in Oxford from about 1129 onwards, at a college of canons called St George's: he may have taught there, although the university had not been formally established. His family were either Welsh or possibly Breton, and he signed himself Geoffrey Arthur, implying that his father was called Arthur. He completed the *History of the Kings of Britain* in about 1136. After a long quest for promotion in the church, to which the dedications of his books bear witness, he became bishop of St Asaph in 1152. His see was in the hands of Welsh rebels, and he probably never visited it before his death in 1154.

Geoffrey begins his book with a long story telling how the British came originally from Troy; his work was based, so he claimed, on 'a very ancient book in the British tongue'. This is a well-known formula in medieval writing: Troy in turn had its fictional history, drawn from a book by 'Dares the Phrygian'. But it is also worth remembering that the distinction between fiction and history is a modern one, and Geoffrey's book is indeed a mixture of the two. It is not a chronicle of contemporary events, but a reconstruction of the past, using the scraps of evidence that were available. It is safe to say that there is very little in Geoffrey's book that his contemporaries could have firmly contradicted as untrue. But they gave it a very different aspect when they used it as a source for the early parts of their own purely factual chronicles.

Geoffrey certainly knew much of the Welsh tradition that has survived, and many of his details can be traced back to this: the names of Arthur's weapons come from this source, as do many names of characters. He used *The History of the Britons* as well, following its outline quite carefully. Geoffrey's real inventions are in the events he describes, both before and after the Roman conquest; we owe to him the story of King Lear as well as that of King Arthur. But it is his portrait of Arthur that is his masterpiece, made up of material borrowed from all kinds of sources. Arthur's birth, which Merlin brings about by disguising Uther Pendragon as the husband of the beautiful Igerna of Cornwall, is an echo of a similar tale in the romances about Alexander the Great. The vast empire which Arthur conquers is a reflection of the ambitious expansion of Norman power in the seventy years before Geoffrey wrote his book. Recent historical events, such as William I's stay at York at Christmas 1069, may have provided copy for some of the details, while contemporary politics also contributed: the Norman interest in bringing Brittany into their sphere of influence is reflected in the large part which the Bretons play in *The History of the Kings of Britain*. Returning crusaders who had been to Constantinople may have given him ideas for the description of Arthur's court at the City of Legions, including the strict segregation of women.

Yet all Geoffrey's efforts would have been in vain if he had not been in tune with what his public wanted. He did not merely write a fictional history: he produced a hero-king who was very much his readers' ideal, and he was also in touch with the latest fashions in courtly behaviour. One of his most remarkable passages (p. 20 below) foreshadows the ideals of courtly love at a time when none of the great courtly stories had yet been written down.

By medieval standards, Geoffrey's work was a best-seller; not only that, but most chroniclers accepted his work as true. Between 1150 and 1420, some fifty chroniclers had used it as the basis for their account of the early history of Britain, while only a handful questioned it. The most sceptical was William of Newburgh, writing at the end of the twelfth century, but his attack went largely unheeded. With the writers of romances, his success was even greater. Two romance histories were based on it within the next twenty years; Gaimar's version is lost, but Wace's *Roman de Brut*, completed in 1155, has survived. Wace, a Norman clerk, followed Geoffrey's work closely, but added some new details of his own, including the first mention of the Round Table, 'of which the Bretons tell many a tale', which Arthur introduced because his barons could not agree on an order of precedence when they sat at table. This work was in turn translated into English by Layamon, a Worcestershire priest, and in the fourteenth century an anonymous poet produced the splendid alliterative poem,

Morte Arthure, the most vigorous of all the versions of Arthur's career. This extract from a description of a hand-to-hand fight at sea gives some idea of its power:

> Then the mariners gather, and masters of ships;
> Merrily each of the mates talks to the others,
> Speaking in their language, telling how things were,
> Drawing bundles on board, tying up sails,
> Crowding on canvas, battening down hatches,
> Brandishing brown steel, blowing their trumpets;
> One stands stiffly at the bows, another steers aft;
> Guiding over the water, the fighting begins,
> The waving wind rises out of the west,
> Blows its burly breath into men's sails,
> Hurling together the stately ships
> So that prows and strakes burst asunder;
> The stern strikes so sharply against the stem
> That the plates of the rudder are dashed in pieces!
> Great ships and small crash against one another.
> Grappling irons are thrown out, as they should be –
> There is keen strife and cracking of ships.
> Great ships of battle are crushed into pieces!

But let us return to Geoffrey of Monmouth's own work. The extract which follows covers the whole of Arthur's career, except for the description of his conception and birth. It is the climax of Geoffrey's work, occupying about one-third of the whole book.

It is foreshadowed in Merlin's marvellous prophecies which immediately precede it; and it is with Merlin's supernatural aid that Arthur is born. Uther falls violently in love with Igerna, wife of his enemy, Gorlois of Cornwall, and is magically transformed (by Merlin) into the latter's likeness. He enters the castle of Tintagel in Gorlois' absence, and begets Arthur by her. On his return, he learns that Gorlois has been killed a few hours earlier, and therefore marries Igerna at the earliest opportunity. Arthur thus enjoys the benefit of being miraculously and yet almost legitimately conceived. The extract begins just after Uther Pendragon's death, when Arthur is fifteen.

Sports and games at the solemn court held at Caerleon by Arthur. The artist has followed Geoffrey's description very closely (*p. 21*). (*Bibliothèque royale, Brussels MS 9243, f.45*)

The History of the Kings of Britain

After the death of Utherpendragon, the leaders of the Britons assembled from their various provinces in the town of Silchester and there suggested to Dubricius, the Archbishop of the City of the Legions, that as their King he should crown Arthur, the son of Uther. Necessity urged them on, for as soon as the Saxons heard of the death of King Uther, they invited their own countrymen over from Germany, appointed Colgrin as their leader and began to do their utmost to exterminate the Britons. They had already overrun all that section of the island which stretches from the River Humber to the sea named Caithness.

Dubricius lamented the sad state of his country. He called the other bishops to him and bestowed the crown of the kingdom upon Arthur. Arthur was a young man only fifteen years old; but he was of outstanding courage and generosity, and his inborn goodness gave him such grace that he was loved by almost all the people. Once he had been invested with the royal insignia, he observed the normal custom of giving gifts freely to everyone. Such a great crowd of soldiers flocked to him that he came to an end of what he had to distribute. However, the man to whom open-handedness and bravery both come naturally may indeed find himself momentarily in need, but poverty will never harass him for long. In Arthur courage was closely linked with generosity, and he made up his mind to harry the Saxons, so that with their wealth he might reward the retainers who served his household. The justness of his cause encouraged him, for he had a claim by rightful inheritance to the kingship of the whole island. He therefore called together all the young men who I have just mentioned and marched on York.

As soon as this was announced to Colgrin, he assembled the Saxons, Scots and Picts, and came to meet Arthur with a vast multitude. Once contact was made between the two armies, beside the River Douglas, both sides stood in grave danger for their lives. Arthur, however, was victorious. Colgrin fled, and Arthur pursued him; then Colgrin entered York and Arthur besieged him there.

As soon as Baldulf, the brother of Colgrin, heard of the latter's flight, he came to the siege with six thousand troops, in the hope of freeing the beleaguered man. At the time when his brother had gone into battle, Baldulf himself had been on the sea-coast, where he was awaiting the arrival of Duke Cheldric, who was on his way from Germany to bring them support. When he was some ten miles distant from the city of York, Baldulf decided to take the advantage of a night march, so that he could launch an unexpected attack. Arthur heard of this and ordered Cador, Duke of Cornwall, to march to meet Baldulf that same night, with six hundred cavalry and three thousand foot. Cador surrounded the road along which the enemy was marching and attacked the Saxons unexpectedly, so that they were cut to pieces and killed, and those who remained alive were forced to flee. As a result Baldulf became extremely worried at the fact that he could not bring help to his brother. He debated with himself how he could manage to talk with Colgrin; for he was convinced that by consulting together it would be possible for them to hit upon a safe solution – that is, if only he could make his way into his brother's presence.

Once Baldulf had come to the conclusion that no other means of access was open to him, he cut short his hair and his beard and dressed himself up as a minstrel with a harp. He strode up and down in the camp, pretending to be a harpist by playing melodies on his instrument. No one suspected him and he moved nearer and nearer to the city walls, keeping up the same pretence all the time. In the end he was observed by the besieged, dragged up over the top of the walls on ropes and taken to his brother. When Colgrin set eyes on Baldulf he had the solace of embracing him and kissing him to his heart's desire, as though Baldulf had been restored to him from the dead. Finally, when, after exhaustive discussions, they had abandoned all hope of ever escaping, messengers returned from Germany to say that they had brought with them to Albany six hundred ships which were commanded by Cheldric and loaded with brave soldiery. When Arthur's advisers learned this, they dissuaded him from continuing the siege any longer, for if so large an enemy force were to come upon them they would all be committed to a most dangerous engagement.

Arthur accepted the advice of his retainers and withdrew into the town of London. There he convened the bishops and the clergy of the entire realm and asked their suggestion as to what it would be best and safest for him to do, in the face of this invasion by the pagans. Eventually a common policy was agreed on and messengers were dispatched to King Hoel in Brittany to explain to him the disaster which had befallen Great Britain. This Hoel was the son of Arthur's sister; and his father was Budicius, the King of the Armorican Britons. As a result, as soon as he heard of the terrifying way in which his uncle was being treated, Hoel ordered his fleet to be made ready. Fifteen thousand armed warriors were assembled and at the next fair wind Hoel landed at Southampton. Arthur received him with all the honour due to him, and each man embraced the other repeatedly.

They let a few days pass and then they marched to the town of Kaerluideoit, which was besieged by the pagans about whom I have already told you. This town is situated upon a hill between two rivers, in the province of Lindsey: it is also called by another name, Lincoln. As soon as they had arrived there with their entire force, keen as they were to fight with the Saxons, they inflicted unheard-of slaughter upon them; for on one day six thousand of the Saxons were killed, some being drowned in the rivers and the others being hit by weapons. As a result, the remainder were demoralized. The Saxons abandoned the siege and took to flight.

Arthur pursued the Saxons relentlessly until they reached Caledon Wood. There they re-formed after their flight and made an effort to resist Arthur. The Saxons joined battle once more and killed a number of the Britons, for the former defended themselves manfully. They used the shelter of the trees to protect themselves from the Britons' weapons. As soon as Arthur saw this, he ordered the trees round that part of the wood to be cut down and their trunks to be placed in a circle, so that every way out was barred to the enemy. Arthur's plan was to hem them in and then besiege them, so that in the end they should die of hunger. When this had been done, he ordered his squadrons to surround the wood and there he remained for three days. The Saxons had nothing at all to eat. To prevent themselves dying of sheer hunger, they asked permission to come out, on the understanding that, if they left behind all their gold and silver, they might be permitted to return to Germany with nothing but their boats. What is more, they promised that they would send Arthur tribute from Germany and that hostages should be handed over. Arthur took counsel and then agreed to their petition. He retained all their treasure, and took hostages to ensure that the tribute should be paid. All that he conceded to the Saxons was permission to leave.

As the Saxons sailed away across the sea on their way home, they repented of the bargain which they had made. They reversed their sails, turned back to Britain and landed on the coast near Totnes. They took possession of the land, and depopulated the countryside as far as the Severn Sea, killing off a great number of the peasantry. Then they proceeded by a forced march to the neighbourhood of Bath and besieged the town. When this was announced to King Arthur, he was greatly astonished at their extraordinary duplicity. He ordered summary justice to be inflicted upon their hostages, who were all hanged without more ado. He put off the foray with which he had begun to harass the Scots and the Picts, and he hastened to break up the siege. Arthur was labouring under very considerable difficulties, for he had left behind in the city of Alclud his cousin Hoel, who was seriously ill. He finally reached the county of Somerset and approached the siege. 'Although the Saxons, whose very name is an insult to heaven and detested by all men, have not kept faith with me,' he said, 'I myself will keep faith with my God. This very day I will do my utmost to take vengeance on them for the blood of my fellow-countrymen. Arm yourselves, men, and attack these traitors with all your strength! With

Christ's help we shall conquer them, without any possible doubt!'

As Arthur said this, the saintly Dubricius, Archbishop of the City of the Legions, climbed to the top of a hill and cried out in a loud voice: 'You who have been marked with the cross of the Christian faith, be mindful of the loyalty you owe to your fatherland and to your fellow-countrymen! If they are slaughtered as a result of this treacherous behaviour by the pagans, they will be an everlasting reproach to you, unless in the meanwhile you do your utmost to defend them! Fight for your fatherland, and if you are killed suffer death willingly for your country's sake. That in itself is victory and a cleansing of the soul. Whoever suffers death for the sake of his brothers offers himself as a living sacrifice to God and follows with firm footsteps behind Christ Himself, who did not disdain to lay down His life for His brothers. It follows that if any one of you shall suffer death in this war, that death shall be to him as a penance and an absolution for all his sins, given always that he goes to meet it unflinchingly.'

Arthur prepares to do battle with the Saxons. From a fifteenth century copy of the Flemish Chronicles of Hainault (*Bibliothèque royale, Brussels, MS 9243, f.36*[v])

Without a moment's delay each man present, inspired by the benediction given by this holy man, rushed off to put on his armour and to obey Dubricius' orders. Arthur himself put on a leather jerkin worthy of so great a king. On his head he placed a golden helmet, with a crest carved in the shape of a dragon; and across his shoulders a circular shield called Pridwen, on which there was painted a likeness of the Blessed Mary, Mother of God, which forced him to be thinking perpetually of her. He girded on his peerless sword, called Caliburn, which was forged in the Isle of Avalon. A spear called Ron graced his right hand: long, broad in the blade and thirsty for slaughter. Arthur drew up his men in companies and then bravely attacked the Saxons, who as usual were arrayed in wedges. All that day they resisted the Britons bravely, although the latter launched attack upon attack. Finally, towards sunset, the Saxons occupied a neighbouring hill, on which they proposed to camp. Relying on their vast numbers, they considered that the hill in itself offered sufficient protection. However, when the next day dawned, Arthur climbed to the top of the peak with his army, losing many of his men on the way. Naturally enough, the Saxons, rushing down from their high position, could inflict wounds more easily, for the impetus of their descent gave them more speed than the others, who were toiling up. For all that, the Britons reached the summit by a superlative effort and immediately engaged the enemy in hand-to-hand conflict. The Saxons stood shoulder to shoulder and strove their utmost to resist.

When the greater part of the day had passed in this way, Arthur went berserk, for he realised that things were still going well for the enemy and that victory for his own side was not yet in sight. He drew his sword Caliburn, called upon the name of the Blessed Virgin, and rushed forward at full speed into the thickest ranks of the enemy. Every man whom he struck, calling upon God as he did so, he killed at a single blow. He did not slacken his onslaught until he had dispatched four hundred and seventy men with his sword Caliburn. When the Britons saw this, they poured after him in close formation, dealing death on every side. In this battle fell Colgrin, with his brother Baldulf and many thousands of others with them. Cheldric, on the contrary, when he saw the danger threatening his men, immediately turned away in flight with what troops were left to him.

As soon as King Arthur had gained the upper hand, he ordered Cador, the Duke of Cornwall, to pursue the Saxons, while he himself hurried off in the direction of Albany. It had reached his ears that the Scots and the Picts had besieged his nephew Hoel[1] in the town of Alclud, where, as I have explained already, Arthur had left him because of his poor health. Arthur therefore hastened to

[1]Geoffrey sometimes calls Hoel Arthur's nephew; in fact, he seems to have intended him to be Arthur's cousin.

his nephew's assistance, for he was afraid that Hoel might be captured by the barbarians.

Meanwhile the Duke of Cornwall, accompanied by ten thousand men, instead of pursuing the fleeing Saxons, rushed off to their boats, with the intention of preventing them from going on board. Once he had seized their boats, he manned them with the best of his own soldiers and gave those men orders that they were to prevent the pagans from going aboard, if these last came running to the boats. Then he hurried off to pursue the enemy and to cut them to pieces without pity once he had found them: this in obedience to Arthur's command.

The Saxons, who only a short time before used to attack like lightning in the most ferocious way imaginable, now ran away with fear in their hearts. Some of them fled to secret hiding-places in the woods, others sought the mountains, and caves in the hills, in an attempt to add some little breathing-space to their lives. In the end they discovered safety nowhere; and so they came to the Isle of Thanet, with their line of battle cut to pieces. The Duke of Cornwall pursued them thither and renewed the slaughter. Cador drew back in the end, but only after he had killed Cheldric, taken hostages, and forced what remained of the Saxons to surrender.

Once peace was restored in this way, Cador set out for Alclud. Arthur had already freed the town from the harassing attentions of the barbarians. He now led his army to Moray, where the Scots and the Picts were under siege. They had fought three times against the King and his nephew, suffering defeat at Arthur's hands and then seeking refuge in this particular district. When they reached Loch Lomond, they took possession of the islands in the lake, hoping to find a safe refuge on them. This lake contains sixty islands and has sixty streams to feed it, yet only one of these streams flows down to the sea. On these islands one can make out sixty crags, which between them support exactly the same number of eagles' nests. The eagles used to flock together each year and foretell any prodigious event which was about to occur in the kingdom: this by a shrill-pitched scream which they emitted in concert. It was to these islands, then, that the enemies of whom I have told you fled, hoping to be protected by the lake, although in effect they gained little help from it. Arthur collected together a fleet of boats and sailed round the rivers. By besieging his enemies for fifteen days he reduced them to such a state of famine that they died in their thousands.

While Arthur was killing off the Scots and the Picts in this way, Gilmaurius, the King of Ireland, arrived with a fleet and a huge horde of pagans, in an effort to bring help to those who were besieged. Arthur raised the siege and began to turn his armed strength against the Irish. He cut them to pieces mercilessly and forced them to return home. Once he had conquered the Irish, he was at liberty once more to wipe out the Scots and the Picts. He treated them with unparalleled severity, sparing no one who fell into his hands. As a result all the bishops of this pitiful country, with all the clergy under their command, their feet bare and in their hands the relics of their saints and the treasures of their churches, assembled to beg pity of the King for the relief of their people. The moment they came into the King's presence, they fell on their knees and besought him to have mercy on their sorrowing people. He had inflicted sufficient suffering on them, said the bishops, and there was no need for him to wipe out to the last man those few who had survived so far. He should allow them to have some small tract of land of their own, seeing that they were in any case going to bear the yoke of servitude. When they had petitioned the King in this way, their patriotism moved him to tears. Arthur gave in to the prayers presented by these men of religion and granted a pardon to their people.

When all this had been accomplished, Hoel took a good look round the side of the loch which I have described to you. He was surprised to see so many rivers, islands, rocks and eagles' nests, and, what is more, to find exactly the same number of each. While he was meditating upon this remarkable circumstance, Arthur came up to him and told him that in the same neighbourhood there was another pool which was even more extraordinary. It was not very far away from where they were standing. It was twenty feet wide and the same distance long, and its depth was just five feet. Whether it had been shaped into a square by the artistry of man, or by nature, it remained true that, while it produced four different kinds of fish in its four corners, the fish of any one corner were never found in any of the others.

Arthur also told Hoel that there was a third pool in the parts of Wales which are near the Severn. The local people call it Lin Ligua. When the sea flows into this pool, it is swallowed up as though in a bottomless pit; and, as the pool swallows the waters, it is never filled in such a way as to overflow the edges of its banks. When the tide ebbs away, however, the pool belches forth the water which it has swallowed, as high in the air as a mountain, and with them it then splashes and floods its banks. Meanwhile, if the people of all that region should come near, with their faces turned towards it, thus letting the spray of the waters fall upon their clothing, it is only with difficulty, if, indeed, at all, that they have the strength to avoid being swallowed up by the pool. If, however, they turn their backs, their being sprinkled has no danger for them, even if they stand on the very brink.

Once he had pardoned the Scottish people, the King moved to York, where he proposed to celebrate the coming feast of the Nativity of our Lord. As he rode into the city, Arthur grieved to see the desolate state of the holy churches. Samson, the saintly Archbishop, had been driven out, and with him all men of the Christian faith. The half-burnt churches no longer celebrated God's holy office. The fury of the pagans had been so great that it had brought everything to an end. Arthur therefore summoned the clergy and the people, and appointed his own chaplain, Piramus, as Metropolitan of that see. He rebuilt the churches, which had been razed to the ground, and he graced them with religious communities of men and women. He restored to their family honours the nobles who had been driven out by the Saxon invasions.

There were in York three brothers sprung from the royal line, Loth, Urian, and Auguselus, who had been Princes in those parts before the Saxon victories. Arthur was determined to do for them what he had done for the others: that is, to grant them back their hereditary rights. He returned the kingship of the Scots to Auguselus; to Urian, the brother of Auguselus, he gave back the honour of ruling over the men of Moray; and Loth, who in the days of Aurelius Ambrosius had married that King's own sister and had had two sons by her, Gawain and Mordred, he restored to the dukedom of Lothian and other near-by territories which formed part of it.

Finally, when he had restored the whole country to its earlier dignity, he himself married a woman called Guinevere. She was descended from a noble Roman family and had been brought up in the household of Duke Cador. She was the most beautiful woman in the entire island.

As soon as the next summer came round, Arthur fitted out a fleet and sailed off to the island of Ireland, which he

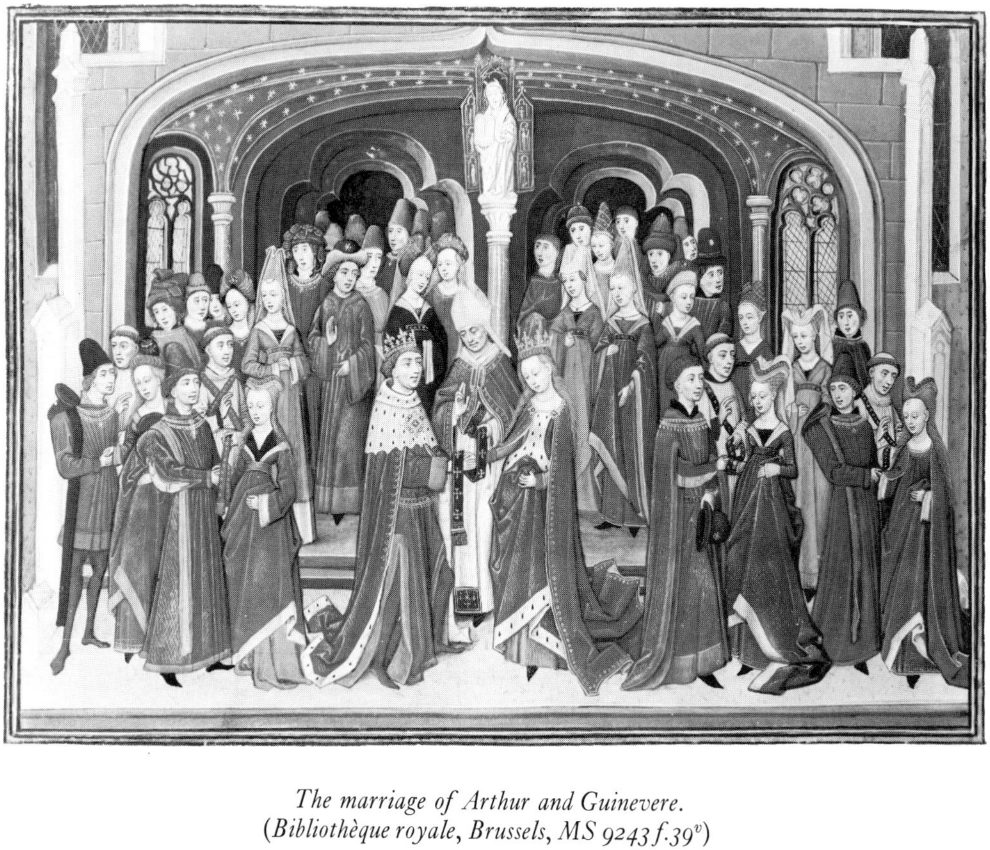

The marriage of Arthur and Guinevere.
(Bibliothèque royale, Brussels, MS 9243 f.39v)

was determined to subject to his own authority. The moment he landed, King Gilmaurius, about whom I have told you before, came to meet him with a numberless horde of his peoples ready to fight against him. However, when Arthur began the battle, Gilmaurius' army, which was naked and unarmed, was miserably cut to pieces where it stood, and ran away to any place where it could find refuge. Gilmaurius himself was captured immediately and forced to submit. The remaining princes of the country, thunderstruck by what had happened, followed their King's example and surrendered. The whole of Ireland was thus conquered.

Arthur then steered his fleet to Iceland, defeated the people there and subdued the island. A rumour spread through all the other islands that no country could resist Arthur. Doldavius, King of Gotland, and Gunhpar, King of the Orkneys, came of their own free will to promise tribute and to do homage.

The winter passed and Arthur returned to Britain. He established the whole of his kingdom in a state of lasting peace and then remained there for the next twelve years.

Arthur then began to increase his personal entourage by inviting very distinguished men from far-distant kingdoms to join it. In this way he developed such a code of courtliness in his household that he inspired peoples living far away to imitate him. The result was that even the man of noblest birth, once he was roused to rivalry, thought nothing at all of himself unless he wore his arms and dressed in the same way as Arthur's knights. At last the fame of Arthur's generosity and bravery spread to the very ends of the earth; and the kings of countries far across the sea trembled at the thought that they might be attacked and invaded by him, and so lose control of the lands under their dominion. They were so harassed by these tormenting anxieties that they re-built their towns and the towers in their towns, and then went so far as to construct castles on carefully-chosen sites, so that, if invasion should bring Arthur against them, they might have a refuge in their time of need.

All this was reported to Arthur. The fact that he was dreaded by all encouraged him to conceive the idea of conquering the whole of Europe. He fitted out his fleets and sailed first of all to Norway, for he wished to give the kingship of that country to Loth, who was his brother-in-law. Loth was the nephew of Sichelm the King of Norway, who had just died and left him the kingship in his will. However, the Norwegians had refused to accept Loth and had raised a certain Riculf to the royal power, for they considered that they could resist Arthur now that their towns were garrisoned. The son of this Loth, called Gawain, was at that time a boy twelve years old. He had been sent by Arthur's brother-in-law to serve in the household of Pope Sulpicius, who had dubbed him a knight. As soon as Arthur landed on the coast of Norway, as I had begun to explain to you, King Riculf marched to meet him with the entire population of the country and then joined battle with him. Much blood was shed on either side, but in the end the Britons were victorious. They surged forward and killed Riculf and a number of his men. Once they were sure of victory, they invested the cities of Norway and set fire to them everywhere. They scattered the rural population and continued to give full licence to their savagery until they had forced all Norway and all Denmark, too, to accept Arthur's rule.

As soon as he had subdued these countries and raised Loth to the kingship of Norway, Arthur sailed off to Gaul. He drew his troops up in companies and began to lay waste the countryside in all directions. The province of Gaul was at that time under the jurisdiction of the Tribune Frollo, who ruled it in the name of the Emperor Leo. The moment Frollo heard of the coming of Arthur, he marched out supported by the entire armed force which he had under command. He was determined to fight against Arthur, but in effect he could offer little resistance. The young men of all the islands which Arthur had subdued were there to fight at his side, and he was reported to have so powerful a force that it could hardly have been conquered by anyone. What is more, the better part of the army of the Gauls was already in Arthur's service, for he had bought them over by the gifts which he had given them. As soon as Frollo saw that he was having the worst of the fight, he quitted the battlefield without more ado and fled to Paris with the few men left to him.

There Frollo reassembled his scattered people, garrisoned the town and made up his mind to meet Arthur in the field a second time. Just as Frollo was considering how to strengthen his army by calling upon neighbouring peoples, Arthur arrived unexpectedly and besieged him inside the city. A whole month passed. Frollo grieved to see his people dying of hunger, and sent a message to Arthur to say that they should meet in single combat and that whichever was victorious should take the kingdom of the other. Being a man of immense stature, courage and strength, Frollo relied upon these advantages when he sent his message, hoping in this way to find a solution to his problem. When the news of Frollo's plan reached Arthur, he was immensely pleased; and he sent word back that he would be willing to hold the meeting that had been suggested. An agreement was come to on both sides and the two met on an island outside the city, the populace gathering to see what would happen to them.

Arthur and Frollo were both fully armed and seated on horses which were wonderfully fleet of foot. It was not easy to foretell which would win. For a moment they stood facing each other with their lances held straight in the air: then they suddenly set spurs to their horses and struck each other two mighty blows. Arthur aimed his lance with more care and hit Frollo high up on his chest. He avoided Frollo's weapon, and hurled his enemy to the ground with all his might. Arthur then drew his sword from the scabbard and was just hurrying forward to strike Frollo when the latter leapt quickly to his feet, ran forward with his lance levelled and with a deadly thrust stabbed Arthur's horse in the chest, thus bringing down both horse and rider. When the Britons saw their King thrown to the ground, they were afraid that he was dead and it was only with great self-control that they restrained themselves from breaking the truce and hurling themselves as one man upon the Gauls. Just as they were planning to invade the lists, Arthur sprang quickly to his feet, covered himself with his shield, and rushed forward to meet Frollo. They stood up to each other hand to hand, giving blow for blow, and each doing his utmost to kill the other. In the end Frollo found an opening and struck Arthur on the forehead. It was only the fact that he blunted the edge of his sword-blade at the point where it made contact with Arthur's metal helmet that prevented Frollo from dealing a mortal blow. When Arthur saw his leather cuirass and his round shield grow red, he was roused to even fiercer anger. He raised Caliburn in the air with all his strength and brought it down through Frollo's helmet and so on to his head, which he cut into two halves. At this blow Frollo fell to the ground, drummed the earth with his heels and breathed his soul into the winds. The moment this was made known throughout the army, the townsfolk ran forward, threw open their gates and surrendered their city to Arthur.

As soon as Arthur had won his victory, he divided his army into two and put one half under the command of Hoel, ordering him to go off to attack Guitard, the leader of the Poitevins. With the other half Arthur busied himself in subduing the remaining provinces which were still hostile to him. Hoel soon reached Aquitania, seized the towns of that region, and, after harassing Guitard in a number of battles, forced him to surrender. He also ravaged Gascony with fire and sword, and forced its leaders to submit.

Nine years passed. Once Arthur had subjected all the regions of Gaul to his power, he returned once more to Paris and held a court there. He called an assembly of the clergy and the people, and settled the government of the realm peacefully and legally. It was then that he gave Neustria, now called Normandy, to his cup-bearer Bedevere, and the province of Anjou to his seneschal Kay. He gave a number of other provinces to the noblemen who had served him. Once he had pacified all these cities and peoples he returned to Britain just as spring was coming on.

When the feast of Whitsuntide began to draw near, Arthur, who was quite overjoyed by his great success, made up his mind to hold a plenary court at that season and place the crown of the kingdom on his head. He decided, too, to summon to this feast the leaders who owed him homage, so that he could celebrate Whitsun with greater reverence and renew the closest possible pacts of peace with his chieftains. He explained to the members of his court what he was proposing to do and accepted their advice that he should carry out his plan in the City of the Legions.

Situated as it is in Glamorganshire, on the River Usk, not far from the Severn Sea, in a most pleasant position, and being richer in material wealth than other townships, this city was eminently suitable for such a ceremony. The river which I have named flowed by it on one side, and up this the kings and princes who were to come from across the sea could be carried in a fleet of ships. On the other side, which was flanked by meadows and wooded groves, they had adorned the city with royal palaces, and by the gold-painted gables of its roofs it was a match for Rome. What is more, it was famous for its two churches. One of these, built in honour of the martyr Julius, was graced by a choir of most lovely virgins dedicated to God. The second, founded in the name of the blessed Aaron, the companion of Julius, was served by a monastery of canons, and counted as the third metropolitan see of Britain. The city also contained a college of two hundred learned men, who were skilled in astronomy and the other arts, and who watched with great attention the courses of the stars and so by their careful computations prophesied for King Arthur any prodigies due at that time.

It was this city, therefore, famous for such a wealth of pleasant things, which was made ready for the feast. Messengers were sent to the different kingdoms and invitations were delivered to all those who were due to come to the court from the various parts of Gaul and from the near-by Islands in the Sea. The following people came: Auguselus,

King of Albany, which is now known as Scotland; Urian, King of the men of Moray; Cadwallo Laurh, King of the Venedoti, who are now called the North Welsh; Stater, King of the Demetae, now the South Welsh; and Cador, King of Cornwall. There came, too, the Archbishops of the three metropolitan sees: London, York, and Dubricius from the City of the Legions. The last named, who was the Primate of Britain and legate of the Papal See, was so remarkably pious that by merely praying he could cure anyone who was ill. The leading men from the principal cities were there: Morvid, Earl of Gloucester; Mauron, Earl of Worcester; Anarauth, Earl of Salisbury; Artgualchar, Earl of Guerensis, which is now called Warwick; Jugein from Leicester; Cursalem from Caistor; Kynniarc, Duke of Durobernia; Urbgennius from Bath; Jonathel of Dorchester; and Boso of Rydychen: that is, Oxford.

In addition to these great leaders there came other famous men of equal importance: Donaut map Papo, Cheneus map Coil, Peredur map Peridur, Grifud map Nogord, Regin map Claut, Eddeliui map Oledauc, Kynar map Bangan, Kynmaroc, Gorbonian map Goit, Worloit, Run map Neton, Kymbelin, Edelnauth map Trunat, Cathleus map Kathel, Kynlit map Tieton and many others whose names it is too tedious to tell. Gilmaurius, King of Ireland, came from the neighbouring islands, with Malvasius, King of Iceland, Doldavius, King of Gotland, Gunhpar, King of the Orkneys, Loth, King of Norway, and Aschil, King of the Danes. From lands across the sea came Holdin, the leader of the Ruteni; Leodegarius, Earl of Hoiland; Bedevere the Cup-bearer, who was Duke of Normandy; Borellus of Cenomania; Kay the Seneschal, who was Duke of Anjou; Guitard of Poitou; the Twelve Peers from the various regions of Gaul, led by Gerin of Chartres; and then Hoel, leader of the Armorican Britons, with the princes who did him homage.

All these marched with a train of accoutrements, mules and horses such as I find it hard to describe. Once they are listed, there remained no prince of any distinction this side of Spain who did not come when he received his invitation. There was nothing remarkable in this: for Arthur's generosity was known throughout the whole world and this made all men love him.

Finally, when they had all assembled in the town and the time of the feast had come, the Archbishops were led forward to the palace, so that they could place the royal crown upon the King's head. Since the plenary court was being held in his own diocese, Dubricius made ready to sing mass in celebration of the moment when the King should place the crown upon his head. As soon as the King was enrobed, he was conducted with due pomp to the church of the metropolitan see. On his right side and on his left there were two archbishops to support him. Four Kings, of Albany, Cornwall, Demetia and Venedotia, preceded him, as was their right, bearing before him four golden swords. A company of clerics of every rank advanced before him, chanting in exquisite harmony.

From another direction the archbishops and bishops led the Queen, adorned with her own regalia, to the church of the dedicated Virgins. Before her walked the four consorts of the Kings already mentioned, carrying four white doves according to the custom. All the married women present followed behind her with great rejoicing.

Afterwards, when the procession was over, so much organ music was played in the two churches and the choirs sang so sweetly that, because of the high standard of the music offered, the knights who were there hardly knew which of the churches to enter first. They flocked in crowds, first to this one, then to the other, so that if the whole day had been spent in celebration they would not have been bored. Finally, high mass was celebrated in both churches.

The King and the Queen then took off their crowns and put on lighter regalia. The King went off with the men to feast in his own palace and the Queen retired with the married women to feast in hers; for the Britons still observed the ancient custom of Troy, the men celebrating festive occasions with their fellow-men and the women eating separately with the other women. When they were all seated as the rank of each decreed, Kay the Seneschal, robed in ermine and assisted by a thousand noblemen who were all clad in ermine too, bore in the food. The same number of men, clad this time in minever, followed Bedevere the Cup-bearer from another entrance, helping him to pass drinks of all sorts in goblets of every conceivable shape. Meanwhile, in the Queen's palace, innumerable servants, dressed in varying liveries, were performing their duties, each according to his office.

If I were to describe everything, I should make this story far too long. Indeed, by this time, Britain had reached such a standard of sophistication that it excelled all other kingdoms in its general affluence, the richness of its decorations, and the courteous behaviour of its inhabitants. Every knight in the country who was in any way famed for his bravery wore livery and arms showing his own distinctive colour; and women of fashion often displayed the same colours. They scorned to give their love to any man who had not proved himself three times in battle. In this way the womenfolk became chaste and more virtuous and for their love the knights were ever more daring.

Invigorated by the food and drink which they had consumed, they went out into the meadows outside the city and split up into groups ready to play various games. The knights planned an imitation battle and competed together on horseback, while their womenfolk watched from the top of the city walls and aroused them to passionate excitement by their flirtatious behaviour. The others passed what remained of the day in shooting with bows and arrows, hurling the lance, tossing heavy stones and rocks, playing dice and an immense variety of other games: this without the slightest show of ill-feeling. Whoever won this particular game was then rewarded by Arthur with an immense prize. The next three days were passed in this way. On the fourth day all those who in the office which they held had done Arthur any service were called together and each rewarded with a personal grant of cities, castles, archbishoprics, bishoprics and other landed possessions.

Then the saintly Dubricius, who for a long time had wanted to live as a hermit, resigned from his position as Archbishop. David, the King's uncle, whose way of life had afforded an example of unblemished virtue to those whom he had instructed in the faith, was consecrated in his place. At the same time Tebaus, the celebrated priest of Llandaff, was appointed in the place of the holy Samson, Archbishop of Dol: this with the approval of Hoel, King of the Armorican Britons, to whom Tebaus' life and saintly habits had commended him. The bishopric of Silchester was given to Maugannius, that of Winchester to Diwanius and that of Alclud to Eledenius.

While Arthur was distributing these benefices among his clergy, twelve men of mature years and respectable appearance came marching in at a slow pace. In their right hands they carried olive branches, to show that they were envoys. They saluted Arthur and handed to him a communication from Lucius Hiberius. This letter read as follows:

'Lucius, Procurator of the Republic, wishes that Arthur, King of Britain, may receive such treatment as he has deserved. I am amazed at the insolent way in which you continue your tyrannical behaviour. I am even more amazed at the damage which you have done to Rome. When I think about it, I am outraged that you should have so far forgotten yourself as not to realize this and not to appreciate immediately what it means that by your criminal behaviour you should have insulted the Senate, to which the entire world owes submission, as you very well know. You have had the presumption to disobey this mighty Empire by holding back the tribute of Britain, which tribute the Senate has ordered you to pay, seeing that Gaius Julius Caesar and other men of high place in the Roman State had received it for many years. You have torn Gaul away from that Empire, you have seized the province of the Allobroges and you have laid hands on all the Islands of the Ocean, the Kings of which paid tribute to my ancestors from the first moment when the might of Rome prevailed in those regions. As a result the Senate has decreed that punishment should be exacted for this long series of wrongs which you have done. I therefore order you to appear in Rome, so that you may submit yourself to your overlords and suffer the penalty of whatever sentence they may pass; and I appoint the middle of next August as the time for your coming. If you fail to arrive, I shall invade your territory myself and do my best to restore to the Roman State all that you have taken from it by your insane behaviour.'

This letter was read aloud in the presence of the kings and the leaders. Arthur then withdrew with them to a gigantic tower near the entrance to the palace, to consider what ought to be done in the face of such a message. As they began to climb the stairs, Cador, Duke of Cornwall, who was a merry man, burst out laughing.

'Until now,' he said to the King, 'I have been afraid that the life of ease which the Britons have been leading might make cowards of them and soften them up during this long spell of peace. Their reputation for bravery on the battlefield, for which they are more famous than any other people, might well have been completely lost to them. Indeed, when it is obvious that men are no longer using their weapons, but are instead playing at dice, burning up their strength with women and indulging in other gratifications of that sort, then without any doubt their bravery, honour, courage and good name all become tainted with cowardice. For the past five years or thereabouts we have thought of nothing but these follies, and we have had no battle experience. It is precisely to free us from this sloth that God has stirred up the resentment of the Romans, so that they may restore our courage to what it used to be in the old days.'

As Cador was saying this to them, and much more in the same strain, they reached their seats. When they had all sat down, Arthur made the following speech:

'You who have been my companions in good times and in bad, you of whose fortitude both in giving advice and in waging war I have had ample proof in the past, give me now your closest attention, every one of you, and in your wisdom tell me what you consider we should do on receiving such a letter as this. Anything which has been planned with great care by man in his wisdom is realised the more easily when the time for action arrives. It follows that we shall be able to bear this attack of Lucius with great equanimity if we have first of all worked out with one accord how we are best to resist him. For myself, I do not consider that we ought to fear his coming very much, seeing with what a trumped-up case he is demanding the tribute which he wants to exact from Britain. He says that he ought to be given it because it used to be paid to Julius Caesar and those who succeeded him. When these men landed with their armed band and conquered our fatherland by force and violence at a time when it was weakened by civil dissensions, they had been encouraged to come here by the disunity of our ancestors. Seeing that they seized the country in this way, it was wrong of them to exact tribute from it. Nothing that is acquired by force and violence can ever be held legally by anyone. In so far as the Roman has done us violence, he pleads an unreasonable case when he maintains that we are his tributaries in the eyes of the law. Since he presumes to exact something illegal from us, let us by a similar argument seek from him the tribute of Rome! Let him who comes out on top carry off what he has made up his mind to take! If the Roman decrees that tribute ought to be paid him by Britain simply because Julius Caesar and other Roman leaders conquered this country years ago, then I decree in the same way that Rome ought to give me tribute, in that my ancestors once captured that city. Belinus, that most glorious of the Kings of the Britons, with the help of his brother Brennius, the Duke of the Allobroges, hanged twenty of the noblest Romans in the middle of their own forum, captured the city and, when they had occupied it, held it for a long time. Similarly, Constantine, the son of Helen, and Maximianus, too, both of them close relations of mine, wearing the crown of Britain one after the other, each gained the throne of imperial Rome. Do you not agree, then, that it is we who should demand tribute of Rome? As for Gaul and the neighbouring Islands of the Ocean, we need send no answer, for when we snatched those lands from their empire they made no effort to defend them.'

[*Hoel speaks in reply to Arthur, and he is supported by Auguselus of Albany. A huge army 183,300 strong excluding footsoldiers, gathered at Barfleur, while Lucius Hiberius assembled an equally vast host and marched north. On landing in Normandy, Arthur, Kay and Bedevere kill a giant who has murdered Hoel's niece and has taken refuge on Mont St Michel. The army then marches south and the envoys of both sides meet near Autun. Provoked by Roman insults, Gawain kills Lucius' nephew and a skirmish follows in which the British are victorious. The next day the Romans ambush the Britons but are driven off with heavy losses.*]

Lucius Hiberius bore all these disasters ill. Harassed as he was by a variety of anxieties, he swayed first this way and then that, for he could not make up his mind whether to engage in a full-scale battle with Arthur or to withdraw inside Autun and there await reinforcements from the Emperor Leo. In the end he let his misgivings take the upper hand. The next night he marched his troops into Langres, on his way to the city of Autun. This move was reported to Arthur. He made up his mind to out-march Lucius along this route. That same night he by-passed the city of Autun on his left hand, and entered a valley called Saussy, through which Lucius would have to pass.

Arthur decided to draw up his troops in battle-formation. He ordered one legion, the command of which he entrusted to Earl Morvid, to stay constantly in reserve, so that, if need arose, he would know where he could withdraw, re-fit his companies, and plan new attacks on the enemy. He drew up the remainder of his troops in seven divisions, to each of which he allocated five thousand, five hundred and fifty-five fully-equipped men. One part of each of the divisions which he drew up consisted of cavalry and the second part of foot soldiers. They were given the following standing-orders: whenever the infantry showed signs of advancing to the attack, the cavalry of that division, moving forward obliquely with closed ranks, should do its utmost to break the force of the enemy. According to the British custom, the infantry battalions were drawn up in a square, with a right and left wing.

Auguselus, the King of Albany, was put in charge of the right wing, and Cador, Duke of Cornwall, of the left wing of the first division. Two famous leaders, Gerin of Chartres and Boso of Rydychen, called Oxford in the Saxon language, were put in command of a second division, with Aschil, King of the Danes, and Loth, King of the Norwegians, in charge of a third. Hoel, King of the Bretons, and Gawain, the King's nephew, commanded a fourth. In support of these, four other divisions were placed in the rear. Kay the Seneschal was put in charge of one, along with Bedevere the Cup-bearer. Holdin, the leader of the Ruteni, and Guitard, Duke of the Poitevins, commanded the second. Jugein of Leicester, Jonathel of Dorchester, and Cursalem of Caistor took charge of the third, and Urbgennius of Bath of the fourth.

Behind all these the King chose a position for himself and for a single legion which he had appointed to remain under his orders. There he set up the Golden Dragon

Arthur addresses his troops before the battle of Saussy. (*Bibliothèque royale, Brussels, MS 9243, f.55*^{v})

which he had as his personal standard. To this point the wounded and exhausted could withdraw in case of necessity, as if to a fortified camp. In the legion which he held back under his own command there were six thousand, six hundred and sixty-six men.

When all his troops were placed in position, Arthur gave them the following order of the day: 'My countrymen, you who have made Britain mistress of thirty kingdoms, I commend you for your courage, which, far from lessening, seems to me to increase in strength every day, despite the fact that you have waged no war for five long years, during which time you have devoted yourselves to the enjoyment of a life of ease rather than to the practice of war. Nevertheless, you do not seem to have degenerated in the least from your inborn valour. On the contrary, you have retained your courage to the full, for you have just put the Romans to flight, at a moment when, encouraged by the pride which came so naturally to them, they were doing their utmost to deprive you of your freedom. Moving forward with the advantage of numbers on their side, it was they who attacked you, but they were not strong enough to resist your advance and they had to withdraw in shame to that city over there. In a short time they will march out again and come through this valley on their way to Autun. You will be able to attack them when they least expect it and slaughter them like so many sheep. No doubt they imagined, when they planned to make your country pay them tribute and to enslave you yourselves, that they would discover in you the cowardice of Eastern peoples. Perhaps they have not heard of the wars you waged against the Danes and Norwegians and the leaders of the Gauls, when you delivered those peoples from their shameful allegiance to the Romans and forced them to submit to my own overlordship. We who had the strength to win a mightier battle will without any doubt at all be successful in this more trifling affair, if only we make up our minds with the same determination to crush these feeble creatures. What rewards you will win, if only you obey my will and my orders, as loyal soldiers ought to do! Once we have beaten the Romans in the field, we can immediately set off for Rome itself. As soon as we march upon Rome, we shall capture it. When we have captured it, you shall occupy it. And yours shall be its gold, silver, palaces, towers, castles, cities and all the other riches of the vanquished!'

As Arthur spoke, they all joined in one great shout of approval, for, as long as he was still alive, they were ready to die rather than leave the battlefield.

Lucius Hiberius found out about the trap which was laid for him. His first inclination was to run away, but he changed his mind. His courage returned to him and he decided to march out to meet the Britons through this same valley. He called his generals together, and delivered the following speech to them:

'My noble leaders,' he said, 'you to whose sovereignty the kingdoms both of the East and of the West owe obedience, remember now the deeds of your ancestors. They did not hesitate to shed their blood in their efforts to conquer the enemies of the Republic. They left an example of bravery and soldierly courage to those who were to come after them, for they fought as if God had decreed that none of them should ever die in battle. They nearly always won, avoiding death in their victory, for they held that no death could come to any man other than that ordained by the will of God. In that way the Republic increased in power as their own prowess became greater. All the integrity, honour and munificence which distinguished men of noble birth flourished in them down the years. This lifted them and their descendants to the overlordship of the whole world. I now want to rouse this same spirit in you. I beg you to remember the bravery of your forefathers. Strong in this courage, you must now march forth to meet your enemies in the valley where they lie in ambush for you. Do your utmost to exact from them what is rightly yours. Do not imagine for a moment that I sought refuge in this city because I feared them, or was afraid of meeting them in battle. On the contrary, I imagined that they would come after us in their senseless bravado and that, as they rushed forward, we might suddenly turn upon them. I thought that we might slaughter them as they tailed out in pursuit. Now, however, since they have behaved in a different way from what we anticipated, we in our turn must make new plans. We must go out to meet them and attack them as bravely as we possibly can. If they have the first advantage, then we must withstand them without letting our lines be broken, and bear the brunt of their initial attack. In this way we shall win without any shadow of doubt. In many a battle the side that stands firm in the first assault achieves victory in the end.'

As soon as Lucius had said these things and added a few other similar remarks, his men agreed with one accord. With heads erect and hands raised they swore an oath, and then armed themselves as quickly as they could. Once they were equipped, they marched out from Langres and made their way to the valley I have described, where Arthur had drawn up his own forces. In their turn they drew up twelve wedge-shaped legions, all of them infantry. They were arranged in wedges, in the Roman fashion, each single legion containing six thousand, six hundred and sixty-six men. Separate commanders were appointed to each of the legions, and according to the orders of these generals so they were to advance to the assault or stand firm when they themselves were attacked.

The Romans placed Lucius Catellus and Ali Fatima, the King of Spain, in command of the first legion; Hirtacius, King of the Parthians, and the Senator Marius Lepidus in command of the second; and Boccus, King of the Medes, with the Senator Gaius Metellus, in command of the third. They gave the command of the fourth legion to Sertorius, the King of Libya, and to the Senator Quintus Milvius. These four legions were placed in the first line. Behind them and in their rear were another four. They placed Serses, King of the Iturei, in charge of the first; Pandrasus, King of Egypt, in charge of the second; Politetes, Duke of Bithynia, in charge of the third; and Teucer, Duke of Phrygia, in charge of the fourth. Behind these again came yet another four legions: to the first of them they appointed the Senator Quintus Carucius; to the second Lelius Hostiensis; to the third Sulpicius Subuculus; and to the fourth Mauricius Silvanus.

Lucius himself moved about among them, now here, now there, making suggestions and telling them how to proceed. He commanded that a golden eagle, which he had brought with him as a standard, should be set up firmly in the centre. He gave orders that anyone whom the tide of battle had cut off from the others should do his utmost to force his way back to this eagle.

Now at last they stood face to face with javelins raised, the Britons on this side and the Romans on that. As soon as they heard the sound of the battle-trumpets, the legion commanded by the King of Spain and Lucius Catellus charged boldly at the division led by the King of Scotland and the Duke of Cornwall, but the latter stood firm, shoulder to shoulder, and the Roman force was not able to breach it. As the Roman legion persisted in its fierce attack, the division commanded by Gerin and Boso moved up at the double. The Roman legion fought bravely, as has already been said, but this fresh division attacked it with a sudden cavalry charge, broke through and came into contact with the legion which the King of the Parthians was directing against the division of Aschil, King of the Danes. Without a moment's delay the two forces met all along the line in a general mêlée, piercing each other's ranks and engaging each other in deadly combat. There ensued the most pitiable slaughter on both sides, with a bedlam of shouting and with men tumbling head foremost or feet first to the ground all over the place and vomiting forth their life with their heart's blood.

At first the Britons had the worst of it, for Bedevere the Cup-bearer was killed and Kay the Seneschal was mortally wounded. When Bedevere met Boccus, the King of the Medes, he was run through by the latter's lance and fell dead inside the enemy lines. Kay the Seneschal did his utmost to avenge Bedevere, but he was surrounded by battalions of Medes and received a mortal wound. Nevertheless, brave soldier as he was, he cut a way through with the force which he was commanding, scattered the Medes and would have retreated to his own support-group with his line of battle unbroken, had he not come up against the legion of the King of Libya, whose counter-attack completely scattered the troops under Kay's command. Even then he fell back with a few men still alive and made his way to the Golden Dragon with the corpse of Bedevere. Now the Neustrians grieved when they saw the body of their leader Bedevere slashed with so many wounds! The Angevins, too, bewailed as they treated the wounds of their leader Kay in every manner they could think of.

This, however, was no moment for weeping and wailing, with the battle-lines meeting on both sides in a bath of blood and giving them little respite for lamentations of this sort before they were compelled to look to their own defence. Hyrelgas, the nephew of Bedevere, was greatly moved by his uncle's death. He gathered round him three hundred of his own men, made a sudden cavalry charge and rushed through the enemy lines to the spot where he had seen the standard of the King of the Medes, for all the world like a wild boar through a pack of hounds, thinking little of what might happen to himself, if only he could avenge his uncle. When he came to the place where he had seen the King, he killed him, carried off his dead body to his own lines, put it down beside the corpse of the Cup-bearer and hacked it completely to pieces. With a great bellow, Hyrelgas roused his fellow-countrymen's battalions to fury, exhorting them to charge at the enemy and to harass them with wave after wave of assault, for now a new-found rage boiled up within them and the hearts of their frightened opponents were sinking. They were drawn up, he shouted, in better order in their battalions than their enemies, fighting hand-to-hand as they were, and they were in a position to attack repeatedly and to inflict more serious losses. The Britons were roused by this encouragement. They attacked their enemy all along the line, and terrible losses were sustained in both armies.

Vast numbers fell on the side of the Romans, including Ali Fatima the King of Spain, Micipsa the Babylonian, and the Senators Quintus Milvius and Marius Lepidus. On the side of the Britons there died Holdin the Duke of the Ruteni, Leodegarius of Boulogne, and the three British leaders Cursalem of Caistor, Guallauc of Salisbury, and Urbgennius of Bath. The troops these men had commanded were greatly weakened and they drew back until they reached the battle-line of the Armorican Britons, which was commanded by Hoel and Gawain. However, this force burst into flame, as it were, rallied those who had been retreating, and compelled the enemy, who, a moment before, had been in pursuit, to withdraw in its turn. The Britons pressed on hard, hurling the fugitives to the ground and killing them. They did not pause in their slaughter until they reached the Emperor's own bodyguard. When he saw what disaster had overtaken his men, the Emperor hurried forward to give them support.

When the battle began again, the Britons were sadly mauled. Chinmarchocus, the Duke of Tréguier, fell dead, and with him there died two thousand men. Three other famous leaders were killed: Riddomarcus, Bloctonius, and Iaginvius of Bodloan. Had these men been rulers of kingdoms, succeeding ages would have celebrated their fame, for their courage was immense. In the attack which they launched with Hoel and Gawain, and which I have described to you, no enemy with whom they came to grips escaped alive from their swords and lances. Eventually they reached the bodyguard of Lucius himself. There they were cut off by the Romans and met their end at the same time as their leader Chinmarchocus and his comrades whom I have mentioned.

No better knights than Hoel and Gawain have ever been born down the ages. When they learned of the death of their followers, they pressed on even more fiercely. They spurred on this way and that, first in one direction, then in another, in their relentless attack on the Emperor's bodyguard. Gawain, fearless in his courage, did his utmost to come up with Lucius himself in the fight. He made every effort to push forward, for he was the bravest of all the knights. He decimated the enemy by his onslaught and as he killed them he moved ever forward. Hoel was in no way less brave. He was raging like a thunderbolt in another sector, encouraging his own men and bringing death to his enemies. He parried their attacks with the utmost courage, giving and receiving blows, but not drawing back for a second. It would be difficult to say which of these two was the braver.

By dint of forcing his way through the enemy troops, as I have said above, Gawain finally found the opening for which he was longing. He rushed straight at the Roman general and fought with him hand to hand. Lucius was in the prime of his youth. He was a man of great courage, strength and prowess, and there was nothing that he wanted more than to join battle with a knight who would force him to prove his worth as a soldier. He accepted Gawain's challenge and fought with him. He was very keen to begin and rejoiced that his opponent was so famous a man. The contest between these two lasted for a long time. They dealt each other mighty blows, holding out their shields to their opponent's onslaught and each planning how he could kill the other.

As Gawain and Lucius fought bitterly in this way, the Romans suddenly recovered. They attacked the Bretons and so brought help to their general. They repulsed Hoel, Gawain and their troops, and began to cut their way into them. It was at this juncture that the Romans suddenly came face to face with Arthur and his division. He had heard a moment before of this slaughter which was being inflicted on his men. He moved up with his own division, drew his wonderful sword Caliburn and encouraged his fellow-soldiers by shouting loudly at them. 'What the devil are you doing, men?' he demanded. 'Are you letting these effeminate creatures slip away unhurt? Not one must escape alive! Think of your own right hands, which have played their part in so many battles and subjected thirty kingdoms to my sovereignty! Remember your ancestors, whom the Romans, then at the height of their power, made tributaries. Remember your liberty, which these halflings, who haven't anything like your strength, plan to take away from you! Not one must escape alive! Not one must escape, I say!'

As he shouted these insults, and many others, too, Arthur dashed straight at the enemy. He flung them to the ground and cut them to pieces. Whoever came his way was either killed himself or had his horse killed under him at a single blow. They ran away from him as sheep run from a fierce lion whom raging hunger compels to devour all that chance throws in his way. Their armour offered them no protection capable of preventing Caliburn, when wielded in the right hand of this mighty King, from forcing them to vomit forth their souls with their life-blood. Ill luck brought two Kings, Sertorius of Libya and Politetes of Bithynia, in Arthur's way. He hacked off their heads and bundled them off to hell.

When the Britons saw their King fighting in this way, they became more bold. They charged as one man at the Romans, attacking them in close formation. While the infantry was assailing them in this way in one sector, the cavalry strove to beat them down and run them through in another. The Romans fought back bitterly. Urged on by Lucius, they strove to take vengeance on the Britons for the slaughter inflicted by their noble King. The fight continued with as much violence on both sides as if they had only just at that moment come to blows with one another. On our side Arthur dealt blow after blow at his enemies (as I have told you already), shouting to the Britons to press on with the slaughter. On their side Lucius Hiberius urged his men on, repeatedly leading them himself in daring counter-attacks. He fought on with his own hand, going the round of his troops in each sector and killing every enemy who came his way, either with his lance or his sword. The most fearful slaughter was done on both sides. At times the Britons would have the upper hand, then the Romans would gain it.

In the end, as the battle continued between them, Morvid, the Earl of Gloucester, moved up at the double with his division, which, as I have told you, had been posted higher up in the hills. He attacked the enemy in the rear, when they were expecting nothing of the kind. His assault broke through their lines. As he moved forward he scattered them with tremendous slaughter. Many thousands of the Romans were killed. In the end, Lucius himself, their general, was brought to bay in the midst of his troops. He fell dead, pierced through by an unknown hand. The Britons followed up their advantage and finally won the day, but only after a supreme effort.

The Romans were scattered. In their terror some fled to out-of-the-way spots and forest groves, others made their way to cities and towns, and all of them sought refuge in the places which seemed safest to them. The Britons pursued them as fast as they could go, putting them to death miserably, taking them prisoner and plundering them: this the more easily as most of them voluntarily held out their hands to be bound, like so many women, in the hope of prolonging their lives a little. All this was ordained by divine providence. Just as in times gone by the ancestors of the Romans had harassed the forefathers of the Britons with their unjust oppressions, so now did the Britons make every effort to protect their own freedom, which the Romans were trying to take away from them, by refusing the tribute which was wrongly demanded of them.

As soon as victory was assured, Arthur ordered the bodies of his leaders to be separated from the carcasses of the enemy. Once they were gathered together, he had these bodies prepared for burial with royal pomp and then they were carried to the abbeys of their own native districts and interred there with great honour. Bedevere the Cup-bearer was borne, with loud lamentations, by the Neustrians to Bayeux, his own city, which his grandfather Bedevere I had founded. There he was laid to rest with all honour, beside a wall in a certain cemetery in the southern quarter of the city. Kay, who was mortally wounded, was carried away to Chinon, the town which he himself had built. Not long afterwards he died from his wound. As was fitting for a Duke of the Angevins, he was buried in a certain wood belonging to a convent of hermits not far from that town. Holdin, the Duke of the Ruteni, was carried to Flanders and laid to rest in his own city of Thérouanne. At Arthur's command, the rest of the leaders and princes were borne to abbeys in the vicinity. He took pity on his enemies and told the local inhabitants to bury them. He ordered the body of Lucius to be carried to the Senate, with a message that no other tribute could be expected from Britain.

Arthur spent the following winter in this same locality and found time to subdue the cities of the Allobroges. When summer came, he made ready to set out for Rome, and was already beginning to make his way through the mountains when the news was brought to him that his nephew Mordred, in whose care he had left Britain, had placed the crown upon his own head. What is more, this treacherous tyrant was living adulterously and out of wedlock with Queen Guinevere, who had broken the vows of her earlier marriage.

About this particular matter, most noble Duke, Geoffrey of Monmouth prefers to say nothing. He will, however, in his own poor style and without wasting words, describe the battle which our most famous King fought against his nephew, once he had returned to Britain after his victory; for that he found in the British treatise already referred to. He heard it, too, from Walter of Oxford, a man most learned in all branches of history.

As soon as the bad news of this flagrant crime had reached his ears, Arthur immediately cancelled the attack which he had planned to make on Leo, the Emperor of the Romans. He sent Hoel, the leader of the Bretons, with an army of Gauls, to restore peace in those parts; and then without more ado he himself set off for Britain, accompanied only by the island kings and their troops. That most infamous traitor Mordred, about whom I have told you, had sent Chelric, the leader of the Saxons, to Germany, to conscript as many troops as possible there, and to return as quickly as he could with those whom he was to persuade to join him. Mordred had made an agreement with Chelric that he would give him that part of the island which stretched from the River Humber to Scotland and all that Hengist and Horsa had held in Kent in Vortigern's day. In obedience to Mordred's command, Chelric landed with eight hundred ships filled with armed pagans. A treaty was agreed to and Chelric pledged his obedience to the traitor Mordred as if to the King. Mordred had brought the Scots, Picts and Irish into his alliance, with anyone else whom he knew to be filled with hatred for his uncle. In all, the insurgents were about eighty thousand in number, some of them pagans and some Christians.

Surrounded by this enormous army, in which he placed his hope, Mordred marched to meet Arthur as soon as the latter landed at Richborough. In the battle which ensued Mordred inflicted great slaughter on those who were trying to land. Auguselus, the King of Albany, and Gawain, the King's nephew, died that day, together with many others too numerous to describe. Ywain, the son of Auguselus' brother Urian, succeeded him in the kingship; and in the wars which followed he became famous because of the many brave deeds which he accomplished. In the end, but only with enormous difficulty, Arthur's men occupied the sea-shore. They drove Mordred and his army before them in flight and inflicted great slaughter on them in their turn. Profiting from their long experience in warfare, they drew up their troops most skilfully. They mixed their infantry with the cavalry and fought in such a way that when the line of foot-soldiers moved up to the attack, or was merely holding its position, the horse charged at an angle and did all that they could to break through the enemy lines and to force them to run away.

However, the perjurer reformed his army and so marched into Winchester on the following night. When this was announced to Queen Guinevere, she gave way to despair. She fled from York to the City of the Legions and there, in the church of Julius the Martyr, she took her vows among the nuns, promising to lead a chaste life.

Now that he had lost so many hundreds of his fellow-soldiers, Arthur was more angry than ever. He buried his dead and then marched on the third day to the city of Winchester and laid siege to his nephew who had taken refuge there. Mordred showed no sign of abandoning his plans. He gave his adherents every encouragement he could think of, and then marched out with his troops and drew them up ready for a pitched battle with his uncle.

Arthur and Mordred at the battle of Camlann.
(*Lambeth Palace Library, MS 6, f.66*[v])

The fight began and immense slaughter was done on both sides. The losses were greater in Mordred's army and they forced him to fly once more in shame from the battlefield. He made no arrangements whatsoever for the burial of his dead, but fled as fast as ship could carry him, and made his way towards Cornwall.

Arthur was filled with great mental anguish by the fact that Mordred had escaped him so often. Without losing a moment, he followed him to that same locality, reaching the River Camblam, where Mordred was awaiting his arrival. Mordred was indeed the boldest of men and always the first to launch an attack. He immediately drew his troops up in battle order, determined as he was either to win or to die, rather than run away again as he had done in the past. From his total force of troops, about which I have told you, there still remained sixty thousand men under his command. From these he mustered six divisions, in each of which he placed six thousand, six hundred and sixty-six armed men. From those who were left over he formed one single division, and, when he had assigned leaders to each of the others, he placed this last division under his own command. As soon as they were all drawn up, he went round to encourage each of them in turn, promising them the possessions of their enemies if only they stood firm and were successful in battle.

On the other side, Arthur, too, was marshalling his army. He divided his men into nine divisions of infantry, each drawn up in a square, with a right and left wing. To each he appointed a commander. Then he exhorted them to kill these perjured villains and robbers who, at the request of one who had committed treason against him, the King, had been brought into the island from foreign parts to steal their lands from them. He told them, too, that this miscellaneous collection of barbarians, come from a variety of countries – raw recruits who were totally inexperienced in war – would be quite incapable of resisting valiant men like themselves, who were the veterans of many battles, provided always that they made up their minds to attack boldly and to fight like men.

While the two commanders were encouraging their men in this way in both the armies, the lines of battle suddenly met, combat was joined, and they all strove with might and main to deal each other as many blows as possible. It is heartrending to describe what slaughter was inflicted on both sides, how the dying groaned, and how great was the fury of those attacking. Everywhere men were receiving wounds themselves or inflicting them, dying or dealing out death. In the end, when they had passed much of the day in this way, Arthur, with a single division in which he had posted six thousand, six hundred and sixty-six men, charged at the squadron where he knew Mordred was. They hacked a way through with their swords and Arthur continued to advance, inflicting terrible slaughter as he went. It was at this point that the accursed traitor was killed and many thousands of his men with him.

However, the others did not take to flight simply because Mordred was dead. They massed together from all over the battlefield and did their utmost to stand their ground with all the courage at their command. The battle which was now joined between them was fiercer than ever, for almost all the leaders on both sides were present and rushed into the fight at the head of their troops. On Mordred's side there fell Chelric, Elaf, Egbrict and Bruning, all of them Saxons; the Irish Gillapatric, Gillasel and Gillarvus; and the Scots and Picts, with nearly everyone in command of them. On Arthur's side there died Odbrict, King of Norway; Aschil, King of Denmark; Cador Limenich; and Cassivelaunus, with many thousands of the King's troops, some of them Britons, others from the various peoples he had brought with him. Arthur himself, our renowned King, was mortally wounded and was carried off to the Isle of Avalon, so that his wounds might be attended to. He handed the crown of Britain over to his cousin Constantine, the son of Cador Duke of Cornwall: this in the year 542 after our Lord's Incarnation.

THE DEATH OF ARTHUR

The cross said to have been found at Glastonbury. From Camden's Britannia *(1610)*

AN ADDITION TO GEOFFREY OF MONMOUTH? · POSSIBLE SOURCES & & &

The piece which follows has never been published before. There are only two surviving manuscripts of it, one a garbled copy and the other a summary, and it is only distantly connected with other versions of King Arthur's death. The most likely explanation for its existence lies in the brief and mysterious account which Geoffrey of Monmouth and his imitators gave of Arthur's death. The piece is headed 'This is the true history of Arthur's death', and the closing words lead into the chapter of Geoffrey of Monmouth's book which follows Arthur's death, as though the story was intended to replace the end of Geoffrey's account by a fuller and more explicit version. It is included here as a reminder that anyone was at liberty to invent a variation on the 'accepted' story of Arthur, though very few of these variations have actually survived.

The main manuscript in which the story is found is fourteenth-century, and probably came from North Wales, but beyond this it is difficult to say when the story was written. There are details in it which echo the romance version of Arthur's death as told by Malory (pp. 135–138 below). However, they are distant echoes: here Arthur is killed by adder's venom, in Malory an adder is the cause of the great last battle; here Arthur's tomb appears miraculously in the place where he was to be buried, in Malory the tomb materialises miles from where he was last seen alive; in both, Arthur is buried at a hermitage. Other details come from Celtic tradition; there was a widespread belief that Arthur was still alive, which Geoffrey hinted at by making him go to the mysterious isle of Avalon, and which we know of from a number of twelfth-century writers. However, the discovery of Arthur's supposed grave at Glastonbury in 1191 had severely shaken belief in this idea, and it would be tempting to say that the present story, which does not mention Glastonbury as the site of the tomb but puts his burial firmly in Gwynedd, was earlier than 1191. But the Glastonbury discovery was not accepted as genuine by everyone, and the writer could simply have ignored it.

Other parts of the narrative seem to be taken from the world of Welsh romance as found in *The Mabinogion* (p. 34 below). For instance, the thunder and mist which descends on Arthur's body is not unlike an episode in the story of Pryderi, when Pryderi and his wife Rhiannon are laid under a spell:

> Rhiannon saw the gate of the caer open; there was no concealment on it, and in she came. And as soon as she came, she perceived Pryderi laying hold of the bowl, and she came towards him. 'Alas, my lord,' said she, 'what dost thou here?' And she laid hold of the bowl with him, and as soon as she laid hold, her own hands stuck to the bowl (of the fountain) and her feet to the slab, so that she too was not able to utter one word. And with that, as soon as it was night, lo, a peal of thunder over them, and a fall of mist, and thereupon the caer vanished, and away with them too.

A bowl and fountain are associated with a violent storm in a French romance based on Celtic stories, Chrétien de Troyes' *Yvain* (p. 59 below), and the disappearance of Arthur's body could have come from a more elaborate version of Pryderi's enchantment. Equally, though there is no exact parallel, the young man with his elm lance could be a magical figure from Welsh romance. Arthur's devotion to the Virgin Mary could be taken from *The History of the Britons*. The general style of the piece is ambitious in its language, and points to a well-educated cleric as the author. Such, in brief, are the few scraps of evidence we have about this curious fragment, which, because of the complex phrasing of the original, is presented here in a fairly free translation.

The Death of Arthur

Therefore, when the battle which was fought between Arthur King of the Britons and Mordred – whom I cannot call his nephew but rather his betrayer – had ended, and Mordred had been handed over to death, there were many dead all around, and many of the enemy were left on the spot. The king, although he had gained the victory, left the field with a heavy heart. He had been wounded; though the wound was not immediately fatal, it threatened to be so in the near future. At length he gave thanks for the victory he had achieved to the Creator of all things and to Our Lord's mother, the blessed Virgin Mary. He tempered the bitterness of his sorrow at the slaughter of his men with the joy of victory. This done, leaning on his shield, he sat down on the ground in order to recuperate. As he was sitting there, he ordered four of the leaders of his people, who had been summoned, to take off his armour carefully, lest a careless movement should increase the pain of his recent wounds. When the king was disarmed, a young man appeared, pleasant-looking, tall in stature, and, from the shape of his limbs, of very great strength; he was making his way on horseback, armed with a shaft of elm in his right hand, which was firm, and neither twisted nor knotty but smooth, with a sharp point like a lance, since at some time in the past it had been hardened with fire by a smith and made harder by being tempered in water. It had been dipped in adder's venom, so that it wounded less by the force of the thrust than by the poison, thus making up for any lack of strength in him who threw it. This high-spirited youth was set to ride over the king, but instead, halting in front of him, he cast the weapon just described at the king, adding to his already serious wounds a yet more serious one. Having done this, he fled in haste, but he did not go far, for the king, acting as quickly as a knight in full health, planted a quivering spear in the back of the fleeing youth, and pierced his heart. Thus wounded, he soon gave up the ghost. So, with the instrument of the king's death dead, the king immediately grew pale and discoloured as if in his last hour, and he told those around that he had not long to live. When they learned this, a flood of tears bathed the faces of those who loved him deeply, and mourning afflicted them all, since they despaired of maintaining Britain's freedom as he had done. As the proverb says, if better rarely follows good, it is much rarer for the best to follow the best. Then the king, recovering for a little, gave orders that he should be carried to Gwynedd, for he intended to stay in the isle of Avalon, a pleasant and delightful place, and very peaceful, where the pain of his wounds would be eased. When they arrived there, doctors used all their art to search the king's wounds; but the king found no relief from their efforts. Despairing of recovery, he sent for the archbishop of London, who came in answer to his summons accompanied by two bishops, Urian of Bangor and Urbegen of Glamorgan. St David, archbishop of Menevia, would have been present if he had not been physically prevented by a serious illness. In the presence of the bishops Arthur made his confession and rendered himself answerable to his Creator's indulgence. Then he rewarded those who had served him with the bounty of royal generosity. And he gave the realm of Britain to Constantine, son of Duke Cador. This done, he was given the Last Sacrament and took his leave of this wicked world. And the story relates that, clad in a hair-shirt, like a true penitent, with his hands outstretched he commended his spirit into the hands of his Redeemer. O what a doleful day, a day worthy of grief and full of mourning, that no inhabitant of Britain can remember without sorrow, and for good reason: for that day in Britain justice faltered, obedience to law became rare, the quietness of peace was disturbed, and noble liberty was imprisoned. For with glorious Arthur taken from their midst, Britain was deprived of victory, since she who was long in power is now entirely subservient to others. But lest I ramble on too long in this vein, let my pen describe the funeral of our dead hero. The three bishops aforesaid commended his spirit to Him who gave it with prayers and devotions. The others laid out the king's body royally, anointing it with balsam and myrrh and preparing it for burial. The next day they took the dead king's body to a little chapel dedicated to the Blessed Virgin, since he had vowed in his lifetime that no other ground should receive him. It was there he wished to be hidden in earth, there that he desired his flesh to return to its origin, there that he commended himself to earth's keeping after his death, in the place which he honoured above all other. But when they arrived at the door of the chapel, the small and narrow entrance prevented them from bringing in the body, because of its size. So the body was left outside by the wall on a bier, because nothing else could be done: for the entry to the aforementioned chapel was so narrow and small that no one could enter it unless, turning sideways, they pushed in with all their might and skill. The inhabitant of this chapel was a certain hermit, who enjoyed the serenity of this most peaceful home all the more for its remoteness from the squalor of everyday business. The senior bishops entered it; the dead man's body remained outside. Meanwhile, while the bishops were performing the last rites, the air thundered, the earth quaked, storms poured down relentlessly from the sky, lightning flashed, and winds blew from every quarter. After this, after the briefest of intervals, the air was filled with a mist which absorbed the brightness of the lightning, and plunged the bier on which the royal corpse lay into such darkness that the attendants could see nothing, though their eyes were wide open. This mist persisted without a break from nine in the morning until three in the afternoon. As the hours passed, the air never grew still from the crash of thunder. Finally, when the mist had lifted, and the air became clear again, they found no trace of the royal corpse, for the king had been carried off to an abode specially prepared for him; they looked at a bier empty of the body which had been left on it. They were seized by disquiet as a result of the removal of the king's body, to such an extent that great doubt as to the truth arose among them: 'Where could this mighty power have come from? By whose violence was he carried off?' Even today, there are shadowy doubts as to where King Arthur was destined to find his place of rest. For this reason certain people say he is still alive, and is both sound and well, since he was carried off without anyone's knowledge. Others contradict this bold guess, saying positively and without the least trace of doubt that he paid the debt of death: they rely on the following argument, that, when the mist already mentioned had lifted and visibility had been restored, a sealed tomb appeared in the sight of those present, both solidly closed and of one piece, so that it seemed indeed to be a single stone, whole and solid, rather than made in pieces with mortar and a builder's skill. They thought that the king was buried in its recesses, since they had discovered it already sealed and closed. And since this discovery was made, there has been no small disagreement among them.

He governed the realm of Britain for thirty-nine years in the power of his strength, the wisdom of his mind, the acuteness of his judgement, and through his renown in battle. In the fortieth year of his reign, he was destined to end his human lot. Therefore, with Arthur dead, Constantine the son of Duke Cador, ascended to the British realm, etc.

THE MABINOGION

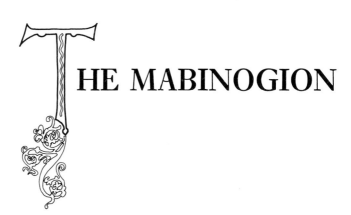

Culhwch and Olwen

Kilhwych, the King's son by A. J. Gaskin (1901)
(Birmingham City Museum and Art Gallery)

THE WELSH ROMANCES · MARVELS AND ADVENTURES · RECITALS AND MANUSCRIPTS & & &

The earliest surviving romances centred on Arthur are in Welsh, and of these the most important is the story of how Arthur's cousin Culhwch won Olwen, daughter of the chief of the giants, Ysbaddaden. It is far removed from the knightly world in which we usually expect to find Arthur, but it has two features which are typical of all the later stories about it. Arthur is ruler of the noblest court in the world, where all the great heroes are to be found, and the adventures that happen are all in some way marvellous and strange. The anonymous author of *Culhwch* was drawing on a tradition that goes back to the stories of ancient Ireland, tales of Cuchulainn and his ilk, and his story is set in a much more primitive society than that depicted by Geoffrey of Monmouth. The central episode, the pursuit of the great boar Twrch Trwyth, is a story to which the author of *The History of the Britons* referred in his account of the marvels of Britain; there is no question of jousting or mail-clad warfare here, but of hunting and journeys on foot through a landscape where anything might happen.

Culhwch and Olwen, along with the other ten tales generally known as *The Mabinogion*, are in fact the only surviving examples of the art of the Welsh bards from this early period, and the material on which they are based is partly a reworking of old tales about the pagan gods of the Britons, just as the Irish tales have a strong mythological streak. This accounts for the readiness with which marvellous happenings are accepted. Such happenings are commonest in the four stories which describe Pryderi's birth and adventures, where the whole chain of events takes place in a remote unworldly atmosphere. *Culhwch* is more artificial than this, as if a masterly and even slightly unorthodox storyteller had decided to take a basic folklore theme, the wedding of the giant's daughter, and to weave around it the most fantastic series of exploits that he could gather together, intertwined with other folklore themes and described in exuberant language. In their introduction to this translation, Gwyn and Thomas Jones write:

> The zest of this unknown storyteller still hits one like a bursting wave; there is magnificence in his self-awareness and virtuosity. One feels how he rejoiced in being equal to all his occasions: the gallant picture of young Culhwch and his steed, the bombast of Glewlwyd Mighty-grasp, the poetic beauty of the episode of the oldest animals, the savage grotesquery of Ysbaddaden Chief Giant, the headlong rush of the hunting of Twrch Trwyth, the lyricism of the description of Olwen.

That so little of the rich tradition of Welsh storytelling has survived is due to the relative isolation of Welsh culture, and to the fact that the Welsh bards were performers who recited their stories rather than wrote them down. Something of the quality of performance survives in *Culhwch*: only part of the achievement of the tasks set is described, as if the storyteller varied his repertoire as the mood took him. What chance led to the recording of these tales we shall never know, but it was the exception rather than the rule. A great mass of material, certainly in Welsh, possibly also in Breton, was in circulation among bards and storytellers, and it was from this that the particular flavour of Arthurian romances was to develop.

Here then is an Arthurian romance untouched by the world of chivalry. The story begins with the birth of Culhwch and the fate pronounced over him by his stepmother, that he shall never have any other wife than Olwen. He sets out to enlist Arthur's help, which Arthur duly gives, and an immense catalogue of all those who aided him in his quest follows, most of them being men with magical powers, like Clust son of Clustfeinad who, even if buried seven fathoms in the earth, could hear an ant leave its nest in the morning fifty miles away. Culhwch takes Cei (Kay) and Bedwyr (Bedivere) with him when he sets out on his journey.

Culhwch and Olwen

Away they went till they came to a wide open plain and saw a fort, the greatest of forts in the world. That day they journeyed. When they thought they were near to the fort they were no nearer than at first. And the second and the third day they journeyed, and with difficulty did they get thereto. However, as they were coming to the same plain as it, they could see a great flock of sheep without limit or end to it, and a shepherd tending the sheep on top of a mound, and a jerkin of skins upon him, and at his side a shaggy mastiff which was bigger than a nine-year-old stallion. It was the way of him that never a lamb had he lost, much less a grown beast. No company had ever fared past him that he did not do it harm or deadly hurt; every dead tree and bush that was on the plain, his breath would burn them to the very ground.

Quoth Cei: 'Gwrhyr Interpreter of Tongues, go and have words with yonder man.' 'Cei, I made no promise to go save as far as thou thyself wouldst go.' 'Then let us go there together.' Quoth Menw son of Teirgwaedd: 'Have no qualms to go thither. I will cast a spell over the dog, so that he shall do harm to none.'

They came to where the shepherd was. Quoth they, 'Things are well with thee, shepherd.' 'May things never be better with you than with me.' 'Yea, by God, for thou art chief.' 'There is no affliction to do me harm save my wife.' 'Whose are the sheep thou tendest, or whose is the fort?' 'Fools of men that you are! Throughout the world it is known that this is the fort of Ysbaddaden Chief Giant.' 'And thou, who art thou?' 'Custennin son of Mynwyedig am I, and because of my wife Ysbaddaden Chief Giant has wrought my ruin. You too, who are you?' 'Messengers of Arthur are here, to seek Olwen.' 'Whew, men! God protect you! For all the world, do not that. Never a one has come to make that request that went away with his life.'

The shepherd arose. As he arose Culhwch gave him a ring of gold. He sought to put on the ring, but it would not go on him, and he placed it in the finger of his glove and went home and gave the glove to his wife. And she took the ring from the glove. 'Whence came this ring to thee, husband? 'Twas not often that thou hast had treasure-trove.' 'I went to the sea, to find sea-food. Lo! I saw a body coming in on the tide. Never saw I body so beautiful as that, and on its finger I found this ring.' 'Alas, husband, since sea does not tolerate a dead man's jewels therein, show me that body.' 'Wife, the one whose body that is, thou shalt see him here presently.' 'Who is that?' the woman asked. 'Culhwch son of Cilydd son of Cyleddon Wledig, by Goleuddydd daughter of Anlawdd Wledig, his mother, who is come to seek Olwen.' Two feelings possessed her: she was glad that her nephew, her sister's son, was coming to her; and she was sad because she had never seen any depart with his life that had come to make that request.

They came forward to the gate of the shepherd Custennin's court. She heard the noise of their coming. She ran with joy to meet them. Cei snatched a log out of the woodpile, and she came to meet them, to try and throw her arms about their necks. Cei thrust a stake between her two hands. She squeezed the stake so that it became a twisted withe. Quoth Cei, 'Woman, had it been I thou didst squeeze in this wise, there were no need for another to love me ever. An ill love, that!'

They came into the house and their needs were supplied. After a while when all were letting themselves be busied, the woman opened a coffer alongside the hearth, and out of it arose a lad with curly yellow hair. Quoth Gwrhyr, ' 'Twere pity to hide a lad like this. I know that it is no fault of his own that is visited upon him.' Quoth the woman, 'He is all that is left. Three-and-twenty sons of mine has Ysbaddaden Chief Giant slain, and I have no more hope of this one than of the others.' Quoth Cei, 'Let him keep company with me, and we shall not be slain save together.'

They ate. Quoth the woman, 'On what errand are you come hither?' 'We are come to seek Olwen.' 'For God's sake, since none from the fort has yet seen you, get you back!' 'God knows we will not get us back till we have seen the maiden. Will she come to where she may be seen?' 'She comes hither every Saturday to wash her head; and in the bowl where she washes she leaves all her rings. Neither she nor her messenger ever comes for them.' 'Will she come hither if she is sent for?' 'God knows I will not slay my soul. I will not betray the one who trusts in me. But if you pledge your word you will do her no harm, I will send for her.' 'We pledge it,' said they.

She was sent for. And she came, with a robe of flame-red silk about her, and around the maiden's neck a torque of red gold, and precious pearls thereon and rubies. Yellower was her head than the flower of the broom, whiter was her flesh than the foam of the wave; whiter were her palms and her fingers than the shoots of the marsh trefoil from amidst the fine gravel of a welling spring. Neither the eye of the mewed hawk, nor the eye of the thrice-mewed falcon, not an eye was there fairer than hers. Whiter were her breasts than the breast of the white swan, redder were her cheeks than the reddest foxgloves. Who so beheld her would be filled with love of her. Four white trefoils sprang up behind her wherever she went; and for that reason was she called Olwen.

She entered the house and sat between Culhwch and the high seat, and even as he saw her he knew her. Said Culhwch to her, 'Ah maiden, 'tis thou I have loved. And come thou with me.' 'Lest sin be charged to thee and me, that I may not do at all. My father has sought a pledge of me that I go not without his counsel, for he shall live only until I go with a husband. There is, however, counsel I will give thee, if thou wilt take it. Go ask me of my father. And however much he demand of thee, do thou promise to get it, and me too shalt thou get. But if he have cause to doubt at all, get me thou shalt not, and 'tis well for thee if thou escape with thy life.' 'I promise all that, and will obtain it,' said he.

She went to her chamber. They then arose to go after her to the fort, and slew nine gatemen who were at nine gates without a man crying out, and nine mastiffs without one squealing. And they went forward to the hall.

Quoth they, 'In the name of God and man, greeting unto thee, Ysbaddaden Chief Giant.' 'And you, where are you going?' 'We are going to seek Olwen thy daughter for Culhwch son of Cilydd.' 'Where are those rascal servants and those ruffians of mine?' said he. 'Raise up the forks under my two eyelids that I may see my future son-in-law.' That was done. 'Come hither tomorrow. I will give you some answer.'

They rose, and Ysbaddaden Chief Giant snatched at one of the three poisoned stone-spears which were by his hand and hurled it after them. And Bedwyr caught it and hurled it back at him, and pierced Ysbaddaden Chief Giant right through the ball of his knee. Quoth he, 'Thou cursed savage son-in-law! I shall walk the worse up a slope. Like the sting of a gadfly the poisoned iron has pained me. Cursed be the smith who fashioned it, and the anvil on which it was wrought, so painful it is!'

That night they lodged in the house of Custennin. And on the morrow with pomp and with brave combs set in their hair they came into the hall. They said, 'Ysbaddaden Chief Giant, give us thy daughter in return for her portion and her maiden fee to thee and her two kinswomen. And unless thou give her, thou shalt meet thy death because of her.' 'She and her four great-grandmothers and her four great-grandfathers are yet alive. I must needs take counsel with them.' 'So be it with thee,' said they. 'Let us go to our meat.' As they arose he took hold of the second stone-spear which was by his hand and hurled it after them. And Menw son of Teirgwaedd caught it and hurled it back at him, and pierced him in the middle of his breast, so that it came out in the small of his back. 'Thou cursed savage son-in-law! Like the bite of a big-headed leech the hard iron has pained me. Cursed be the forge wherein it was heated. When I go uphill, I shall have tightness of chest, and bellyache, and a frequent loathing of meat.' They went to their meat.

And the third day they came to court. Quoth they, 'Ysbaddaden Chief Giant, shoot at us no more. Seek not thy harm and deadly hurt and death.' 'Where are my servants? Raise up the forks – my eyelids have fallen over the ball of my eyes – so that I may take a look at my future son-in-law.' They arose, and as they arose he took the third poisoned stone-spear and hurled it after them. And Culhwch caught it and hurled it back, even as he wished, and pierced him through the ball of the eye, so that it came out through the nape of the neck. 'Thou cursed savage son-in-law! So long as I am left alive, the sight of my eyes will be the worse. When I go against the wind they will water, a headache I shall have, and a giddiness each new moon. Cursed be the forge wherein it was heated. Like the bite of a mad dog to me the way the poisoned iron has pierced me.' They went to their meat.

On the morrow they came to court. Quoth they, 'Shoot not at us. Seek not the harm and deadly hurt and martyrdom that are upon thee, or what may be worse, if such be thy wish. Give us thy daughter.' 'Where is he who is told to seek my daughter?' ' 'Tis I who seek her, Culhwch son of Cilydd.' 'Come hither where I may see thee.' A chair was placed under him, face to face with him.

Said Ysbaddaden Chief Giant, 'Is it thou that seekest my daughter?' ' 'Tis I who seek her.' 'Thy pledge would I have that thou wilt not do worse by me than is just.' 'Thou shalt have it.' 'When I have myself gotten that which I shall name to thee, then thou shalt get my daughter.' 'Name what thou wouldst name.'

'I will,' said he. 'Dost see the great thicket yonder?' 'I see.' 'I must have it uprooted out of the earth and burnt on the face of the ground so that the cinders and ashes thereof be its manure; and that it be ploughed and sown so that it be ripe in the morning against the drying of the dew, in order that it may be made into meat and drink for thy wedding guests and my daughter's. And all that I must have done in one day.'

'It is easy for me to get that, though thou think it is not easy.'

'Though thou get that, there is that thou wilt not get. A husbandman to till and prepare that land, other than Amaethon son of Dôn. He will not come with thee of his own free will, nor canst thou compel him.'

'It is easy for me to get that, though thou think it is not easy.'

'Though thou get that, there is that thou wilt not get. Gofannon son of Dôn to come to the headland to set the irons. He will not do work of his own free will, save for a king in his own right, nor canst thou compel him.'

'It is easy for me to get that, though thou think it is not easy.'

'Though thou get that, there is that thou wilt not get. The two oxen of Gwlwlydd Wineu, both yoked together to plough well the rough ground yonder. He will not give them of his own free will, nor canst thou compel him.'

'It is easy for me to get that, though thou think it is not easy.'

'Though thou get that, there is that thou wilt not get. The Melyn Gwanwyn and the Ych Brych, both yoked together, must I have.'

'It is easy for me to get that, though thou think it is not easy.'

'Though thou get that, there is that thou wilt not get. The two horned oxen, one of which is beyond Mynydd Bannawg, and the other this side – and to fetch them together in the one plough. Nyniaw and Peibiaw are they, whom God transformed into oxen for their sins.'

'It is easy for me to get that, though thou think it is not easy.'

'Though thou get that, there is that thou wilt not get. Dost see the hoed tilth yonder?' 'I see.' 'When first I met the mother of that maiden, nine hestors of flax seed were sown therein; neither black nor white has come out of it yet, and I have that measure still. I must have that in the new-broken ground yonder, so that it may be a white head-dress for my daughter's head on the day of thy wedding-feast.'

(*And so the catalogue continues, ending with the hunting of Twrch Trwyth and the obtaining of Wrnach's sword.*)

'It is easy for me to get that, though thou think it is not easy.'

'Though thou get that, there is that thou wilt not get. Wakefulness without sleep at night shalt thou have in seeking those things. And thou wilt not get them, nor wilt thou get my daughter.'

'Horses shall I have and horsemen, and my lord and kinsman Arthur will get me all those things. And I shall win thy daughter, and thou shalt lose thy life.'

'Set forward now. Thou shalt not be answerable for food or raiment for my daughter. Seek those things. And when those things are won, my daughter too thou shalt win.'

That day they journeyed till evening, until there was seen a great fort of mortared stone, the greatest of forts in the world. Lo, they saw coming from the fort a black man, bigger than three men of this world. Quoth they to him: 'Whence comest thou, fellow?' 'From the fort you see yonder.' 'Whose is the fort?' 'Fools of men that you are! There is none in the world does not know whose fort this is. It belongs to Wrnach the Giant.' 'What usage is there for a guest and far-comer alighting at this fort?' 'Ah, chieftain, God protect you! No guest has ever come thence with his life. None is permitted therein save him who brings his craft.'

They made their way to the gate. Quoth Gwrhyr Interpreter of Tongues, 'Is there a porter?' 'There is. And thou, may thy head not be thine, that thou dost ask!' 'Open the gate.' 'I will not.' 'Why wilt thou not open it?' 'Knife has gone into meat, and drink into horn, and a thronging in Wrnach's hall. Save for a craftsman who brings his craft, it will not be opened again this night.' Quoth Cei, 'Porter, I have a craft.' 'What craft hast thou?' 'I am the best furbisher of swords in the world.' 'I will go and tell that to Wrnach the Giant and will bring thee an answer.'

The porter came inside. Said Wrnach the Giant, 'Thou hast news from the gate?' 'I have. There is a company at the entrance to the gate who would like to come in.' 'Didst thou ask if they had a craft with them?' 'I did, and one of them declared he knew how to furbish swords.' 'I had need of him. For some time I have been seeking one who should polish my sword, but I found him not. Let that man in, since he had a craft.'

The porter came and opened the gate, and Cei came inside all alone. And he greeted Wrnach the Giant. A chair was placed under him. Said Wrnach, 'Why, man, is this true which is reported of thee, that thou knowest how to furbish swords?' 'I do that,' said Cei. The sword was brought to him. Cei took a striped whetsone from under his arm. 'Which dost thou prefer upon it, white-haft or dark-haft?' 'Do with it what pleases thee, as though it were thine own.' He cleaned half of one side of the blade for him and put it in his hand. 'Does that content thee?' 'I would rather than all that is in my dominions that the whole of it were like this. It is a shame a man as good as thou should be without a fellow.' 'Oia, good sir, I have a fellow, though he does not practise this craft.' 'Who is he?' 'Let the porter go forth, and I will tell his tokens: the head of his spear will leave its shaft, and it will draw blood from the wind, and settle upon the shaft again.' The gate was opened and Bedwyr entered in. Said Cei, 'A wondrous gift has Bedwyr, though he does not practise this craft.'

And there was great debate betwixt those men outside. Cei and Bedwyr came inside. And a young lad came inside with them, the shepherd Custennin's only son. He and his comrades, who stayed close to him, crossed the three baileys as though this were a thing less than naught to them, until they came inside the fort. Quoth his comrades of Custennin's son, 'Best of men is he.' From then on he was called Goreu son of Custennin. They dispersed to their lodgings that they might slay those who lodged them, without the Giant knowing.

The furbishing the sword was done, and Cei gave it into the hand of Wrnach the Giant, as though to see whether the work was to his satisfaction. Said the giant, 'The work is good, and I am content with it.' Quoth Cei, 'It is thy scabbard has damaged thy sword. Give it to me to take out the wooden side-pieces, and let me make new ones for it.' And he took the scabbard, and the sword in the other hand. He came and stood over the giant, as if he would put the sword into the scabbard. He sank it into the giant's head and took off his head at a blow. They laid waste the fort and took away what treasures they would. To the very day at the end of a year they came to Arthur's court, and the sword of Wrnach the Giant with them.

They told Arthur how it had gone with them. Arthur said, 'Which of those marvels will it be best to seek first?' 'It will be best,' said they, 'to seek Mabon son of Modron, and there is no getting him until his kinsman Eidoel son of Aer is got first.' Arthur rose up, and the warriors of the Island of Britain with him, to seek for Eidoel; and they came to Glini's outer wall, to where Eidoel was in prison. Glini stood on the rampart of the fort, and he said, 'Arthur, what wouldst thou have of me, since thou wilt not leave me alone on this crag? I have no good herein and no pleasure, neither wheat nor oats have I, without thee too seeking to do me harm.' Arthur said, 'Not to thy hurt have I come hither, but to seek out the prisoner that is with thee.' 'I will give thee the prisoner, though I had not bargained to give him up to any one. And besides this, my aid and my backing thou shalt have.'

The men said to Arthur, 'Lord, get thee home. Thou canst not proceed with thy host to seek things so petty as these.' Arthur said, 'Gwrhyr Interpreter of Tongues, it is right for thee to go on this quest. All tongues hast thou, and thou canst speak with some of the birds and the beasts. Eidoel, it is right for thee to go along with my men to seek him – he is thy first cousin. Cei and Bedwyr, I have hope that whatever you go to seek will be obtained. Go then for me on this quest.'

They went on their way as far as the Ouzel of Cilgwri. 'For God's sake,' Gwrhyr asked her, 'knowest thou aught of Mabon son of Modron, who was taken when three nights old from betwixt his mother and the wall?' The Ouzel said, 'When first I came hither, there was a smith's anvil here, and as for me I was a young bird. No work has been done upon it save whilst my beak was thereon every evening. Today there is not so much of it as a nut not worn away. God's vengeance on me if I have heard aught of the man you are asking after. Nevertheless, that which it is right and proper for me to do for Arthur's messengers, I will do. There is a kind of creature God made before me;

I will go along as your guide thither.'

They came to the place where the Stag of Rhedynfre was. 'Stag of Rhedynfre, here we have come to thee, Arthur's messengers, since we know of no animal older than thou. Say, knowest thou aught of Mabon son of Modron, who was taken away from his mother when three nights old?' The Stag said, 'When first I came hither, there was but one tine on either side of my head, and there were no trees here save a single oak sapling, and that grew into an oak with a hundred branches, and the oak thereafter fell, and today there is naught of it save a red stump; from that day to this I have been here. I have heard naught of him you are asking after. Nevertheless I will be your guide, since you are Arthur's messengers, to the place where there is an animal God made before me.'

They came to the place where the Owl of Cwm Cawlwyd was. 'Owl of Cwm Cawlwyd, here are Arthur's messengers. Knowest thou aught of Mabon son of Modron, who was taken away from his mother when three nights old?' 'If I knew it, I would tell it. When first I came hither, the great valley you see was a wooded glen, and a race of men came thereto and it was laid waste. And the second wood grew up therein, and this wood is the third. And as for me, why! the roots of my wings are mere stumps. From that day to this I have heard naught of the man you are asking after. Nevertheless I will be a guide to Arthur's messengers until you come to the place where is the oldest creature that is in this world, and he that has fared furthest afield, the Eagle of Gwernabwy.'

Gwrhyr said, 'Eagle of Gwernabwy, we have come to thee, Arthur's messengers, to ask whether thou knowest aught of Mabon son of Modron who was taken away from his mother when three nights old?' The Eagle said, 'I came here a long time ago, and when first I came hither I had a stone, and from its top I pecked at the stars each evening; now it is not a hand-breadth in height. From that day to this I have been here, but have heard naught of him you are asking after. Save that at one faring I went to seek my meat as far as Llyn Llyw, and when I came there I sank my claws into a salmon, thinking he would be meat for me many a long day, and he drew me down into the depths, so that it was with difficulty I got away from him. And my whole kindred and I went after him, to seek to destroy him. But he sent messengers to make peace with me, and came to me in person to have fifty tridents taken out of his back. Unless he knows something of what you seek, I know none who may. Nevertheless, I will be your guide to the place where he is.'

They came to the place where he was. The Eagle said, 'Salmon of Llyn Llyw, I have come to thee with Arthur's messengers to ask whether thou knowest aught of Mabon son of Modron who was taken away from his mother when three nights old?' 'As much as I know, I will tell. With every tide I go up along the river till I come to the bend of the wall of Caer Loyw; and there I found such distress that I never found its equal in all my life; and, that you may believe, let one of you come here on my two shoulders.' And Cei and Gwrhyr Interpreter of Tongues went upon the salmon's two shoulders, and they journeyed until they came to the far side of the wall from the prisoner, and they could hear wailing and lamentation on the far side of the wall from them. Gwrhyr said, 'What man laments in this house of stone?' 'Alas, man, there is cause for him who is here to lament. Mabon son of Modron is here in prison; and none was ever so cruelly imprisoned in a prison house as I; neither the imprisonment of Lludd Silver-hand nor the imprisonment of Greid son of Eri.' 'Hast thou hope of getting thy release for gold or for silver or for worldly wealth, or by battle and fighting?' 'What is got of me, will be got by fighting.'

They returned thence and came to where Arthur was. They told where Mabon son of Modron was in prison. Arthur summoned the warriors of this Island and went to Caer Loyw where Mabon was in prison. Cei and Bedwyr went upon the two shoulders of the fish. Whilst Arthur's warriors assaulted the fort, Cei broke through the wall and took the prisoner on his back; and still he fought with the men. Arthur came home and Mabon with him, a free man.

Arthur said, 'Which of the marvels is it now best to seek first?' 'It is best to seek for the two whelps of the bitch Rhymhi.' 'Is it known where she is?' asked Arthur. 'She is,' said one, 'at Aber Deu Cleddyf.' Arthur came to the house of Tringad in Aber Cleddyf and asked him, 'Hast thou heard of her in these parts? In what shape is she?' 'In the shape of a she-wolf,' answered he, 'and she goes about with her two whelps. Often has she slain my stock, and she is down in Aber Cleddyf in a cave.'

Arthur went to sea in his ship Prydwen, and others by land to hunt the bitch, and in this wise they surrounded her and her two whelps, and God changed them back into their own semblance for Arthur. Arthur's host dispersed, one by one, two by two.

And as Gwythyr son of Greidawl was one day journeying over a mountain, he heard a wailing and a grievous lamentation, and these were a horrid noise to hear. He sprang forward in that direction, and when he came there he drew his sword and smote off the anthill level with the ground, and so saved them from the fire. And they said to him, 'Take thou God's blessing and ours, and that which no man can ever recover, we will come and recover it for thee.' It was they thereafter who came with the nine hestors of flax seed which Ysbaddaden Chief Giant had named to Culhwch, in full measure, with none of it wanting save for a single flax seed. And the lame ant brought that in before night.

As Cei and Bedwyr were sitting on top of Pumlumon on Carn Gwylathyr, in the highest wind in the world, they looked about them and they could see a great smoke towards the south, far off from them, and not blowing across with the wind. And then Cei said, 'By the hand of my friend, see yonder the fire of a warrior.' They hastened towards the smoke and approached thither, watching from afar as Dillus the Bearded was singeing a wild boar. Now, he was the mightiest warrior that ever fled from Arthur. Then Bedwyr said to Cei, 'Dost know him?' 'I know him,' said Cei; 'that is Dillus the Bearded. There is no leash in the world may hold Drudwyn the whelp of Greid son of Eri, save a leash from the beard of him thou seest yonder. And that too will be of no use unless it be plucked alive with wooden tweezers from his beard; for it will be brittle, dead.' 'What is our counsel concerning that?' asked Bedwyr. 'Let us suffer him,' said Cei, 'to eat his fill of meat and after that he will fall asleep.' Whilst he was about this, they busied themselves making tweezers. When Cei knew for certain that he was asleep, he dug a pit under his feet, the biggest in the world, and he struck him a blow mighty past telling, and pressed him down in the pit until they had entirely twitched out his beard with the tweezers; and after that they slew him outright.

And then the two of them went to Celli Wig in Cornwall, and a leash from Dillus the Bearded's beard with them. And Cei gave it into Arthur's hand, and thereupon Arthur sang this englyn:

Cei made a leash
From Dillus' beard, son of Eurei.
Were he alive, thy death he'd be.

And because of this Cei grew angry, so that it was with difficulty the warriors of this Island made peace between Cei and Arthur. But nevertheless, neither for Arthur's lack of help, nor for the slaying of his men, did Cei have aught to do with him in his hour of need from that time forward.

And then Arthur said, 'Which of the marvels will it now be best to seek?' 'It will be best to seek Drudwyn the whelp of Greid son of Eri.'

A short while before this Creiddylad daughter of Lludd Silver-hand went with Gwythyr son of Greidawl; and before he had slept with her there came Gwyn son of Nudd and carried her off by force. Gwythyr son of Greidawl gathered a host, and he came to fight with Gwyn son of Nudd. And Gwyn prevailed, and he took prisoner Greid son of Eri, Glinneu son of Taran, and Gwrgwst the Half-naked and Dyfnarth his son. And he took prisoner Pen son of Nethawg, and Nwython, and Cyledyr the Wild his son, and he slew Nwython and took out his heart, and compelled Cyledyr to eat his father's heart; and because of this Cyledyr went mad. Arthur heard tell of this, and he came into the North and summoned to him Gwyn son of Nudd and set free his noblemen from his prison, and peace was made between Gwyn son of Nudd and Gwythyr son of Greidawl. This is the peace that was made: the maiden should remain in her father's house, unmolested by either side, and there should be battle between Gwyn and Gwythyr each May-calends for ever and ever, from that day till doomsday; and the one of them that should be victor on doomsday, let him have the maiden.

And when those lords had been thus reconciled, Arthur obtained Dun-mane the steed of Gweddw, and the leash of Cors Hundred-claws.

After that Arthur made his way to Llydaw, and with him Mabon son of Mellt and Gware Golden-hair, to seek the two dogs of Glythfyr Ledewig. And when he had obtained them, Arthur went to the west of Ireland to seek out Gwrgi Seferi, and Odgar son of Aedd king of Ireland along with him. And after that Arthur went into the North and caught Cyledyr the Wild; and he went after Ysgithyrwyn Chief Boar. And Mabon son of Mellt went, and the two dogs of Glythfyr Ledewig in his hand, and Drudwyn the whelp of Greid son of Eri. And Arthur himself took his place in the hunt, and Cafall, Arthur's dog, in his hand. And Cadw of Prydein mounted Llamrei, Arthur's mare, and he was the first to bring the boar to bay. And then Cadw of Prydein armed him with a hatchet, and boldly and gallantly set upon the boar and split his head in two. And Cadw took the tusk. It was not the dogs which Ysbaddaden had named to Culhwch which killed the boar, but Cafall, Arthur's own dog.

And after Ysgithyrwyn Chief Boar was slain, Arthur and his host went to Celli Wig in Cornwall; and thence he sent Menw son of Teirgwaedd to see whether the treasures were between the two ears of Twrch Trwyth – so mean a thing would it be to go to fight with him, had he not those treasures. However, it was certain that he was there; he had already laid waste the third part of Ireland. Menw went to seek them out. He saw them in Esgeir Oerfel in Ireland. And Menw transformed himself into the likeness of a bird and alighted over his lair and sought to snatch one of the treasures away from him. But for all that he got nothing save one of his bristles. The other arose in his might and shook himself so that some of his poison caught him. And after that Menw was never without scathe.

After that Arthur sent a messenger to Odgar son of Aedd king of Ireland, to ask for the cauldron of Diwrnach the Irishman, his overseer. Odgar besought him to give it. Said Diwrnach, 'God knows, though he should be the better for getting one glimpse of it, he should not have it.' And Arthur's messenger came back from Ireland with a nay. Arthur set out and a light force with him, and went in Prydwen his ship, and came to Ireland, and they made for the house of Diwrnach the Irishman. The hosts of Odgar took note of their strength; and after they had eaten and drunk their fill Arthur demanded the cauldron. He made answer that were he to give it to any one, he would have given it at the word of Odgar king of Ireland. When he had spoken them nay, Bedwyr arose and laid hold of the cauldron and put it on the back of Hygwydd, Arthur's servant; he was brother by the same mother to Cacamwri, Arthur's servant. His office was always to carry Arthur's cauldron and to kindle fire under it. Llenlleawg the Irishman seized Caledfwlch and swung it in a round and he slew Diwrnach the Irishman and all his host. The hosts of Ireland came and fought with them. And when the hosts were utterly routed Arthur and his men went on board ship before their very eyes, and with them the cauldron full of the treasures of Ireland. And they disembarked at the house of Llwydeu son of Cel Coed, at Porth Cerddin in Dyfed. And Mesur-y-Peir is there.

And then Arthur gathered together what warriors there were in the Three Realms of Britain and its three adjacent islands, and where there were in France and Brittany and Normandy and the Summer Country, and what there were of picked dogs and horses of renown. And with all those hosts he went to Ireland, and at his coming there was great fear and trembling in Ireland. And when Arthur had come to land, there came to him the saints of Ireland to ask his protection. And he granted them protection, and they gave him their blessing. The men of Ireland came to Arthur and gave him a tribute of victuals. Arthur came to Esgeir Oerfel in Ireland, to the place where Twrch Trwyth was, and his seven young pigs with him. Dogs were let loose at him from all sides. That day until evening the Irish fought with him; nevertheless he laid waste one of the five provinces of Ireland. And on the morrow Arthur's war-band fought with him: save for what evil they got from him, they got nothing good. The third day Arthur himself fought with him, nine nights and nine days: he slew of his pigs but one pigling. His men asked Arthur what was the history of that swine, and he told them: 'He was a king, and for his wickedness God transformed him into a swine.'

Arthur sent Gwrhyr Interpreter of Tongues to seek to have word with him. Gwrhyr went in the form of a bird and alighted above the lair of him and his seven young pigs. And Gwrhyr Interpreter of Tongues asked him, 'For His sake who made thee in this shape, if you can speak, I beseech one of you to come and talk with Arthur.' Grugyn Silver-bristle made answer. Like wings of silver were all his bristles; what way he went through wood and meadow one could discern from how his bristles glittered. This was the answer Grugyn gave: 'By Him who made us in this shape, we will neither do nor say aught for Arthur. Harm enough hath God wrought us, to have made us in this shape, without you too coming to fight with us.' 'I tell you, Arthur will fight for the comb, the razor and the shears which are between the two ears of Twrch Trwyth.' Said Grugyn, 'Until first his life be taken, those treasures will not be taken. And tomorrow in the morning we will set out hence and go into Arthur's country, and there we will do all the mischief we can.'

They set out by sea towards Wales; and Arthur and his hosts, his horses and his dogs, went aboard Prydwen, and in the twinkling of an eye they saw them. Twrch Trwyth came to land at Porth Cleis in Dyfed. That night Arthur came as far as Mynyw. On the morrow Arthur was told they had gone by, and he overtook him killing the cattle of Cynwas Cwryfagyl, after slaying what men and beasts were in Deu Gleddyf before the coming of Arthur.

From the time of Arthur's coming, Twrch Trwyth made off thence to Preseleu. Arthur and the hosts of the world came thither. Arthur sent his men to the hunt, Eli and Trachmyr, and Drudwyn the whelp of Greid son of Eri in his own hand; and Gwarthegydd son of Caw in another quarter, with the two dogs of Glythfyr Ledewig in his hand; and Bedwyr with Arthur's dog Cafall in his hand. And he ranged all the warriors on either side the Nyfer. There came the three sons of Cleddyf Difwlch, men who had won great fame at the slaying of Ysgithyrwyn Chief Boar. And then he set out from Glyn Nyfer and came to Cwm Cerwyn, and there he stood at bay. And he then slew four of Arthur's champions, Gwarthegydd son of Caw,

Tarawg of Allt Clwyd, Rheiddwn son of Eli Adfer, and Isgofan the Generous. And after he had slain those men, again he stood at bay against them there, and slew Gwydre son of Arthur, Garselit the Irishman, Glew son of Ysgawd, and Isgawyn son of Banon. And then he himself was wounded.

And the morrow's morn at point of day some of the men caught up with him. And then he slew Huandaw and Gogigwr and Penpingon, the three servants of Glewlwyd Mighty-grasp, so that God knows he had never a servant left to him in the world, save only Llaesgymyn, a man for whom none was the better. And over and above those he slew many a man of the country, and Gwlyddyn the Craftsman, Arthur's chief builder. And then Arthur caught up with him at Peluniawg, and he then slew Madawg son of Teithion, and Gwyn son of Tringad son of Neued, and Eiriawn Penlloran. And thence he went to Aber Tywi. And there he stood at bay against them, and he then slew Cynlas son of Cynan and Gwilenhin king of France. Thereafter he went to Glyn Ystun, and then the men and dogs lost him.

Arthur summoned to him Gwyn son of Nudd and asked him whether he knew aught of Twrch Trwyth. He said he did not. Thereupon all the huntsmen went to hunt the pigs as far as Dyffryn Llychwr. And Grugyn Silver-bristle and Llwydawg the Hewer dashed into them and slew the huntsmen so that not a soul of them escaped alive, save one man only. So Arthur and his hosts came to the place where Grugyn and Llwydawg were. And then he let loose upon them all the dogs that he been named to this end. And at the clamour that was then raised, and the barking, Twrch Trwyth came up and defended them. And ever since they had crossed the Irish Sea, he had not set eyes on them till now. Then was he beset by men and dogs. With might and with main he went to Myndydd Amanw, and then a pigling was slain of his pigs. And then they joined with him life for life, and it was then Twrch Llawin was slain. And then another of his pigs was slain, Gwys was his name. And he then went to Dyffryn Amanw, and there Banw and Benwig were slain. Not one of his pigs went with him alive from that place, save Grugyn Silver-bristle and Llwydawg the Hewer.

From that place they went on to Llwch Ewin, and Arthur caught up with him there. Then he stood at bay. And then he slew Echel Big-hip, and Arwyli son of Gwyddawg Gwyr, and many a man and dog besides. And after that they went on to Llwch Tawy. Grugyn Silver-bristle then parted from them, and Grugyn thereafter made for Din Tywi. And he proceeded then into Ceredigiawn, and Eli and Trachmyr with him, and a multitude along with them besides. And he came as far as Garth Grugyn. And there Grugyn was slain in their midst, and he slew Rhuddfyw Rhys and many a man with him. And then Llwydawg went on to Ystrad Yw. And there the men of Llydaw met with him, and he then slew Hir Peisawg king of Llydaw, and Llygadrudd Emys and Gwrfoddw, Arthur's uncles, his mother's brothers. And there he himself was slain.

Twrch Trwyth went then between Tawy and Ewyas. Arthur summoned Cornwall and Devon to meet him at the mouth of the Severn. And Arthur said to the warriors of this Island: 'Twrch Trwyth has slain many of my men. By the valour of men, not while I am alive shall he go into Cornwall. I will pursue him no further, but I will join with him life for life. You, do what you will.' And by his counsel a body of horsemen was sent, and the dogs of the Island with them, as far as Ewyas, and they beat back thence to the Severn, and they waylaid him there with what tried warriors there were in this Island, and drove him by sheer force into Severn. And Mabon son of Modron went with him into Severn, on Gwyn Dun-mane the steed of Gweddw, and Goreu son of Custennin and Menw son of Teirgwaedd, between Llyn Lliwan and Aber Gwy. And Arthur fell upon him, and the champions of Britain along with him. Osla Big-knife drew near, and Manawydan son of Llŷr, and Cacamwri, Arthur's servant, and Gwyngelli, and closed in on him. And first they laid hold of his feet, and soused him in Severn till it was flooding over him. On the one side Mabon son of Modron spurred his horse and took the razor from him, and on the other Cyledyr the Wild, on another horse, plunged into Severn with him and took from him the shears. But or ever the comb could be taken he found land with his feet; and from the moment he found land neither dog nor man nor horse could keep up with him until he went into Cornwall. Whatever mischief was come by in seeking those treasures from him, worse was to come by in seeking to save the two men from drowning. Cacamwri, as he was dragged forth, two quernstones dragged him into the depths. As Osla Big-knife was running after the boar, his knife fell out of its sheath and he lost it; and his sheath thereafter being full of water, as he was dragged forth, it dragged him back into the depths.

Then Arthur went with his hosts until he caught up with him in Cornwall. Whatever mischief was come by before that was play to what was come by then in seeking the comb. But from mischief to mischief the comb was won from him. And then he was forced out of Cornwall and driven straight forward into the sea. From that time forth never a one has known where he went, and Aned and

Aethlem with him. And Arthur went thence to Celli Wig in Cornwall, to bathe himself and rid him of his weariness.

Said Arthur, 'Is there any of the marvels still unobtained?' Said one of the men, 'There is: the blood of the Black Witch, daughter of the White Witch, from the head of the Valley of Grief in the uplands of Hell.' Arthur set out for the North and came to where the hag's cave was. And it was the counsel of Gwyn son of Nudd and Gwythyr son of Greidawl that Cacamwri and Hygwydd his brother be sent to fight with the hag. And as they came inside the cave the hag grabbed at them, and caught Hygwydd by the hair of his head and flung him to the floor beneath her. And Cacamwri seized her by the hair of her head, and dragged her to the ground off Hygwydd, but she then turned on Cacamwri and dressed them down both and disarmed them, and drove them out squealing and squalling. And Arthur was angered to see his two servants well nigh slain, and he sought to seize the cave. And then Gwyn and Gwythyr told him, 'It is neither seemly nor pleasant for us to see thee scuffling with a hag. Send Long Amren and Long Eiddil into the cave.' And they went. But if ill was the plight of the first two, the plight of those two was worse, so that God knows not one of the whole four could have stirred from the place, but for the way they were all four loaded on Llamrei, Arthur's mare. And then Arthur seized the entrance to the cave, and from the entrance he took aim at the hag with Carnwennan his knife, and struck her across the middle until she was as two tubs. And Cadw of Prydein took the witch's blood and kept it with him.

And then Culhwch set forth, and Goreu son of Custennin with him, and every one that wished ill to Ysbaddaden Chief Giant, and those marvels with them to his court. And Cadw of Prydein came to shave his beard, flesh and skin to the bone, and his two ears outright. And Culhwch said, 'Hast had thy shave, man?' 'I have,' said he. 'And is thy daughter mine now?' 'Thine,' said he. 'And thou needst not thank me for that, but thank Arthur who has secured her for thee. Of my own free will thou shouldst never have had her. And it is high time to take away my life.' And then Goreu son of Custennin caught him by the hair of his head and dragged him behind him to the mound, and cut off his head, and set it on the bailey-stake. And he took possession of his fort and his dominions.

And that night Culhwch slept with Olwen, and she was his only wife so long as he lived. And the hosts of Arthur dispersed, every one to his country.

And in this wise did Culhwch win Olwen daughter of Ysbaddaden Chief Giant.

MARIE DE FRANCE

The Lay of Sir Launfal

The Modena archivolt

ARTHUR AND THE BRETONS · THE MODENA ARCHIVOLT · THE *Lais* & & &

If there is little enough surviving Welsh literature, it is positively abundant compared with the surviving material from Brittany, where the few genuine fragments are so rare that nineteenth-century forgers attempted to fill the gap. Yet the Bretons were as famous as the Welsh for their minstrels; the belief in Arthur's survival and eventual return is consistently referred to as 'the Breton hope'; and there are numerous references to their songs and stories about Arthur. Whether these were the same as those of the Welsh, or whether the Breton idea of Arthur was quite different, we shall never know. But we do know that songs and stories about Arthur were widespread decades before Geoffrey of Monmouth produced *The History of the Kings of Britain*, and that the Bretons played a large part in making such tales popular.

The best evidence for this is not found in written records, but in a carving over the north doorway (Porta della Pescheria) of Modena Cathedral. On the semicircular frieze of the archivolt is carved what is generally agreed to be a scene from Arthurian romance. Reading from left to right, we have the following figures, identified by carved labels above them. First, an unnamed knight on horseback, fully armed, follows Isdernus (Ider), bareheaded but mounted and equipped with spear and shield. He is preceded by Artus de Bretania (Arthur), armed and mounted, who is attacking Burmaltus (Durmart), the latter on foot wielding a hammer, without mail. A barbican and moated castle at the top of the arch contain a woman, Winlogee (Guinevere), who is accompanied by an unarmed man, Mardoc. To the right of this, an armed knight, Carrado (Caradoc), rides out to attack Galvagin (Gawain). There follow Galvariun (Galeron) and Che (Kay), with their lances on their shoulders. All the last three are armed and mounted: Artus, Galvariun and Che have pennants on the ends of their lances.

The scene occurs both in a much later French romance, and in a rather different version in one of the Welsh saints' lives; it was later to become part of the story of Lancelot and Guinevere.

So far there is nothing remarkable in the carving, a not unfamiliar Arthurian scene, albeit rather far afield. But when it comes to the date of the work, there is much to explain. For although art historians cannot agree as to the exact date of the sculpture, and the style has been variously dated, it is generally believed that this work was executed between 1100 and 1120, before any Arthurian romances of any sort other than those in Welsh had been written down. This dating is confirmed by the record of the building of the cathedral, which tells us that a considerable part of the cathedral had been built and the sculptures placed in position by 1100. This probably included the west front, which was usually one of the first parts of a Romanesque cathedral to be built. It has on it carvings so similar in style to those on the 'Porta della Pescheria' that they cannot be more than a decade or two later or earlier. Hence the latest date for the Arthurian frieze is 1130, more than twenty years before the earliest known written romance.

However incredible this sculpture may appear to be, and however difficult to accept, we have to explain how it came to be produced in Italy at a time when we have no recorded legends of any substance about Arthur on his native soil. Such slender evidence as we have already discussed shows that some sort of legend about Arthur was current among popular storytellers of Wales, Cornwall and Brittany; in fact among the Celtic races descended from the Britons of Arthur's day. And when the Continental romances of two or three decades later are examined, they are full of Celtic names and incidents. We can find parallels to some of these names and incidents in Welsh stories; but often there are bewildering and quite inexplicable discrepancies in an otherwise recognisable Welsh tale. Many hypotheses have been put forward to cover these facts and weld them into a rational whole, and long and complex arguments have resulted.

On the face of it, only one factor appears to reconcile the three points: Celtic tales, French romances, and Italian sculpture – namely the Bretons. The Bretons came of Celtic stock, and had many points of contact with France and indeed throughout Europe. Records show that they travelled widely, and were found in Wales as well as in France at this time; and it seems that it must have been they who transmitted the tales. At Modena, this is confirmed by the name Winlogee, which is a form of Guinevere's name found only in Breton. This would explain the strange discrepancies between the Welsh originals and the French versions. But there remains the major obstacle already mentioned: there is no written trace of any Breton version of these legends.

This need not necessarily deter us; for most of the Welsh legends were only recorded in the memory of the bards, and told or sung at feasts. Similarly, the Bretons must have had their bards; their material may well have been the same as the Welsh, but they were free to wander beyond their own borders into France in search of an audience. The mysterious figure of Master Blihis, who appears as author or source in some romances, might be such a travelling poet, though there is evidence to connect him with Wales. The stories told by such bards would have attracted the writers and poets of the newly-developed French language, the vernacular tongue as opposed to the Latin of Church and Court officials, and in much elaborated forms they then passed into literature proper.

Such, drastically compressed, is the core of the argument in favour of the Breton origin of the French romances. Many minor points support it; Bretons are recorded both in Yorkshire, near the monastery where Ailred of Rievaulx wrote of the 'fables about Arthur', and in northern Italy, on their way to the First Crusade in 1096, near Modena and the carving on its cathedral. The names in the French romances appear to show traces of a double translation, and are closer to Breton than Welsh: Owein ap Urien of the triads appears as Yvain in French and Ivan in Breton, to name but one of many such examples. The Bretons would be more likely to know French tastes, and to cater for them accordingly, whereas the Welsh, while knowing the stories better, were less likely to be able to present them in a popular form. Nor were the Bretons an intellectually backward race: among other major figures of the period of Breton stock we find Peter Abelard and another philosopher, Bernard of Chartres.

On the other hand, we know very little about Welsh contacts abroad through Norman French culture. None of the evidence comes from areas which were not also subject to Norman influence (except the Modena sculpture); and even this could have been the work of an itinerant northern French craftsman. It is unlikely that any certain answer will ever emerge; two or three lost manuscripts of early French translations of Welsh stories would suffice to fill the gap between *The Mabinogion* and Chrétien de Troyes, and jongleurs or travelling minstrels were just as likely to have been French as Breton. All that is certain is the Celtic origin of the French romances, though many of the details have been added or altered in the process of translation and transmission.

But the very small group of surviving poems which have a Breton background have very little link with the main Arthurian romances. They are charming short fairy-tales or episodes from romance, some of which are set at Arthur's court, though the original tale was usually complete in itself and has merely had Arthur's name attached to it. One *lai*, *The Honeysuckle*, is a very early fragment from the story of Tristan and Iseult: Tristan compares himself and the queen to the honeysuckle and the hazel-tree, so entwined that one cannot live without the other. The *lai* which is printed here is more elaborate, but it nonetheless has the peculiarly 'other world' simplicity of these short poems. Launfal's love has little to do with courtliness or chivalry; and the action is a contest between magic and everyday life, between the world of beautiful fairies and the hardships and pitfalls of court life. The translation, by Eugene Mason, has its own interest as an Edwardian period piece; the original vocabulary and style are simple and in no way consciously old fashioned.

The Lay of Sir Launfal

I will tell you the story of another Lay. It relates the adventures of a rich and mighty baron, and the Breton calls it, the Lay of Sir Launfal.

King Arthur – that fearless knight and courteous lord – removed to Wales, and lodged at Caerleon-on-Usk, since the Picts and Scots did much mischief in the land. For it was the wont of the wild people of the north to enter the realm of Logres, and burn and damage at their will. At the time of Pentecost, the King cried a great feast. Thereat he gave many rich gifts to his counts and barons, and to the Knights of the Round Table. Never were such worship and bounty shown before at any feast, for Arthur bestowed honours and lands on all his servants – save only on one. This lord, who was forgotten and misliked of the King, was named Launfal. He was beloved by many of the Court, because of his beauty and prowess, for he was a worthy knight, open of heart and heavy of hand. These lords, to whom their comrade was dear, felt little joy to see so stout a knight misprized. Sir Launfal was son to a King of high descent, though his heritage was in a distant land. He was of the King's household, but since Arthur gave him naught, and he was of too proud a mind to pray for his due, he had spent all that he had. Right heavy was Sir Launfal, when he considered these things, for he knew himself taken in the toils. Gentles, marvel not overmuch hereat. Ever must the pilgrim go heavily in a strange land, where there is none to counsel and direct him in the path.

Now, on a day, Sir Launfal got him on his horse, that he might take his pleasure for a little. He came forth from the city, alone, attended by neither servant nor squire. He went his way through a green mead, till he stood by a river of clear running water. Sir Launfal would have crossed this stream, without thought of pass or ford, but he might not do so, for reason that his horse was all fearful and trembling. Seeing that he was hindered in this fashion, Launfal unbitted his steed, and let him pasture in that fair meadow, where they had come. Then he folded his cloak to serve him as a pillow, and lay upon the ground. Launfal lay in great misease, because of his heavy thoughts, and the discomfort of his bed. He turned from side to side, and might not sleep. Now as the knight looked towards the river he saw two damsels coming towards him; fairer maidens Launfal had never seen. These two maidens were richly dressed in kirtles closely laced and shapen to their persons and wore mantles of a goodly purple hue. Sweet and dainty were the damsels, alike in raiment and in face. The elder of these ladies carried in her hands a basin of pure gold, cunningly wrought by some crafty smith – very fair and precious was the cup; and the younger bore a towel of soft white linen. These maidens turned neither to the right hand nor to the left, but went directly to the place where Launfal lay. When Launfal saw that their business was with him, he stood upon his feet, like a discreet and courteous gentleman. After they had greeted the knight, one of the maidens delivered the message with which she was charged.

'Sir Launfal, my demoiselle, as gracious as she is fair, prays that you will follow us, her messengers, as she has a certain word to speak with you. We will lead you swiftly to her pavilion, for our lady is very near at hand. If you but lift your eyes you may see where her tent is spread.'

Right glad was the knight to do the bidding of the maidens. He gave no heed to his horse, but left him at his provand in the meadow. All his desire was to go with the damsels, to that pavilion of silk and divers colours, pitched in so fair a place. Certainly neither Semiramis in the days of her most wanton power, nor Octavian, the Emperor of all the West, had so gracious a covering from sun and rain. Above the tent was set an eagle of gold, so rich and precious, that none might count the cost. The cords and fringes thereof were of silken thread, and the lances which bore aloft the pavilion were of refined gold. No King on earth might have so sweet a shelter, not though he gave in fee the value of his realm. Within this pavilion Launfal came upon the Maiden. Whiter she was than any altar lily, and more sweetly flushed than the new born rose in time of summer heat. She lay upon a bed with napery and coverlet of richer worth than could be furnished by a castle's spoil. Very fresh and slender showed the lady in her vesture of spotless linen. About her person she had drawn a mantle of ermine, edged with purple dye from the vats of Alexandria. By reason of the heat her raiment was unfastened for a little, and her throat and the rondure of her bosom showed whiter and more untouched than hawthorn in May. The knight came before the bed, and stood gazing on so sweet a sight. The Maiden beckoned him to draw near, and when he had seated himself at the foot of her couch, spoke her mind.

'Launfal,' she said, 'fair friend, it is for you that I have come from my own far land. I bring you my love. If you are prudent and discreet, as you are goodly to the view, there is no emperor nor count, nor king, whose day shall be so filled with riches and with mirth as yours.'

When Launfal heard these words he rejoiced greatly, for his heart was litten by another's torch.

'Fair lady,' he answered, 'since it pleases you to be so gracious, and to dower so graceless a knight with your love, there is naught that you may bid me do – right or wrong, evil or good – that I will not do to the utmost of my power. I will observe your commandment, and serve in your quarrels. For you I renounce my father and my father's house. This only I pray, that I may dwell with you in your lodging, and that you will never send me from your side.'

When the Maiden heard the words of him whom so fondly she desired to love, she was altogether moved, and granted him forthwith her heart and her tenderness. To her bounty she added another gift besides. Never might Launfal be desirous of aught, but he would have according to his wish. He might waste and spend at will and pleasure, but in his purse ever there was to spare. No more was Launfal sad. Right merry was the pilgrim, since one had set him on the way, with such a gift, that the more pennies he bestowed, the more silver and gold were in his pouch.

But the Maiden had yet a word to say.

'Friend,' she said, 'hearken to my counsel. I lay this charge upon you, and pray you urgently, that you tell not to any man the secret of our love. If you show this matter, you will lose your friend, for ever and a day. Never again may you see my face. Never again will you have seisin of that body, which is now so tender in your eyes.'

Launfal plighted faith, that right strictly he would observe this commandment. So the Maiden granted him her kiss and her embrace, and very sweetly in that fair lodging passed the day till evensong was come.

Right loath was Launfal to depart from the pavilion at the vesper hour, and gladly would he have stayed, had he been able, and his lady wished.

'Fair friend,' said she, 'rise up, for no longer may you tarry. The hour is come that we must part. But one thing I have to say before you go. When you would speak with me I shall hasten to come before your wish. Well I deem that you will only call your friend where she may be found without reproach or shame of men. You may see me at your pleasure; my voice shall speak softly in your ear at will; but I must never be known of your comrades, nor must they ever learn my speech.'

Right joyous was Launfal to hear this thing. He sealed the covenant with a kiss, and stood upon his feet. Then there entered the two maidens who had led him to the pavilion, bringing with them rich raiment, fitting for a knight's apparel. When Launfal had clothed himself therewith, there seemed no goodlier varlet under heaven, for certainly he was fair and true. After these maidens had refreshed him with clear water, and dried his hands upon the napkin, Launfal went to meat. His friend sat at table with him, and small will had he to refuse her courtesy. Very serviceably the damsels bore the meats, and Launfal and the Maiden ate and drank with mirth and content. But one dish was more to the knight's relish than any other. Sweeter than the dainties within his mouth was the lady's kiss upon his lips.

When supper was ended, Launfal rose from table, for his horse stood waiting without the pavilion. The destrier was newly saddled and bridled, and showed proudly in his rich gay trappings. So Launfal kissed, and bade farewell, and went his way. He rode back towards the city at a slow pace. Often he checked his steed, and looked behind him, for he was filled with amazement, and all bemused concerning this adventure. In his heart he doubted that it was but a dream. He was altogether astonished, and knew not what to do. He feared that pavilion and Maiden alike were from the realm of faery.

Launfal returned to his lodging, and was greeted by servitors, clad no longer in ragged raiment. He fared richly, lay softly, and spent largely, but never knew how his purse was filled. There was no lord who had need of a lodging in the town, but Launfal brought him to his hall, for refreshment and delight. Launfal bestowed rich gifts. Launfal redeemed the poor captive, Launfal clothed in scarlet the minstrel. Launfal gave honour where honour was due. Stranger and friend alike he comforted at need. So, whether by night or by day, Launfal lived greatly at his ease. His lady, she came at will and pleasure, and, for the rest, all was added unto him.

Now it chanced, the same year, about the feast of St John, a company of knights came, for their solace, to an orchard, beneath that tower where dwelt the Queen. Together with these lords went Gawain and his cousin, Yvain the fair. Then said Gawain, that goodly knight, beloved and dear to all.

'Lords, we do wrong to disport ourselves in this pleasaunce without our comrade Launfal. It is not well to slight a prince as brave as he is courteous, and of a lineage prouder than our own.'

Then certain of the lords returned to the city, and finding Launfal within his hostel, entreated him to take his pastime with them in that fair meadow. The Queen looked out from a window in her tower, she and three ladies of her fellowship. They saw the lords at their pleasure, and Launfal also, whom well they knew. So the Queen chose of her Court thirty damsels – the sweetest of face and most dainty of fashion – and commanded that they should descend with her to take their delight in the garden. When the knights beheld this gay company of ladies come down the steps of the perron, they rejoiced beyond measure. They hastened before to lead them by the hand, and said such words in their ear as were seemly and pleasant to be spoken. Amongst these merry and courteous lords hasted not Sir Launfal. He drew apart from the throng, for with him time went heavily, till he might have clasp and greeting of his friend. The ladies of the Queen's fellowship seemed but kitchen wenches to his sight, in comparison with the loveliness of the Maiden. When the Queen marked Launfal go aside, she went his way, and seating herself upon the herb, called the knight before her. Then she opened out her heart.

'Launfal, I have honoured you for long as a worthy knight, and have praised and cherished you very dearly. You may receive a queen's whole love, if such be your care. Be content: he to whom my heart is given, has small reason to complain him of the alms.'

'Lady,' answered the knight, 'grant me leave to go, for this grace is not for me. I am the King's man, and dare not break my troth. Not for the highest lady in the world, not even for her love, will I set this reproach upon my lord.'

When the Queen heard this, she was full of wrath, and spoke many hot and bitter words.

'Launfal,' she cried, 'well I know that you think little of woman and her love. There are sins more black that a man may have upon his soul. Traitor you are, and false. Right evil counsel gave they to my lord, who prayed him to suffer you about his person. You remain only for his harm and loss.'

Launfal was very dolent to hear this thing. He was not slow to take up the Queen's glove, and in his haste spake words that he repented long, and with tears.

'Lady,' said he, 'I am not of that guild of which you speak. Neither am I a despiser of woman, since I love, and am loved, of one who would bear the prize from all the ladies in the land. Dame, know now and be persuaded, that she, whom I serve, is so rich in state, that the very meanest of her maidens, excels you, Lady Queen, as much in clerkly skill and goodness, as in sweetness of body and face, and in every virtue.'

The Queen rose straightway to her feet, and fled to her chamber, weeping. Right wrathful and heavy was she, because of the words that had besmirched her. She lay sick upon her bed, from which, she said, she would never rise, till the King had done her justice, and righted this bitter wrong. Now the King that day had taken his pleasure within the woods. He returned from the chase towards evening, and sought the chamber of the Queen. When the lady saw him she sprang from her bed, and kneeling at his feet, pleaded for grace and pity. Launfal – she said – had shamed her, since he required her love. When she had put him by, very foully had he reviled her, boasting that his love was already set on a lady, so proud and noble, that her meanest wench went more richly, and smiled more sweetly, than the Queen. Thereat the King waxed marvellously wrathful, and swore a great oath that he would set Launfal within a fire, or hang him from a tree, if he could not deny this thing, before his peers.

Arthur came forth from the Queen's chamber, and

called to him three of his lords. These he sent to seek the knight who so evilly had entreated the Queen. Launfal, for his part, had returned to his lodging, in a sad and sorrowful case. He saw very clearly that he had lost his friend, since he had declared their love to men. Launfal sat within his chamber, sick and heavy of thought. Often he called upon his friend, but the lady would not hear his voice. He bewailed his evil lot, with tears; for grief he came nigh to swoon; a hundred times he implored the Maiden that she would deign to speak with her knight. Then, since the lady yet refrained from speech, Launfal cursed his hot and unruly tongue. Very near he came to ending all this trouble with his knife. Naught he found to do but to wring his hands, and call upon the Maiden, begging her to forgive his trespass, and to talk with him again, as friend to friend.

But little peace is there for him who is harassed by a King. There came presently to Launfal's hostel those three barons from the Court. These bade the knight forthwith to go with them to Arthur's presence, to acquit him of this wrong against the Queen. Launfal went forth, to his own deep sorrow. Had any man slain him on the road, he would have counted him his friend. He stood before the King, downcast and speechless, being dumb by reason of that great grief, of which he showed the picture and image.

Arthur looked upon his captive very evilly.

'Vassal,' said he, harshly, 'you have done me a bitter wrong. It was a foul deed to seek to shame me in this ugly fashion, and to smirch the honour of the Queen. Is it folly or lightness which leads you to boast of that lady, the least of whose maidens is fairer, and goes more richly, than the Queen?'

Launfal protested that never had he set such shame upon his lord. Word by word he told the tale of how he denied the Queen, within the orchard. But concerning that which he had spoken of the lady, he owned the truth, and his folly. The love of which he bragged was now lost to him, by his own exceeding fault. He cared little for his life, and was content to obey the judgment of the Court.

Right wrathful was the King at Launfal's words. He conjured his barons to give him such wise counsel herein, that wrong might be done to none. The lords did the King's bidding, whether good came of the matter, or evil. They gathered themselves together, and appointed a certain day that Launfal should abide the judgment of his peers. For his part Launfal must give pledge and surety to his lord, that he would come before this judgment in his own body. If he might not give such surety then he should be held captive till the appointed day. When the lords of the King's household returned to tell him of their counsel, Arthur demanded that Launfal should put such pledge in his hand, as they had said. Launfal was altogether mazed and bewildered at this judgment, for he had neither friend nor kindred in the land. He would have been set in prison, but Gawain came first to offer himself as his surety, and with him, all the knights of his fellowship. These gave into the King's hand as pledge, the fiefs and lands that they held of his Crown. The King having taken pledges from the sureties, Launfal returned to his lodging, and with him certain knights of his company. They blamed him greatly because of his foolish love, and chastened him grievously by reason of the sorrow he made before men. Every day they came to his chamber, to know of his meat and drink, for much they feared that presently he would become mad.

The lords of the household came together on the day appointed for this judgment. The King was on his chair, with the Queen sitting at his side. The sureties brought Launfal within the hall, and rendered him into the hands of his peers. Right sorrowful were they because of his plight. A great company of his fellowship did all that they were able to acquit him of this charge. When all was set out, the King demanded the judgment of the Court, according to the accusation and the answer. The barons went forth in much trouble and thought to consider this matter. Many amongst them grieved for the peril of a good knight in a strange land; others held that it were well for Launfal to suffer, because of the wish and malice of their lord. Whilst they were thus perplexed, the Duke of Cornwall rose in the council, and said:

'Lords, the King pursues Launfal as a traitor, and would slay him with the sword, by reason that he bragged of the beauty of his maiden, and roused the jealousy of the Queen. By the faith that I owe this company, none complains of Launfal, save only the King. For our part we would know the truth of this business, and do justice between the King and his man. We would also show proper reverence to our own liege lord. Now, if it be according to Arthur's will, let us take oath of Launfal, that he seek this lady, who has put such strife between him and the Queen. If her beauty be such as he has told us, the Queen will have no cause for wrath. She must pardon Launfal for his rudeness, since it will be plain that he did not speak out of a malicious heart. Should Launfal fail his word, and not return with the lady, or should her fairness fall beneath his boast, then let him be cast off from our fellowship, and be sent forth from the service of the King.'

This counsel seemed good to the lords of the household. They sent certain of his friends to Launfal, to acquaint him with their judgment, bidding him to pray his damsel to the Court, that he might be acquitted of this blame. The knight made answer that in no wise could he do this thing. So the sureties returned before the judges, saying that Launfal hoped neither for refuge nor for succour from the lady, and Arthur urged them to a speedy ending, because of the prompting of the Queen.

The judges were about to give sentence upon Launfal, when they saw two maidens come riding towards the palace, upon two white ambling palfreys. Very sweet and dainty were these maidens, and richly clothed in garments of crimson sendal, closely girt and fashioned to their bodies. All men, old and young, looked willingly upon them, for fair they were to see. Gawain, and three knights of his company, went straight to Launfal, and showed him these maidens, praying him to say which of them was his friend. But he answered never a word. The maidens dismounted from their palfreys, and coming before the dais where the King was seated, spake him fairly, as they were fair.

'Sire, prepare now a chamber, hung with silken cloths, where it is seemly for my lady to dwell; for she would lodge with you awhile.'

This gift the King granted gladly. He called to him two knights of his household, and bade them bestow the maidens in such chambers as were fitting to their degree. The maidens being gone, the King required of his barons to proceed with their judgment, saying that he had sore displeasure at the slowness of the cause.

'Sire,' replied the barons, 'we rose from Council, because of the damsels who entered in the hall. We will at once resume the sitting, and give our judgment without more delay.'

The barons again were gathered together, in much thought and trouble, to consider this matter. There was great strife and dissension amongst them, for they knew not what to do. In the midst of all this noise and tumult, there came two other damsels riding to the hall on two Spanish mules. Very richly arrayed were these damsels in raiment of fine needlework, and their kirtles were covered by fresh fair mantles, embroidered with gold. Great joy had Launfal's comrades when they marked these ladies. They said between themselves that doubtless they came for the succour of the good knight. Gawain, and certain of his company, made haste to Launfal, and said,

'Sir, be not cast down. Two ladies are near at hand, right dainty of dress, and gracious of person. Tell us truly, for the love of God, is one of these your friend?'

But Launfal answered very simply that never before had he seen these damsels with his eyes, nor known and loved them in his heart.

The maidens dismounted from their mules, and stood before Arthur, in the sight of all. Greatly were they praised of many, because of their beauty, and of the colour of their face and hair. Some there were who deemed already that the Queen was overborne.

The elder of the damsels carried herself modestly and well, and sweetly told over the message wherewith she was charged.

'Sire, make ready for us chambers, where we may abide with our lady, for even now she comes to speak with thee.'

The King commanded that the ladies should be led to their companions, and bestowed in the same honourable fashion as they. Then he bade the lords of his household to consider their judgment, since he would endure no further respite. The Court already had given too much time to the business, and the Queen was growing wrathful, because of the blame that was hers. Now the judges were about to proclaim their sentence, when, amidst the tumult of the town, there came riding to the palace the flower of all the ladies of the world. She came mounted upon a palfrey, as white as snow, which carried her softly, as though she loved her burthen. Beneath the sky was no goodlier steed, nor one more gentle to the hand. The harness of the palfrey was so rich, that no king on earth might hope to buy trappings so precious, unless he sold or set his realm in pledge. The Maiden herself showed such as I will tell you. Passing slim was the lady, sweet of bodice and slender of girdle. Her throat was whiter than snow on branch, and her eyes were like flowers in the pallor of her face. She had a witching mouth, a dainty nose, and an open brow. Her eyebrows were brown, and her golden hair parted in two soft waves upon her head. She was clad in a shift of spotless linen, and above her snowy kirtle was set a mantle of royal purple, clasped upon her breast. She carried a hooded falcon upon her glove, and a greyhound followed closely after. As the Maiden rode at a slow pace through the streets of the city, there was none, neither great nor small, youth nor sergeant, but ran forth from his house, that he might content his heart with so great beauty. Every man that saw her with his eyes, marvelled at a fairness beyond that of any earthly woman. Little he cared for any mortal maiden, after he had seen this sight. The friends of Sir Launfal hastened to the knight, to tell him of his lady's succour, if so it were according to God's will.

'Sir comrade, truly is not this your friend? This lady is neither black nor golden, mean nor tall. She is only the most lovely thing in all the world.'

When Launfal heard this, he sighed, for by their words he knew again his friend. He raised his head, and as the blood rushed to his face, speech flowed from his lips.

'By my faith,' cried he, 'yes, she is indeed my friend. It is a small matter now whether men slay me, or set me free; for I am made whole of my hurt just by looking on her face.'

The Maiden entered in the palace – where none so fair had come before – and stood before the King, in the presence of his household. She loosed the clasp of her mantle, so that men might the more easily perceive the grace of her person. The courteous King advanced to meet her, and all the Court got them on their feet, and pained themselves in her service. When the lords had gazed upon her for a space, and praised the sum of her beauty, the lady spake to Arthur in this fashion, for she was anxious to begone.

'Sire, I have loved one of thy vassals – the knight who stands in bonds, Sir Launfal. He was always misprized in thy Court, and his every action turned to blame. What he said, that thou knowest; for over hasty was his tongue before the Queen. But he never craved her in love, however loud his boasting. I cannot choose that he should come to hurt or harm by me. In the hope of freeing Launfal from his bonds, I have obeyed thy summons. Let now thy barons look boldly upon my face, and deal justly in this quarrel between the Queen and me.'

The King commanded that this should be done, and looking upon her eyes, not one of the judges but was persuaded that her favour exceeded that of the Queen.

Since then Launfal had not spoken in malice against his lady, the lords of the household gave him again his sword. When the trial had come thus to an end the Maiden took her leave of the King, and made her ready to depart. Gladly would Arthur have had her lodge with him for a little, and many a lord would have rejoiced in her service, but she might not tarry. Now without the hall stood a great stone of dull marble, where it was the wont of lords, departing from the Court, to climb into the saddle, and Launfal by the stone. The Maiden came forth from the doors of the palace, and mounting on the stone, seated herself on the palfrey, behind her friend. Then they rode across the plain together, and were no more seen.

The Bretons tell that the knight was ravished by his lady to an island, very dim and very fair, known as Avalon. But none has had speech with Launfal and his faery love since then, and for my part I can tell you no more of the matter.

CHRETIEN DE TROYES

Yvain or The Knight with the Lion

Lancelot crossing the sword bridge, from a thirteenth century capital in St Pierre, Caen. In Chrétien de Troyes' Lancelot *Guinevere was abducted by Meleagant, and in order to rescue her Lancelot had to brave various perils, of which this was one. (Photo James Austin).*

CHRETIEN AND HIS CIRCLE; EREC · REALITY AND FANTASY · CLIGES · LANCELOT · PERCEVAL & & &

Arthur reached his greatest fame in a world far removed from his Celtic origins, and when we think of him today it is usually in the character given him by twelfth- and thirteenth-century French romances. We have already touched on the difficult problem of how the Celtic stories which provided these writers with their material, the *matière de Bretagne* or 'matter of Britain', were transplanted across the channel. Within the framework of Arthur's Court as depicted by Geoffrey and his followers, and drawing on both Celtic and classical stories for the events, Chrétien de Troyes and his successors introduce the two essential elements of chivalry and courtly love, and transplant the exotic adventures of the Welsh heroes to the civilised courts and castles of England and France.

The earliest romance proper seems to have been a *Tristan* of about 1150, but it is Chrétien de Troyes, who began to write soon after this, who represents the mainstream of strictly Arthurian literature. Born before 1130, Chrétien was closely associated with the Court of Champagne and particularly with the Countess Marie, daughter of Eleanor of Aquitaine. From her mother, Marie had inherited a taste for literature, particularly that of the Provençal troubadours; and the ideal of courtly love flourished in her circle. Chrétien's first works seem to have been a translation of Ovid's *Art of Love*, a popular work in the Middle Ages, and a version of the Tristan legend. Both of these are lost, and the *Erec* of about 1170 is his earliest surviving piece. It was followed by *Cligès*, which is hardly Arthurian at all, drawn largely from classical legend and using Arthur's Court merely as a backdrop. Then came the important *Lancelot, or The Knight of the Cart*, *Yvain, or the Knight with the Lion*, both written about 1179, and *Perceval, or the History of the Grail.* The last was left unfinished, and dates from 1180–90.

Chrétien's handling of *Erec* sets certain patterns which were to endure throughout medieval Arthurian romance. Erec wins Enide as his bride by achieving two quests, perhaps separate stories linked by Chrétien. He then brings her to Arthur's court, where she is received with great honour; and this affords an opportunity for Chrétien to describe the characters of the court and its splendours, and to display his own learning in Arthurian matters. The main psychological action follows: how Erec abandons knightly ways for Enide's charms, and, on hearing her reproach herself for this, mistakenly suspects her fidelity. The testing of both Erec's knightly prowess and his wife's faithfulness is worked out in a series of loosely-linked adventures, again drawn from Celtic prototypes and including such themes as an encounter with a dwarf king, which recur in many later works. When both Erec and Enide have been proved true, a last section forms the climax: Erec breaks an enchantment by which a king and his Court are bound. It is as though the power to do this had only been established by his previous trials, though Chrétien does not make this explicit. The poem ends with the coronation of Erec and Enide as heirs to his father's kingdom.

The framework, with its three clearly defined divisions, betrays a mind trained in formal literary conventions, and is certainly Chrétien's own device. The actual content of the story is centred on the folklore theme of Patient Griselda, which accounts for the main action; and the details are drawn from the Celtic–French material already described, though only the last exploit, the so-called *Joie de la Cort*, has the characteristic fey quality of such adventures, with half-explained enchantments and disenchantments whose logic is not that of the rational world. The great appeal of this combination to contemporary audiences was its presentation of a familiar world with this fantastic surrounding of adventure. The familiar world is also transformed but only by making everything more splendid and dramatic until it transcends reality. Arthur's court is like any ordinary court, but peopled with heroes and bedecked in the richest furnishings; Arthur himself is a king such as every knight dreamed of, generous and a great encourager of prowess, quite untrammelled by everyday considerations.

Chrétien's next romance, *Cligès*, illustrates the way in which quite different stories could be drawn into the Arthurian web simply by using Arthur's court as a background. On this point, it is interesting that Chrétien, the first so to depict the Round Table as a great centre of chivalry, was also the first to name Arthur's capital Camelot, a name he may have found in *Camulodunum*, the Roman name for Colchester. *Cligès* tells of the love of Alexander and Fenice, and of their son Cligès for Soredamors; much of the action takes place in Constantinople, and lacks the mysterious atmosphere of the other romances; as a result, none of the characters or episodes play an important part in later Arthurian stories.

In *Lancelot*, or as it is more often known, *Le Chevalier de la Charette* (The Knight of the Cart), Chrétien introduced for the first time one of the most important elements of the romances: the idea of courtly love. It is important to distinguish between the passionate, unrestrained love of Tristan and Isolt and the carefully restrained code of courtly love. The latter (with which Chrétien does not seem to have altogether sympathised, since he firmly declares that he only wrote the tale at Marie de Champagne's bidding, and left it to another poet to finish) was derived from the literature of southern France, where, from the beginning of the twelfth century, the troubadours had elaborated on the theme of the superiority of the lady and the moral worth to which the worshipping lover could attain, investing the beloved with an aura of divinity which still lingers about Guinevere in Chrétien's tale. Utter obedience was required if the lover was to gain solace, though in the strictest schools such solace was no more than a chaste kiss. Hence Lancelot is rebuked for hesitating a moment in mounting an executioner's cart, when his duty to Guinevere required him to do so after his horse had been slain as he rode to her rescue. Chrétien does not hold to the principle of courtly love with its implied adultery, probably because of the original from which he was working: his own view of love was much more moral, as witness Fenice's proud rejection, in *Cligès*, of Isolt's fate: 'Never could I agree to live the life that Isolt lived; love was debased in her for her body was at the disposal of two, and her heart was wholly for one. . . . Let him who has the heart have the body and exclude all others.'

The story of *The Knight of the Cart* is that of Guinevere's abduction by Meleagant which appears in Malory's last book. The all-important theme is that of Lancelot as lover and rescuer, whether performing heroic feats, falling into an ecstasy at the sight of his mistress' golden hairs on a comb she has left behind, or playing the coward at a tournament at her command. The adventures are full of marvels and mysteries, of perilous beds and flaming lances; perhaps the most famous is that of the bridge made of a single sharp sword blade which Lancelot has to crawl across in order to reach Guinevere's prison. However much Chrétien may disclaim his responsibility for both subject and moral, he has succeeded in combining all the essential ingredients of Arthurian romance for the first time, quite apart from his own masterly portrait of the lovelorn Lancelot and his distant divine lady. The weakness of the poem is in the mechanism of the action, which remains unexplained and unmotivated except where the lovers are concerned. A wider canvas was needed in order to give the causes and consequences of the adventures, and the final effect is of a cameo rather than a complete work of art.

Chrétien's last, unfinished work, *Perceval* or *Le Conte du Graal* (*The History of the Grail*) once again points the way forward. The plot, that of a simpleton, who, brought up far from the haunts of men, wins his own way in the world through a series of adventures caused by his ignorance, contained the germs of the development of the whole spiritual element in the Arthurian cycle. What Chrétien himself intended by the Grail we shall never know. Such evidence as there is points to a kind of dish of plenty for which Chrétien chose to use a rare French word *graal*, from the late Latin *gradalis*. Such all-providing dishes or cauldrons are fairly frequent in Celtic literature; Arthur himself seizes one from the High Steward of the King of Ireland in *Culhwch and Olwen*. Furthermore, the cauldron was a symbol of spiritual nourishment, the source of poetic inspiration or *awen* in some Welsh tales, which would suggest more mysterious functions than mere feasting. There are difficulties and inconsistencies in plenty in Chrétien's account, and for once it seems as though the marvels of the Celtic original proved too much for his more rational approach. While he usually makes clear how any given marvel happened, he is never particularly troubled by the why or wherefore. Here, however, the Grail procession, the wounded king and the asking of a ritual question are all interlinked and Chrétien does not seem to be able to explain why this should be so. Perhaps it was difficulties with his material rather than lack of opportunity that led him to leave the tale incomplete. His failure to finish the story meant that other writers were able to continue it, and to shape the idea of the Grail into its final form, that of the chalice used by Our Lord at the Last Supper.

Yvain or the Knight with the Lion is perhaps Chrétien's masterpiece, in which marvels and courtly love, spectacular adventures and finely drawn characters blend into a well-wrought unity. The theme is similar to that of Erec, and Gawain's speech to Yvain (p. 70 below) echoes the reproaches addressed to Erec. What follows is the first part of the poem; the second part tells how Yvain, failing to keep his promise to Laudine, goes mad when she sends a messenger to reproach him. He is befriended by a lion, cured of his madness, and with the lion's help rescues various unfortunate ladies, including Lunete, who is to be burnt at the stake because of his desertion. He goes on to break various evil enchantments, and Lunete at last contrives to reconcile him to Laudine.

Yvain kills Esclados and is introduced by Lunete to Laudine; two scenes from an early fourteenth century embroidery made at Freiburg for Johannes Malterer, a banker, and his wife Anna. The designer has run together different moments in the story: the fight is shown as taking place during the magic storm (lightning and hailstones), and Lunete appears to be giving Yvain the ring which makes him invisible at the moment when he meets Laudine. (Augustinermuseum, Freiburg im Breisgau)

Yvain or The Knight with the Lion

Arthur, the good King of Britain, whose prowess is a lesson in courtesy and bravery to us all, held a rich and royal court at the feast of Whitsuntide. The King was at Carduel in Wales, and after dinner the knights flocked to where the ladies and damsels and young girls summoned them. Some told stories, others talked about love, its pains and sorrows, and the great benefits that the disciples of its teaching often gained; in those days they were plentiful and flourishing, but nowadays there are only a few left. Almost everyone has given up love, which has come down in the world. In those days anyone who was a lover earned a name for courtesy, bravery, generosity and honour. Nowadays love is just a word, because those who have never felt love declare that they are in love: but they are lying; and people who are mere boasters, without any right to do so, tell stories and lies like these. But let us leave those who are still living to talk of the men of other days, because a courteous man dead is worth far more than a live rogue. So I would prefer to tell a story about that king, who was so famous that men far and near still talk about him today: as to that, I agree with the Bretons who say that his name will live for ever. His name reminds us also of the good knights he chose, who always strove to win honour.

But that day they were very surprised to see the King leave them; some of them were angry and talked much of it, because they had never before seen him go to his chamber to rest or sleep on such a feast day. But on this day it did happen, for the Queen detained him and he stayed so long with her that he forgot himself and went to sleep. Outside the door of his chamber were Dodinel, Sagremor, Kay, Gawain and Yvain as well; and Calogrenant was with them, a promising knight who had begun to tell them a story, which was not to his own credit, but rather to his shame. The Queen heard them, and got up from beside the King; she came up to them so quietly that she was in their midst before they had noticed her. Only Calogrenant jumped to his feet in time to greet her. And Kay, who was always quarrelsome, treacherous, cutting and abusive said to him: 'By God, Calogrenant, you are very brave and forward, and I'm pleased to see that you are the most courteous among us; and I know that you are so stupid enough to think so too. It is right that milady thinks that you are as brave and courteous as all of us put together, because we were too lazy to get up, or did not bother. On my word, that is not true, sir; it was only because we did not see milady until you had got up.' 'Really, Kay,' said the Queen, 'you would burst if you could not pour out your poison. You are nothing but a common bore when you abuse your comrades.' 'Lady, if we are no better off for your company,' said Kay, 'at least don't let us lose by it. I don't think that I have said anything wrong, so please say no more. There is no sense or manners in a fool's quarrel, so let it be and don't continue it. But make him carry on with the story which he had begun to tell us.' At this Calogrenant speaks out and answers: 'Sir, I have no time for a quarrel, which means nothing to me. If you have slandered me, it will do me no harm, for you have often troubled wiser and braver men than me, Sir Kay, for it is your habit, just as the manure-heap always stinks, the gad-fly stings and the bees hum. But I will not continue with my story today, if milady will allow it; I beg her to say no more about it and not to order me to do something I don't wish to.' 'Lady,' said Kay, 'everyone here will be grateful to you if you do, because they all want to hear it. Don't do it for my sake, but by your loyalty to the king, do order him to go on and you will do well!' 'Calogrenant,' said the Queen, 'don't be disturbed by Kay the Seneschal's attack. He is used to saying evil things, and it is no good punishing him for it. I command and beg you not to be angry because of him, nor to stop telling a story we would like to hear; if you want my favour, please start again from the beginning.' 'Milady, you order me to do something I do not wish to do: I would rather lose an eye, but it would anger you if I did not continue, so I will do as you ask, much as it grieves me.

It happened, almost seven years ago, that, as lonely as a peasant, I was seeking adventures, fully armed as a knight ought to be. I found a road to the right, through a thick forest. The road was an evil one, full of thorns and briars; with some difficulty and pain I managed to keep to this path. I rode for almost a whole day until I came out of the forest, in Broceliande. From the forest I entered open country, and saw a wooden tower half a Welsh league or so away. Riding faster than walking pace, I saw the palisade with a moat made around it, and standing on the draw-bridge I saw the owner of the fortress, with a moulted falcon on his wrist. I had scarcely greeted him before he came to take my stirrup and told me to dismount. I got off, for there was no denying that I needed lodging for the night. And he repeated more than a hundred times that blessed was the road by which I had come there. Soon we entered the courtyard, passing through the gate and across the bridge. In the middle of the court of this baron (to whom God repay the joy and honour he gave me that night) there hung a gong: I do not think there was any iron in it, or anything except copper. The baron struck this gong three times with a hammer which hung on a nearby post. The people who were upstairs in the house heard the noise and his voice and came out of the house. Some of them took my horse, which the good baron was holding; and I saw a beautiful gentle girl come towards me. Looking at her closely I saw she was tall and slim and graceful. She took off my armour skilfully and well, and then put a short cloak on me lined with miniver and made of scarlet and blue material. All the others went away, and no one remained with the two of us, to my delight; for I did not want to see anyone else. She led me to a seat in the most beautiful little garden in the world, enclosed by a low wall round it. I found her so well-bred, well spoken, and well informed, so pleasing in looks and character, that I was delighted to be there, and had no desire to move. But the onset of night disturbed me, for then the baron came in search of me, for it was suppertime. So I could not linger there but did as he told me. I will only say of the supper that it was just what I wanted, once the girl I had been talking to sat down facing me. After supper the baron admitted that although he had had many wandering knights as his guests, he could not remember when he last had one who was in search of adventures. And he begged me to return by way of his castle, as a favour, if I was able to. And I said: 'I will be glad to, sir', for it would have been rude to refuse such a small request on my host's part.

That night I was made welcome as a guest, and my horse was ready as soon as it was daybreak, just as I had requested the night before. My good host and his dear daughter I commended to the Holy Ghost and said fare-well at once, leaving as soon as I could. I had scarcely left the castle when I came to a clearing where wild bulls were fighting amongst themselves, making such a noise and looking so fierce, that, to tell the truth, I beat a retreat; for there is no animal as fierce and dangerous as a bull. I saw a peasant, black as a mulberry, extremely huge and hideous – indeed, I cannot describe how ugly he was – sitting on a stump with a great club in his hand. I approached him and saw that his head was bigger than a horse's; he had tousled hair, but he was bald in front, with a forehead a foot high, and had great hairy ears like an elephant's. Huge eyebrows overhung his flat face, with its owl's eyes and cat's nose, a long wolf's mouth and sharp yellow teeth like a boar's. He had a black beard and tangled moustache, and although he was tall his body was twisted. He leaned on his club, dressed in a strange garment, not made of linen or cotton, but of two newly-flayed hides from bulls or oxen, fastened round his neck. As soon as he saw me approach, the peasant got up; I did not know if he was going to attack me, or what he was going to do, but I prepared to defend myself until I saw that when he stood up properly on a tree trunk, he was over seventeen feet tall. He looked at me without a word, just like a dumb animal, and I thought that he was an idiot and could not speak. Anyway, I plucked up courage and said to him: 'Go on, tell me if you are friend or enemy.' He answered: 'I am a man.' 'What kind of man?' 'Just as you see me, never different.' 'What do you do here?' 'I live here, keeping these cattle in the wood.' 'Keeping them? By St Peter of Rome, they would not obey a man, and anyway, how can you keep cattle in the open or in a wood without a place to shut them in?' 'I keep them in such a way that they never leave this clearing.' 'And you can make them obey? Tell me how do you do it.' 'None of them dares to move off when they see me coming, because when I get one into my hard strong hands I give its horns such a twisting that the others tremble with fear, and gather round me as if to beg for mercy. Only I can come here, because anyone else would be killed by them at once. So I am lord of my cattle; and now it is your turn to tell me who you are and what you seek.' 'I am a knight, and I seek something I cannot find; indeed I have sought it for a long time and still cannot find it.' 'And what are you after?' 'Adventures to prove my courage and boldness, so please tell me if you know of any adventure or marvel.' 'You will have to do without "adventures" because I know nothing about such things, and have never heard of them. But if you go to a fountain near here, you won't come back without difficulty, if you follow the custom. Near here there is a path which leads straight to it, but make sure that you follow the straight path because there are many other paths on which to lose your way. There you will see a fountain of boiling water which is colder than marble. It is shaded by the finest tree that Nature ever made. Its leaves last for ever, it does not lose them in winter; from it hangs an iron bowl on a chain so long that it reaches the fountain. By the fountain there is a great stone – you will see it, but I can't describe it, because I've never seen one like it – and on the other side a chapel, which is small but very beautiful. If you scoop up some water in the bowl and pour it on the stone, you will see such a storm that no wild animal will stay in the forest; every dog, stag, deer and boar and all the birds will leave it in terror, because you will see such lightning, wind and shattering of trees, rain and thunder, that if you get away unharmed you will be luckier than any of the knights who have been there before.'

So I left the peasant who had shown me the way. It must have been after nine, and getting on towards noon when I saw the tree and the chapel. The tree was the finest pine-tree that ever grew on the earth; however hard it rained, not a drop of water would have penetrated its branches. I saw the bowl hanging from the tree, made of finer gold than you can buy at any fair, and believe me, the fountain was boiling like hot water. The stone was an emerald, with a hole in it like a flask, set with four rubies, brighter and more brilliant red than the sun when it rises in the east. And every word of what follows is true. I wanted to see the marvellous storm and tempest, which was not a wise thing to do, for I would have been glad to stop it, if I could have done so, as soon as I had poured water from the bowl onto the stone. I must have poured too much, for the sky was so stormy that lightning struck from more than fourteen directions at once, and snow, hail and rain fell from the clouds all at once. The storm was so violent that a hundred times I expected to be killed by the thunderbolts and shattered trees that fell all around me, and I was terrified as long as the storm lasted. But God comforted me, because the tempest did not last long, and the winds, which obey His commands, died down. I was delighted to see the air become clear and pure, and my joy made me forget my fear. As soon as the storm passed, I saw gathered on the great pine tree so many birds that every branch and leaf was covered with them, making the tree even more beautiful; they all began to sing, and although they were in perfect harmony, none of them sang the same song. Their joyful song was a delight, and I listened to them until they had finished their 'service'; I do not think that anyone else will find such pleasure in singing unless he hears those same birds, which almost sent me out of my mind with ecstasy.

Then I heard a knight approaching: indeed I thought there were ten knights, he made such a noise. When I saw that he was alone, I held my horse and mounted at once. He rode towards me angrily, faster than a swallow and fiercer than a lion, challenging me in a loud voice: 'Vassal, you never challenged me but have done me much harm just the same. If you have a quarrel with me, you should have challenged me, but now I demand satisfaction as you have declared war on me. If I can I shall take revenge for the damage which you can see you have done: look at my woods, which you have destroyed. I accuse you of driving me from my house by storms and rain. You have caused me such harm to my woods and castle that no men-at-arms nor walls could have protected me from it; no-one would have been safe even in a stone fortress. So there can never be any truce or peace between us.'

At these words we charged at each other, each gripping his shield to protect himself. The knight had a good horse and a stout lance, and was at least a head taller than I. So I was in a bad way, being smaller than him, while his horse was stronger than mine. I am telling the truth, to cover up my shame. I gave him as hard a blow as I could, trying with all my might, and struck him at the top of the shield; I put such force into it that my lance flew in pieces and his remained whole; it was no light one – indeed, it was heavier than any knight's lance I have ever seen. And the knight struck me so forcefully that he bore me clean off my horse and laid me flat on the ground, where he left me ashamed and exhausted; he did not look at me again. He took my horse and left me, returning the way he had come. And I, completely at a loss, was left in pain and troubled. I sat for a little while by the fountain and rested; I did not dare follow the knight, for that would have been sheer madness, and I did not know what had become of him even if I had dared to go after him. In the end, I thought that I would keep my promise to my host, and return by way of his house. The idea pleased me, and I did so, first taking off my armour in order to walk more easily; and so I returned shamefacedly. When I came to his home at nightfall, I found my host just as before, just as cheerful and courteous, as I had before. I did not notice that either his daughter or himself were less glad to see me, or treated me less honourably than they had done the night before. Everyone in the house treated me with great respect, for which I thank them; and they said that no-one of whom they knew or had heard had ever escaped from the place I had been to without either being killed or captured. That is the story of my journey and return; on the way back I thought I was a fool, and like a fool I have told you the story which I never wanted to tell you.'

'By my head,' said Sir Yvain, 'you are my cousin-german, and we ought to be close to one another, but I call you a fool for concealing this from me for so long. If I call you a fool, do not hold it against me, because if I can and am allowed to, I shall go and avenge your shame.' 'It is obviously after dinner,' said Kay, who could not keep quiet: 'for there are more words in a jar full of wine than in a whole barrel of beer. They say that a cat grows gay when it is full. After dinner no one moves, but everyone is off to kill Nur-ed-din and wants to avenge King Forré! Are your saddlebags filled and your greaves polished and your banners unfurled? Come on, tell us, fair sir, when you are off to your martyrdom, for we would like to send you on your way. All the provosts and constables will be glad to go with you. And I beg you, whatever happens, that you will not go without saying goodbye; and if you have a bad dream tonight, then stay at home!' 'By the devil, Sir Kay, are you mad,' said the Queen, 'and does your tongue never make an end? Shame on your tongue, which is so full of bitterness; it must hate you for it always says the worst things it can about everyone . . .' 'Really, my lady, his rudeness does not worry me,' said Sir Yvain. 'In every court, Sir Kay is so able, wise and worthy that he will never be deaf or dumb. He can always deal with meanness, and answer it with wisdom and courtesy, and has always done so. You know perfectly well that I am not lying. But I do not want to quarrel, or start a foolish dispute. He who deals the first blow does not always start a fight, but whoever tries to strike back. It is better to fight a stranger than your companion. I don't want to be like a watchdog who bristles and growls when another dog barks at him.'

As he spoke, the King came out of his chamber, where he had been for a long time, for he had slept until just then. And the lords saw him and all got to their feet, but he told them to sit down again. The Queen told him of Calogrenant's adventures, word for word, and made a good story of it. The King listened willingly, and swore three great oaths, by the soul of Utherpendragon, and of his son and of his mother, that he would go and see the spring before a fortnight had passed, and the storm and the marvels as well; he would be there on St John's eve and would spend the night there, and he said that anyone who wanted to could come with him. The whole court was delighted with the King's plan, for both lords and knights were keen to go. But although everyone else was pleased, Sir Yvain was annoyed, because he had intended to go by himself and was angry that the King was intending to go. The cause of his anger was that he knew that if Sir Kay asked for the favour, he would be allowed to fight the stranger, as would Sir Gawain if he asked for it first. If either of them asked for the favour, they would never be refused. But he had no desire for their company, so he did not wait for them, but wanted to go off all by himself, whether things turned out well or badly. And whoever might be left behind, he wanted to be in Broceliande within three days and to seek out the narrow wooded path which he longed to see, and the heath, and the castle, and the joy and pleasure of the courteous girl who was so charming and beautiful, and, besides his daughter, the lord of the house as well, who tried to honour his guests because he himself was so noble and well-bred. Then he would see the bulls in the clearing, and the huge peasant who guards them. He very much wanted to see this fellow, who was so ugly, huge, hideous, misshapen and black as a smith. Then he would see, if he could, the stone, the fountain and the basin, and the birds in the pine tree, and he would make the rain come and the winds blow. But he would not seek to boast of this, nor would anyone know of his desire until he had earned great honour or great shame; then everything could be known.

But Sir Yvain slipped away from the court so that no one met him, and went alone to his lodging. He found all his household there and ordered his horse to be saddled; he called a squire of his, from whom he hid nothing: 'Come on,' he said, 'follow me and bring my armour. I shall go out by that gate on my palfrey. Be sure not to delay, because I have a long way to go, and have my horse well shod. But I order you to be sure not to answer any questions that are asked of me. Otherwise, however much you trust me, you can never rely on me again.' 'Sir,' he said, 'everything will be all right. No one will learn anything from me. Go, and I will follow you.'

Sir Yvain mounted at once, hoping to avenge his cousin's shame before he returned, if he could. The squire ran for his armour and horse, and mounted at once; there was no need for delay, because the horse was already shod. He followed his master's tracks until he saw that he had dismounted and was waiting for him in a secluded place far from the road. He had brought all his harness and equipment, and he armed him; but Sir Yvain did not wait for a moment once he was armed. He made his way each day over mountains and down valleys, the length of wide forests, through strange and savage places. He passed many dangerous spots, many perils and many hazards, until he

Yvain is welcomed by the host of the castle near the spring and his daughter.
(Paris, Bibliothèque Nationale, MS Fr 1433 f.67^v)

came to the path he sought, dark and full of thorns. Then he was sure that he could not lose his way. Whatever the cost, he would not stop until he had seen the pine which shaded the spring and stone, and the storm which hailed and rained and thundered and blew. That night he was lodged as he wished; for he found more riches and honour than he had been told of at the baron's house, and saw a hundred times more wit and beauty in the girl than Calogrenant had described; no one could describe the qualities of either the girl or her father. When a man like him turns to good deeds, it is impossible to describe him, for no tongue could recount the honour of such a man. Sir Yvain was well looked after that night, much to his pleasure; and the next day he went to the clearing and saw the bulls and the peasant, who told him the way. But he crossed himself more than a hundred times in amazement at the way in which Nature had created such an ugly and evil creature. Then he rode as far as the fountain, and saw everything there that he wanted to see. Without stopping or resting, he poured the basin full of water on the stone: and then it blew and rained and made the storm which he expected. And when God brought back the clear sky, the birds gathered on the pine and made a marvellous, joyous noise above the perilous fountain. When their joy had died down, the knight came, burning with more wrath than a log on fire and making more noise than if he were hunting a rutting stag. And when they saw each other, they charged as though they were mortal enemies. Each had a strong stout lance, and they gave each other such great blows that they thrust through each other's shields and tore their mailcoats. The lances broke into splinters and the butts flew in the air. They attacked each other with swords, and in the clash of weapons their shield-straps were cut and the shields hacked in pieces above and below until pieces hung off them and they served neither as cover nor as defence. For they had shredded them so much that their white swords fell on each other's sides and arms and thighs. They attacked each other murderously, but they did not move from their place any more than two blocks of stone. Two knights were never so engrossed in bringing about each other's death. They were careful not to waste their blows, so that they could use them to best effect. They dented and bent their helmets and sent the rings of their mailcoats flying until they drew blood enough; for their hauberks were so hot from their own heat that they were scarcely more use than a coat. As they lunged at each other's faces, it was amazing how long such a fierce and hard-fought battle lasted; but both were so stout-hearted that neither would retreat a foot until his enemy had wounded him to death. Even so they were very conscious of honour and did not wish or deign to wound or harm each other's horse; but they remained on horseback, and never dismounted, which made the fight more handsome. At last Sir Yvain hacked off the other knight's helmet; he was so stunned and faint that he passed out; he had never had such a vicious blow before, and under his cap his head was cut to the brain, and brain and blood stained the rings of bright mailcoat; it caused him such pain that his heart almost failed. Then he fled, and he was not wrong to do so, for he felt himself wounded to death, and no defence could help him. With this thought he fled as quickly as he could to his castle; the drawbridge was lowered and the gate opened wide. Sir Yvain spurred after him as quickly as he could. But Yvain was like a gerfalcon stooping on a crane that it has seen from far off, which approaches it, thinking that it will seize it, and yet does not touch it; and the result of his hunt was the same. He could almost throw his arms around him and yet he could not reach him: he was so close that he could hear him groan with pain, but his enemy still fled. He strove to catch him, thinking that all his efforts were in vain if he could not take him dead or alive: for he remembered Sir Kay's mockery. He was not yet quit of the pledge he had given his cousin, and no one would believe him if he did not produce proof. The other knight had led him to spur his horse up to the gate of the castle, and both entered; they found neither man nor woman in the streets, and they both came to the palace gate.

The gate was very high and wide, but the entrance was so narrow that neither two men nor two horses could go through it together nor pass each other in the gateway. For it was built just like the trap laid for a rat when he comes to take the bait, with a blade above which is released and strikes and catches the rat; if anything touches the spring, however softly, it comes down. In the same way there were two thongs which held up an iron portcullis, with sharpened cutting ends. If anything came onto this machine the gate above dropped down and anyone below who was touched by the gate was caught and cut to pieces. The safe way through was exactly in the middle, as narrow as a beaten track. The knight charged through on the right path, with Yvain galloping after him. He was so close to him that he had gripped the back of his saddle; and it was just as well for him that he was stretching forward for his horse touched the beam which held up the iron gate. The gate came down like a devil out of hell. It struck the saddle and the horse's rump and cut it clean in two. But, thank God, it did not touch Sir Yvain except to shave his back so closely that it cut off both his spurs level with his heels. He fell off, dismayed, while the mortally wounded knight escaped as follows. There was another gate behind the first, just like it; the knight fled through it, and the gate fell behind him. So Sir Yvain was captured; full of fear and much disturbed, he walked round this hall, which was studded with gilded nails, and the walls were skilfully painted in rich colours. But he was grieved by nothing so much as not knowing where the knight had gone. Then, while he was in this narrow place, he heard a narrow door being opened in a little room nearby, and a very charming and beautiful girl came out alone, shutting the door behind her. When she found Sir Yvain, she was much disturbed at first. 'Indeed, knight,' she said, 'I fear you are unwelcome. If anyone sees you here, you will be hacked in pieces; for my lord is mortally wounded, and I know that you killed him. My lady is in such grief and her people are

Yvain's horse is cut in half by the descending portcullis, shown on a misericord from Lincoln cathedral.

weeping around her, and I fear they will kill themselves with grief; and they know that you are inside! But their grief is still so great that they cannot yet deal with you. If they want to kill or imprison you, they cannot fail to do so when they come to attack you.' And Sir Yvain replied: 'Yet, if God pleases, they will not kill me, nor will I be captured.' 'No,' she said, 'because I will do my best for you. He who is fearful is no true knight. I think you a brave man when I see that you are not afraid. And I assure you that if I could I would help you and treat you with honour, as you once did to me. My lady once sent me with a message to the King's court; I suppose that I was not as wise or courteous or of such bearing as a girl should be, but there was not a single knight there who deigned to speak a single word to me except yourself; but you – and I thank you for it – respected me and helped me. I shall reward you now for the respect you showed me then. I know your name, for I have recognised you: you are King

Urien's son, and are called Sir Yvain. You can be quite sure that if you trust me you will neither be caught nor ill-treated. Take this little ring of mine, which you will return when I have set you free.' When she had given him the ring, she explained that its power was such that it was like the bark that covers the wood of a tree, so that you cannot see it; but it had to be put on so that the stone in the ring was covered by the palm. Then the wearer of the ring had nothing to fear; no-one, however sharp-eyed, could see him, any more than he could see the wood beneath the covering bark. Sir Yvain was pleased with this, and when she had told him about it, she led him to a seat on a couch covered with such a rich quilt that the Duke of Austria has none like it. She told him that she would bring him something to eat if he wanted it; and he said that he would be glad of it. The girl ran quickly to her room, and soon came back with a roasted chicken and a cake, a cloth and a jug full of excellent wine covered by a bright goblet, and offered him this for his meal. He was in need of it and ate and drank heartily.

When he had eaten and drunk, the knights who were in search of him came that way, wanting to avenge their lord. The girl said to him: 'Friend, listen, they are already looking for you! There is a great deal of noise and disturbance. But whoever comes or goes, do not move because of it, because you will never be found if you do not move from this bed. You will see the room full of angry, hostile people who hope to find you here. I think they will bring the body here before the burial, and will begin to look for you under the benches and couches. All this will be amusing to a man who has no fear, for everyone will seem to be blind; they will all be so blind, and upset and deluded that they will be beside themselves with fury. That is all I can tell you, and I dare not stay any longer. But I thank God that I have had the chance to help you, because I wanted very much to do so.' Then she went back the way she had come, and when she had gone, all the people gathered on both sides of the gates, bearing clubs and swords; there was a great crowd of them. They saw the half of the horse which had been cut in two outside the gate, and thought that when the gates were opened they would be sure to find him who they wished to kill. Then they drew up the gates, which had killed many men, but no thongs or traps were set in their path, so they all came in at once. They found the other half of the dead horse on the threshold, but none of them had eyes to see Sir Yvain, whom they would gladly have killed. And he saw them grow very angry and furious. They said: 'How can this happen? There is no gate or window here through which anyone could go, except for a bird which could fly out, or a squirrel of some kind, or something as small or smaller than that: the windows are barred, and the gates were closed as soon as our lord passed through. The body is in here, dead or alive, for it is certainly not outside. More than half the saddle is in here, as we can see; but all we can see of him is his cut-off spurs, which fell from his feet. Let's stop chattering and search every corner. He is either still here or we are under a spell, or evil beings have taken him from us.' So, burning with rage, they searched up and down the room, beating the walls and the couches and benches. But the couch where he was sitting was not touched, so that he escaped unharmed. They barged around and made a great disturbance there with their clubs, like blind men tapping their way in search of something. As they were hunting around under the couches and stools, there came in one of the most beautiful ladies that any earthly being ever saw. No one has ever described such a very beautiful Christian lady. But she was so mad with grief that she almost killed herself. Again and again she cried out, until she could not continue and fell down in a faint. When she was set on her feet again she started to tear her clothes and her hair. She tore her hair and her dress, and fainted at every step, and nothing could comfort her. When she saw her lord brought before her dead on a bier, she never expected to be comforted again: so she lamented loudly. The holy water, cross and candles were carried before the bier by the ladies of a convent, and missals and censers and clergy followed, who were to pronounce the last absolution which heals the soul in misery.

Sir Yvain heard the cries and mourning, which cannot be described; no one could describe it, or put such a thing down in a book. The procession passed, but in the middle of the room a great crowd gathered around the bier; for the warm clear red blood was flowing from the dead man's wound. This was a true sign that he who had fought the battle and overcome and killed him was still there. So they searched and hunted everywhere, turning everything over, until everyone was in a sweat from anguish and from their toil, all because of the red blood which had flowed before their eyes. Sir Yvain was much beaten and barged where he lay, but he did not move a finger. And everyone was more and more disturbed by the wounds which had burst open; they wondered why they bled, nor could they tell who was at fault. They all said to each other: 'The man who killed him is still among us, but we cannot see him. This is a marvel and a devil's trick.' At this the lady was so overcome by grief that she went almost mad, and cried as if beside herself: 'Ah God, aren't we going to find the murderer, the traitor, who has killed my good lord? Good? The best of lords! Indeed, God, it will be Your fault if You let him escape like this. I cannot blame anyone except You, because You are hiding him from my sight. Such violence and wrong was never seen as You are doing me by not letting me see him who is so close to me. I am sure, because I cannot see him, that some ghost or hostile spirit has put himself between us, and I am bewitched by a phantom. Either that, or he is a coward and afraid of me. He must be a coward to fear me; it is out of cowardice that he dare not show himself before me. Ah, you ghost and coward! why are you such a coward towards me when you were so bold when faced with my lord? Vain and empty creature, why can't I have you in my power now? Why can't I seize you? How can you have killed my lord except by treachery? I am sure my lord would never have been defeated by you if he had seen you. Neither God nor man have ever known his like in this world, nor is there anyone now who is a match for him. If you were a mortal man, you would not have dared to fight with my lord, for no one could get the better of him.'

Thus the lady argued with herself, tormenting herself with the conflict in her mind until she was exhausted. Her people joined in, and made the greatest possible mourning. They bore the body away and buried it. They had hunted up and down with such energy that they were weary of searching, and so they abandoned it from weariness when they could not see anyone who might be guilty. The nuns and the priests had finished the service and returned from the church; now they arrived at the burial place. But the girl in the chamber was not interested in all this; she thought of Sir Yvain, and went quickly to him. 'Fair sir,' she said, 'these people have been looking for you in a great mob. They have raised a great tumult here and have hunted out every corner more closely than a hound after a partridge or a quail. I'm sure you were frightened.' 'By my faith,' he said, 'you're right! I never thought I would be so full of fear. Now, if possible, I would like to watch the procession and the body from some window or arrow-slit.' But he had no eyes for the body or for the procession; he would have gladly seen them all burnt, even if it had cost him a thousand marks. A thousand? No, three thousand. He only said this for the sake of the lady of the town, whom he wanted to see. The girl put him at a little window, always wanting to repay the respect he had shown her. Through the window, Sir Yvain saw the beautiful lady, who was saying: 'Fair lord, may God indeed have mercy on your soul. For I never knew of a knight in the saddle who was your equal! No knight, fair dear lord, was your equal in honour, nor in courtesy. Generosity was your friend, and boldness your companion. May your soul join the company of the saints, fair dear lord!' Then she beat herself and tore everything that came to hand. Sir Yvain only prevented himself with great difficulty from running out and restraining her. But the girl begged and advised and ordered him strictly, though with courtesy and grace, not to do anything foolish, saying: 'You are well off here. Don't move for anything until this grief has abated, and the people are tired and have gone away, as they soon will. If you follow my advice, you will do well out of it. You can stay sitting here and watch the people outside going up and down the street; and no one can see you; that is the best thing to do. But be careful not to say anything that might offend; for anyone who forgets himself and is carried away, and does something violent when he has the chance, is, I would say, wicked rather than bold. If you are thinking of doing anything foolish, make sure that you don't do it. A wise man conceals his wild thoughts and puts goodness to work if he can. So behave like a wise man and do not risk your head: you would never be put to ransom. Have a care for yourself and remember my advice. I dare not stay here any longer. I might stay so long that perhaps I would be suspected when I was not seen among the others in the crowd, and I would suffer for it.'

Then she went away, leaving him there not knowing what to do. He was reluctant to see the corpse buried without having been able to take anything to show as clear evidence that he overcame and killed the knight. If he had no evidence or proof, Kay was so evil and perverse, so mocking and irritating, that he could never convince him. He would go about every day offering him insults and hurling mockery and abuse at him as he did the other day. His taunts then were still fresh and troubling his heart, but with her sugar and honeycombs a new Love softened him; Love had hunted on his lands and gathered all his prey. His enemy took away his heart, and he loved the creature who most hated him. The lady had indeed avenged her Lord's death, though she did not know it. She had taken worse revenge than she ever could have done if Love had not avenged him, who attacked him so softly that he wounded his heart through his eyes. And this wound lasts longer than those made by lance or sword: sword thrusts can be cured and healed quickly as soon as a doctor attends to it, while Love's wound gets worse the nearer it is to its doctor. Sir Yvain was thus wounded, and would never recover from it, for he had surrendered entirely to Love. Love had abandoned his old haunts and lodged only here, wanting no other lodging or host except him; he was sensible to abandon poorer hostelries in favour of such a man. It is shameful that Love should ever be so base as to settle in the meanest place he can find just as readily as the best. But now he was welcome and honoured and he settled happily there. Love should act like that, who is such a noble creature that it is amazing that he ever dares to stoop to vile places. He is like a man who spreads rich ointment on dust and ashes, hating honour and loving shame, mixing sugar with gall, and suet with honey. But this time he had done nothing of the kind and had lodged in a noble place, where no one could wrong him.

When they had buried the dead man, all the people went home. Of all the clergy, knights, men-at-arms and ladies, only she remained who was unable to hide her grief. But she stayed there all alone, often clasping her throat, wringing her hands and beating them together as she read the psalms in a psalter illuminated with golden letters. Sir Yvain was still at the window watching her, and the more he was aware of her the more he loved her and the more beautiful she seemed. He wished that she would stop weeping and reading and that she would like to talk to him. Love, who caught him at the window, put this desire into him. But he despaired of achieving his wishes, for he could not think or believe that his wishes could come true, and said: 'I am a fool to long for something I can never have. I killed her lord, and yet I hope to be at peace with her? By my faith, I think all I shall learn is that she now hates me more than any other being, and she will be right, "Now", did I say? That was wise, for women have a thousand moods. Her present mood may perhaps change – indeed, she will change it, without "perhaps", so I am a fool to despair. And God grant that she changes it soon. I must be in her power now, since Love so wishes. Anyone who does not welcome Love as soon as he comes to him is a wicked traitor, and I say (hear it who will) that such a man deserves neither well-being nor happiness. So I will love my enemy, for I must not hate her unless I want to betray Love. I will love whatever Love wishes. And should she treat me as a friend? Yes indeed, because I love her. And I call her my enemy, because she hates me and is not wrong to do so, because I have killed the man she loved. And am I therefore her enemy? No indeed, but her friend; for I never loved any creature so much before. I grieve for her fair hair, finer than fine gold, it shines so brightly; I feel rage and anguish when I see her cut and tear it; nor can the tears be stemmed which fall from her eyes. All these things displease me. Though they are filled with tears which never cease to flow, yet eyes were never so beautiful as these. I grieve for her weeping, but nothing distresses me more than her face, which she so unjustly wounds. I never saw a face so well formed and fresh in colour. And it wrings my heart to see her put her hands to her throat. She is not just pretending when she does the worst she can to herself. And yet no crystal or mirror is so clear and so polished. God! Why does she act so foolishly, and why does she not hurt herself less? Why does she wring her hands and beat her breast and tear at it? Wouldn't she be a real marvel to look at if she was happy, when she is so lovely in her trouble? Yes indeed, I swear it; Nature will never be able to surpass her beauty, because she has so excelled herself here. Did she never equal such work? How could it have happened, where could such beauty have come from? Surely God himself made her with His own hands, to give Nature a rest. Nature would waste her time trying to make a copy, for she would never succeed in doing it. Even God could not match her, I think, if He wished to try, for He could never make her equal however hard He tried.'

In this way Sir Yvain thought about the lady who was destroyed by grief; I do not think that it has ever come about that someone in prison and in fear of his life, like Sir Yvain, was so madly in love that he did not make some plea on his behalf when no one else was likely to do so. He stayed at the window until he saw the lady go away and both the portcullises were lowered again. Anyone else would have been sorry at this and would have preferred to escape rather than stay there. But for him it was all the same whether they were closed or open. He certainly would not leave if they were open, nor even if the lady gave him leave and graciously pardoned the death of her lord. Love and shame held him back, one on each side. He would be ashamed if he went, because no one would believe in his exploit; and he was so eager at least to see the beautiful lady, if nothing else, that he did not worry about being in prison: he would rather die than leave. But now the girl returned, to keep him company and cheer him up, and bring him whatever he wanted. She found him thoughtful and weary because of his love. She said to him: 'Sir Yvain, how have you got on today?' 'Pleasantly enough,' he said. 'Pleasantly? By God, are you telling the truth? How can you have a pleasant time when everyone is hunting for you to kill you, unless you long for your own death?' 'It is true, my sweet friend,' he said, 'that I would not wish to die; but, in God's sight, what I have seen today was very pleasing, and will always please me.' 'Let it be for now,' she said, 'because I know what you're talking about. I'm not so simple or stupid as not to understand your meaning; but now follow me, because I will soon find a method of getting you out of prison. I will set you free, if you wish, tonight or tomorrow. Come now, I will show you the way.' He answered 'I assure you, I will never leave secretly like a thief. When everyone has gathered in the streets outside, then I can leave with honour, but not by creeping out at night.' With these words he followed her into a little room. The girl was kind, and anxious to help him; she got for him whatever he wanted. And at the right moment she remembered what he had said to her: that he had been very pleased by what he saw when everyone was searching for him in the room in order to kill him.

The girl was in such favour with her lady, that she was not afraid of telling her anything, whatever the implications, for she was her adviser and trusted friend. So why should she be afraid of comforting her lady and giving her advice that would bring her honour? The first time that they were alone together she said: 'My lady, I am astonished that you behave so foolishly; do you think this mourning will bring your dead lord back to life?' 'Not at all,' she said; 'I would rather be dead of grief.' 'Why?' 'To follow him.' 'To follow him? May God preserve you from it, and give you another lord as good as him, for He can certainly do so.' 'Don't talk such nonsense! He could never find one like him.' 'He will give you a better one, if you will accept him, and I will prove it myself.' 'Go away! Be quiet! I will never find a man like that.' 'You will indeed, my lady, if it pleases you. But now tell me, if you will, who will defend your lands when King Arthur arrives, who is coming here next week to the stone and fountain. You had a message about it in the letter which the Damsel Sauvage sent you. Ah, what good use you make of the letter! You ought to hold council as to how to defend your fountain, and all you do is go on weeping! Please do not delay, my dear lady! The knights you have are no better than chambermaids. The best of them will never take shield or lance in hand. You have many cowardly servants but not one brave enough to mount a horse to go to war; and the King is coming with such a large army that he will take everything without opposition.' The lady knew quite well in her own mind that the girl was giving good advice; but she, like other women, was unreasonable, and would not admit she was wrong, while she said no to what she really desired. 'Go away,' she said, 'say no more! If you ever refer to it again, you will do so in a bad moment, unless you leave me altogether. Your talk wearies me!' 'Very well, my lady,' she said, 'I can see you are a true woman, because you grow angry when someone tries to help you.'

Then she went away and left her, and the lady realised that she was in the wrong. She would have dearly loved to know how she could prove that she could find a knight who was better than her lord, and would have been glad to hear the answer, but she had forbidden the girl to speak. In this mood, she waited until the girl returned. It was clear that her warning had had no effect, for the latter at once said: 'My lady, is it right that you should kill yourself with grief? By God, control yourself, and at least show enough dignity to stop your lamenting. For such a noble lady as you should not mourn for so long. Remember your honour and high birth! Do you think that all courage was slain with your lord? There are a hundred as good as he in this world!' 'You are telling lies, God confound me! Name a single one who is acknowledged to be the peer of my lord!' 'Very well, I will tell you, in spite of everything, even if you are angry and start to threaten me again.' 'I won't, I assure you.' 'Then I hope that everything will turn out well for you, if you can agree to it, and God give you pleasure of it! I cannot see why I should keep quiet; no-one can hear our conversation. You will think that I am bold, but I will speak out. When two knights meet in battle, which do you think is the better, when one defeats the other? For my part, I would give the prize to the winner. What do you think?' 'I think you are laying traps for me, and want to catch me out.' 'By my faith, let me tell you that I am right, and so I have proved beyond argument that the man who defeated your lord was the better of the two. Not only did he defeat him, but he was bold enough to pursue him here, until he had imprisoned him in his house.' 'This is the greatest nonsense,' she said, 'that I have ever heard. Go away, you evil spirit, foolish and malicious girl! Don't tell such lies again, and never try to come back to speak for him again!' 'Very well, my lady, I know that I will never be in your favour again, and I told you so beforehand. But you promised that you would bear no ill will towards me, and that you wouldn't be angry. You haven't kept your promise very well, and what has happened is that you have spoken as you pleased, and I lost by breaking my silence.'

So she went back to the room where Sir Yvain was waiting, whom she kept in great comfort. But nothing pleased him when he was unable to see the lady, and he paid no attention to the proposal she made to him. The lady spent the whole night in a state of great concern: she was very worried as to how she could defend the fountain, and began to regret having blamed and insulted and rejected the girl. She felt quite sure that the girl would not have mentioned the knight because of a bribe or reward, or even out of love for him; the girl loved her more than him, and would never do anything to embarrass or trouble her, for she was far too loyal a friend. So the lady changed her mind about the girl who she had just insulted, and felt that she would never at any price be entirely devoted to her again. And as for the knight, who she had rejected, she now loyally pardoned, because there were good arguments in his favour, and he had done her no wrong. She began to imagine that he was in her presence and to argue with him as follows: 'Come,' she says, 'can you deny that my lord was killed by you?' 'I cannot deny it,' he says, 'but freely admit it.' 'Why? Did you do it to harm me, out of hate or spite?' 'May death not spare me if I did it in order to harm you.' 'So you have not wronged me, and you cannot have wronged him, for he would have killed you if he could. So, to the best of my knowledge, I have summed up the case well.' So, having proved by reason, right and commonsense, that she had no right to hate him, she said what she desired to admit; and at the same time she kindled love, like a bush which only smokes when lit until someone blows on the flames. If the girl had come in now, she would have won her argument which she had pleaded so hard, and for which she had been abused.

Next morning, she did come in, and began her speech again where she had left off. The lady sat with bowed head, knowing that she had done her wrong; for now she wanted to make amends and ask the knight's name and standing and descent. She behaved humbly and wisely, and said: 'I want to ask your forgiveness for the angry and proud things I foolishly said to you; I will take your advice. But please tell me – if you know – what kind of man and from what family is the knight on whose behalf you argued for so long? If he is a suitable match for me – and if he does not refuse me – I will make him lord of my lands and of myself. But it must be done in such a way that no one can mock me and say: "She was the woman who married her husband's killer." ' 'In God's name, it will be so, my lady. You shall have the noblest, gentlest and most handsome lord there ever was among Abel's descendants.' 'What is he called?' 'Sir Yvain.' 'By my faith, he is no common man, but one of the most noble, as I know indeed; he is King Urien's son.' 'Indeed, my lady, you tell the truth.' 'When can we have him here?' 'In five days' time.' 'That would be too long; I wish he were here already. Get him to come tonight or tomorrow at the latest.' 'My lady, I don't think that even a bird could fly that far in one day. But I will send one of my servants, who runs very quickly and will reach King Arthur's court by tomorrow evening at least; that is where he is to be found.' 'That is too long. The days are long. But tell him that tomorrow night he must be back here, and he must go quicker than he usually does. Because if he is prepared to try, he can do two days' journey in one, and tonight the moon will shine, making the night like day. I will give him whatever he wants when he returns.' 'Leave this all to me; you shall have him here the day after tomorrow at the latest. Meanwhile, send for your people, and ask their advice about the approach of the King. You will need counsel as to how to maintain the custom of defending your fountain. And no one will be so proud as to boast that he will go there. You can tell them plainly that you must marry. A very famous knight has sought your hand, but you dare not accept, unless they all agree. And I can guarantee the result; I know they are all such cowards that they will fall at your feet and thank you, so that their burden, which would be too much for them, can be put on someone else's shoulders. Anyone who is frightened of his own shadow is only too glad to avoid encountering lances and arrows; cowards do not like that kind of game.' And the lady answered: 'By my faith, that is how I want it to be, and I agree, for I had already thought of this plan, and we will carry it out. But why are you waiting? Be off, and don't delay any longer. Do everything to get him here. I shall stay with my people.'

So their conversation ended, and the girl pretended that she had sent for Sir Yvain from his own lands; every day she had him bathed, washed and made elegant. Besides, she prepared a scarlet robe trimmed with brand-new fur. She lent him everything that he needed to adorn him: a golden collar for his neck, worked with precious stones which make people look handsome, a belt and a purse made of rich embroidery. She saw to it that he was well-dressed, and told her lady that her messenger had come back, and had done his work cleverly. 'What!' she said, 'when will Sir Yvain come?' 'He is here.' 'Here? Let him come at once, secretly and quietly, while no-one is with me. See that no-one else comes, because I would hate to have a fourth person here.' The girl left at once and went back to her guest. But she did not let her face show the joy in her heart; instead, she said that her lady knew that she had kept him hidden there, and said. 'Sir Yvain, by God, it is no use hiding you any longer. News of you has got out and my lady knows you are here; she is very angry with me, and blames me for it, and has reproached me severely. But she has given her promise that I may lead you to her, without angering or annoying her. I do not think you will be grieved at this, except that – and I will not betray you by lying – she wishes to imprison you, in such a way that both body and heart shall be hers!' 'Indeed,' he said, 'I am very willing, and it will not grieve me at all. I will be happy to be her prisoner.' 'So you will be; I swear it by this right hand by which I hold you. Now come on, and I advise you to behave so humbly to her that she will not imprison you harshly. But do not let it alarm you: I don't think your imprisonment will be a great trouble to you.' So the girl led him along, first dismaying him, then reassuring him, and talking obliquely about the prison in which he would be put; for every lover is a prisoner. She was right to talk of imprisonment, for everyone who loves is certainly in prison.

The girl led Sir Yvain by the hand to the place where he was to be held dear, but he thought he would be unwelcome, and it is hardly surprising that he thought so. They found the lady sitting on a red cushion. I warrant you that Sir Yvain was very frightened as he went into the room; there he found the lady, who did not say a word. That made him even more frightened, and he was quite beside himself with fear at the thought that he had been betrayed. He stood there so long that in the end the girl spoke, and said: 'Five hundred curses on my soul for bringing into a beautiful lady's room a knight who neither approaches her nor has a tongue, a mouth or any sense to introduce himself.' With these words she took him by the arm and said: 'Come forward, knight, and do not be afraid of my lady; she will not bite you. But try to win her goodwill and be reconciled. I will ask her, too, to forgive you the death of her lord Esclados the Red.' But Sir Yvain now clasped his hands and knelt, saying like a true lover: 'Lady, I will not beg for mercy, but will thank you for whatever you want to do to me. Nothing you do could displease me.' 'No, sir? Not even if I had you put to death?' 'Lady, I thank you; you will never hear me say otherwise.' 'Indeed,' she said, 'I have never heard of anything like this: you are putting yourself in my power without being forced to do so.' 'Lady, I do not lie when I say that there is no force as strong as the one which makes me consent to the least of your wishes. I am not afraid of carrying out anything you order me to do. If I can make amends for the death, which was not my fault, I will certainly do so without hesitating.' 'What?' she said, 'tell me, and you shall be forgiven, why you did no wrong in killing my lord.' 'Lady,' he said, 'do not be offended; when your lord attacked me, was I wrong to defend myself? If anyone who wants to kill or capture someone else is killed by the latter in self-defence, has he done anything wrong?' 'No, if you consider it properly. And I think that there would have been no point in putting you to death. But I would like to know where this power comes from which makes you agree to anything I wish without opposition. I forgive you all your misdeeds and crimes. But sit down, and tell me now why you are so meek and mild.' 'Lady,' he said, 'the power comes from my heart, which favours you: my heart put me in this mood.' 'And what decided your heart, my handsome, gentle friend?' 'Lady, my eyes.' 'And what influenced your eyes?' 'The great beauty that I see in you.' 'How has beauty wronged you?' 'By making me fall in love.' 'In love? With whom?' 'You, dear lady.' 'Me?' 'Yes, indeed.' 'Indeed? And in what way?' 'I could not be more in love; my heart cannot tear itself away from you, nor will you find it anywhere else. I cannot think of anything else, and surrender entirely to you, loving you more than myself; I love you so absolutely that at your wish I will live or die for you.' 'And would you dare to undertake the defence of the fountain for me?' 'Yes indeed, my lady, against all comers!' 'Very well then, our peace is made.' So they were quickly reconciled! And the lady, who had already held council with her barons, said: 'Now we will go from here to the great hall,' and she led Yvain to the hall, which was full of knights and men-at-arms, who all looked at him with amazement, and stood up and bowed as he entered, thinking to themselves: 'This is the man our lady will marry. Curses on anyone who opposes the match, because he seems to be an amazingly fine man. The Empress of Rome would be well matched if she married him. If only he had already given her his word, and she were to marry him today or tomorrow!' That is what they said to themselves. At the upper end of the hall there was a bench, where the lady sat down and Sir Yvain made as if he wanted to sit at her feet, but she made him get up, and summoned her seneschal to speak so that all could hear his speech. Then the seneschal, who was neither reluctant nor slow of speech: 'Lords,' he said, 'war is ahead. Every day the king is making ready, with all the haste he can, to come and lay waste our lands. Before a fortnight has passed, everything will be laid waste, unless we have a good defender. When my lady first married, less than seven years ago, she did so on your advice. Her lord is dead, to her great grief. He who held this land, and brought it prosperity, has now only six feet of earth. It is a great pity that his life was so short. A woman cannot bear a shield or set a lance in rest. It would be greatly to her advantage if she could marry a good lord. The need for it was never greater than it is now! You should all advise her to take a husband, so that the custom of this castle, which has been upheld for more than six hundred years, can continue.' At these words, the whole gathering said that it seemed the right thing to do, and they all knelt at her feet. They urged her to do as she wished, for she had got them to ask her to do what she wanted, until, although apparently unwilling, she granted them what she would have done anyway, even if they had all opposed her, saying: 'Lords, since it is your wish, this knight who is sitting beside me has wooed me and begged for my hand. He wishes to put himself in my service and to defend my honour, and I thank him for it, as you will, too! Indeed, though I have never met him before, I have often heard him spoken of. He is of very high birth, I can tell you, for he is King Urien's son. Besides being of high birth, he is very valiant, courteous and wise, so no-one should dissuade me from marrying him. I think you have all heard people talk about Sir Yvain, and he it is who has asked me to marry him. When I am wedded to him, I shall have a nobler lord than I deserve.' They all said: 'If you act wisely, do not let this day pass without celebrating the marriage, for anyone who delays, for even an hour, doing something to his advantage is foolish.' They beseeched her so urgently that she granted what she would have done anyway. For Love ordered her to do the deed about which she asked for council and advice; but she married him more honourably when it was by her people's advice. Their requests did not annoy her in the least, for they only urged her heart to do as it wished. A horse which is not going slowly will go even faster when spurred. In the sight of all her barons the lady gave herself to Lord Yvain; from the hand of one of her chaplains, he took the Lady Laudine de Landuc as his wife, daughter of the Duke Laudunet whose song you know. That very day, without delay, he married her and they celebrated the wedding. There were enough mitres and croziers there, for the lady had sent for her bishops and abbots. There was great rejoicing and happiness, crowds of people and much wealth – more than I can tell you about, even if I thought about it for a long while. It is better for me to be silent than say too little. Now Sir Yvain was Lord, and the dead man was forgotten. He who killed him was married to his wife, and they lay together; and the people loved their living lord more than they ever did the dead man. They held his wedding feast in style; it lasted until the evening before the day when the King came to see the marvel of the stone and fountain, with all his companions. All his household came on this expedition; not a single one was missing. And Sir Kay said: 'What has happened to Yvain, who has not come? He was the one who boasted after dinner that he would go and avenge his cousin. It is clear that it was a drunken boast. My guess is that he has run away; he did not dare come and be shown up. He was very boastful and proud; anyone who boasts of doing something which someone else has not praised him for, and has no witness of his feats except false flattery, is very bold. There is a great difference between a coward and a brave man: a coward by the fireside tells tall tales of himself, thinking everyone else fools, who don't know him. A brave man would be very distressed if he heard his feats told by someone else. All the same, I quite agree that a coward is right to praise himself and boast, for no-one else will do it for him. If he doesn't say it, who will? Everyone else will keep quiet, even the heralds, for they proclaim the deeds of the brave, but cast aside the cowards.' That was how Sir Kay spoke, and Sir Gawain said: 'Enough, Sir Kay! If Sir Yvain is not here, you do not know what duty has called him. He never debased himself to say mean things about you, but was always courteous.' 'Sir,' said Kay, 'I will be quiet. I will not speak another word today, since you are offended by my speech.' And the King poured a full basin of water onto the stone beneath the pine, and at once it teemed with rain. It was not long before Sir Yvain entered the forest, fully armed, and came at a full gallop on a great sleek horse, strong and bold and swift. Then Sir Kay wanted to ask for the first encounter for, whatever the result, he always wanted to start a battle or joust, or he became very angry. In front of every one, he asked the King to allow him the encounter. 'Kay,' said the King, 'since you want to, and were the first to ask, no-one should forbid you.' Kay thanked him and mounted. If he could now give him cause to be ashamed, Sir Yvain would be happy to do so; he recognised him by his arms. He grasped his shield by the straps, and Kay did likewise; they charged, spurring their horses, and gripping their lances, which they couched. Then they put them forward a little, until they held them by the leather-covered butt so that when they met they could give such blows that both lances would shiver down to the butts. Sir Yvain gave Kay such a blow that he turned a somersault out of his saddle and his helmet struck the ground first. Sir Yvain did him no further harm; but dismounted and took his horse; this pleased many of the onlookers, who said: 'Ha, ha, how you lie there, you mocker of others. And yet we ought to forgive you this time, because it never happened to you before.' Meanwhile Sir Yvain went up to the King, leading the horse by the bridle to give it to him. He said to him: 'Sire, take this horse; If I were to keep anything of yours, it would be unjust.' 'And who are you?' asked the King. 'I cannot recognise you unless you tell me your name or take off your helm.' Then Sir Yvain revealed his name, and Kay was overcome with shame, completely humbled and mortified, for having said that he had fled. All the rest are delighted and pleased to honour him. The King was very joyful, and Sir Gawain a hundred times as joyful as the rest. And the King begged and requested him to tell them how he had got on, if he was willing to do so, for he was very anxious to know all about his adventure, and made him promise to tell the truth. And he told him all about the service which the girl had done him, and how good she had been to him, nor did he leave out a single word or event. And after that he begged the King that he and all his knights should come to visit him, saying that it would be an honour and a pleasure if they would be his guests. And the King said that he would gladly be entertained and honoured by him for a whole week. Sir Yvain thanked him, and they did not delay any longer there. They mounted, and rode straight to the castle. Sir Yvain sent a squire before the company bearing a crane-falcon, so that they would not surprise his lady, and so that his people could decorate their houses for the King's arrival. When the lady heard the news that the King was coming, she was delighted. There was no-one who heard the news and did not rejoice and feel happy. And the lady summoned them all, and asked them to go to meet him; they did not make excuses or argue, because they were all eager to do as she told them.

They went to meet the King of Britain mounted on great Spanish horses and proudly greeted first King Arthur and then all his companions. 'Welcome to this company,' they said, 'which is so full of valiant men! A blessing on him who brings them here, and gives us such excellent guests.' The whole castle resounded with joy at the King's arrival. Silken hangings were brought out and hung as tapestries, and carpets spread on the pavement, and draped along the streets, as they awaited the King; and in addition they covered the streets with awnings against the heat of the sun. The church bells, horns and trumpets made the castle ring with noise until you could not have heard God himself thundering. Young girls danced out to meet him, while flutes and pipes were played as well as drums, large and small, and cymbals. Elsewhere supple youths leapt and tumbled; all tried to show their joy. And joyfully they received the King, as they should have done. The lady had come out, dressed like an empress in a brand-new ermine robe, a diadem of rubies on her head. There was no anger in her look; indeed, she was so gay and full of smiles that in my opinion she was more beautiful than any goddess. The crowd thronged close around her, and all shouted: 'Welcome to the King, lord of all kings and rulers of the world.' The King could not reply to them all before he saw the lady coming up to him to hold his stirrup: and he did not want to wait for this but was quick to dismount as soon as he caught sight of her. She greeted him saying: 'A hundred thousand welcomes to the King, my Lord, and blessing on Lord Gawain, his nephew.' 'Gentle and lovely lady, fair of face, all joy and good fortune to you,' replied the King, and embraced her, clasping her round the waist, and she threw her arms about him. I will not say any more of the way in which she welcomed them, but I never heard of any people who were so well received, honoured and looked after. I would be wasting words if I told you any more about the rejoicing, but I would like to mention a certain private encounter between the moon and the sun. Do you know who I mean? He who was the lord of knights and the most famous of all might well be called the sun, and by that I mean Sir Gawain, by whom all knighthood was made more splendid, just as the morning sun spreads its rays and light appears everywhere. And by the moon I mean someone who can only be very wise and courteous. But I call her that not all because of her high reputation, but also because she is called Lunete.

The girl was called Lunete; she was very attractive, with dark brown hair, sensible, shrewd and well-mannered. She and Sir Gawain came to know each other, and he thought much of her and loved her, calling her his beloved; because she had saved his companion and friend from death he became her servant. And she told the whole story of how difficult it had been to win over her lady to take Yvain as her husband, and how she saved him from those who sought to kill him, he was among them, but they did not see him. Sir Gawain laughed at the story, and said: 'My, girl, I give you a knight, such as I am, to be at your service, both when you need him and when you don't. Don't exchange me for anyone else if you want to better yourself. I am yours, and you shall be my lady from now on.' 'Thank you, sir,' she said. So these two became close friends, and the others were pairing off as well, for there were about ninety ladies there, each beautiful, gentle, noble, well-mannered, virtuous and wise, all girls of high birth; so the men were able to find pleasure in embracing and kissing them, talking to them and looking at them and sitting with them; they managed to get that far, at least. Sir Yvain was delighted that the King was staying with him. His lady did them all such honour, each by himself and all together, that a fool might have thought that she was in love with them all by the attention she paid them. But anyone who thinks that a lady is in love with him or some other unlucky man just because she is courteous and attentive and embraces him deserves to be called a fool. A fool is made happy by a kind word, and is easily taken in.

They spent a whole week in this joyful way; there was much sport to be had in the woods and along the rivers for those who wanted it. And those who wanted to see the

The Coronation of Arthur
This miniature is probably by one of the greatest of medieval English artists, Matthew Paris, and was drawn about 1230–1250. (Chetham's Library, Manchester, MS 6712, col. 185)

Illustrations from a North French manuscript of the romance of Lancelot, produced between 1300 and 1320, showing the adventures of Lancelot and the other knights of the Round Table, as well as the story of Lancelot's love for Guinevere. (Pierpont Morgan Library, New York, MSS 805–806)

Lancelot and Guinevere embrace, while Galehault looks on, a famous scene referred to by Dante in his Inferno. *At the right, Galehault's seneschal sits outside and talks to two ladies. (f.67)*

Gawain arrives at the tent of a lady whom Hector loves, and is told their story by the girl's uncle, the dwarf Groadan. (f.73)

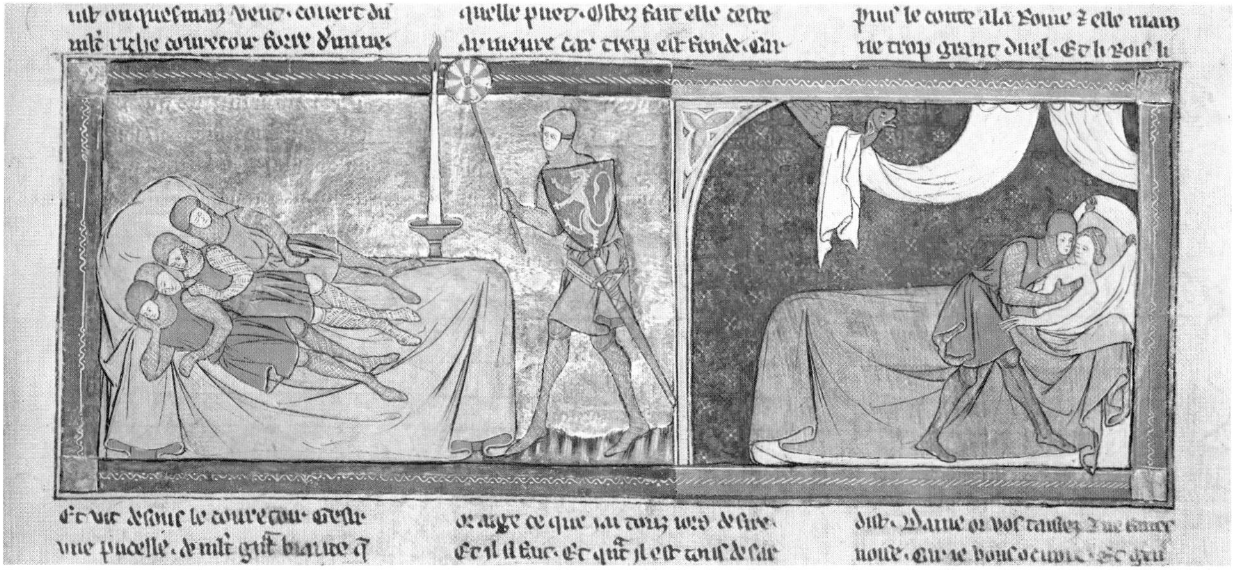

Gawain enters the anteroom of the bedchamber of the King of Norgales' daughter, where knights are keeping guard, and puts out the candle with a flabellum or extinguisher. He then enters her room, where she is lying naked in bed and kisses her. (*f.99*)

Lancelot, driven mad by his love for Guinevere, is found by the Queen, who hangs a magic shield (sent by the Lady of the Lake) round his neck. He recovers his senses and recognises the Queen. On the right, the Lady of the Lake treats him with an ointment which makes him sleep and restores him to health. (*f.109*)

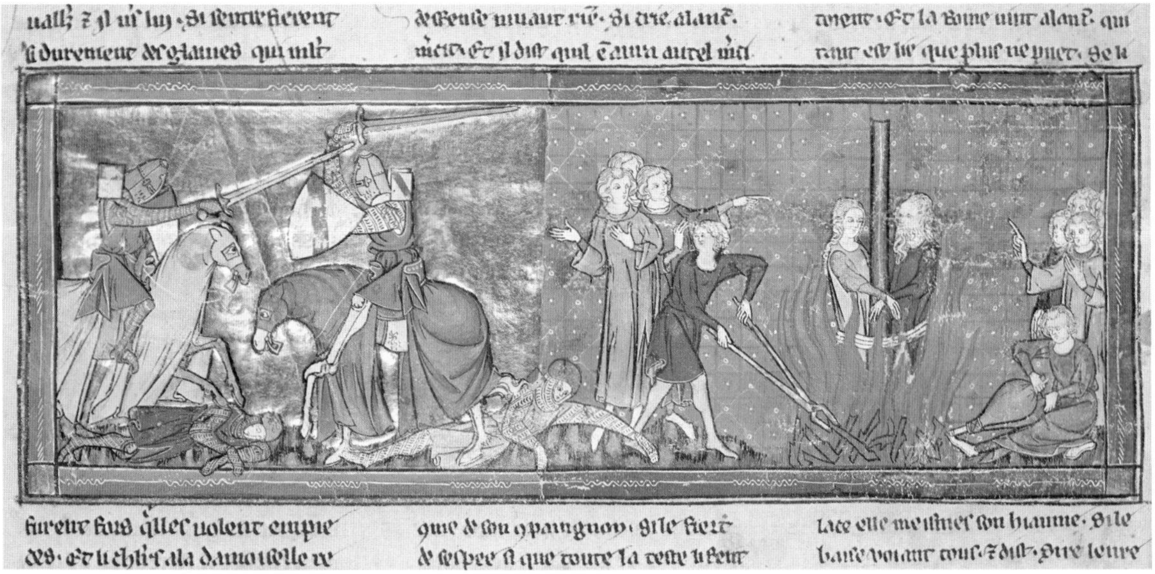

The false Guinevere, created by Morgan le Fay, is overcome. On the left, her supporters are vanquished by Lancelot, and on the right she and her accomplice are burnt at the stake. (f.119v)

In the Valley of False Lovers, Lancelot strangles a dragon with his hands; he then overcomes three knights defending a magic bridge, killing one and making the others vanish by using a ring given him by the Lady of the Lake. On a staircase above a wall of flames, he defeats two more knights and hurls them into the fire. (f.139)

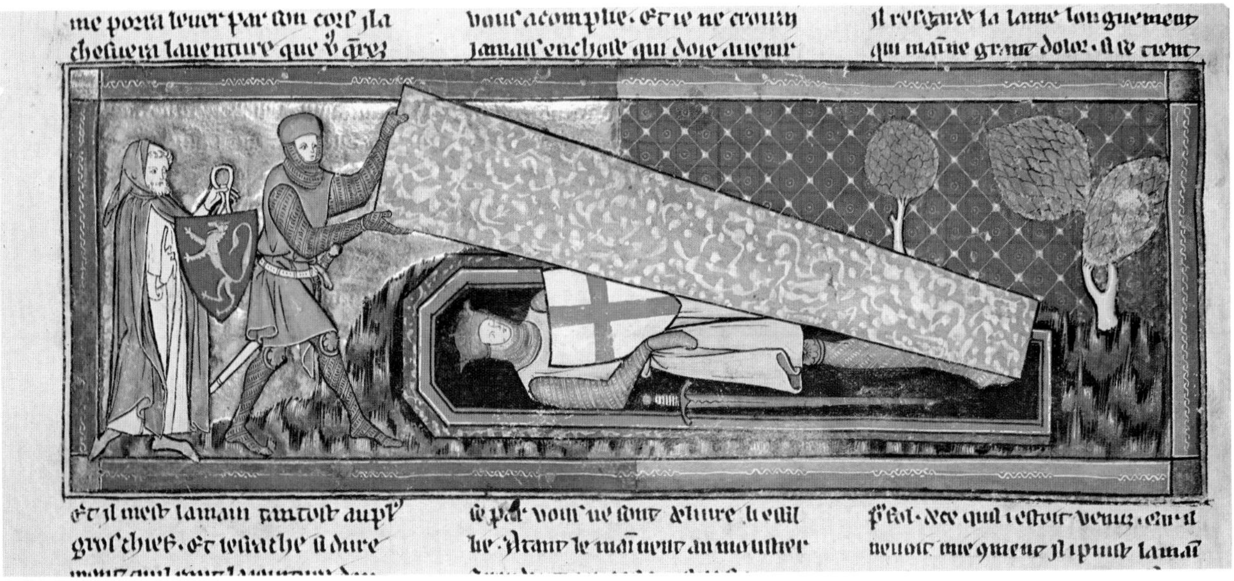

Lancelot, at an ancient monastery, is told that the knight who will free Arthur's subjects held captive in the land of Gorre will be able to lift the cover of a rich tomb in the cemetery. He does so, revealing the body of his ancestor, the son of Joseph of Arimathea. (*f.161ᵛ*)

Gawain and Hector enter the Perilous Cemetery, to find the tombs of the twelve brothers of Chanaan which burn continuously and have pointed swords erected on them. First Gawain, and then Hector (*right*)*, attempts to reach the tombs, but the swords rise up and strike them.* (*f.207*)

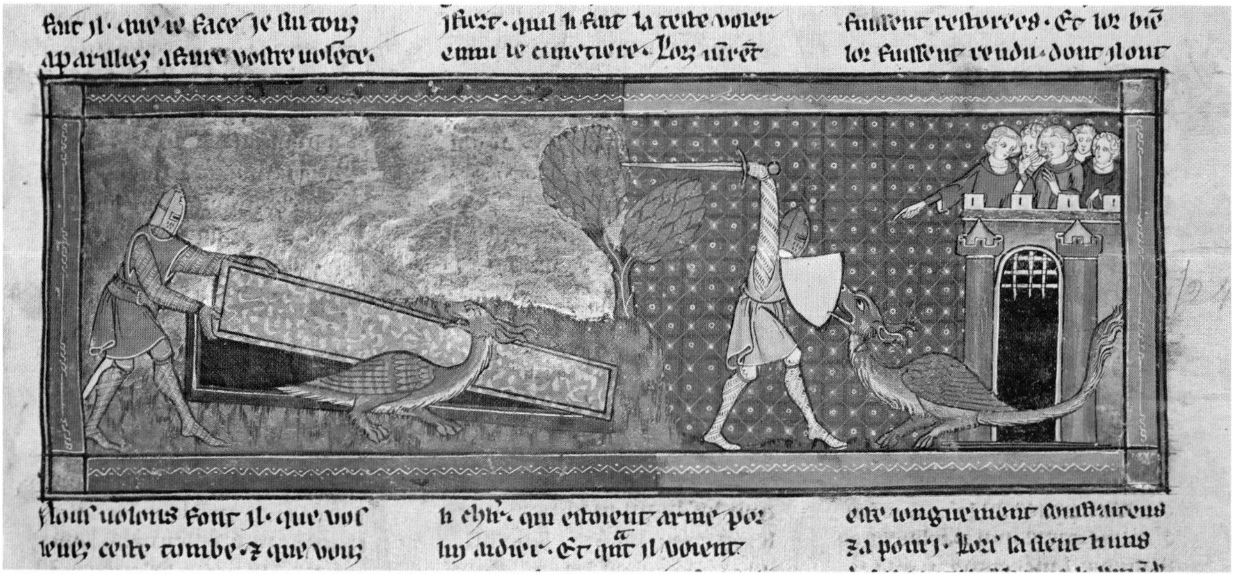

Lancelot opens an enchanted tomb, from which a dragon emerges. He slays the dragon and breaks the spell. (*f.241*)

The tourney at Camelot. Lancelot is told by the Queen to fight incognito on King Baudemagus' side, and is victorious until he catches sight of the Queen. He falls into a swoon and has to be rescued by Baudemagus (*left*). (*f.262*)

se confesse a lui.
dist li contes que trois iours fist

Lancelot, on the quest for the Holy Grail, confesses to a hermit living in a wicker hut in a tree; from a French manuscript of c. 1300. (Bodleian Library, MS Douce 215, f.14)

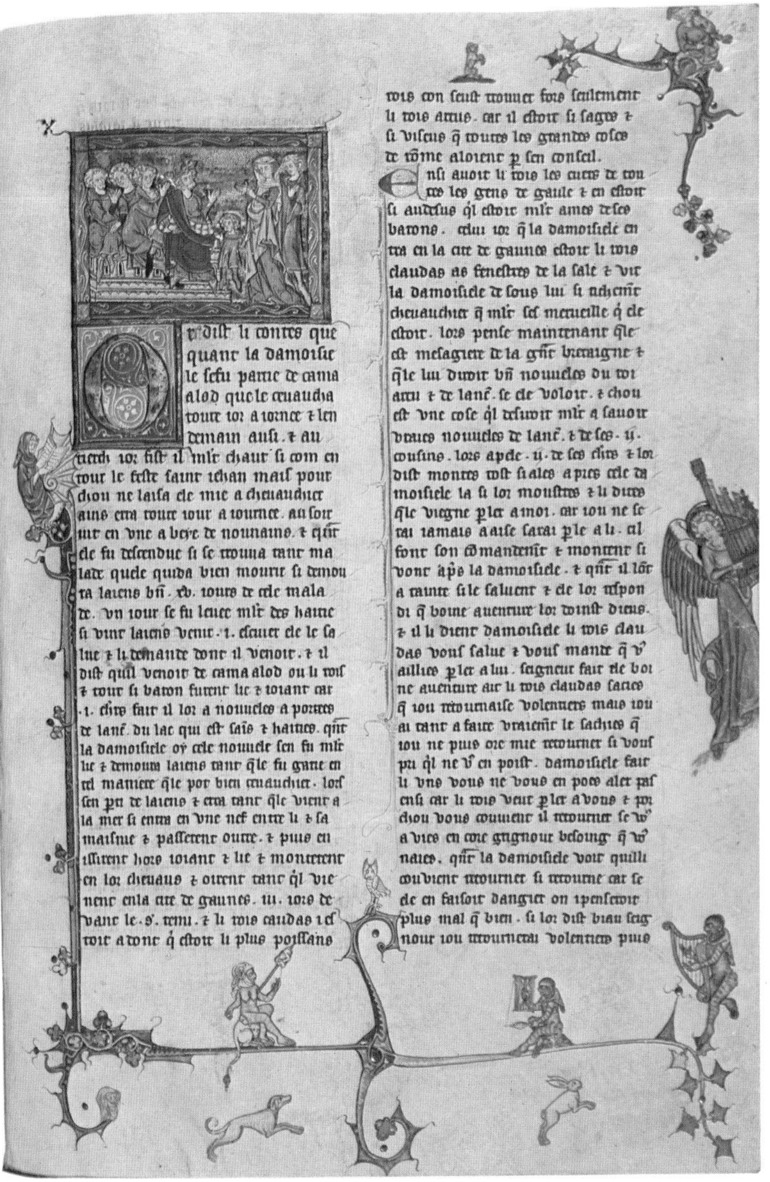

A lady brings news of King Arthur and Lancelot to Lancelot's uncle, King Claudas of Gaul. Decorated page from an early fourteenth-century French manuscript.
(Manchester, John Rylands Library, MS Fr. 1, f.212)

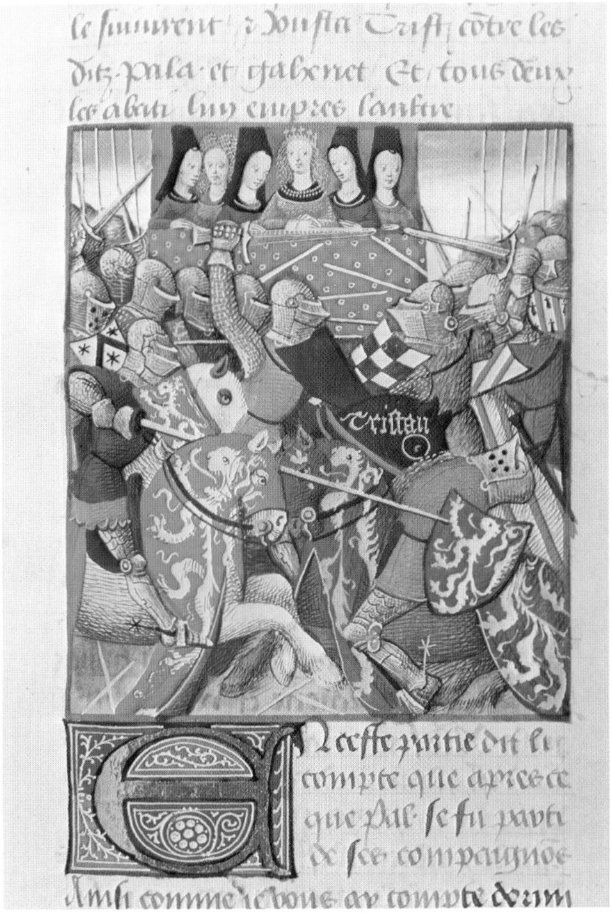

Illuminations by Everard d'Espingues for a three-volume Tristan *written for Jean du Cas, seigneur de l'Isle, 1479–80. (Musée Condé, Chantilly, MS 315–317). Left, Tristan fights his rival Palamedes in a tournament. Right, Tristan and Iseult embark for England.*

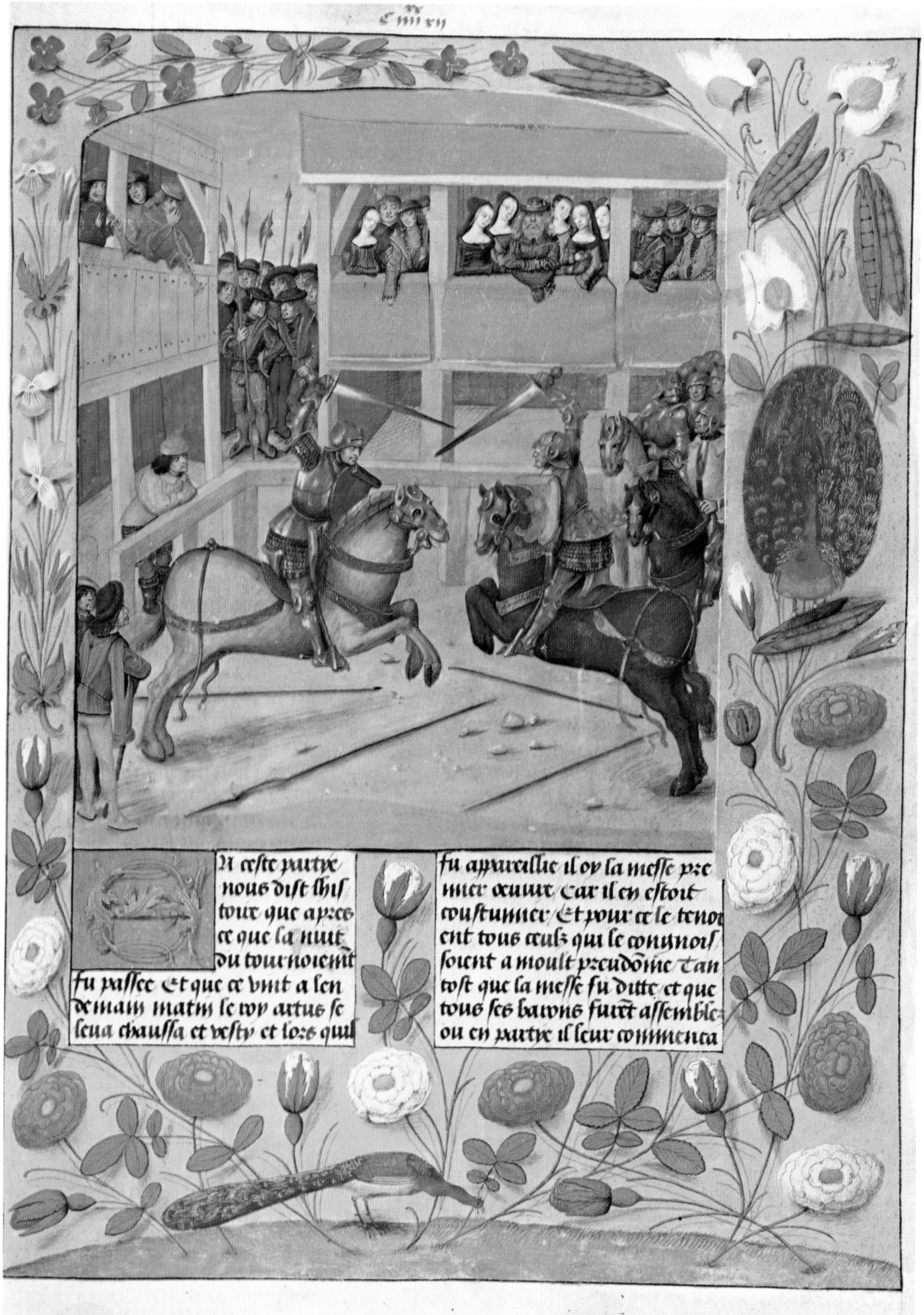
n ceste partye
nous dist lhis
toire que apres
ce que la nuit
du tournoiemt
fu passee Et que ce vint a len
demain matin le roy artus se
leua chaussa et vesty et lors quil
fu appareillie il oy la messe pre
mier oeuure car il en estoit
coustumier Et pour ce le tenoi
ent tous ceulz qui le connoi
soient a moult preudomme tan
tost que la messe fu ditte et que
tous ses barons furet assemble
ou en partye il leur commenca

Two miniatures from a de luxe manuscript of the late romance of Guiron le Courtois by Hélie de Borron, written for Engelbert, Count of Nassau and Vianden, a knight of the Order of the Golden Fleece, c. 1475–1500, and illuminated by a Flemish artist. Above, a tournament in King Arthur's presence. (*Bodleian Library, MS Douce 383 f.16*)

The arrival of a damsel at the court of King Arthur, the usual prelude to an adventure. Arthur is shown dressed as a fifteenth-century prince would be, sitting at table. (*f.17*)

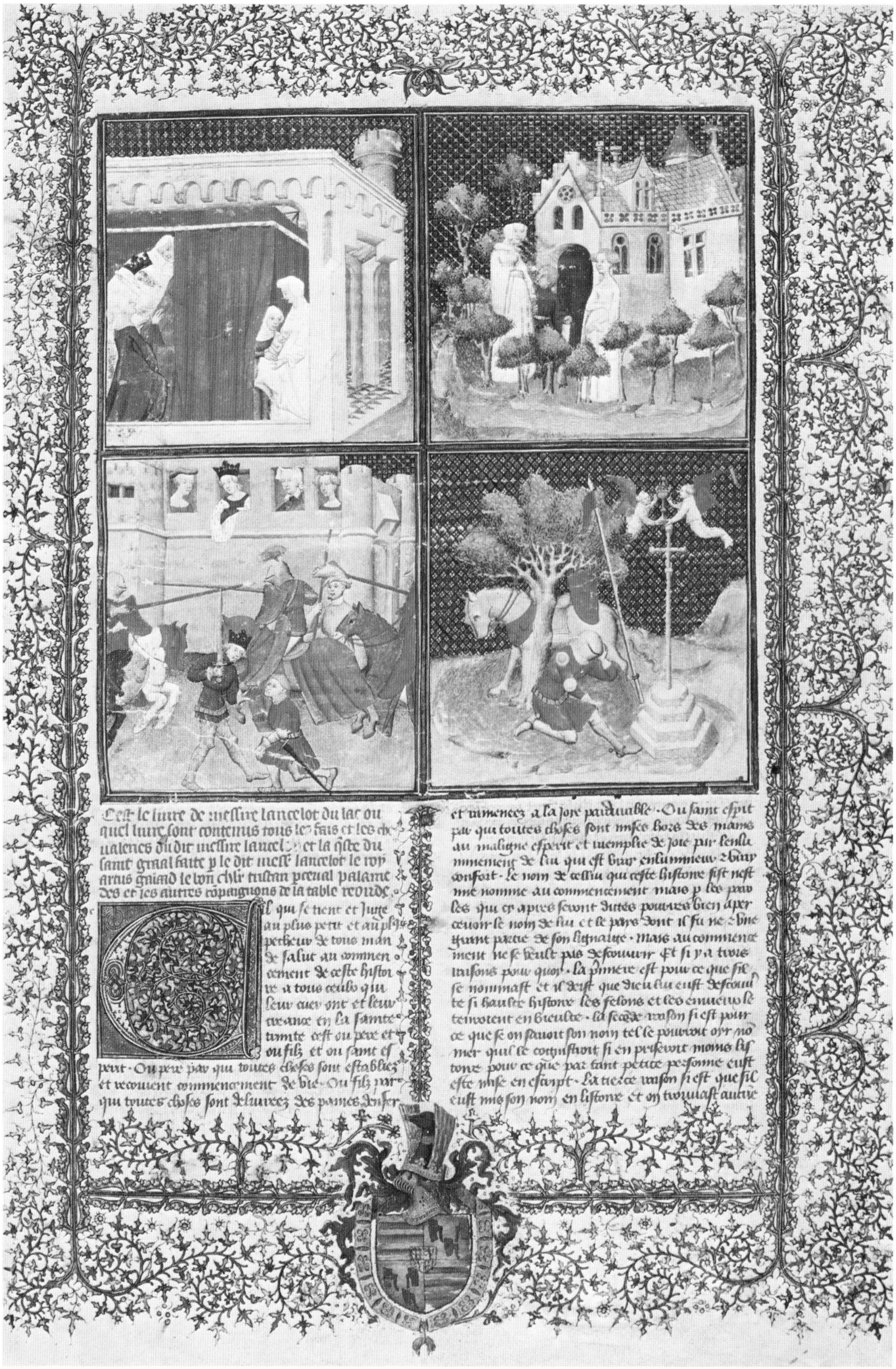

Frontispiece to a manuscript of the romance of Lancelot, c. 1400, which may possibly have been commissioned by Marshal Boucicaut, and which belonged to Jean duc de Berry. The scenes show Lancelot's birth, his upbringing by the Lady of the Lake, Lancelot in combat, and his vision of the Grail at the wayside cross.
(*Paris, Bibliothèque Nationale, MS Arsenal 3479, f.1. Photo Giraudon*)

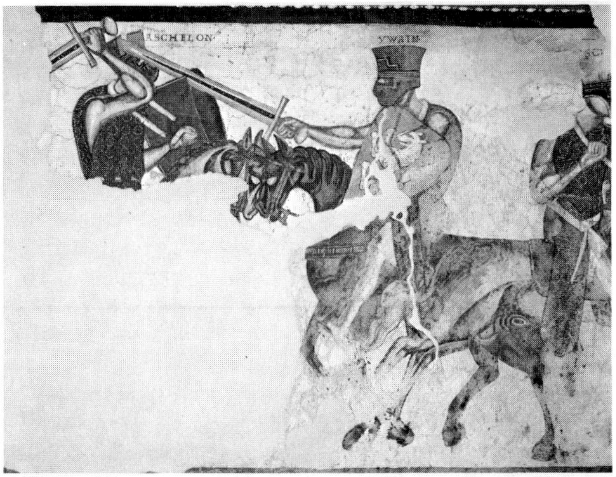

Yvain fights the defender of the spring (here called Askelon rather than Esclados, following a German translation of Chrétien); a fresco from Schloss Rodeneck in South Tirol dating from 1200–1215, rediscovered in 1973.
(Photo H. Walder, courtesy Soprintendenza Provinciale Beni Culturali, Bolzano).

lands which Sir Yvain had won along with the lady whom he had married could go and amuse themselves by staying at castles two or three or four leagues away. When the King had stayed for as long as he wished, he made ready for his departure. But throughout the week they had begged as hard as they could that Sir Yvain should go with them. 'What!' said Sir Gawain, 'are you going to be one of those knights who are less brave once they are married? By the Virgin, shame on him who is the worse for being married! Whoever has a beautiful lady, either as mistress or wife should be the better for it, and it is not right that she should love him once his fame and worth are at an end. Surely even now you would regret being in love if you are the worse for it, for a woman soon takes back her love, and rightly so, if she comes to despise a man who has become lord of a realm and is yet the worse for it. Now of all times your fame should grow! Break the bridle and halter, and we two will go in search of tournaments, so that no-one says you are a jealous husband. Now you must no longer dream idly, but frequent tournaments and joust well, whatever the cost. He who cannot stir has been idle for long enough. But you must come, for I shall be with you. Be careful that our friendship does not come to an end through you; if it does so, it will not be my fault. It is strange that people like a life of ease, which they can have at any time. Pleasures grow more sweet by postponing them, and a little pleasure, if delayed, is better than a great pleasure enjoyed without waiting. Love's joys, when they come late, are like a green bush in a fire; the longer you put off lighting it, the greater heat it will give. You can get into habits which are very difficult to shake off, and when you want to be rid of them you cannot. It is true that if I had a mistress as beautiful as yours, by God and all the saints, I would be reluctant to leave her! I think I would be mad about her. But a man may give someone else advice which he does not follow himself, like those deceitful cheats the preachers, who teach us and tell us to do things they would never do themselves.'

Sir Gawain spoke so often in this way, and begged him again and again that he promised him that he would tell his wife and would go with him, if she would give him leave. Whether he was wise or foolish to do so, he would not fail to ask her permission to return to Britain. So he talked to his wife, who had no idea that he was going to ask to go away, and said: 'My dearest lady, you are my heart and soul, my wealth, joy and health: grant me one thing, for your honour and mine.' The lady granted it, without knowing what he would ask, saying: 'Fair lord, tell me what it is, as long as it seems good to you.' Sir Yvain asked her permission to escort the King home and to go to tournaments, so that he did not appear to be idle. And she said: 'I grant you leave until a certain date; but the love I bear you will turn to hate, be sure of it, if you stay away beyond the day I fix. I tell you that I am not lying. If you break your word, I will keep mine. If you want my love, and I am dearer to you than anyone else, remember to come back at the latest a year from today, a week after Midsummer Eve, for today is a week after that day. You will be deprived of my love if you have not come back to me by that day.'

Tristan's boyhood, from a German manuscript of c. 1230–40, probably illustrated c. 1300. At the top, Tristan is baptized; then he is trained in different skills – reading, athletics, music. Below this, his voyage to Cornwall is shown. (Munich, Staatsbibliothek, MS Germ, 51, f.15^{v})

GOTTFRIED VON STRASSBURG

Tristan

THE ORIGINS OF THE TRISTAN STORY · EARLY VERSIONS · THOMAS · GOTTFRIED AND THE NATURE OF LOVE & & &

Chrétien de Troyes worked largely on material which he shaped in general outline and content, using details borrowed from Celtic tradition. When we come to the story of Tristan and Isolt the reverse is true: the plot and events remain constant, while it is the details which tend to change for each new audience. Marie de France and two of the troubadours mention Tristan as an ideal lover in the 1160s, and Chrétien himself claimed to have made a version of the legend. The earliest surviving fragments of any poem about Tristan are of a version by Thomas, who wrote at the Plantagenet Court in England some time after 1150. He was followed by Eilhart von Oberge in about 1170, and by another Norman poet, Béroul, about 1190.

The central theme of these romances, the love of Tristan for Isolt, wife of his uncle Mark, is found in Welsh literature and scholars generally accept that the original Tristan was Drust, son of the Pictish King Talorc who ruled in Scotland about 780, and that the legends were later given a new setting in Cornwall. The so-called Tristan stone at Castledore refers to another character of similar name, and its only connection with the legend is that it may have suggested the new site of the stories. In Welsh legend, Essyllt's lover is always Tristan 'son of Tallwch' and the Cornish Drustanus' father is named in the inscription as Cunomorus. The shape of the legend was drawn by Welsh writers from Irish sources, by adding the story of Diarmaid and Grainne to an episode about Drust which told how he rescued a foreign king from having to surrender his daughter as tribute, by defeating a hero in single combat. This theme, similar to the story of Theseus in Greek myth, suggested the addition of other details from the Theseus legends: the half-bestial nature of his adversary (as with the Minotaur) and the use of the black and white sails as a signal of failure or success. Other incidents were drawn into the story from sources as far afield as India and Arabia, brought perhaps by travelling merchants; and merchants figure in the poem as the cause of Tristan's arrival in Cornwall from Brittany. The power of the central love-story has attracted all kinds of lesser folklore in which the same triangle of characters is repeated.

The story as given in the original version runs as follows. Tristan is the son of Rivalen and Blancheflor, the sister of King Mark of Cornwall. His father was slain in battle and his mother died in childbirth; hence his name, implying sorrow (*tristesse*). He came incognito to Mark's Court, and soon distinguished himself by knightly feats, in particular by slaying the Irish champion Morholt, who came every seven years to demand a tribute of young men and girls from the Cornish king. Morholt's body was taken back to Ireland, where his niece, the Princess Isolt, removed a piece of Tristan's sword, swearing to use it to trace his slayer and exact vengeance. Tristan came to Ireland in search for a bride for King Mark and won Isolt by slaying a dragon, but he was overcome by the dragon's poison, and a seneschal falsely claimed to have achieved the exploit. As Isolt tended Tristan's wounds, she noticed the gap in the blade of his sword, but since only he could save her from the seneschal, refrained from killing him when he was unarmed. Tristan duly took her back to Cornwall as his uncle's bride, but on the voyage a magic philtre intended for her wedding night was given to the pair by mistake. Brangain, Isolt's faithful maid, took her place on her wedding night in King Mark's bed; and the lovers yielded to their passion, resorting to all kinds of trickery to deceive King Mark. When Mark, at last convinced of their guilt, made Isolt swear that she was faithful by the ordeal of holding a red-hot iron, she arranged for Tristan to disguise himself as a pilgrim. As she approached the place of the ordeal, she stumbled into his arms, and altered the oath to swear that she had never been touched by any man save her husband and the pilgrim. She survived the ordeal unscathed, but Mark later banished the lovers. Hunting in the forest, he once came across them asleep, with a naked sword between them, which again persuaded him of their innocence. As a precaution, he banished Tristan, who crossed to Brittany and married Isolt of the White Hands, sister of Prince Kaherdin. However, he never consummated the marriage, and when this came to light, persuaded Kaherdin that he meant no insult and offered to show him the Irish Isolt. They travelled in disguise to Cornwall where Kaherdin fell in love with Brangain. They had to return to Brittany, where after a number of adventures, Tristan was wounded by a poisoned arrow. Sending for Isolt of Ireland to heal him, he instructed the messenger to hoist black sails if he returned without her, white sails if his quest was successful. Isolt of Brittany, jealous of the other Isolt, falsely told him that the sails were black. At this, Tristan died of grief, as did Isolt of Ireland on finding she had arrived too late.

Eilhart and Béroul took this relatively sophisticated

story, with its complex sequence of episodes, and did little more than retell it in their own way, making minor alterations but leaving the working of the tragedy of guilty love unchanged. Neither poet takes a 'courtly' attitude towards the lovers. Some episodes are of a primitive cruelty, as when Isolt is about to be burnt for adultery and a company of lepers suggest that a more fitting fate would be for her to be given to them as their whore. There are a few psychological elaborations, and the lovers' passion is neither praised nor blamed by either writer. Eilhart sees the love-potion as the one cause of their woe; once they have tasted 'the most unlucky drink', they are doomed. Béroul, on the other hand, apportions no moral blame but sees Mark's conduct towards the lovers in terms of strictly legal rights. Mark refuses Tristan the customary trial by battle and thenceforward is in the wrong, since Tristan is never legally proved guilty; and the episode of the ambiguous oath fits in with this legalistic attitude very well. These two early versions of the legend are more realistic and down to earth than what followed, but the lovers lack fire and character: the mainspring of their actions is scarcely more than physical desire, however fierce or passionate.

With Thomas the emphasis changes considerably. The story is subordinated to the study of feeling, much in the manner of Chrétien's *Cligès*, and from physical realism we move into emotional realism. The crux is therefore the truth of Tristan and Isolt's love: the effect of the love-potion does not abate, as in Eilhart and Béroul, because it is not an external force but a symbol of an internal emotion, and Tristan's marriage to the second Isolt becomes another of the tests of the lovers' fidelity. Likewise, Thomas introduces the *Salle aux Images* (hall of statues) to which Tristan retreats secretly to worship an image of Isolt of Cornwall, an idea which comes near to the veneration of the troubadours for their ladies. But there is none of the restraining *mezura* ('measure in all things') of the Provençal poets here, no holding back from the physical consummation of spiritual desire. Yet Thomas does not entirely achieve the glorification of love which he attempts, because he is too respectful of the original version.

It was only his German translator, Gottfried von Strassburg, who realised the full possibility of the story. Gottfried's *Tristan* begins with an account of the hero's father and his exploits. Tristan himself appears as the image beyond all words of the perfect courtier and knight, every skill is at his command, no virtue is too taxing. Strong, handsome, gay, he turns his hand to chess, harping, the arts of venery or war, speaks several languages, is at ease from the moment he sets foot in a strange Court.

With such a beginning, we might well expect to find ourselves in the world of Chrétien, amidst yet more extravagant fantasies. Instead, the fantasies are kept to a minimum; the descriptions are extraordinarily real, yet none the less beautiful for it. The courtly world needs no apology, no excusing ethos; for Gottfried it is normal and natural. Tristan's loyalty to Mark, his duty to his subjects as ruler of Parmenie are part of this world; his adventures, until he meets Isolde, are purely chivalrous and of a very simple type. The slaying of Morold is treated in an antique heroic manner, as is the theme of the poisoned sword whose wounds only the dead man's relatives can heal.

Gottfried uses this perfect, self-contained world only as a starting-point. Because Tristan and Isolde are already perfect, they alone are fit for the transcending experience. The mysticism of love is his theme, and he speaks only to those 'noble hearts' who can understand his message.

The crux of the story, the famous scene where Tristan and Isolde drink the love-potion, thinking it is common wine, has been given many different meanings. Gottfried uses the idea skilfully. He leaves us uncertain whether the drink merely confirms a love already begun, or is in itself the *coup de foudre*. For his own purposes he is well enough content to let it be regarded as a supernatural force; with this excuse he can tell his story of open adultery, treachery and broken oaths as a special case, and invoke magic as the cause of each transgression. On the other hand, the 'noble hearts' who understood his true meaning could see the potion merely as surrogate of love's power, a symbol of its workings.

Tristan and Isolde's love puts their relationship above the everyday ways of the world. They are no longer subject to the ordinary laws of men, and can only be judged in terms of their fidelity to each other and to love's ideals. The conflict and tension that arises between the two worlds, their unresolved discontent, shows that this is not an intensified version of courtly love, but a more disturbing force. Passion is the word we have now come to use for this force, and it is a commonplace of our view of love. But to Gottfried's contemporaries, despite Chrétien's tentative descriptions of the symptoms, this was novelty indeed.

Tristan and Isolde are equal in love. There is no question of knight serving lady; instead, they are both servants of *Frau Minne*, Lady Love. Caution becomes impossible, compromise unthinkable once her mystic joys have been tasted; Love becomes the fountain of all goodness, and even provides them with physical sustenance. The extract which follows, the episode in the Cave of Lovers, is the climax of Gottfried's poem.

But if love is a higher ideal than those of the courtly world in which the lovers move, it affords them no protection. Its joys are balanced by its sorrows; and its sorrows stem from the lovers' concern for their reputation. When Mark discovers them lying with a naked sword between them and is persuaded of their innocence, they return to Court 'for the sake of God and their place in society'. Mark represents the opposite side of love: lust and appetite aroused by Isolde's beauty. As such he cannot find peace either; a pitiful figure, he wavers between the unpalatable truth and the comfort of illusion. Despite its outward gaiety, the Court of Cornwall which he rules is similarly tainted; suspicion is everywhere, misunderstanding and distrust abound. Only Brangane and Kurvenal remain loyal; and even their steadfastness is tested. Isolde, fearing lest Brangane should reveal their secrets, tries to have her killed, but repents as soon as she fears the deed is really done. For loyalty only exists between the lovers themselves; all external claims are brushed aside and there is left

A man, a woman; a woman, a man:
Tristan, Isolde; Isolde, Tristan.

Their true world is an enclosed, charmed garden; in the everyday world, no matter how splendid and gay, they moved guiltily, forced to deny their desires, and the air grows thick with sorrow and evil.

Gottfried did not complete his poem; whether by design or accident, we cannot tell for certain. It ends with Tristan's thoughts as he is torn between the idea of marrying Isolde of the White Hands, whose love he has won during his self-imposed exile from Cornwall, or remaining single for Isolde of Ireland's sake; and it seems likely that Gottfried was similarly torn between faithfully following the story as given in his original, and the loyalty in love which had become both his main theme and the excuse for his hero and heroine's misdeeds. That this ideal meant a great deal to him is plain enough, and there are veiled references to personal experiences of such a love throughout the poem. Yet, even as a guiding light for those 'noble hearts' to whom he addresses himself, it is an uncertain star. Gottfried makes sensual love sublime by his artistry; it is the one way in which the great tale he tells can come to life, but the philosophy of it is incomplete and less subtle than that of the troubadours and *minnesangers*. Indeed, it is scarcely a philosophy at all, though Gottfried would like us to think it was; it is a mysticism without a goal, the exaltation of emotion to the level of the divine through the element of suffering that emotion arouses. What he does tell us a great deal about is the psychology of love, how lovers behave and how their minds work; and his audience of 'noble hearts' are lovers who seek to find distraction for their own sorrows and perhaps a reflection of their own dilemmas.

The king of Ireland prevents his wife from killing Tristan while he is in his bath; she has just discovered that he killed Morholt, her intended son-in-law, because a piece missing from his sword corresponds with that found in Morholt's body.
(*Paris, Bibliothèque Nationale, MS. Fr100 f.50, late fourteenth century*).

Tristan

For a summary of the early part of the plot see p. 74 above. *This extract begins after Mark has married Isolde, and Tristan has become her lover.*

Melot left, and he at once rode to the forest and found Mark. He told the King that he had got to the bottom of the matter, and reported what had happened at the brook. 'If you will ride there with me tonight, Sire, you can see the truth for yourself. There is nothing on which I count with greater confidence than that they will meet there this very night, however they manage to do so. Then you can see for yourself how they behave.'

The King rode back with Melot to spy on his own chagrin. When they entered the orchard after dark and set about their business, the King and his dwarf failed to find any cover that would serve them for a lurking-place. Now beside the running brook there stood an olive-tree of some size, its foliage low, yet ample and spreading. Into this they climbed after some effort, sat, and said not a word.

When night was drawing on, Tristan stole out on his way again. Arriving in the orchard he took his 'messengers', placed them in the stream and sent them floating along. They always told love-lorn Isolde that her lover was at hand. Tristan at once crossed the brook to where the olive cast its shadow on the grass. There he took his stand, pondering his secret woes. And so it chanced that he noticed Mark's and Melot's shadows, for the moon was shining down through the tree very brightly. When he had made out these two forms distinctly, he was seized with great anxiety, for he realised in a flash that he was in a trap. 'Almighty God,' he thought, 'protect Isolde and me! If she fails to detect this trap from the shadow in time, she will come straight on towards me. And if that happens we shall be in a sad predicament! O Lord in thy mercy and goodness have us both in thy keeping! Stand guard over Isolde on this path! Guide her every step! Make the blameless woman somehow aware of this vile ambush which has been set for us, lest she say or do anything that could give rise to ugly thoughts. O my Lord, have pity on her and me! I commend our lives and honour this night to Thee!'

His lady the Queen and their friend, noble Brangane, went out unaccompanied to their garden of sorrows, where they always used to go to commiserate with each other when there was no danger in their doing so, to keep watch for Tristan's messengers. They walked up and down, sorrowing and lamenting, and sadly conversing of love. But Brangane soon noticed the message-bearing shavings in the current and beckoned to her mistress. Isolde retrieved and examined them. She read both 'Isolde' and 'Tristan'.

Quickly taking her cloak, Isolde wound it round her head and stole through the flowers and grass towards the tree by the brook. When she was near enough for them both to see each other, Tristan remained standing where he was, a thing that he had never done before – she had never approached him without his having come a long way to meet her. Thus Isolde was much puzzled to know what this could mean, and her heart sank within her. She dropped her head and walked towards him with apprehension – her going filled her with horror. As she softly drew near to the tree she caught sight of the shadows of three men, yet, to her knowledge, only one was there. From this, but also from Tristan's behaviour, she recognised at once that it was a trap. 'Oh what will come of this plot to have us murdered? What lies behind this ambush? I'll wager my master has a hand in it, wherever he may be lurking. I am sure we have been betrayed! Protect us, O Lord. Help us to leave this place without dishonour! Lord, watch over him and me!' But then she thought: 'Is Tristan aware of this calamity, or does he not know of it?' Then it struck her that, judging from his behaviour, he had discovered the trap.

She halted some way off and said: 'Lord Tristan, I am sorry you count with such assurance on my simplicity as to expect me to talk to you at this time of night. If you were to guard your reputation towards your uncle and me that would be more seemly and accord better with your allegiance and my honour than putting me to so late and secret a parley. Now tell me, what is it you want? I stand here in great fear because Brangane insisted on my coming and meeting you here in order to learn what was troubling you; after leaving you today she begged and urged me to do so. But it was very wrong of me to give way to her. She is sitting somewhere near by, and however safe I am here, I assure you, such is my dread of wicked people, I would rather lose a finger than that anyone should learn I had met you here. People have spread such tales about us; they would all take their oaths on it that we are embroiled in an illicit love-affair! The court is full of that suspicion. But God Himself knows how my feelings stand towards you. And I will go a little farther. May God be my witness when I say it – may I never be rid of my sins by any other test than the measure of my affection for you! For I declare before God that I never conceived a liking for any man but him who had my maidenhead, and that all others are barred from my heart, now and for ever. I swear to Heaven, Lord Tristan, that it is very wrong of my lord Mark to suspect me so strongly on your account, fully acquainted as he is with the state of my feelings towards you. God knows, those who have got me talked about are very rash: they have no idea what my heart is really like. I have put on a friendly mien for you a hundred thousand times from affection for the man whom it is mine to love – not with intent to deceive, Heaven knows full well! It seems right to me and very much to my credit, that I should show honour to anyone, knight or page, who is dear or near to Mark. Yet people twist it against me! But, for my part, I will never bear you any ill will as a result of all their lies. My lord, tell me what you have to tell me, for I wish to go – I cannot stay here any longer.'

'Good lady,' answered Tristan, 'I do not doubt that you would speak and act both virtuously and honourably if you had your way, but liars do not permit you, such as have brought suspicion upon you and me and lost us my lord's favour without cause, wholly innocent though we are, as God must recognise. Consider it, good lady, noble Queen, reflect how altogether guiltless I am with regard to you and Mark, and urge my lord of his courtesy to hide the animosity which he bears me without cause, and to put a good face on the matter for no more than this coming week. Till then let both of you behave towards me as though I enjoyed your favour. Meanwhile I shall make my preparations to leave. We shall lose our good name, my lord the King, and you and I. For, if you behave as you do when I go away, our enemies will say: "There was most certainly something in it – see how my lord Tristan left court in the King's disfavour!" '

'Lord Tristan,' answered Isolde, 'I would sooner suffer death than ask my lord to do something for my sake that had anything to do with you. Surely you know that he has been ungracious towards me for a long time now on your account, so that, if he knew that I was alone with you at night at this very moment, I would be the subject of such a scandal that he would never again show me honour or kindness. Whether in fact he ever will, I truly do not know, and I am altogether puzzled as to how my lord Mark came by this suspicion, and who it was inspired it; while I for my part have never noticed (as women very quickly do, you know) that you have ever dissembled towards me, nor was I ever guilty of any falsity or laxness towards you. I cannot imagine of what treachery we are the victims, for your affairs and mine are in an ugly and lamentable state – may God Almighty remember them in time and mend and rectify them! Now, my lord, pardon me, I must go, as you must, too. God knows, I regret your vexation and troubles. I could claim that you have given me good cause to hate you, but I waive it now: rather am I sorry that you, through no fault, should now be in trouble because of me. I shall accordingly overlook your offence. And when the day comes for you to go away, may God preserve you, sir! May the Queen of Heaven watch over you! If I could be sure that the mission with which you have charged me would be furthered by any assistance that I could give, I would advise and act in any way I thought might help you. But I fear that Mark will misinterpret it. Yet whatever comes of it, and at whatever risk to me, I will give you your due for having acted loyally and honestly towards my lord and me. Whatever my success, I will further your suit as best I can!'

'Thank you, my lady,' answered Tristan. 'Let me know at once what response you meet with. But if I notice anything amiss and perhaps go away and never see you again, whatever comes of me then, may Heaven bless you, noble Queen! For God knows, neither land nor sea ever sustained so blameless a lady! Madam, I commend your body and soul, your life and honour, to God!'

And so they took leave of one another. The Queen went away sighing and sorrowing, pining and languishing, with secret pain both of body and of heart. Melancholy Tristan too went sorrowfully away amid a flood of tears. Sorrowful Mark sitting in the tree was moved to sadness by it, and was deeply distressed for having suspected his wife and nephew of infamy. He called down a thousand curses on those who had led him into it – in his heart and also aloud. He roundly accused Melot the dwarf of deceiving him and of slandering his wife. They descended from their tree and rode back to the hunt in a state of great dejection. But Mark and Melot were aggrieved for very different reasons: Melot because of the deception that he was alleged to have practised; Mark because of the suspicion which had induced him to put his wife and his nephew, and most of all himself, to such annoyance and get them so ill spoken of, both at court and in the country.

Next morning he lost no time in having it announced to the hunt that they should remain and carry on with their hunting: but he himself returned to court.

'Tell me, madam the Queen, how have you passed the time?'

'I have had needless sorrow to occupy me: to distract me the harp and the lyre.'

'Needless sorrow?' asked Mark. 'What was that, and why?'

Isolde's lips parted in a smile. 'Whatever the reason, it happened,' said she, 'and it will go on happening today and ever after. It is my nature like that of all other women to be sad and despondent without reason. We purify our hearts and brighten our eyes with it. We often conceive some great secret sorrow for a mere nothing, then suddenly abandon it.' And she went on trifling in this vein.

But Mark was passing it all through his mind and noting her words and meaning. 'Now, madam, tell me,' he said, 'do you or does anyone at court here know how Tristan is? When I rode away recently I was told he was in pain.'

'And you were told the truth, Sire,' was the Queen's answer. (She meant with regard to love – she was well aware that love was the cause of his suffering.)

'What do you know about it, and who told you?' continued the King.

'I only know what I suspect, and what Brangane told me of his illness a short time past. She saw him yesterday during the day and brought me a message from him asking me to bring you his complaint and beg you in God's name not to entertain thoughts so hurtful to his honour and to moderate your harshness towards him this coming week, so as to allow him time to prepare for his departure; and then to let him leave your court and go abroad with honour. This he asks of us both.' And she repeated his whole request in full, as he had made it beside the brook and as Mark himself had heard it, and the whole course of their conversation.

'May that man be eternally damned who led me into this, ma'am!' rejoined the King. 'I bitterly regret that I ever brought suspicion to bear on him, for only a short while ago I learned of his complete innocence and got to the bottom of it all! And, my dear Queen, if you have any affection for me, let this quarrel be yours to decide – whatever you do will be acceptable. Take the two of us, him and me, and compose the difference between us!'

'Sire, I do not wish to take such a labour upon myself, for were I to settle your quarrel today you would resume your suspicions tomorrow as before.'

'No, indeed, ma'am, never again. I will never again harbour thoughts that are injurious to his honour, nor shall I ever suspect you, my lady Queen, for any outward show of friendship!' This was duly vowed.

Thereupon Tristan was summoned, and suspicion was buried at once in amity and sincerity. Isolde was entrusted to Tristan's keeping with all due form, and he guarded and advised her in every way. She and her apartment were at his sole discretion. Tristan and his lady enjoyed a pleasant life again. The measure of their joy was full. Thus, following after their troubles, they now had a life of bliss again, however short-lived it was before fresh woes were on them.

I say quite openly that no nettle has so sharp a sting as a sour neighbour, nor is there a peril so great as a false housemate. This is what I call false: the man who shows his friend the face of a friend and is his enemy at heart. Such comradeship is terrible, for all the time he has honey in his mouth, but venom on his sting! Such venomous spite puffs up ill fortune for his friend in all that he sees or hears, and one cannot keep anything safe from him. On the other hand, when a man lays his snares for his enemy openly I do not account it falseness. As long as he remains an overt foe he does not do too much harm. But when he feigns friendship for a man, let his friend be on his guard!

This is what Melot and Marjodoc did. With deceit in their hearts they often sought Tristan's company, and, the one like the other, offered him their devoted friendship with cunning and dissembling. But Tristan had been amply warned, and he warned Isolde in turn. 'Now, queen of my heart,' he said, 'guard yourself and me in what you say and do. We are beset by great dangers. There are two poisonous snakes in the guise of doves who with their suave flattery never leave your sides – be on the alert for them, dear Queen! For when one's house-mates are faced like doves and tailed like the serpent-brood, one should cross oneself before the hailstorm and say a prayer against sudden death! Dearest lady, lovely Isolde, be much on your guard against Melot the Snake and Marjodoc the Cur!' Indeed, that is what they were – the one a snake, the other a cur, who were always laying their traps for the two lovers, whatever they did, wherever they went, like cur and snake. Morning and night they treacherously worked upon Mark with schemes and accusations till he began to waver in his love again and suspect the lovers once more and lay traps and make trial of their intimacy.

One day, on the advice of his false counsellors, Mark had himself bled, and Tristan and Isolde, too. They had no suspicion that any sort of trouble was being prepared for them and were entirely off their guard. Thus the King's intimate circle lay pleasurably at ease in their room.

On the evening of the following day, when the household had dispersed and Mark had gone to bed, there was no one in the chamber but Mark, Isolde, Tristan, Melot, Brangane, and one young lady-in-waiting, as had been planned beforehand. Moreover, the light of the candles had been masked behind some tapestries to dim their brightness. When the bell for matins sounded, Mark silently dressed himself, absorbed in his thoughts as he was, and told Melot to get up and go to matins with him. When Mark had left his bed, Melot took some flour and sprinkled it on the floor so that if anyone should step to or away from the bed his coming or going could be traced. This done, they both went to church, where their observance had little concern with prayer.

Meanwhile, Brangane had at once seen the stratagem from the floor. She crept along to Tristan, warned him, and lay down again.

This trap was mortal pain for Tristan. His desire for the woman was at its height and his heart yearned in his body as to how he could get to her. He acted in keeping with the saying that passion should be without eyes, and love knows no fear when it is in deadly earnest. 'Alas,' he thought, 'God in Heaven, what shall I do in face of this cursed trap? This gamble is for high stakes!' He stood up in his bed and looked all about him to see by what means he could get there. Now there was light enough for him to see the flour at once, but he judged the two positions too far apart for a leap; yet on the other hand he dared not walk there. He was nevertheless impelled to commit himself to the more promising alternative. He placed his feet together and ran hard at his mark. Love-blind Tristan made his gallant charge too far beyond his strength; he leapt on to the bed, yet lost his gamble, for his vein opened and this caused him much suffering and trouble in the outcome. His blood stained the bed and its linen, as is the way with blood, dyeing it here, there, and everywhere. He lay there for the briefest space, till silks and gold brocades, bed and linen, were altogether soiled. He leapt back to his bed as he had come and lay in anxious thought till the bright day dawned.

Mark was soon back and gazing down at the floor. He examined his trap and found no trace. But when he went along and studied the bed, he saw blood everywhere. This caused him grave disquiet.

'How now, your Majesty,' asked Mark, 'what is the meaning of this? How did this blood get here?'

'My vein opened, and it bled from it. It has only just stopped bleeding!'

Then, as if in fun, he turned to examine Tristan. 'Up you get, lord Tristan!' he said, and threw back the coverlet and found blood here as there.

At this Mark fell silent and said not a word. He left Tristan lying there and turned away. His thoughts and all his mind grew heavy with it. He pondered, like a man for whom no pleasant day has dawned. Indeed, he had chased and all but caught up with his mortal sorrow, yet he had no other knowledge of their secret and the true state of affairs than he was able to see from the blood. But this evidence was slender. Thus he was now yoked again to the doubts and suspicions which he had utterly renounced. Having found the floor before the bed untrodden, he imagined that he was free of misdemeanour from his nephew. But again, finding the Queen and his bed all bloody, he was at once assailed by dark thoughts and ill humour, as always happens to waverers. Amid these doubts he did not know what to do. He believed one thing, he believed another. He did not know what he wanted or what he should believe. He had just found Love's guilty traces in his bed, though not before it, and was thus told the truth and denied it. With these two, truth and untruth, he was deceived. He suspected both alternatives, yet both eluded him. He neither wished the two of them guilty, nor wished them free of guilt. This was a cause of lively grief to that waverer.

Mark, lost man that he was, was now weighed down more than ever before by pondering on how he might find a way out and compose his doubts, how he might throw off his load of uncertainty and wean the court from the suspicions with which it was so busy concerning his wife and nephew. He summoned his great nobles, to whom he looked for loyalty, and acquainted them with his troubles. He told them how the rumour had sprung up at court, and that he was much afraid for his marriage and his honour, and he declared that in view of how the allegation against them had been made public and noised about the land, he felt no inclination to show favour to the Queen or to be on terms of intimacy with her till she had publicly vindicated her innocence and conjugal fidelity towards him, and that he was seeking their general advice as to how he could eliminate all doubt concerning her delinquency, one way or the other, in a manner consonant with his honour.

His kinsmen and vassals advised him forthwith to hold a council at London in England and make known his troubles to the clergy, to those shrewd prelates so learned in canon law.

The council was promptly called to meet in London after Whitsun week when May was drawing to a close. A great number of clergy and laymen arrived on the appointed day in answer to the royal summons. And now Mark and Isolde arrived, both weighed down with sorrow and fear – Isolde in great fear of losing her life and her honour, Mark in great sorrow that through his wife Isolde he might cripple his happiness and noble reputation.

When Mark had taken his seat at the council he complained to his great nobles of the vexation to which this slander was subjecting him and begged them earnestly for the sake of God and of their honour, if they had the skill, to devise some remedy whereby he could exact satisfaction and justice for this delict and settle the issue in one sense or another. Many aired their views on this topic, some well, others ill, one man this way, another that.

Then one of the great lords present at the council rose to his feet, a man well fitted by sagacity and age to offer good advice, the Bishop of the Thames, who was old and distinguished in appearance and as grey as he was wise.

'My lord King, hear me,' said the bishop, leaning over his crook. 'You have summoned us, the nobles of England, into your presence to hear our loyal advice, in dire need of it as you are. I am one of the great nobles, too, Sire. I have my place among them, and am of an age that I may well act on my own responsibility, and say what I have to say. Let each man speak for himself. Your majesty, I will tell you my mind, and if it meets with your approval and pleases you, be persuaded by me and follow my advice.

'My Lady Isolde and Lord Tristan are suspected of serious transgressions, yet judging by what I have heard, they have not been proved guilty by any sort of evidence. How can you allay this evil suspicion with evil? How can you sentence your nephew and your wife to forfeit their honour or their lives, seeing that they have not been caught in any misdemeanour and very likely never will be? Somebody makes this allegation against Tristan; but he does not attest it on Tristan, as by rights he ought to do. Or someone spreads rumours about Isolde; but that someone cannot prove them. Nevertheless, since the court so strongly suspects that they have misconducted themselves, you must deny the Queen community of bed and board till such time as she can prove her innocence before you and the realm, which knows of this report and busies itself with it daily. For alas, true or false, people's ears are eager for such rumours. Whatever is made common gossip when someone impugns a reputation, whether there be truth or falsehood behind it, it excites our baser feelings. However the matter stands here, whether it be true or not, reports and allegations have been gossiped about to such a point that you have taken offence and the court is scandalised.

'Now this is my advice, Sire: that since madam the Queen has had this fault imputed to her, you summon her here into the presence of us all, so that your indictment and her reply may be heard in such terms as shall please the court.'

'I will do so, my lord,' answered the King. 'What you have said by way of advice appears to me appropriate and acceptable.' Isolde was sent for, and she came into the Palace to the council. When she had taken her seat, the grey, wise Bishop of the Thames did as the King had bidden him.

He rose and said: 'Lady Isolde, noble Queen, take no offence at what I say – my lord the King has ordered me to be his spokesman and I must obey his command. Now may God be my witness that, if there is anything that will compromise your honour and rob you of your spotless reputation, I shall bring it to light most reluctantly.

Would that I might be spared it! My good and gracious Queen, your lord and consort commands me to indict you in respect of a public allegation. Neither he nor I knows whether perhaps someone is paying back a grudge; but your name has been linked with his nephew Tristan's both at court and in the country. If God so will, you shall be innocent and free of this fault, madam. Yet the King views it with suspicion because the court declares it to be so. My lord himself has found nothing but good in you. It is from rumours fostered by the court that he brings suspicion to bear on you, not from any evidence; and he indicts you so that kinsmen and vassals can hear the case and discover whether, with our joint advice, he can perhaps root out this slander. Now I think it would be wise if you were to speak and account to him for this suspicion, in the presence of us all.'

Since it was for her to speak, Isolde, the sharp-witted Queen, rose in person, and said: 'My lord Bishop, you Barons here, and the Court! You shall all know this for a fact: whenever I am called upon to answer for my lord's dishonour and for myself, I shall most assuredly answer, now and at all times. You lords, I am well aware that this gross misbehaviour has been imputed to me for the past year, at court and in the country. But it is well known to you all that there is none so blessed by heaven as to be able to live to everybody's liking all the time, and not have vices attributed to him. And so I am not surprised that I too am the victim of such talk. There was no chance that I should be passed over and not be accused of improper conduct, for I am far from home and can never ask here for my friends and relations. Unfortunately, there is scarcely a soul in this place who will feel disgraced with me – rich or poor, you are each one of you very ready to believe in my depravity! If I knew what to do or what remedy there were for it, so that I could persuade you all of my innocence in accordance with my lord's honour, I would gladly do so. Now what do you advise me to do? Whatever procedure you subject me to, I gladly accept it so that your suspicions may be set aside, yet more, by far, in order to vindicate my lord's honour and mine.'

'I am content to leave it there, your Highness,' answered the King. 'If I am to have satisfaction from you as you have proposed to us, give us your surety. Step forward at once and bind yourself to the ordeal of the red-hot iron, as we shall instruct you here.' The Queen complied. She promised to submit to their judgement in six weeks' time in Carleon in accordance with the terms laid down for her. Then the King, his peers, and indeed the whole council withdrew.

Isolde, however, remained alone with her fears and her sorrows – fears and sorrows that gave her little peace. She feared for her honour and she was harassed by the secret anxiety that she would have to whitewash her

Mark talks to Iseult (top) *and tells his lords and prelates of his suspicions; at the bottom, Iseult vows to undergo an ordeal to clear herself.*
(*Munich Staatsbibliothek MS Germ.51 f.82*)

falseness. With these two cares she did not know what to do: she confided them to Christ, the Merciful, who is helpful when one is in trouble. With prayer and fasting she commended all her anguish most urgently to Him. Meanwhile she had propounded to her secret self a ruse which presumed very far upon her Maker's courtesy.

She wrote and sent a letter to Tristan which told him to come to Carleon early on the appointed day when he could seize his chance, as she was about to land, and to watch out for her on the shore.

This was duly done. Tristan repaired there in pilgrim's garb. He had stained and blistered his face and disfigured his body and clothes. When Mark and Isolde arrived and made land there, the Queen saw him and recognised him at once. And when the ship put to shore she commanded that, if the pilgrim were hale and strong enough, they were to ask him in God's name to carry her across from the ship's gangway to the harbour; for at such a time, she said, she was averse to being carried by a knight. Accordingly, they all called out, 'Come here, good man, and carry my lady ashore!' He did as he was bidden, he took his lady the Queen in his arms and carried her back to land. Isolde lost no time in whispering to him that when he reached the shore he was to tumble headlong to the ground with her, whatever might become of him.

This Tristan duly did. When he came to the shore and stepped on to dry land the wayfarer dropped to the ground, falling as if by accident, so that his fall brought him to rest lying in the Queen's lap and arms. Without a moment's delay a crowd of attendants ran up with sticks and staves and were about to set upon him. 'No, no, stop!' said Isolde. 'The pilgrim has every excuse – he is feeble and infirm, and fell accidentally!' They now thanked her and warmly commended her, and praised her in their hearts for not punishing the poor man harshly. 'Would it be surprising if this pilgrim wanted to frolic with me?' asked Isolde with a smile. They set this down in her favour as a mark of her virtue and breeding, and many spoke highly in praise of her. Mark observed the whole incident and heard various things that were said. 'I do not know how it will end,' continued Isolde. 'You have all clearly seen that I cannot lawfully maintain that no man other than Mark found his way into my arms or had his couch in my lap.' With much banter about this bold rogue they set out towards Carleon.

There were many barons, priests, and knights and a great crowd of commoners there. The bishops and prelates who were saying mass and sanctifying the proceedings quickly dispatched their business. The iron was laid in the fire. The good Queen Isolde had given away her silver, her gold, her jewellery, and all the clothes and palfreys she had, to win God's favour, so that He might overlook her very real trespasses and restore her to her honour.

Meanwhile Isolde had arrived at the minister and had heard mass with deep devotion. The wise, good lady's worship was most pious: she wore a rough hair-shirt next her skin and above it a short woollen robe which failed to reach to her slender ankles by more than a hand's breadth. Her sleeves were folded back right to the elbow; her arms and feet were bare. Many eyes observed her, many hearts felt sorrow and pity for her. Her garment and her figure attracted much attention. And now the reliquary was brought, on which she was to swear. She was ordered forthwith to make known to God and the world how guilty she was of the sins that were alleged against her. Isolde had surrendered her life and honour utterly to God's mercy. She stretched out her hand to take the oath upon the relics with fearful heart, as well she might, and rendered up heart and hand to the grace of God, for Him to keep and preserve.

Now there were a number present who were so very unmannerly as to wish to phrase the Queen's oath in a way that aimed at her downfall. That bitter-gall, Marjodoc the Steward, plotted her ruin in many devious ways, but there were no few who treated her courteously and gave things a favourable turn for her. Thus they wrangled from side to side as to what her oath should be. One man wished her ill, another well, as people do in such matters.

'My lord King,' said the Queen, 'my oath must be worded to your pleasure and satisfaction, whatever any of them says. Therefore see for yourself whether, in my acts and utterances, I frame my oath to your liking. These people give too much advice. Hear the oath which I mean to swear: "That no man in the world had carnal knowledge of me or lay in my arms or beside me but you, always excepting the poor pilgrim whom, with your own eyes, you saw lying in my arms." I can offer no purgation concerning him. So help me God and all the Saints that be, to a happy and auspicious outcome to this judgement! If I have not said enough, Sire, I will modify my oath one way or another as you instruct me.'

'I think this will suffice, ma'am, so far as I can see,' answered the King. 'Now take the iron in your hand and, within the terms that you have named to us, may God help you in your need!'

'Amen!' said fair Isolde. In the name of God she laid hold of the iron, carried it, and was not burned.

Thus it was made manifest and confirmed to all the world that Christ in His great virtue is pliant as a wind-blown sleeve. He falls into place and clings, whichever way you try Him, closely and smoothly, as He is bound to do. He is at the beck of every heart for honest deeds or fraud. Be it deadly earnest or a game, He is just as you would have Him. This was amply revealed in the facile

Queen. She was saved by her guile and by the doctored oath that went flying up to God, with the result that she redeemed her honour and was again much beloved of her lord Mark, and was praised, lauded, and esteemed among the people. Whenever the King observed that her heart was set on anything, he sanctioned it at once. He accorded her honour and rich gifts. His heart and mind were centred only upon her, wholly and without guile.

His doubts and suspicions had been set aside once more.

When Isolde's companion Tristan had carried her ashore at Carleon and done as she had asked him, he at once sailed from England to Duke Gilan in Swales. Gilan was young, wealthy, and single, as free as he was gay. Tristan was heartily welcome to him, since Gilan had heard a great deal in former days about his exploits and strange adventures. He was solicitous of Tristan's honour, and of his happiness and ease. Whatever offered a prospect of pleasing him Gilan sought most assiduously. Only melancholy Tristan was always fettered by his thoughts, moping and brooding on his fate.

One day, as Tristan sat beside Gilan, lost in doleful thoughts, he happened to sigh without knowing it. But Gilan noticed it and sent for his little dog Petitcreiu, his heart's delight and balm to his eyes, which had been sent to him from Avalon. His command was duly performed – a rich and noble purple, most rare and wonderful and suitably broad, was spread on the table before him with a tiny dog upon it. It was an enchantment, so I heard, and had been sent to the Duke by a goddess from the fairy land of Avalon as a token of love and affection. It had been so ingeniously conceived in respect of two of its qualities, namely its colour and magic powers, that there was never a tongue so eloquent or heart so discerning that they could describe its beauty and nature. Its colour had been compounded with such rare skill that none could really tell what it was. When you looked at its breast it was so many-coloured that you would not have said otherwise than that it was whiter than snow; but at the loins it was greener than clover; one flank was redder than scarlet, the other yellower than saffron; underneath, it resembled azure, but above there was a mixture so finely blended that no one hue stood out from all the others – for here was neither green, nor red, nor white, nor black, nor yellow, nor blue, and yet a touch of all, I mean a regular purple. If you looked at this rare work from Avalon against the grain of its coat, no one, however discerning, could have told you its colour. It was as bewilderingly varied as if there were no colour at all.

Round the dog's little neck went a chain of gold on which hung a bell so sweet and clear that, as soon as it began to tremble, melancholy Tristan sat there rid of the sorrows of his attachment and unmindful of his suffering for Isolde. The tinkling of the bell was so sweet that none could hear it without its banishing his cares and putting an end to his pain. Tristan saw and listened to this marvel of marvels, he studied and observed both the dog and its bell and examined each in turn – the dog and its wonderful coat, the bell and its sweet music. They both filled him with wonder. Yet, as he looked, the marvel of the dog appeared to him more marvellous than the dulcet sound of the bell that sang into his ears and took his sadness away. He thought it a wonderful thing that his eyes, wide open though they were, should be deceived by this medley of colours and that he could identify none, however much he looked at them. He gently stretched out his hands to stroke the dog, and as he fondled it, it seemed to him as though he were fingering the very finest silk, so soft and smooth was it everywhere. The dog neither growled nor barked nor showed any sign of vice, whatever games you played with it. It neither ate nor drank, so the tale declares.

When Petitcreiu had been carried out again, Tristan's sadness was as fresh as ever. It returned with heightened intensity, so that he gave his deepest thoughts to considering by what happy inspiration or ingenious idea he might obtain the little dog for his lady the Queen, in order that her longing might be eased. But he could not conceive how this should ever come to pass, either by entreaty or artifice, for he was well aware that Gilan would not part with it for any precious thing that he had ever seen, except to save his life. Such thoughts and anxieties weighed continually on his heart, yet he never gave a sign.

As the authentic history of Tristan's exploits tells us, there was at this time a giant who had settled near the land of Swales, a haughty and arrogant man who had his dwelling on the bank of a river, and who was called Urgan li vilus. Gilan and his land of Swales were subject to this giant and, in return for his allowing his people to live free of molestation, were obliged to pay him tribute.

During this time it was announced at court that the giant Urgan had arrived, and that he had gathered together what passed for his tribute – cattle, sheep, and pigs – and was having it driven off ahead of him. Hereupon Gilan told his friend Tristan how this tribute had first been imposed on them by force and villainy.

'Now tell me, my lord,' said Tristan, 'if I succeed in ridding you of this trouble, and quickly help you to be free of the tribute for the rest of your days, what will you give me in return?'

'Indeed, sir,' answered Gilan, 'I shall willingly give you anything I have!'

'If you will promise this, my lord,' continued Tristan, 'by whatever means I achieve it, I shall most certainly help you to be rid of Urgan for ever in a short space, or else die in the attempt!'

'Believe me, sir, I will give you whatever you fancy,' answered Gilan. 'You have only to say the word.' And he gave Tristan his hand on it.

Tristan's horse and armour were sent for, and he asked to be shown the way along which that brat of the devil would have to return with his plunder. They promptly directed him to Urgan's tracks leading into the wildest of forests, which abutted on the giant's territory in the region where the plundered cattle regularly crossed by a bridge. And now the giant and his booty were approaching. But Tristan was there before them and was barring the way of the stolen herds. Seeing the turmoil at the bridge, that damned giant Urgan immediately turned towards it with his huge long pole of steel, holding it poised in the air.

When Urgan saw the knight before the bridge so well armed, he addressed him scornfully:

'My friend on the horse, who are you? Why don't you let my cattle cross? That you have barred the way, I swear, will cost you your life, unless you surrender at once!'

'Friend, my name is Tristan,' answered the man on the horse. 'Believe me, I am not in the least bit afraid of you or your pole, so be off with you! And take my word for it that your plunder will not get any farther, so far as I can prevent it!'

'Oh yes, Lord Tristan,' rejoined the giant, 'you plume yourself on having fought Morold of Ireland, with whom you arranged a combat under no provocation at all, and whom you killed from over-weening pride! But I am a different sort of person from the Irishman whose favour you gained with your strumming, and from whom you stole Isolde in the flower of her beauty, though he wished to fight a duel for her! No, no, this riverside is my home and my name is Urgan li vilus! Quick, get out of the way!'

With these words Urgan began to measure off, using both hands, a mighty long swing and a throw straight at Tristan. He aimed its sweep and fall with the precise intention of making an end of him – but as Urgan was in the act of hurling the pole, Tristan swerved aside, yet not enough to escape having his mount cloven in two, forward of the croup. The grisly giant let out a roar.

'So God help you, Lord Tristan!' he shouted with a grin. 'Don't be in a hurry to ride away! Do please wait for me, so that I can beg you on bended knee to permit me quietly and honourably to go on driving off my revenues!'

Tristan alighted on the grass, for his horse had been killed. Making for Urgan with his lance, he wounded him in one eye. With this blow the damned villain was hit fair and square. The grisly giant tore across to where his pole had fallen and, as he lowered his hand to lay hold of it, Tristan, having thrown down his spear, came up at top speed with his sword and struck him just where he wished to, for he cut off his hand as it sought for the pole so that it came to rest on the ground. He then gave the giant a second blow, on the thigh, and drew aside. The injured giant Urgan groped down with his left hand, snatched up the pole, and ran at his deadly enemy. He chased Tristan beneath the trees, with many a fearful twist and turn. In this way the gush of blood that issued from Urgan's wound grew so great that the fiendish man began to fear that his strength and spirit would shortly ebb away. He therefore let the knight and his plunder be, found his hand, picked it up, and at once returned home to his stronghold, while Tristan stayed in the forest with the booty. He was not a little afraid at Urgan's having escaped alive. He sat down on the grass pondering deeply and reflecting that, since he had no proof of his exploit apart from the stolen tribute, the terror and toil he had endured for it would not advance him one jot, and he judged that Gilan would not honour his oath, in view of the terms they had agreed on. He immediately made after Urgan and ran at an even speed along the track where the latter had run in advance of him, and where the grass and soil were dyed red with his blood.

When he came to the castle Tristan searched for Urgan here, there, and everywhere, but found neither him nor any living person. For, as the story tells us, the wounded man had laid his lost hand on a table in the hall and run down the hill from the castle to grub for herbs with which to treat his wound and which he knew had the power to heal him. And indeed, Urgan had calculated that, once he had joined his hand to his arm in good time before it was quite dead, by a means that he was versed in, he would have emerged well from this peril with his hand, though minus an eye. But this was not to be. For Tristan came in at once, caught sight of the hand there, and finding it undefended, took it and immediately returned by the way that he had come.

Now Urgan came back and, to his sorrow and anger, perceived that he had forfeited his hand. Casting his simples to the ground he turned to pursue Tristan, who was now across the bridge and well aware that he was pelting after him. Tristan quickly took the giant's hand and hid it beneath a fallen tree-trunk. Now at last he was seriously alarmed at the monster, for it was plain that one of them must die, either he or the giant.

Tristan made for the bridge and met Urgan with his spear, thrusting at him with such force that it snapped; and as soon as he had made his thrust, cursed Urgan was upon him with his pole and he struck at him so avidly that, but for the blow overshooting its mark, Tristan would never have survived it, though he had been made of bronze. But Urgan's craving to get at him aided his escape, for the giant had come in too close and aimed the sweep of his blow too far to Tristan's rear. And now, before the gruesome man could withdraw his pole, Tristan feinted and pierced him in the eye – there was no denying he had pierced him in his other eye! Urgan now lashed out like the blinded man he was, and there was such a rain of blows that Tristan ran to cover out of range and left him to blunder about, striking with his left hand. Eventually it happened that Urgan stepped so near to the end of the bridge that Tristan ran up at speed and put his utmost strength into this exploit: he raced up to Urgan and, turning him with both hands from the bridge to where he must pitch headlong, thrust him down so that his monstrous bulk was shattered on the rock.

Elated with his victory, Tristan now took Urgan's hand and, making all speed, soon came upon Duke Gilan, who was riding from the opposite direction. Gilan deeply regretted in his heart that Tristan had ever taken it upon himself to join this battle, for it never occurred to him that he would emerge from it alive as in fact he had. Seeing Tristan running towards him, he joyfully addressed him. 'Welcome, noble Tristan!' cried Gilan. 'Tell me, dear man, how are you? Are you safe and well?' Tristan at once showed him the dead hand of the giant and told him of the good fortune which had blessed the whole enterprise, exactly as it had happened. Gilan was heartily glad of it. They then rode back to the bridge and found a man who had been dashed to pieces in accordance with Tristan's testimony, just as Gilan and his men had been told; and they accounted it a marvel. They thereupon turned back and happily drove the stolen beasts into their territory again. This gave rise to great rejoicing in Swales. They sang praise, honour, and glory to Tristan – never in that land was one man's valour held in higher esteem.

When Gilan and victorious Tristan had arrived back home and resumed their talk of their good fortune, Tristan, the wonder-worker, addressed the Duke without delay.

'My lord Duke, let me remind you of the pledge and the terms that we agreed on, and what you promised me.'

'My lord, I willingly recall it. Tell me, what would you like? What do you desire?'

'Lord Gilan, I desire that you give me Petitcreiu!'

'But I have a better proposal,' answered Gilan.

'Well, then, tell me,' said Tristan.

'Leave me my little dog and take my handsome sister together with half my possessions!'

'No, my Lord Gilan, I must remind you of your word; for I would not take all the kingdoms in the world in exchange, if I were given the choice. I killed Urgan li vilus with the sole object of winning Petitcreiu.'

'If your wishes run more on him than on what I have proposed to you, I will keep my promise and grant you what you want – I will use no trickery or cunning in this affair. Though I am very loth to do so, your wishes shall be met!' He thereupon ordered the little dog to be set before him and Tristan. 'Look, sir,' he said, 'I declare to you on oath by all my hopes of bliss that there is nothing I could have or that I ever cherished, apart from my life and honour, that I would not much rather give you than my dog Petitcreiu. Now take him and keep him, and may God give you joy of him! In him you deprive me of my eyes' rarest pleasure and much delight to my heart.'

When Tristan had gained possession of the little dog, he would truly have rated Rome and all the kingdoms, lands, and seas, as nothing in comparison. He had never felt so happy as then, except in Isolde's company. He took a Welsh minstrel into his confidence, an intelligent and well-versed man, and instructed him in a convenient stratagem by which he could give fair Isolde, the Queen, her happiness again. He shrewdly hid Petitcreiu in the Welshman's crwth. He wrote a letter to her in which he told her how and where he had acquired the dog for love of her. The minstrel set out on his journey in accordance with his instructions, and duly arrived at Mark's castle in Tintagel without mishap on the way. He got into conversation with Brangane and handed her the dog and letter, and she conveyed them to Isolde.

Isolde examined intently this marvel of marvels which

she found in the dog and its bell, both one by one and together. She rewarded the minstrel there and then with ten marks of gold. She wrote and dispatched by him a letter in which she told Tristan with great urgency that her Lord Mark was most favourably inclined towards him and would hold nothing that had happened against him, and that he must return without fail, since she had settled their differences.

Tristan did as he was bidden and returned home without delay. The King and his court and the land and its people all held him in high esteem, as before. He had never been shown greater honour at court, except inasmuch as Marjodoc honoured him on the outside of his heart, as did his yoke-mate Petit Melot. But, whatever the honour shown him by those who had been his enemies, there was little honour in it. State your opinions, all of you, on this point: where you have only the semblance, is that honour or no? I myself say both yes and no. No and yes both have their share in it. 'No' for the man who renders honour: 'yes' for the one who receives it. These two are found between the pair of them – both 'yes' and 'no' are found there. What more is there to say? Here we have honour without honour.

Now, as to the little dog, Queen Isolde told her lord that her mother the wise Queen of Ireland had sent him to her with instructions to make him a delightful little kennel of gold and precious things, such as one might dream of. Inside, they spread a rich brocade for him to lie on. In this way Petitcreiu was under Isolde's observation day and night, in public and in private – such was her custom wherever she was or wherever she rode. He never came out of her sight, he was always led or carried where she could see him. Nor did she have this done for any relief it might give her. She had it done (so we are told) to renew her tender love-pangs out of affection for Tristan, who had been moved by love to send her Petitcreiu.

Isolde had no relief from Petitcreiu, she did not depend on him for solace. For as soon as the faithful Queen had received the dog and heard the bell which made her forget her sorrow, she had reflected that her friend Tristan bore a load of troubles for her sake, and she immediately thought to herself: 'O faithless woman, how can I be glad? Why am I happy for any time at all while Tristan, who has surrendered his life and joy to sorrow for my sake, is sad because of me? How can I rejoice without him, whose sorrow and joy I am? And however can I laugh when his heart can find no ease, unless my heart has a share in it? He has no life but me. Should I now be living without him, happily and pleasantly, while he is pining? May the good God forbid that I should ever rejoice away from him!' So saying, she broke off the bell, leaving the chain round the little dog's neck. From this the bell lost its whole virtue. It no longer sounded with its old music. They say that it never again quenched or made away with sorrow in any heart, however much one heard it. But this meant nothing to Isolde; she did not wish to be happy. This constant, faithful lover had surrendered her life and joy to the sadness of love and to Tristan.

Once more Tristan and Isolde had surmounted their cares and perils, once more they were happy at court, which again overflowed with their honours. Never had they enjoyed such esteem. They were as intimate again as ever with Mark their common lord. They also hid their feelings very thoroughly; for, when it was not propitious for them to seize their chance together, they deemed the will sufficient, which often consoles a pair of lovers. Hope and expectation of how to accomplish the desire on which the heart is set never fail to give it a blossoming vigour and a living ecstasy. Here is true attachment, such are the best instincts in matters of love and affection – that where one cannot have the deed in a way that is serviceable to love, one should forgo it, and take the will for the deed. Wherever there is a sure will but no good opportunity, lovers should assuage their longing with that same sure will. Companions in love should never want what opportunity denies them, or they will want their sorrow. To desire when the means are lacking is a very impolitic game. When you have the means – that is the time for desiring. This game is rich in opportunities, it is not fraught with sorrow. When these partners Isolde and Tristan were unable to seize their opportunity, they let the occasion pass, content in their common will, which, never tiring, stole tenderly and lovingly from one to the other. A common desire and affection seemed sweet and good to them.

The lovers hid their love at all times from the court and from Mark, as much and as well as they were allowed to do by the blind passion that would not leave them. But the seed of suspicion in love is of a nature so accurst that it takes root wherever it is cast. It is so fertile, so fecund, and so sturdy, that even lacking moisture and all but dying, it can never die entirely.

Busy suspicion shot up luxuriantly and began once more to play about Tristan and Isolde. Here was excess of moisture, of their tender looks and signs in which Love's proofs were ever visible. How right he was who said that however one guards against it, the eye longs for the heart, the finger for the pain. The eyes, those lodestars of the heart, long to go raiding to where the heart is turned: the finger and the hand time and time again go towards the pain. So it was always with these lovers. However great their fears, they had not the power to refrain from nourishing suspicion with many a tender look, often and all too often. For alas, as I have just said, that friend of the heart, the eye, was ever turned towards the heart, the hand would go to the pain. Many a time did they enmesh their eyes and hearts with looks that passed between them, so intimately that they often failed to disengage them before Mark had found Love's balm in them, for he was always watching them. His eye was always on them. He secretly read the truth in her eyes many, many times, and indeed in nothing but her glance – it was so very lovely, so tender, and so wistful that it pierced him to the heart, and he conceived such anger, such envy and hatred from it that he forsook his doubt and suspicion; for now pain and anger robbed him of measure and reason. It was death to his reason that his darling Isolde should love any man but himself, he valued nothing above Isolde, and in this he never wavered. For all his anger, his beloved wife was a dear and dearer to him than life. Yet however dear she was to him, this vexation and maddening pain brought him to such a frenzy that he was rid of his affection and wholly taken up by his anger – he was past all caring whether his suspicions were true or false.

In his blind agony Mark summoned them both to court in the Palace before the household. Addressing Isolde publicly in full sight and hearing of the court, he said: 'My Lady Isolde of Ireland, it is well known to my land and people under what dire suspicion you have long stood with regard to my nephew Tristan. Now I have subjected you to tests and trials of many kinds to discover whether, for my sake, you would restrain yourself from this folly; but I see that you will not leave it. I am not such a fool as not to know or see from your behaviour in public and in private that your heart and eyes are for ever fixed on my nephew. You show him a kinder face than ever you show me, from which I conclude that he is dearer to you than I am. Whatever watch I set on you or him, it is of no avail. It is all to no purpose, whatever lengths I go to. I have put a distance between you so often that I never cease to marvel that you remain so one at heart all this long while. I have severed your tender glances so many times, yet I fail to sunder your affections. In this I have over-indulged you. But now I will tell you how it is to end. I will bear with you no longer the shame and grief that you have caused me, with all its suffering. From now on I will not endure this dishonour! But neither shall I revenge myself on you for this

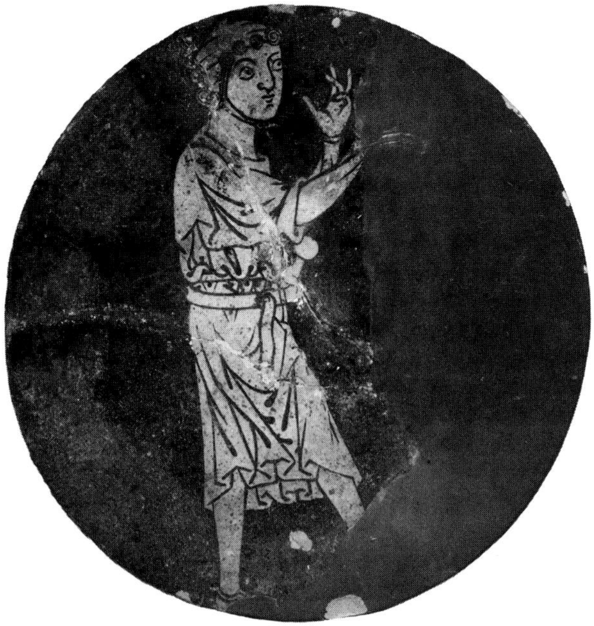

Tristan; a tile made at Chertsey Abbey, near Windsor, in about 1270.
(British Museum).

state of affairs to the extent that I am entitled, did I wish to be revenged. Nephew Tristan, and my Lady Isolde, I love you too much to put you to death or harm you in any way, loth as I am to confess it. But since I can read it in the pair of you that, in defiance of my will, you love and have loved each other more than me, then be with one another as you please – do not hold back from any fear of me! Since your love is so great, from this hour I shall not vex or molest you in any of your concerns. Take each other by the hand and leave my court and country. If I am to be wronged by you I wish neither to see nor hear it. This fellowship between the three of us can hold no longer; I will leave you two together, and I alone shall quit it, however I succeed in freeing myself. Such fellowship is vile – I mean to be rid of it! For a King to be partnered in love with open eyes is beneath contempt! Go, the two of you, with God's protection. Live and love as you please; this companionship in love is ended!'

It duly happened as Mark commanded. With moderate distress and cool regret, Tristan and his Lady Isolde bowed to their common lord, the King, and then to the royal retainers. Then these steadfast companions took each other by the hand and crossed the court. They told

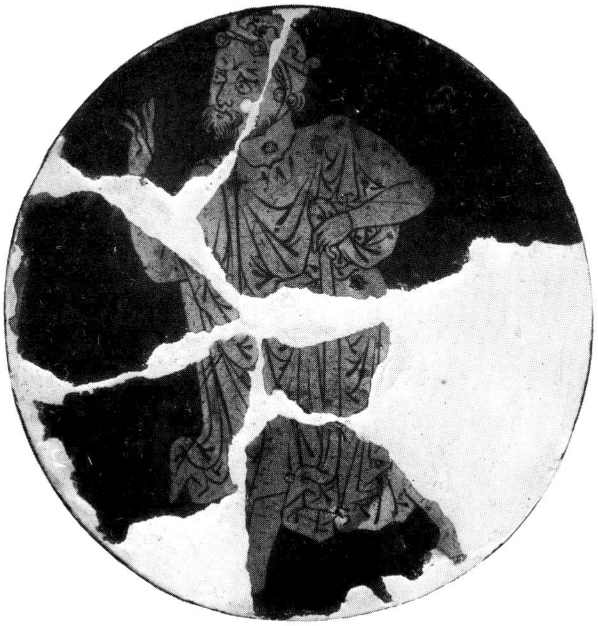

Mark; from a tile made at Chertsey Abbey, near Windsor in about 1270.
(*British Museum*)

their friend Brangane to keep well, and asked her to remain and pass the time at court until she should hear how they were faring – this they urgently commended to her. Of Isolde's store of gold, Tristan took twenty marks for Isolde and himself for their needs and sustenance. They also brought him his harp, his sword, his hunting-bow, and his horn, which he had asked them to fetch for his journey. In addition he had chosen one of his hounds, a handsome, slender animal called Hiudan, and he took charge of it himself. He commended his followers to God, telling them to return him to his father Rual, all except for Curvenal, whom he retained in his own party. He gave Curvenal his harp to carry, but took his crossbow himself, and his horn and hound too – Hiudan, not Petitcreiu. And so the three of them rode from the court.

Comely Brangane remained in grief and sadness, utterly alone. This sorrowful event and most hateful parting from her two dear friends wrung her heart so cruelly that it was a marvel she did not die of grief. They, too, took their leave of her in great sorrow, except that they left her with Mark and told her to stay for a while, so that she might bring about a reconciliation between themselves and him.

The three of them together made steadily for the wilds, journeying over forest and heath for well on two days. Tristan had long known of a cavern in a savage mountainside, on which he had chanced when his way had led him there out hunting. The cavern had been hewn into the wild mountain in heathen times, before Corynaeus' day, when giants ruled there. They used to hide inside it when, desiring to make love, they needed privacy. Wherever such a cavern was found it was barred by a door of bronze, and bore an inscription to Love – *la fossiure a la gent amant*, which is to say 'The Cave of Lovers'.

The name was well suited to the thing. The story tells us that this grotto was round, broad, high, and perpendicular, snow-white, smooth, and even, throughout its whole circumference. Above, its vault was finely keyed, and on the keystone there was a crown most beautifully adorned with goldsmiths' work and encrusted with precious stones. Below, the pavement was of smooth, rich, shining marble, as green as grass. At the centre there was a bed most perfectly cut from a slab of crystal, broad, high, well raised from the ground, and engraved along its sides with letters, announcing that the bed was dedicated to the Goddess of Love. In the upper part of the grotto some small windows had been hewn out to let in the light, and these shone in several places.

Where one went in and out there was a door of bronze. Outside, above the door, there stood three limes of many branches, but beyond them not a single one. Yet everywhere downhill there were innumerable trees which cast the shade of their leafy boughs upon the mountainside. Somewhat apart, there was a level glade through which there flowed a spring – a cool, fresh brook, clear as the sun. Above that, too, there stood three limes, fair and very stately, sheltering the brook from the sun and rain. The bright flowers and the green grass, with which the glade was illumined, vied with each other most delightfully, each striving to outshine the other. At their due times you could hear the sweet singing of the birds. Their music was so lovely – even lovelier here than elsewhere. Both eye and ear found their pasture and delight there: the eye its pasture, the ear its delight. There were shade and sunshine, air and breezes, both soft and gentle. Away from the mountain and its cave for fully a day's journey there were rocks unrelieved by open heath, and wilderness and wasteland. No paths or tracks had been laid towards it of which one might avail oneself. But the country was not so rough and fraught with hardship as to deter Tristan and his beloved from halting there and making their abode within that mountain-cave.

When they had taken up their quarters they sent Curvenal back to put it out at court and wherever else was necessary that, after many griefs and hardships, Tristan and fair Isolde had arrived back in Ireland in order to proclaim their innocence before the land and people. Further, he was to take up residence at court as Brangane should instruct him and earnestly assure the true-hearted girl, their common friend, of their love and friendship. He was also to find out what was rumoured of Mark's intentions – whether he might be plotting some villainy against their lives, and in that case inform them at once. And they begged him to keep Tristan and Isolde in his thoughts and to return once every twenty days with such intelligence as would enable them to counter such moves. He did as he was asked. Meanwhile Tristan and Isolde had taken up their abode together in this wild retreat.

Some people are smitten with curiosity and astonishment, and plague themselves with the question of how these two companions, Tristan and Isolde, nourished themselves in this wasteland? I will tell them and assuage their curiosity. They looked at one another and nourished themselves with that! Their sustenance was the eye's increase. They fed in their grotto on nothing but love and desire. The two lovers who formed its court had small concern for their provender. Hidden away in their hearts they carried the best nutriment to be had anywhere in the world, which offered itself unasked ever fresh and new. I mean pure devotion, love made sweet as balm that consoles body and sense so tenderly, and sustains the heart and spirit – this was their best nourishment. Truly, they never considered any food but that from which the heart drew desire, the eyes delight, and which the body, too, found agreeable. With this they had enough. Love drove her ancient plough for them, keeping pace all the time, and gave them an abundant store of all those things that go to make heaven on earth.

Nor were they greatly troubled that they should be alone in the wilds without company. Tell me, whom did they need in there with them, and why should anyone join them? They made an even number: there were simply one and one. Had they included a third in the even pair which they made, there would have been an uneven number, and they would have been much encumbered and embarrassed by the odd one. Their company of two was so ample a crowd for this pair that good King Arthur never held a feast in any of his palaces that gave keener pleasure or delight. In no land could you have found enjoyment for which these two would have given a brass farthing to have with them in their grotto. Whatever one could imagine or conceive elsewhere in other countries to make a paradise, they had with them there. They would not have given a button for a better life, save only in respect of their honour. What more should they need? They had their court, they were amply supplied with all that goes to make for happiness. Their loyal servitors were the green lime, the sunshine and the shade, the brook and its banks, flowers, grass, blossoms, and leaves, so soothing to the eye. The service they received was the song of the birds, of the lovely, slender nightingale, the thrush and blackbird, and other birds of the forest. Siskin and calander-lark vied in eager rivalry to see who could give the best service. These followers served their ears and sense unendingly. Their high feast was Love, who gilded all their joys; she brought them King Arthur's Round Table as homage and all its company a thousand times a day! What better food could they have for body or soul? Man was there with Woman, Woman there with Man. What else should they be needing? They had what they were meant to have, they had reached the goal of their desire.

Now some people are so tactless as to declare (though I do not accept it myself) that other food is needed for this pastime. I am not so sure that it is. There is enough here in my opinion. But if anyone has discovered better nourishment in this world let him speak in the light of his experience. There was a time when I, too, led such a life, and I thought it quite sufficient.

Now I beg you to bear with me while I reveal to you on account of what hidden significance that cave was thus constructed in the rock.

It was, as I said, round, broad, high, and perpendicular, snow-white, smooth, and even, throughout its whole circumference. Its roundness inside betokens Love's Simplicity: Simplicity is most fitting for Love, which must have no corners, that is, Cunning or Treachery. Breadth signifies Love's Power, for her Power is without end. Height is Aspiration that mounts aloft to the clouds: nothing is too great for it so long as it means to climb, up and up, to where the molten Crown of the Virtues gathers the vault to the keystone. The Virtues are invariably encrusted with precious stones, inlaid in filigree of gold and so adorned with praise, that we who are of lower aspiration – whose spirits flag and flutter over the pavement and neither settle nor fly – we gaze up intently at the masterpiece above us, which stands amid the Virtues and descends to us from the glory of those who soar in the clouds and send their refulgence down to us! – we gaze at their Virtues and marvel! From this grow the feathers by which our spirit takes wing and, flying, earns praise for its virtues.

The wall was white, smooth, and even: such is Integrity's nature. Her brilliant and uniform whiteness must never be mottled with colour, nor should Suspicion find any pit or ridge in her. In its greenness and firmness the marble floor is like Constancy; this meaning is the best for it in respect of colour and smoothness. Constancy should be of the same fresh green as grass, and smooth and gleaming as glass.

At the centre, the bed of crystalline Love was dedicated to her name most fittingly. The man who had cut the crystal for her couch and her observance had divined her nature unerringly: Love *should* be of crystal – transparent and translucent!

On the inside, across the door of bronze, there ran two bars. Inside, too, there was a latch most ingeniously let through the wall, where Tristan, indeed, had found it. This latch was governed by a lever, which passed from the outside to the inside and guided it this way and that. There was neither lock nor key to it, and I will tell you why. There was no lock for this reason – than any device which one applies to a door (I mean on the outside) for the purpose of opening and shutting it, betokens Treachery. For when anyone enters at Love's door who has not been admitted from within, it cannot be accounted Love, since it is either Deceit or Force. Love's gate is there to prevent it, the door of bronze bars the way, and none can get the better of it, unless it be by Love. Indeed, it is made of bronze so that no tool, whether of force or of violence, cunning or artifice, treachery or falsehood should ever have power to harm it. Within, two bars, two seals of love, were turned towards each other on either side, the one of cedar, the other of ivory. Now hear their interpretations. The bar of cedar stands for the Discretion and Understanding of Love; the other of ivory for her Purity and Modesty. With these two seals, with these chaste bars, Love's house is guarded, and Deceit and Force locked out. The secret lever which had been let into the latch from without was a spindle of tin, while the latch was of gold, as it should be. Neither the one nor the other, latch or lever, could have been better applied in respect of their innate virtues: tin means Willing Thought for a secret affair of the heart, but gold stands for Success. Tin and gold are appropriate here. Any man can mould his thoughts to his will, narrow, broaden, shorten, lengthen them, free them, or confine them, here or there, this way or that, with very little effort, as is the case with tin, and there is no great harm in that. But if a man can set his thoughts on love with a true will, this lever of humble tin will carry him on to golden success and the tender transports of love.

Mark sends Tristan and Iseult into exile (top); he later finds them asleep in the cave of lovers, with a sword between them, and, convinced of their innocence, allows them to return. (Munich, Staatsbibliothek, MS. Germ.51 f.90)

Overhead, three little windows in all had been hewn through the solid rock into the cave, very secretly and neatly, through which the sun would shine. The first stood for Kindness, the second for Humility, the third for Breeding. Through these three, the sweet light, that blessed radiance, Honour, dearest of all luminaries, smiled in and lit up that cave of earthly bliss.

It also has its meaning that the grotto was so secluded in the midst of this wild solitude, in that one may well compare it with this – that Love and her concerns are not assigned to the streets nor yet to the open country. She is hidden away in the wilds, the country that leads to her refuge makes hard and arduous going – mountains are strewn about the way in many a massive curve. The tracks up and down are so obstructed with rocks for us poor sufferers that, unless we keep well to the path, if we make one false step we shall never get back alive. But whoever is so blessed as to reach and enter that solitude will have used his efforts to most excellent purpose, for he will find his heart's delight there. Whatever the ear yearns to hear, whatever gratifies the eye, this wilderness is full of it. He would hate to be elsewhere.

I know this well, for I have been there. I, too, have tracked and followed after wildfowl and game, after hart and hind in the wilderness over many a woodland stream and yet passed my time and not seen the end of the chase. My toils were not crowned with success. I have found the lever and seen the latch in that cave and have, on occasion, even pressed on to the bed of crystal – I have danced there and back some few times. But never have I had my repose on it. However hard the floor of marble beside it, I have so battered the floor with my steps that, had it not been saved by its greenness, in which lies its chiefest virtue, and from which it constantly renews itself, you would have traced Love's authentic tracks on it. I have also fed my eyes on the gleaming wall abundantly and have fixed my gaze on the medallion, on the vault and on the keystone, and worn out my eyes looking up at its ornament, so bespangled with Excellence! The sun-giving windows have often sent their rays into my heart. I have known that cave since I was eleven, yet I never set foot in Cornwall.

Those true-hearted denizens, Tristan and his mistress, had arranged their leisure and exertions very pleasantly in the woods and glades of their wilderness. They were always at each other's side. In the mornings they would stroll to the meadow through the dew, where it had cooled the grass and the flowers. The cool field was their recreation. They talked as they walked to and fro, and they listened as they went to the sweet singing of the birds. Then they would turn aside to where the cool spring murmured, and would hearken to its music as it slid down on its path. Where it entered the glade they used to sit and rest and listen to its purling and watch the water flow, a joy they never tired of.

But when the bright sun began to climb and the heat to descend, they withdrew to their lime-tree in quest of its gentle breezes. This afforded them pleasure within and without their breasts – the tree rejoiced both their hearts and their eyes. With its leaves the fragrant lime refreshed both air and shade for them; from its shade the breezes were gentle, fragrant, cool. The bench beneath the lime was flowers and grass, the best-painted lawn that ever lime-tree had. Our constant lovers sat there together and told love-tales of those whom love had ruined in days gone by. They debated and discussed, they bewept and bewailed how Phyllis of Thrace and poor Canacea had suffered such misfortune in Love's name; how Biblis had died broken-hearted for her brother's love; how love-lorn Dido, Queen of Tyre and Sidon, had met so tragic a fate because of unhappy love. To such tales did they apply themselves from time to time.

When they tired of stories they slipped into their refuge and resumed their well-tried pleasure of sounding their harp, and singing sadly and sweetly. They busied their hands and their tongues in turn. They performed amorous lays and their accompaniments, varying their delight as it suited them: for if one took the harp it was for the other to sing the tune with wistful tenderness. And indeed the strains of both harp and tongue, merging their sound in each other, echoed in that cave so sweetly that it was dedicated to sweet Love for her retreat most fittingly as '*La fossiure a la gent amant*'.

All that had been rumoured in tales of old on the subject of the grotto was borne out in this pair. Only now had the cave's true mistress given herself to her sport in earnest. Whatever frolics or pastimes had been pursued in this grotto before, they did not equal this; they were neither so pure nor so unsullied in spirit as when Tristan and Isolde disported themselves. These two beguiled Love's hour in a way no lovers surpassed – they did just as their hearts prompted them.

There were amusements enough for them to follow by day. They rode out into their wilderness: hunting wildfowl and game with their crossbow now and then, when fancy took them, and sometimes they chased the red deer with Hiudan their hound, who as yet could not run without giving tongue. But it was not long before Tristan had trained him to run most perfectly through field and forest on the scent of hart and hind and of all varieties of game without giving cry. And so they spent many a day, not for what such sport brings the hunting-bag, but solely for the amusement it affords. They exercised hound and bow, I am convinced, more for their pleasure and recreation than for their table. What they did was entirely as they pleased, and as they felt inclined.

WOLFRAM VON ESCHENBACH

Parzival

The beginning of the adventures of Perceval (Parzival) as depicted on a Parisian ivory casket of c. 1400: Perceval is seen in his simple rustic clothing, holding a bow, watching three knights in amazement. (Musée du Louvre)

APPROACHES TO ROMANCE · A HERO'S ODYSSEY · PARZIVAL'S ADVENTURES · THE GRAIL AND THE SPIRITUAL WORLD & & &

The great German writers took their material – that is, the outline and main episodes of their stories – from French romances. Their contribution was only occasionally in the shape of new characters and adventures; they were much more concerned with the inner meanings of the romances, as we have seen in the case of Gottfried von Strassburg. Gottfried's contemporary and rival, Wolfram von Eschenbach, writing in a very different style and with very different ideas, nonetheless shares with him a spiritual approach to their subject which only the *Quest for the Holy Grail* among the French romances begins to rival. In his *Parzival* Wolfram writes of strange adventures and marvels much as Chrétien had done, but he adds to them an exploration of the highest philosophical themes, notably a coherent idea of knightly behaviour. Within the framework of romance, he portrays a world in which chivalry becomes an ideal fulfilling all man's highest aspirations, crowned by its own religious order, the knights of the Grail, and which is nonetheless real and actual.

Wolfram was a Bavarian knight, from the village now known as Wolframseschenbach. His family were *ministeriales*, knights in imperial service who remained officially serfs. Of his life we know only what he himself tells us: that he was poor – 'at home the mice rarely have enough to eat' – that he had various misfortunes in love (though he implies that he was happily married in the end), that he was widely travelled in Germany. He came at some point in his journeyings to the Court of Hermann of Thuringia, where other great poets such as Walter von der Vogelweide had been honoured guests, and where, between about 1300–1310, he wrote *Parzival*. His view of courtly life is not entirely approving; he has some sharp words for the disorderliness of Hermann's halls, where every insolent fellow who pretended to sing or make verses gained easy entrance. Addressing Hermann himself, he says 'you would need someone like Kay [who appears in the romances as an uncompromising and forthright seneschal] to deal with an unruly mob like that'. And in another passage he attacks the morals that all too often lay behind the outward show of courtly love, saying that he would not care to take his wife to King Arthur's Court, where everyone's thoughts were always occupied with love. 'Someone would soon be telling her that he was transfixed by love for her, and blind with the joy it caused him; if she could cure his pain, he would always serve her. I should take her away from there before anyone had a chance to do this'. Wolfram's wry humour marks him as a man with a down-to-earth view of life, at first blush an unlikely guide through the exotic forests and spellbound adventures of his chosen subject.

The theme which Wolfram makes central to the story, Parzival's courtly and spiritual progress, is only vaguely explored in Chrétien. The old folk-tale of the prince brought up in ignorance, the 'pure fool' of noble birth, was merely another inherited motif from the Celtic past which served as a starting point for the romance. Wolfram turns this into a deeply-felt heroic example, yet does not preach or point a conscious moral. Indeed, his portrait of Parzival's innocence is delightful and natural. The boy, kept from the ways of knighthood that have caused his father's death, is brought up by his mother in the depths of the forest with no knowledge of the glittering world that is his birthright, with no knowledge of even the simplest ideas about life; he has learnt who God is, and that 'his love helps all who live on earth'. When he meets a knight who has fled deep into the forest to escape his pursuers, he can only imagine that this superior being is God: and though he is duly disillusioned, his natural instinct for knighthood has been aroused.

Wolfram makes great play with the idea that nobility is an inherited trait. Parzival's nature predisposes him to knighthood. From his father's family he inherits love as his destiny; from his mother's, the service of the Grail. This idea of a place in life, at once foreordained and inherited, is at the root of Wolfram's concept of society, which he sees as a series of orders crowned by knighthood. Man should not question his appointed lot, even if it be a less honourable one than knighthood.

So Parzival sets out: dressed in fool's clothing and with the briefest of advice from his mother. She hopes that his attire will draw mockery upon him and send him back to her; and he has misunderstood her advice. This provides the matter of his first adventures, and the wrongs he unwittingly inflicts he will have to atone for later, including the killing of Ither, a knight who has done him little harm, but whose splendid armour he covets. It is not until he reaches the castle of Gurnemanz that he finds a mentor who is prepared to educate him in matters of chivalry. His fool's attire, which he still wears beneath the real armour, is taken from him, and with it his foolish ways. Gurnemanz instructs him in courtesy, and, more important, in the ethics behind courtesy. 'Never lose your sense of shame' is his first precept, and the second to show compassion to those who suffer. Parzival remembers, but does not understand; he has learnt the outward forms but not the inner meaning.

His second series of exploits starts auspiciously. He wins the heart of Condwiramurs, and marries her. The contrast with Chrétien is sharp. Perceval and Blancheflor are deeply in love but their ties are only casual. Here Parzival and Condwiramurs are bound by the ideal love to which the concept of Minne or love-devotion aspires, the conjugal love of marriage and passionate physical love. When Condwiramurs comes to Parzival's room at dead of night to pour out her troubles to him, they do not even kiss; it is an astonishing scene, when such nocturnal adventures have only one ending in every other romance. And when they marry, their love is so ethereal, 'they so shared togetherness', that Parzival does not think of making love to her for three nights after the wedding. The strength and joy of their earthly loves shines clearly through the beautiful scene when Parzival, now at the end of his adventures, comes to meet his wife at the edge of the lands of Munsalvaesche, the Grail castle, in the grey light of dawn, and finds her asleep with their twin sons. The seneschal wakes the Queen. Clad only in her shift, and a sheet hastily flung round her, with one impetuous movement she is in Parzival's arms. Parzival embraces her; the children wake, and he stoops to kiss them too. The old seneschal and the attendant ladies discreetly retire with the children, and leave the pair alone to prolong the night until the sun stands high in the heavens.

In this ideal marriage Parzival fulfils one half of his nature, the steadfastness in love inherited from his father. Most heroes of romance win their ladies only at the end of the tale. Even apparent exceptions such as Erec and Yvain do not finally secure their beloved's affections until their adventures are over, and their deeds are always carried out with the idea of gaining favour in their lady's eyes. To Parzival, Condwiramurs is both the lady of his love-service and his sustaining hope in his adventures. At one moment, like Chrétien's hero, we find him sunk in ecstasy over three drops of blood in the snow, which remind him of the complexion of his beloved. If we remember that she is also his wife, the difference between Chrétien and Wolfram is evident. The idea for this relationship may well be evolved from Chrétien's married heroes, yet it is transformed by Wolfram's complete acceptance of the situation. Chrétien cannot quite believe that knighthood and marriage are compatible; for Wolfram they are the most natural companions in the world. Even Gawan, whose adventures occupy about half the romance, ends by marrying the proud Orgeluse. Orgeluse is in the French romance an irrational, scornful figure, and it would seem difficult for even Wolfram to make her a convincing character. Yet she becomes entirely human in his hands; her pride and scorn are partly the result of the loss of her lover, partly a test by which she will find the hero who can revenge her on her lover's killer.

Parzival's other inheritance takes us into the moral and religious spheres which are notably absent from Chrétien's unfinished poem. After a time, Parzival asks Condwiramurs to let him go in search of his mother; 'loving him truly, she could not disagree', and he sets out on a quest which, though he does not know it, is to lead not to his mother, but to his fulfilment of his part as guardian of the Grail. It is a task for which he is not yet ready; for though he comes to Munsalvaesche, the Grail castle, he heeds only Gurnemanz's warning that curiosity is rude, and does not ask the crucial question on seeing the Grail borne in procession, and the agony of the Grail-king, Anfortas. (It is noteworthy that Wolfram has his own ideas about the Grail, which he presents as a stone of strange powers which fell from heaven during the struggle between Lucifer and the angels, and which has the power to attract the highest and best in men). The offence of the Grail-king has been to pursue earthly love without permission, thus breaking the laws of the Grail community, and he now lies wounded between the thighs in punishment, until such time as an unknown knight shall come and ask him: 'Lord, what ails thee?' Parzival may observe the outward forms of courtesy and suppress his curiosity, leaving the crucial question unasked: but he forgets its inward essence, humility and compassion. He leaves the desolate castle – which had shone with all the show of a splendid feast on the previous night – in a dark and lonely dawn, with only the curses of the gatekeeper to speed him on his way. As if to show that ordinary men cannot judge between inward and outward courtesy, Parzival rides on to his greatest triumph yet at Arthur's Court, only to have it shattered by the arrival of Cundry, the hideous messenger from the Grail castle, who roundly curses him for his 'falseness', both to his nature and to his destiny.

However, Parzival can only ask the question when he is spiritually ready to do so; and his reactions to Cundry's message show that he is far from such a state of mind or spirit. In the grip of black despair, he curses God for not rewarding his faithful service, and departs in search of the Grail again. He is now farther than ever from it, seeking it *despite* God: the lesson he has to learn is not only compassion and humility, but penitence and the real nature of man's relationship to God.

The extract which follows is the scene in which Parzival is brought to understand these things by his uncle, the hermit Trevrizent. It is the crux of the romance, and what follows it is the accomplishment of his quest.

When 'the story comes to its rightful theme' again after a long digression concerning Gawan's adventures, Parzival and Gawan fight a duel as strangers, in which Parzival is victor, though – as usual in the romances – he recognises Gawan before they have done each other serious injury. A similar combat ensues with Parzival's half-brother Feirefiz, in which the combatants are equally matched; again, they recognise each other in time. In the meanwhile, he has also fought a mutual enemy of his and Gawan's, Gramoflanz. Each of these battles, at this stage of Parzival's spiritual progress, must represent more than another episode in the romance, or they would reduce Parzival to the level of a mere knight-errant like Gawan again. So in the wider symbolism of the poem, Gawan represents earthly chivalry and Gramoflanz pride: both earthly chivalry and pride must be overcome. And Feirefiz, Parzival's pagan half-brother from his father's marriage to the heathen Belakane, is the archetype of natural goodness; despite his strange black and white striped skin, he is as courteous as any of the knights of the Round Table, and as virtuous as any Christian. It is Feirefiz who is the one knight chosen by Parzival to go with him on his journey to claim the kingship of the Grail.

Thus Parzival's trials are now at an end: and on the day of Feirefiz's admission to the Round Table, a day of 'sweet pure clarity', the messenger from the Grail castle returns, to announce that he has been named as King of the Grail, letters which have appeared on the magical stone itself. He rides to Munsalvaesche; the compassionate question is asked, Anfortas healed. The story moves swiftly to its end, telling how Condwiramurs rejoins Parzival, how Feirefiz is converted and married to the bearer of the Grail. The two ways are reconciled; earthly and spiritual chivalry move in harmony.

Parzival is at once the greatest and most human figure in the romances; in him the highest ideal of chivalry is shot through with a warmth and natural ease which owes little to convention. By contrast, Gawan, the secondary hero of the story, is a formal figure, moving within a limited world, but perfect within his own established limits. The idea of orders, levels of achievement according to man's power, enables Wolfram to transcend the old ideals of knighthood, and to set a higher goal without contradicting these cherished images. For this is his real insight: that the chivalry underlying the stories is not merely a matter of rules of good behaviour, of a code of courtly love, or even of religious service. Its strength lies in its appeal to man's better nature while remaining in close contact with the realities of life. The marvellous is only an outward trapping, corresponding to the splendours of Court festivals; what matters is the effect of these great ideals on the mind and soul. Chrétien had started to explore the effect of idealism in love on men's minds; in Parzival, Wolfram extends and completes the search, until his framework of an imaginary world contains the history of the way of Everyman to Salvation.

Wolfram's style is exceptionally difficult, and even his contemporaries, such as Gottfried von Strassburg, found him obscure and puzzling. The translation used here, by M. F. Richey is stylised, but in many ways the language reflects the original rather than being an affectation on the part of the translator. No wholly satisfactory version has yet appeared.

Parzival

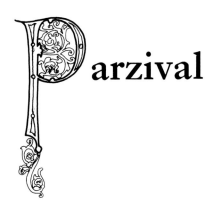

'Open!' To whom? Who are you? 'I would fain come into thy heart to thee.' 'Tis a small space you crave! 'How, shall I scarce find lodging-room? If I press in and enter, thou needst not rue it! I will tell thee of wondrous things.' Yes, is it you, my Lady Adventure? How fares that lovely knight? I mean the noble Parzival, whom Cundrie with harsh words drove forth to seek the Graal, there, where many a lady made lament that nought could avert his going. From Arthur of Britain did he then depart; how fares he now? Take up that tale and say, whether he be all joyless, or has he won high renown? – whether his unbroken prowess be waxen long and broad, or is it shortened or grown small? Tell us of all his hands have wrought! Has he seen Munsalvaesche since that day, and the gentle Anfortas, whose heart was so pierced with sighs? Of your goodness, give us sure tidings now, whether he be released from suffering. Let us hear if Parzival was there, your lord and mine. Declare and show me all his doings! Sweet Herzeloyde's child, how has he fared, that son of Gahmuret, since he left Arthur's court? Has he won victory or defeat in strife? Does he keep to the open, or has he since lain down to take his ease? Tell me of all his ways and doings!

The story tells us that he had passed through many a land on horseback, and in ships crossed the sea, and that whomsoever he met, none ever jousted with him and kept his seat. In many hard fights had he proved his victorious valour, and had caused the renown of others to flag and fail. The sword which Anfortas had given him snapped, as was prophesied, in the first encounter; but the spring which rises near Karnant, whose name is Lac, made it new and whole. That sword brought him many a triumph.

The story tells us how, one day, Parzival, the hardy knight, came riding into a forest, I know not at what time. There his eyes lit on a cell, new-built, with a swift stream flowing through (it was built on one bank and jutted out over the stream). The young undaunted knight rode seeking adventure, and God took thought for his guidance. He found a recluse living there, who had dedicated her virgin life to God and renounced all joy. Sorrow deep-rooted in her woman's heart put forth new blossoms daily; yet the troth from which it had sprung was no wise new.

Schionatulander and Sigune found he there once more. The warrior lay at rest within. She, bowed down upon his coffin, drew breath with anguish still. Duchess Sigune heard no Mass chanted, yet was her whole life here one ceaseless prayer. Her red lips, warm and full, were blanched and pale, since the day when the world's joy forsook her. No maid ever pined so cruelly; because of her grief she dwelt alone.

And because of his love who died for her, whose life was split ere he had won her, she, living, loving, cherished his dead corpse. Had she become his wife, i'faith, Dame Lunet would have made ill speed with that quick counsel which blew the change in her own mistress' mind. We may still see many a one like Lunet ride fast on the trail of some scheme or other. She now, whom constraining modesty and wifely fellowship so rule that no strange love can woo her from her mate, if while he lives she shuns all other pledge, that man, methinks, has found in her his chief desire. Afterwards, let her do as her heart instructs her. Yet, if she still keeps faith, she wears a garland brighter than if she went crowned in mirth to the festive dance.

Why do I measure mirth at all with that stern suffering which Sigune's faithfulness decreed her? Let me forbear to speak of both together!

Over fallen tree-trunks, where no path lay, straight ahead rode Parzival, till he halted before that window, all too near, indeed! – he was vexed when he knew that. But he wished to enquire about the forest, or in what direction his journey tended, and cried out, hoping for answer: 'Is any one within?' 'Yes', answered she. When he heard that it was a woman's voice which spoke, with sudden haste he turned his horse aside on the untrodden grass, chiding himself because he had not lighted down before. His tardiness stung him with shame.

Then he tethered his horse to the branch of a fallen tree. His battle-pierced sword he hung there too. When this was done, and the brave yet gentle knight had of his courtesy loosed his sword from off him, he again approached the window to ask for tidings. The cell was empty of joy, bare of all pleasance; nought found he there but sorrow exceeding great. Then, when he desired her to come to the window, the pale-cheeked maiden rose, meekly courteous, from her bended knees. And as yet he neither knew nor guessed who she was or might well prove to be. She wore a hair-shirt next her skin under her grey gown. Great sorrow was her close companion; that had subdued her proud blithe spirit, overburdened her heart with sighs.

Courteously the maid now came to the window, and with sweet words received the stranger there. She held a psalter in her hand. Parzival the warrior saw that and marked at the same time a ring she wore, which the hardest penance could not wrest from her, but as true love counselled her, she wore it still. A garnet set in the ring glittered out through the darkness like a spark of fire. The fillet that bound her hair was of Sorrow's binding. 'Outside by the wall,' said she, 'Sir, you will find a bench. Sit down, if you care to rest and are travel-weary. For the greeting which calls me hither may God reward you! – even as He rewards all true words spoken.'

The knight, as she then advised him, sat down by the window, in like manner begging her to sit down within. She said: 'It is something new for me to sit and hold converse with any man.' The knight, much wondering at that, began to question her concerning her manner of life and means of living. 'Strange that you dwell so far from the beaten road in this lonely place! Lady, I marvel how you can live at all, where all round you is but waste and wold.'

She said: 'There comes to me sure provision sent thither from the Graal. The sorceress Cundrie takes thought for that; each Saturday night without fail she brings me food enough for the whole week following. If in all else it were well with me, I could content me with the poorest fare; of that I take no heed, I am well sufficed.'

Then Parzival thought she spoke false and that she wished to deceive him in other ways too. Mockingly he asked her: 'For whose sake do you wear that ring? I have always heard say that hermitess or hermit were sworn to shun all amorous dealings.' She said: 'If your speech had power to hurt, you fain would slander me, 'tis clear. If ever I learn to deal falsely and you are present, accuse me then! 'Fore God, I am free of stain; no skill is mine to deceive. This bridal gift I wear for the sake of a dead man, whose love I never won to my possessing with bodily act; the counsels of my virgin heart urge this bestowal of my love upon him.' She paused, and added: 'I have him here within, whose jewel I have kept and worn from the time that the spear of Orilus smote him down.

'All the days and years of my mourning I will give him love in sooth. The guerdon of true love is mine to give him, which he with knightly strength of hand, with shield and spear, valiantly strove to win, until he died in my service. I am a maid, and single, yet in the sight of God he is my husband. If thoughts have the strength of deeds, I know no pretext, none, which can sever henceforth my marriage-tie. His death changed my life to mourning. This ring shall be the token of my marriage-right when we stand in God's presence. The sure pledge of my troth it is; and the tears that spring from my heart bear witness too.

'I am here with another. Schionatulander is the one, the other I myself.' Then Parzival understood that it was Sigune, whereat the shadow of her grief oppressed him too. Straightway and ere he spoke to her again he doffed his coif, and showed her his face uncovered. Then the maiden, perceiving how fair his complexion shone through the iron-grime which stained it, forthwith recognised the hardy knight, and quickly spoke: 'It is you, Sir Parzival! Then say, how fares your seeking of the Graal? Have you yet discovered its true nature, or how has your journey thriven?'

He said to that maiden of noble lineage: 'Much joy did I lose thereby. Sorrow enough and to spare the Graal has brought me! I left behind me a land where I wore crown, and, more, the loveliest wife on earth; of humankind was never a wight so fair. I yearn for the grace of her gentle presence, for her love I mourn, for that, and the far high goal of my striving, to behold Munsalvaesche, and the Graal; unattained is it still. Cousin Sigune, thou doest cruelly to wreak thy hatred on me, seeing thou knowest the burden of my cares, how great it is.' The maid replied: 'All my condemnation of thee, cousin, I here abjure. Thou hast lost much joy indeed through thy delaying of that wondrous question, then, when the gentle Anfortas was thy host, and guardian of thy luck unseen. Hadst thou but questioned, it had won thee in that hour undreamed-of guerdon. Now is thy joy waxed feeble, thy soaring spirit flags with lame wing. Thy heart has made care familiar, which had been all unknown to thee, if touching that matter thou hadst made question then.'

'I did as one whom an ill fate overruleth,' said he. 'Dear cousin, give me counsel, remember how near we are of kin, and tell me also, how stands thy case with thee? I would make lament for thy sorrow, were not my own grief passing heavy, too great for man to bear.'

She said: 'Now may help come to thee from the hand of Him to Whom all care is known, that so thou mayest light on a certain track which will lead thee to Munsalvaesche, whereon, as thou tellest me, thy joy depends. The sorceress Cundrie rode hence but now; always, when she comes, her mule stands waiting, yonder, where the spring gushes from the rock. I would I had asked her if her way lay thither or elsewhere. I counsel thee that thou ride after her. Perchance she is not yet so far but that thou mayest with good speed outride her.' Then was made no long tarrying; the hero bade farewell and, riding forward, came immediately on that fresh track. He followed, but so wild the way became which Cundrie's mule had taken that the forest maze soon blotted out all trace of guidance. And thus, once more, the Graal was lost to him, and joy passed from his mind forgotten. Methinks, if he had then come to Munsalvaesche, he would have questioned, aye, and boldly too, and the tale had been other than it was before.

Now let him ride on his way, wherever it lead him. There came spurring to meet him along that path a knight, bareheaded, clad in a mantle of rich cost and in shining mail. Except for his head, he was fully armed. Towards Parzival he rode at a great pace, crying out: 'Sir, it likes me not that you forge a way through my lord's forest thus! You may look for a sharp reproof to dash your spirits. Munsalvaesche is not wont to let intruders ride so near, an they be not ready to face perilous strife, ay, pay the forfeit which outside these forest bounds is known as death!'

In his hand he carried a helmet with silken cords and a sharp new spear. With angry gesture he bound the helmet on, and addressed himself to do combat. Parzival thought: 'I should be slain forthwith, if I rode over this man's corn! There would be no end to his wrath if that had happened. Here, after all, I do but trample down wild fern. An my two hands fail me not, I will buy the right to pursue my way without check from him!'

With that, they both clashed together; nor did the lance of either knight miss its aim. Many a hostile stroke did Parzival ward off from him. His trained hand and the impulse of his will drove the answering thrust to the point where shield and helmet meet, which hurled the champion of Munsalvaesche from his horse, down an incline so steep that he found no place to rest in.

Parzival came on behind. His horse was too speedy to halt in time, and fell over the edge of the slope right to the bottom, where it lay dashed to pieces. Parzival gripped a cedar branch with his hands, and with his feet caught hold of a ledge of rock. He saw his horse lying dead in the wild ravine. The knight was making good his escape up the opposite side. Parzival climbed back again. The horse, which the other knight had left behind, its feet caught in the reins, stood waiting there. That gain outweighed the loss of his splintered spear. He swung himself on the steed's back and rode, he knew not whither. But he met with no further attack from Munsalvaesche. The Graal evaded him as before, to his great sorrow.

Whoso cares to hear, him will I tell, how after this his fortune fared.

I number not the weeks, nor strive to reckon how long Parzival rode seeking adventure as before. One morning, after a fall of snow, just heavy enough to make the day seem winter, he saw, as he rode through a wide forest, a knight coming towards him, whose beard was grey, his complexion fresh and fair. His wife had the same look of youthful age. Both of them wore cloaks of hodden grey, nothing between that and their skins, for they were on pilgrimage that day. Their children, two young maids who were a joy to look on, were clad the same. All four, as their pure hearts counselled it, walked barefoot. Parzival saluted the old grey knight, by whose counsel he was to find the luck he needed. He looked like a man of high degree. The ladies had with them little dogs, which ran beside them; behind, with lowly mien, knights and squires were walking reverently, all pilgrims, many of them quite young, with faces smooth.

Parzival, the noble knight, had taken fine care of his body's pride, so that now his plumed helmet and glittering arms made a brave show, quite unlike the plain grey garb of the grey-haired man. As they met, he turned his horse aside, then asked what their journey meant, and was told the reason. And the old knight grieved to find that that holy day meant so little to him, seeing he had not learned to ride unarmed, or to walk barefoot, and to celebrate the season's rite.

Parzival answered him: 'Sir, I have no notion what time of the year it is – how the weeks pass and the days are called is a thing I know not. I served one whose name is God, before it pleased him to put me to open shame. My mind had never swerved from him, in whose help I trusted; yet for all that his help has failed me.'

Then said the old grey knight: 'Do you mean God, Whom the Virgin bare? If you believe what He, made man, suffered for us as on this day, which this day's season celebrates, it is not right for you to wear armour thus. To-day is Good Friday, whereon the whole world has cause to rejoice and mourn. Where in all time was shown a love more faithful than when God proved His love for us, Who for our sakes on the Cross was hung? Sir, if you are a Christian, you should mourn for that dire exchange. He gave, to redeem us, His glorious life, made death His price, because mankind was lost, condemned to hell. If you are not a heathen, sir, remember this! Ride further, following our track; there lives not far from here a holy man, he will give you counsel, chasten you where you have gone astray and, if you repent and confess, from sin absolve you.'

His daughters then took up the word. 'Father, what is there to punish? In bad weather like this, what advice to give him! Why not bring him to where he could get warm? His iron-clad arms, for all they appear so knightly, must surely be very cold; he would freeze, were he three times as strong. Thou hast thy lodgings close by, thick warm tents of esclavine; were King Arthur thy guest, thou couldst entertain even him with the food we have. Now be a good host, and invite this knight to come with us.' The old knight said: 'Sir, my daughters speak truth. From a place close by, I come the same time each year to this wild forest, always, be it warm or cold, as it draws towards the Passion and Death of Him, Whose award is sure. Whatever food I have brought I will gladly share with you, God's blessing on it.'

Then the damsels, who much desired it, eagerly begged him to stay and be their guest. He should be welcome, they said, and in truth they meant it. Parzival looked at them and saw that, despite the frost, their mouths were red, warm and full, not sad, as the day prescribed. If I had some little thing to avenge on them, I would fain take a kiss from those lips as forfeit, if they were willing! Women are what they always are – just women! Many a strong man have they enthralled, they best know how.

Parzival heard their sweet entreaty, voices of father, mother, children, pleading in turn. He thought: 'If I turn back, I shall feel ill at ease riding on horseback, with these fair girls, and the rest of them, all on foot. Better to part, since I am at strife with Him Whom they love from their hearts, and Whose help they look to. He has been sparing of His help to me, and has not preserved me from trouble!'

So he said: 'Sir, and lady, let me take leave of you now. May fortune bless you, and give you increase of joy! Sweet maidens, this grace you own, may it bring you a fair reward for your kindness towards me! Let me say farewell.' He bowed, and those others bowed also. And they did not conceal how grieved they were to lose him.

So they parted, and Herzeloyde's child rode on. His manly breeding in itself disposed him to thoughts pure and charitable. But Herzeloyde had bequeathed him more: she, his young mother, bestowed on him at birth true depth of feeling. Repentance stirred in him. Now for the first time verily he thought on his Creator, how great He was. And he said: 'What if God's help can quell my sorrow? Loved He ever a knight, rewarded He ever a knight his service, or, put it thus, if shield and sword be worthy of help from Him, and true knightly prowess, whence His Help may amend my need, if to-day is His day for helping, then let Him help, if help He can!'

He looked back at the spot whence he had ridden. They were still standing there, sorry, kind folk that they were, to see him going. The maidens gazed after him, and he, too, looking back, knew in his heart that he liked to see them, they were so fair.

He said: 'If God's power is so lordly that it can guide both horse and hind, and people too, then will I praise His power. Be it true that God's power can aid, let it guide this charger of mine the best way possible for my journey's goal. That help shall declare His goodness. Forward, as God shall choose!' He let the reins fall on his horse's neck, hurried it with the spur; and the way the steed went led him straight to a place he knew: Fontane la Salvatsche, where he and Orilus had plighted troth. Here lived Trevrizent the Pure, who many a Monday was wont to fast, many a full week too. Wine and bread did he eschew, nor would he touch aught, whether flesh or fish, in which there had been blood. God had so minded him to live out his days in holiness, so to make ready to meet the heavenly host. With stern fastings he chastised and purified himself to withstand the devil.

From him, then, Parzival learned the marvellous hidden history of the Graal. [*Wolfram goes off on a long digression as to how he himself had learned this history, before returning to the matter in hand.*]

He knew a place, though the snow covered it now, where bright flowers had grown before, hard by a mountain wall – the spot where his strong right hand had reconciled Jeschute's lord to her. But the track led further yet, to a spring, and the hermitage near it: Fontane la Salvatsche that place was called. He found the Hermit there who, coming forward to meet him, addressed him thus.

'Alas, sir, what has happened to you, this holy day? Has sharp necessity forced you to don your arms, or have you no call to fight? Another garb, in that case, would beseem you better, if pride could see it. Please to alight, sir – I take it, you will be nothing loath – and warm yourself at a fire. Was it some adventure drew you forth to win love's guerdon? Then, if you treasure a love that is deep and true, love otherwise, give your heart to this day's love. Do service some other day for a lady's smile! Dismount, I pray you.'

Parzival the warrior dismounted forthwith as the Hermit bade, and with great modesty stood facing him. Then he said: 'Sir, give me counsel! I am a man who has sinned.'

'Counsel I guarantee you. By whose direction found you the way hither?'

'Sir, in the forest I met an old grey knight who spoke to me very kindly, so did those with him. He, like a true friend, sent me here to you.'

'That was Kahenis,' the Hermit said. 'He is a man right noble, stands high, and comes of the best blood in Punturteis. His sister is wedded to a king, and he too, is of royal lineage. There are no children born more sweetly mannered than those two fair maids of his whom you saw and spoke to. Each year he comes to me here on pilgrimage.'

Parzival said to his host: 'When I saw you first, were you afraid at all, as I rode up to you? Did you apprehend aught from my coming?' The Hermit answered: 'Sir, believe me, I have been startled oftener by bear or stag than by the approach of man. To speak truth, I fear nothing that man can do: I am skilled to meet it. But that I might seem to vaunt, I could say that not once in my life here I turned to flee. Never, in all my fighting days, did my heart betray me. I was a knight as you are, one, also, who strove to win a fair lady's love. Many a time have I let sinful thoughts mingle with what was pure. My life did I prank out, that a woman I knew might show me favour. All this have I long forgot.

'Give me the rein. There, under that ridge of rock is your horse's stable. We will pluck fir twigs and clumps of fern for him later on; indeed, I have no other fodder.' Parzival wanted him not to take the rein. 'Your good manners should teach you not to resist your host,' was the answer, and he gave way. The Hermit then took and put his horse for him in that same wild stable, under a great shady rock by a rushing stream.

Parzival stood on the snow, and the keen air smote through him: frailer than he could have ill endured the cold feel of his armour. His host took and led him into a cave, which shut out the wind: on the hearth a fire burned. The sight of the glowing coals made the guest feel glad. His host lit a candle for him; by this light the warrior doffed his arms. A pile of brushwood and fern made a pleasant seat. His limbs grew warm, his skin glowed rosy. Well might he be forest-weary, for he had spent last night, and many a night, with no roof to his head, had ridden many a desolate track for weeks together. Now he found a good host and true.

A mantle lay there. His host lent him this to put on and led him into another cave, where lay the holy books from which he read. An altarstone, bare in accordance with that day's custom, stood there, and a casket on it. This Parzival knew at once for the one whereon he had sworn an unperjured oath that had changed Jeschute's grief to joy. And he said to his host: 'Sir, I know the look of this casket and recognise it, for on it I swore an oath one time when I stopped here in passing. I found here, beside it, a gilded spear. I took that away with me, sir, and, from what I have heard, won some glory by it. Thus it was: I fell to thinking about my wife, and so lost myself in thought that my senses left me. With that spear in my hand I fought two fair jousts, nothing knowing. *Then* I stood high in honour; *now* there is no man more burdened with care than I. Sir, of your courtesy, tell me, how long may it be since I took that spear away?'

The holy man said: 'My friend Taurian forgot it and left it here; he rued that later. Five years and three days have passed since then: if you will listen to me, I can

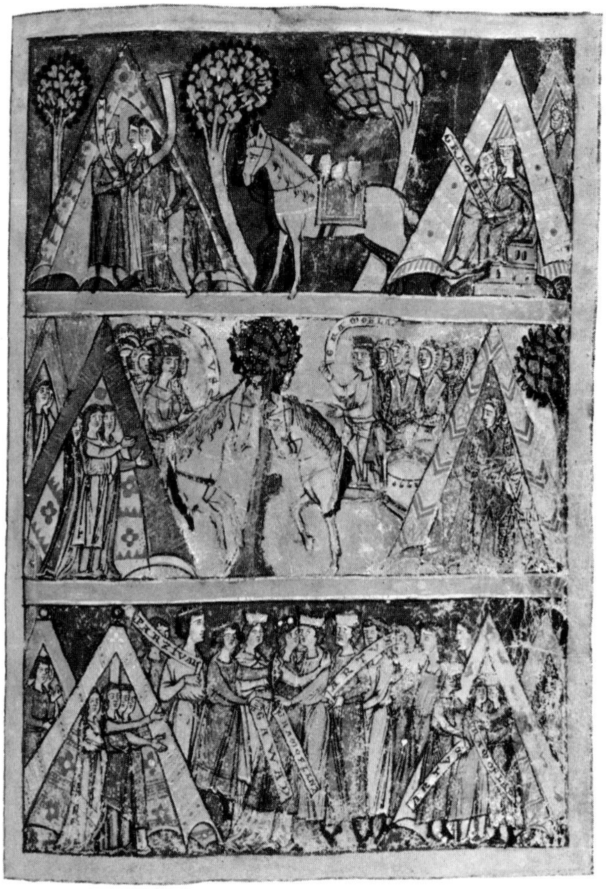

Illustrations for Wolfram von Eschenbach's Parzival, *from a thirteenth century manuscript. All the episodes are from the last three books: these pictures deal with the adventures of Gawain, showing his reconciliation with his enemy Gramoflanz. (Munich, Staatsbibliothek, MS Germ.19 f.49)*

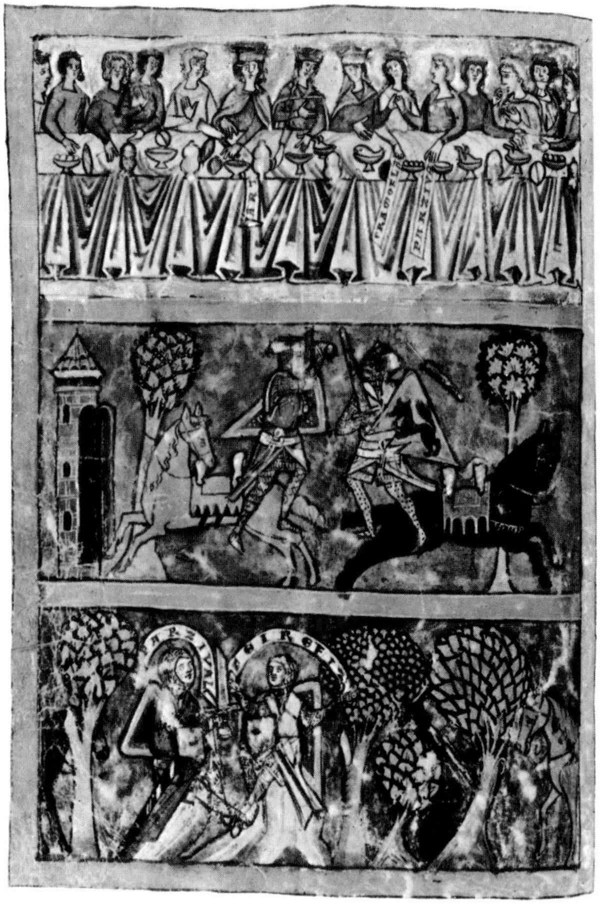

The adventures of Gawain and Parzival continued: in the top scene Gramoflanz weds Gawain's sister, while in the centre Parzival fights his half-brother Feirefiz. The bottom scene shows them recognizing each other. (f.49^{v})

show you how.' From his psalter he read the tale of the years and weeks which lay between. 'Now for the first time do I perceive,' said Parzival, 'how long I have gone unguided, lorn of joy. To me, joy is a dream, grief, the burdensome yoke under which I labour.

'Sir, I will tell you more. Wherever, in church or minster, God's praise was sung, no eye has seen me since that day. I have cared for nought else but fighting. Yes, and I bear great enmity towards God, for He has fathered my sorrows and made them mighty. My joy is buried alive. If God's power were ready to help, what an anchor my joy would have been! Now it has nought to hold to, grief sucks it down. If my hope is wounded past help, or if it survives the scar wherewith sorrow's sharp crown has branded my knightly prowess, each way I maintain, it is a shame of Him Who has power to help, if all they say of His help be true, that He helps not me!'

His host sighed, and looked at him. Then he said: 'Sir, if you are wise, put your trust in God. He will help you, for he is sworn to help. May God help us both! Sir, you had best explain (please to sit down), tell me calmly and with temperate speech how that wrath was kindled, which has caused you to war with God. Of your courtesy, hear me first with patience: let me prove His innocence, ere you accuse Him to me. His help has never been known to fail.

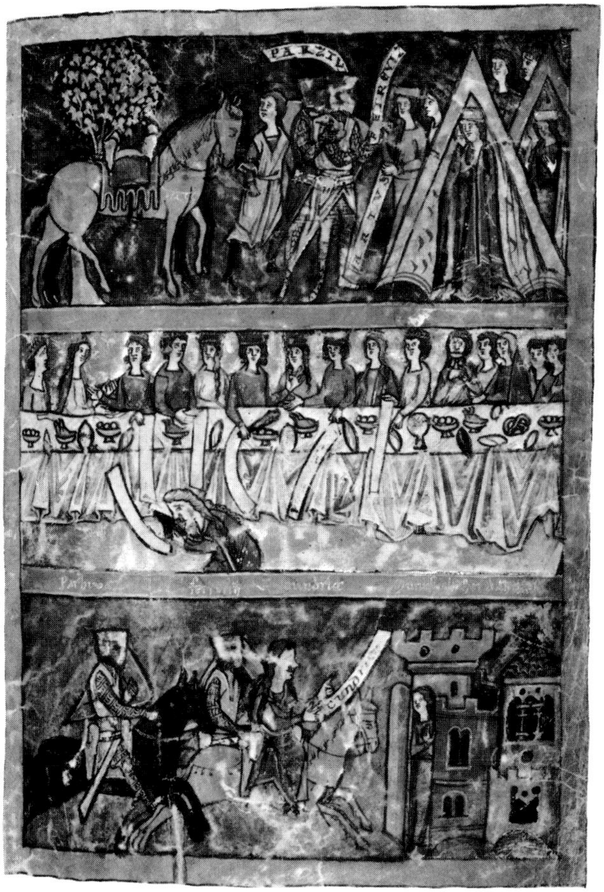

The adventures of Parzival continued. He and Feirefiz arrive at Arthur's court, where (centre) the Grail messenger Kundrie begs for his forgiveness, and (below) leads him to the Grail castle. (f.50)

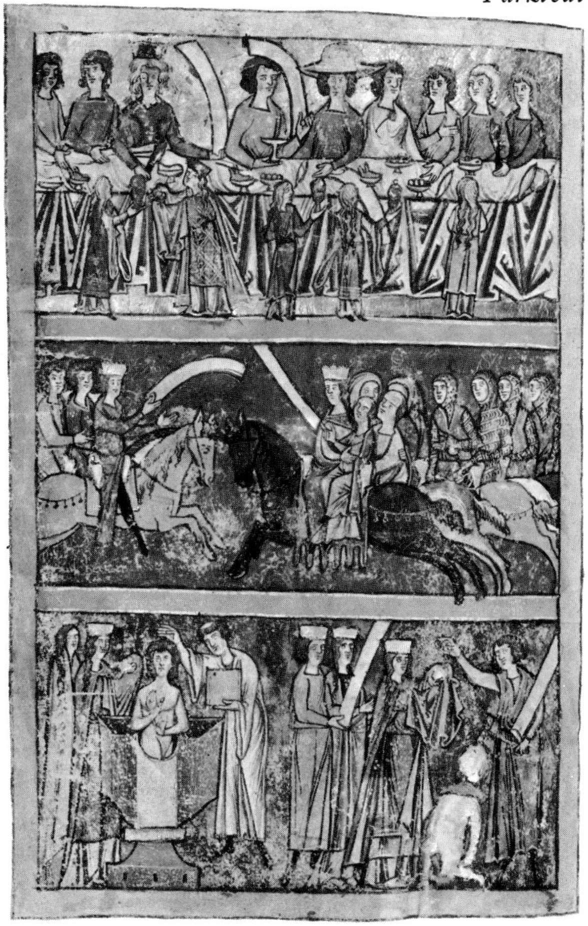

The conclusion of Parzival's adventures. The Grail feast is shown at the top; in the centre, Parzival and his beloved Kondwiramurs are reunited, and at the bottom Feirefiz is baptised in the presence of the girl whom he loves, Repanse de Schoye, bearer of the Grail. (f.50ᵛ)

'While I was yet a layman, even then I knew how to read and write what the Scriptures taught, how a man should steadfastly serve Him Who never wearies in giving help to sustain the soul. Be true, nothing wavering, since God Himself is Truth: all false arts to him are alien. We must believe in Him, He has done so much for us, seeing His high and glorious strain humbled itself to become like man. God is, as He is called, our Surety. All false ways does He abhor. Think upon that: He can forsake no man. Learn to do likewise, be on your guard and see you are true to Him.

'You can win nothing from Him by rage or hate. Whoever saw you strive to contend with *Him* would take you for a fool! Now mark how Lucifer fared, he and his fellows. They were once without gall: God only knows whence sprang that malice in them which, grown to everlasting strife, reaps bitter reward in hell. Astiroth and Belcimon, Belet and Radamant, that shining heavenly host became through malice and hatred black as hell.

'When Lucifer passed hellward with his host, after that, to succeed him, a man was made. God from the earth fashioned the noble Adam. From Adam's body He took and severed Eve who, through neglect of her Creator's bidding, brought misery on us. Of these, two sons were born. One, puffed up by his intemperate will to pride insatiate, robbed his ancestress of her maidenhead. Many a man, when he hears this, waits not to hear more but straightway questions how that could be. Howbeit, the tale of that guilt is no vain fable.'

Parzival answered: 'Sir, I do not think it could have been. How was that man born by whom, as you say, his ancestress was robbed of her maidenhead? You should not have told me *that*.'

'I will solve you the riddle,' the Hermit said. 'The earth was Adam's mother: on the fruits of the earth was he reared. The earth, at that time, was virgin soil. Cain, son of Adam, slew Abel his brother for the sake of a little wealth: when that blood was shed on the earth, her virgin purity was smirched and fouled. That was the first strife between man and man; and so it has continued from age to age.

'In the world there is nothing so pure as a stainless maid. God Himself was the maiden's child. There were two men thus born. God took on Himself a countenance and form like that of the first maiden's child: that was a gracious bending of His high will. Of Adam's race sorrow and joy are sprung, since He, Whom all angels serve, stooped to be of our kin, and since the legacy of our kin is guilt and evil. May the power of Him, with Whom compassion dwells, have mercy on us, since His true manhood strove so faithfully against all things false and wicked.

'You must make peace with Him, if you treasure your soul's salvation. Atone for sin; be not so free in words and works; for he who wreaks his own sufferings with wanton speech shall at last learn that his own mouth condemns him. Hear what was said of old: Plato the sage and the prophetic Sibyl foretold, long ages past, the coming of Him by Whom all debts were paid. The hand of the Highest with divine true love freed us all from hell save those, whose wantonness condemned them.

'Of that True Lover are these sweet tidings told: He is a clear-shining light, and swerves not in His love. Well for him, to whom His love is shown. All men are free to choose His love or brook His wrath. Think, which of these two is better? The unrepentant sinner shuns the offer of divine true love. He who atones for his sins shall earn the grace of Him Who penetrates our thoughts to the very core. Though thought can shut out the sun, though it need no lock to guard its secret, though it be dark as night, yet the brightness of the Godhead glances through it, pierces that screen of darkness and, spear-like, drives home with soundless thrust the unseen stroke which shakes and thrills the heart. There is no thought so swift but, ere it flash into utterance, it is judged and known. God sees, and approves the thoughts that are pure and humble. Then if God so tries our inmost thoughts, what hope for deeds unsound? When a man so forfeits His grace by sinful deeds, whereat the Godhead veils its light for shame, to what end was he reared and bred, where shall the wretched soul find sanctuary? Then, since God offers you choice of wrath and love, wronging Him, you work out your own perdition. Come, change your heart, that He in His goodness may draw near and bless you!'

Parzival answered: 'Sir, I am very glad you have told me of Him Who, I see now, leaves nothing unrewarded, whether it be good or ill. I have spent my youth in care to this day and, because I continued faithful, have been sore troubled.'

The Hermit said: 'If there is nought to hide, speak, I will gladly hear what trouble and what sin you harbour. If you will lay them before me, I can perhaps give you counsel which you yourself have not.' Parzival answered and said: 'My chief need is for the Graal, after that, for my own wife – no fairer creature ever drew suck from its mother's breast. My heart yearns for them both.'

The Hermit said: 'Sir, you speak truth: you are indeed hard pressed, since it is for your own wife you pine so sorely. If you are true to wedlock, then, though you suffer the pangs of hell, that distress will pass: God will deliver you straightway. You say also, you long for the Graal. Foolish man, I am grieved to hear it! No one can ever find where the Graal lies hid, save the Graal's elect, whose name is foretold of heaven. That is the truth: I have proved it with my own eyes and know for sure.'

Parzival said: 'Were you there?' The Hermit replied: 'Sir, I was.' Parzival did not tell that he also had come thither. He asked to hear all about the Graal, what was its nature.

The Hermit told him. 'It is well known to me how that many a warrior, valiant and strong of hand, dwells at Munsalvaesche to guard the Graal. These at all times ride forth and hazard their lives in combat. Be the end defeat or victory, these knights, these templars, make atonement both ways for sin.

'By the strength of that war-like band the place is guarded. I will tell you now how they are fed. They are nourished by a stone most precious: its name is *lapsit exillis*. By the power of that stone the phoenix, lighting upon it, is burnt to ashes; but the ashes then quicken it back to life, when, with bright new wings, it springs from the pyre revived and beautified. There was never a man so ill, but on whatever day he beheld that stone, for the space of the whole week following he cannot die. Nor shall his colour fade. Be it maid or man, whoso beholds that stone shall keep the freshness of life's prime. If one looked at that stone for two hundred years, but for the hair grown grey, no other sign of age would appear. Such power comes from the stone that flesh and bones are made young by it. Its other name is the Graal.

'There comes to it this day an embassy, whereon its chief power depends. It is Good Friday to-day, at which season a dove flies down from heaven, carrying in its beak a small white ubbly, and leaves it on the stone, then spreads its glistening wings and flies back to heaven. Always on Good Friday it brings, I tell you, that from which the stone receives in essence all the earth can yield of food or beverage, savours of Paradise, to have, and to give anew: fish, flesh or fowl. By the power of the Graal that knightly brotherhood receives food daily.

'Hear next, how those chosen to serve the Graal are named and known. Name and lineage of each one chosen for that blest journey, boy or maid, appears inscribed on the stone in magic letters, when the time is due. None dare efface those characters, they remain until they are read, then fade away. All who have grown up in that company were children when they came. From many lands are they gathered and brought thither. Rich and poor rejoice in like measure, whose children are summoned to join that band. There they are evermore immune from sin and shame, and have good reward in heaven.

'They who took neither side, when Lucifer and the Trinity joined battle, those fair high angels were sent down to earth, to have charge of that stone. I know not if God forgave them in the end or condemned them further. Since then, the stone has been in the keeping of those whom God elected and to whom He sent his angel. Sir, such is the nature of the Graal.'

Then answered Parzival: 'If knightly prowess can win renown in this life, Paradise for the soul as well, with shield and spear, I am one whose thoughts have turned always to deeds of prowess. I fought wherever I found cause to fight, and in such wise, that honour lies within reach of my strong right hand. If God is a judge of fighting, He should elect me to that company, that they may know me for what I am: no shunner of battle!' His host made answer: 'Nay, but there you would have to humble your will and beware of pride. Your youth may easily tempt you to excess. Pride always sank and fell,' said the Hermit, and his eyes filled with tears as he recalled a tale, which he now told.

'Sir,' he said, 'there was a king; he was called and is still called Anfortas. You and I, poor though I be, should never cease to pity from our hearts his sad affliction, which was the reward of pride. His youth and princely pride turned to his hurt, and to the world's grief concerning him, because he set his desire on a love unchartered.

'That way runs counter to the Graal's decree. Under this, both knight and squire are pledged to resist all wantonness. Humility has ever vanquished pride. There dwells a noble brotherhood, whose armed strength has warded off the people of all lands, so that the Graal is unknown, save to those who are singled out by name to join the company of Munsalvaesche. Only one came there unsummoned: that was a young fool, who took sin away with him, since he spoke not a word to his host touching the misery he saw him bear. I will reproach no man; but yet, he must pay dear for that sin, inasmuch as he did not ask his host what ailed him. He was so bowed and stricken, anguish the fellow of his was never known.

'Before that, King Lehelin came riding thither, to the shores of Lake Brumbane, where brave Lybbeals stood ready to oppose him, who in that fight was slain. Then Lehelin took and led away his horse; and so robbed the dead.

'Sir, are you Lehelin? There stands in my stable a horse like those belonging to the knightly bands which serve the Graal. The saddle shows the device of the turtle-dove: that horse comes from Munsalvaesche! It was Anfortas bade that the steeds, too, should wear the emblem which, from earliest times, their shields had borne. Titurel bequeathed this to his son, King Frimutel, who, wearing it, was struck down in combat. *He* loved his own wife so dearly, no woman since was so beloved of man. You should renew his custom and love your wife from your heart. You should be like him: your looks resemble his. Ah, sir, whence come you then? Pray let me know your lineage!'

Each one looked hard at the other. Parzival said to his host: 'Sir, I was born of a man who lost his life fighting, because of his valiant heart. Sir, of your goodness, give him a place in your prayers! My father was called Gahmuret, and was an Angevin by birth. Sir, I am not Lehelin. If ever I robbed the dead, it was when I had no wisdom. Nevertheless, so I did: I must confess that crime. Ither of Cumberland was slain by my sinful hand. I laid him dead on the grass, and took, what there was to take.'

'O world, why doest thou so?' said the Hermit, he was vexed at those tidings. 'Thou givest thy people more cumber and rue than joy: such is thy guerdon! So ends thy song and thy story.' Then he said: 'Dear sister's son, what help could I give thee now? Thou hast slain thine own life. If thou bring thy guilt before God, then, since you were both of one blood, if God exacts the penalty that is just, thy life is forfeit. What recompense wilt thou give Him for Ither of Gaheviez? Such nobleness did God reveal in him as left this world the purer. 'Twere right if women spurned thee for his fair sake. So loyally did he serve them so well, all women's eyes shone for joy when they saw him. May God have mercy on thee for a sin so grievous! My sister, too, died sorrowing after thee, thy mother Herzeloyde.'

'No, no, dear sir, what do you tell me now?' said Parzival. 'If I were lord of the Graal, that could never compensate me for these last news. If I am your sister's child, deal truly by me, and tell me faithfully, are these tidings sure?'

Then answered that good man: 'I am not one who can deceive. Thy mother's loving heart so wrought with her that, on thy parting from her, she straightway died. Thou wast the dragon which, suckled at her breast, flew far away, as came to pass in the dream she had, ere in love she bore thee.

'Of two more sisters I have still to tell. One, Schoysiane, died when her child was born. Duke Kyot of Katelangen was her husband, who, when he lost her, renounced all other joy. Sigune, his little daughter, was left in thy mother's care. Deep in my heart, the death of Schoysiane grieves me still. A steadfast sanctuary of grace was her pure spirit. Another sister of mine, Repanse de Schoye, in stainless purity lives yet, and is guardian of the Graal which weighs so heavy that no false wight can raise it. Her brother and mine is Anfortas who, by right of birth, both was, and is, Lord of the Graal. From him, alas, all joy is fled, but that he hopes his suffering will one day bring him to everlasting peace. It is a strange tale which I will tell thee, nephew, how he came to that dolorous pass. Thou wilt pity his misery then, if thy heart be true.

'When Frimutel, my father, lost his life, his eldest son was chosen to succeed him, as king, and as captain of the Graal's elect. That was my brother Anfortas, who was worthy of crown and realm. We were both small at the time. My brother now reached the age when, at the dawning of manhood, Youth is wont to contend with Love. Herein Love is to blame, that she presses her friends too sorely. But if any lord of the Graal seek love outside his ordinance, he must suffer hard punishment for it, and grievous bale.

'My lord and my brother chose him a lady for his love, as seemed to him then, in fair knightly fashion. Who she was does not matter now. In her service he fought with a spirit that knew no fear: many a shield was pierced through by his princely hand. He, in the flower of his sweet youth, with hazardous deeds achieved such glory that, in all lands where chivalry held sway, he knew no rival. *Amor* was his battlecry! But that watchword does not go far to correct and humble.

'One day the king rode out alone (much did his people rue it), in quest of adventure, in the hope of love's guerdon. Love's desire pricked him to it. Then was he wounded by an envenomed spear, was thy sweet uncle, smitten in combat through the privy parts with hurt so sore that it has never healed. 'Twas a heathen who fought with him there and dealt that stroke, one born in Ethnise, where from Paradise the Tigris flows. This same heathen was sure that his valour would win him mastery of the Graal. In the spear his name was graven. He was come into far-off lands in quest of chivalry, drawn by the Graal and by no other power. By the stroke of his lance our joy lay slain.

'Thy uncle's fighting was worthy of all praise. With the spear in his body he rode thence. When that young, gallant man was come home to his own, great indeed was their sorrow! The heathen lay slain where he left him. We will spare our lament for *him*!

'When the king returned to us so pale, and with his strength all ebbing, came a physician who, plucking at the wound, found the spear-head and a splinter of the shaft embedded in it, and pulled them out. Then I fell on my knees in prayer. And I vowed, in supplication to God's power, that I would nevermore do deeds of prowess, so that God, for His great name's sake, might help my brother from that sore pass. I also forswore meat, bread and wine, and all things with blood in their veins, saying I would nevermore desire them. That was new cause of lament to our people, dear nephew, as I may tell thee, that I parted thus from my sword. They said: "Who shall be guardian now of the Graal's mystery?" Bright eyes grew dim with weeping.

'Straightway, looking for help from God, they carried the king to where he could see the Graal. When he beheld the Graal, his anguish deepened, since he could not die, for to die beseemed him not, seeing I had given myself to a life poor and needy and the lordship of that high race on his weak life hung. The king's wound was poisoned in such wise that all the books of medicine which we searched proved barren, and all the cures which wise physicians knew, as antidotes to all stings of venomous reptiles, could yield no help. God Himself refused their aid to us.

'We sought help of Geon and Fison, Eufrates and Tigris, the four streams of Paradise, to find if they had drifted any herbs whose Eden fragrance, not yet lost, could cure our bane. That was lost labour.

'Yet we tried other and diverse cures. The bough wherewith the Sibyl declared Eneas proof against hell's pestilence and the reek of Phlegethon we tried, if perchance that hateful spear had been tempered in hell's hot venom. But it was not so. We took of the pelican's blood and smeared it on the wound, as we best knew how; that did not help us. We tried the unicorn's heart, the carbuncle lodged in its forehead beneath the horn, the potent herb which is called dracontea. Nought availed us.

'Then we fell on our knees before the Graal. All at once we saw written thereon that a knight should come thither, from whose lips a question heard would end our trouble, but if anyone, child, maid or man, warned him at all, his question would give no help, we should be in ill case as before, our hearts the sadder. The writing said: "Do you understand? Your warning may turn to hurt. If he does not question the first night here, the question will lose its power. But if in the right hour that word is spoken, he shall be king, and an end shall be made of your cumber by God's high hand. Then Anfortas shall be healed, but shall rule no longer."

'So we read on the Graal that the sufferings of Anfortas would cease, when the question was put to him. And we salved the wound with anything that could soothe it, nard and theriak, and with their sweetness mingled the fragrant smoke of lignum aloae, for he was in pain at all times. Then I withdrew to this place. A joyless lot is my life's portion. Since then, a knight came riding to Munsalvaesche. He might have spared his coming! Of him I told thee before, how he brought shame on himself by his conduct there, seeing he beheld that great and real affliction yet said not to his host: "Sir, what has caused your suffering?" Since his stupidity held him from questioning then, he missed great blessing by it.'

They were both sad at heart. By that time, it was almost noon. The Hermit said: 'Let us go look for food. Thy horse is without provision; so are we, unless God show us where. There is little smoke from my kitchen! Thou must excuse this lack, both to-day, and so long as thou art my guest. I could teach thee the virtue of roots and herbs, if the snow would let us. God grant, that it soon thaw! Meanwhile, let us break yew twigs for fodder. Thy horse, I fear, will not fare so well here as at Munsalvaesche! – yet no host could gladlier serve it and thee, if the means lay ready.'

They went out, then, to hunt for food. Parzival saw to the steed's provender. The Hermit dug roots for their own meal, then, since his rule forbade him to break fast before nones, hung them on branches of shrubs and searched for more. Many a day he went without food entirely, having missed the place where it hung.

The two companions went to wash herbs and roots in the running stream. No sound of mirth came from their lips. In silence they washed their hands. Parzival twisted the sprigs of yew wreathwise and gave them his horse to feed on. Then they went back to their seats by the coal fire. There was no meat to boil or roast, and no need of kitchen. Parzival, out of the true affection he bore his host, thought wisely that here was enough and better fare than when he had supped with Gurnemanz, and afterwards when, in the presence of many fair ladies at Munsalvaesche, he had had rich entertainment from the Graal.

The Hermit said: 'Nephew, thou must not despise this fare. Poor though it be, thou wilt not quickly find a host more loving.' Parzival answered: 'Sir, may I lose God's blessing, if ever I found entertainment that liked me better.'

When they had finished, they rose and went out, Parzival and the holy man, to the horse's stable. The kindly host spoke to the steed in mournful tones: 'I grieve for thy hunger, thou wearing a saddle stamped with the very arms which Anfortas bore in battle!'

And now that the steed had been fed and groomed, they faced new sorrow. Parzival said to his host: 'Sir, my dear uncle, if I dared speak for shame and tell you of it, I would, and make lament for my ill-luck. Of your gentleness, pray you, forgive! My love, trusting you, flies to you for refuge. I have committed a wrong so great that, if you let me pay the price, there is no hope for me, nor shall I ever again be free from sorrow. Pity my folly then, and give me counsel! He who came riding to Munsalvaesche, he who beheld that real and true distress and, seeing it, put no question, that was I, wretched wight! In this way, sir, did I sin.'

'Nephew,' the Hermit said, 'what sayest thou now? We may both take grief to our hearts and let joy slide, since thy wisdom knew no better than to spurn its blessing. Those five senses God had given thee, it seems, denied thee counsel. What a slack watch did they keep on thy true heart just then, when the wound of Anfortas was thy concern!

'Yet I will not falter in counsel, nor shouldst thou grieve too sorely. Thou shouldst in right measure grieve and abstain from grieving. Human nature has its own strange ways. It may hap, that youth is on the right road to wisdom; then if age in its turn act stupidly and clog with gloom young ways that are clear and honest, that, indeed,

Perceval, on his first visit to the Grail castle sees the Grail procession and fails to ask the vital question, 'Whom does the Grail serve?' From a North French manuscript dated 1274.
(Paris, Bibliothèque Nationale, MS Fr. 342 f.84v)

may sully whiteness, and wither the green plant from which many a noble flower might bud and blow. If I could renew thy verdure and embolden thy heart, and so quicken thee to win high honour and put thy trust in God, thou mightest thrive so nobly as to find recompense therein: God Himself would not forsake thee.

'Thus, in God's place, acting as surety for Him, I give thee counsel.

'Now tell me, didst thou see the spear at Munsalvaesche, in the palace hall? When the star of Saturn had run its course, that was made known to us by the wound, and by the summer snow. Thy sweet uncle then, as the frost smote through him, suffered worse anguish than frost before this had caused him. There was no help but to thrust the spear into the wound; one agony cured the other; it was this that stained the spear blood-red. Certain stars in their courses augment the people's woe; likewise the changes of the moon gall the wound right sorely. At the season which I have named, the king can find no ease: the frost so pierces him that his flesh grows colder than snow. Then since the venom on the spear is hot, they lay it on the wound; that draws the frost out of the body, when it hardens, and cleaves to the spear as ice. There is then no way to sever it from the spear but by the means which Trebuchet wrought for that purpose, the cunning smith, two silver knives that cut clean through the ice and break it. Asbestos, they say, is a wood that can never burn; yet, let a particle of this glass fall on it, sparks fly, and fire is kindled. So potent is that venom!

'The king can neither ride nor walk, nor stand nor lie. He leans, without sitting, as sore experience has taught him. When the moon changes, he suffers much. There is a lake called Brumbane: thither, when the wound grows noisome, they bear the king, that the sweet air may cleanse it. He calls that his fishing day, whence the tale grew that he was a fisherman! That name has clung to him, howbeit scarce likely it is that he, in his suffering state, can catch salmon or lamphreys or ply any sport at all, to cheer his sorrow.'

'On that lake,' said Parzival, 'I saw the king, in a boat which lay anchored. I had ridden many a mile that day, on the way thither, had left Pelrapeire about mid-morning. That evening I wondered where I could find lodging for the night. My uncle it was, who directed me where to go.'

'That was a perilous ride,' the Hermit said, 'through many an outpost well guarded. Each has its own strong garrison, whence not often a man has contrived to pass unchallenged. It is dangerous work to encounter those armed guards. They accept no man's surrender; they stake their lives against the invader's life. In such wise it is granted them to atone for sin.'

'Well, that time,' said Parzival, 'I passed through unattacked till I found the king. His palace hall, as I witnessed it that evening, was filled with lament and dolour. A squire rushed in by the door, at whose coming lament broke forth and the walls resounded. He held in his hands a spear, which he bore to each of the four walls in turn; the uplifted point was stained red with blood. At the sight of that the people lamented greatly.'

His host replied: 'Nephew, never before nor since was the king so tortured with pain as then, when the star Saturn proclaimed its coming, with measure more fierce than its wont of frost and snow. It was no use to lay the spear on the wound, as at other times: it had to be thrust right in. The sphere of Saturn revolves at a height so far, that the frost was felt by the wound before it came. The snow, for all its speed, fell not before the second night of that summer storm. It was while they strove to combat the king's frost that the people took part in his suffering, and mourned for sorrow.'

Parzival said to his uncle: 'I saw twenty-five maidens there, who in fair order stood before the king.' The Hermit answered: 'Maidens, by God's decree, are elected to serve the Graal which, in the order of their ministry, thou sawest, they walked before. Knights, also, are appointed to guard the Graal in pure and faithful service. And (as I said) the seasons when the high stars have run their courses bring great suffering on the people there, both old and young. God has been wroth with them too long: when shall they see joy?

'Nephew, now will I tell thee what thou mayest accept as true. A twofold chance is theirs, which occurs often, to give, and to receive, blessing and boon. They receive young children sent thither to join that service, fair children of high degree. And wherever a land is left lordless, if the people have faith in God and pray for a lord to be sent them from the Graal, that prayer is granted. Him they must serve in pure allegiance: the blessing of God watches over him while he is there.

'God sends the men forth secretly; maids are openly bestowed in marriage. Know, that King Castis desiring to wed thy mother, she, Herzeloyde, with all fair circumstance was given him then to wife. He, however, was fated not to enjoy her love: death laid him in the grave too soon. Ere that befell, he had endowed her with Waleis and Norgals, two lands, and their cities, Kanvoleis and Kingrivals, to hold in her own right. The king might live no longer. It was on the way home that he lay down to die. Then was she crowned queen over two lands. And hence it came, that Gahmuret fought and won her.

'Thus the maids are sent forth openly from the Graal, the men in secret, that their fruit may be gathered back into the Graal's service, if so be their children are destined to join the elect of that band. God's will is well able to point them the way thither.

The procession of the Grail, from an early fourteenth century Parisian manuscript. (Paris, Bibliothèque Nationale, MS Fr. 12577, f.84v)

'He who has pledged himself to serve the Graal must forego love towards women. Only the king is allowed in single purity a wife by law, and otherwise those who are sent to rule over lordless lands. I overstepped that command and joined Love's soldiery. My fresh-blown youth and a fair lady's grace so fired my blood that, in her service, I rode full oft a-jousting where strife was peril. Wild adventures seemed to me so delightful that I cared not for tilt or tourney. Her love brought joy to my heart; for her sake I fought many a combat. The power of her love forthsped me to seek out hazardous occasions in far strange lands. Thus did I earn her love: all who fought with me, baptized or heathen, were the same to me in strife. Methought her guerdon was all I could desire.

'So for my lady's sake I went warfaring over three parts of the earth, in Europe and in Asia and far-off in Africa. When I wished to fight great combats I rode towards Gauriun. I have also fought many a joust before Mont Famorgan. I waged splendid warfare where Agremontin bars the way. On one side of that mountain, he who seeks combat there sees fiery men come forth to the encounter; on the other, no flame gives aid to the men who fight. I jousted there; and when after that I had journeyed towards Rohas, still seeking adventure, out came a valiant host of Wends to give answering battle.

'From Seville I sailed all round the sea till I arrived in Cilli, out past Aquileia through Friuli. O joy and woe that ever I saw thy father, whom, in the course of that journey, I chanced to meet. For, as I entered Seville, I found the noble Angevin lodged there before me; nor can I cease, even now, to rue his journey, which led him deathward oversea to Baldac's walls. There he lay slain in battle. Even as thou has said. I know it, to my great sorrow.

'It was my brother's custom to send me forth, secretly, on many a chivalrous emprise in ways unknown. When I left Munsalvaesche, I would take with me his seal, and so came first to the castle of Karchobra, to the meeting of sea and river where, on the seal's authority, the castellan gave me squires to go with me, and rich equipment for the wild perils of knighthood whereto I journeyed. In giving, he spared no cost. I had to come there alone. On my return I would stop with him again to leave my retinue; and so rode back alone towards Munsalvaesche.

'Now, my dear nephew, listen. When thy noble father saw me, for the first time, there in Seville, although he had never seen my face before, straightway he declared I was the brother of his own wife, Herzeloyde. And, in truth, there is no denying. I was as fair a man then as any alive – I was still young and beardless. He visited me in my lodging. To what he said I swore many a contradiction, but since he persisted in his claim I at last gave way, telling him as a secret who I was, to his great joy.

'We made an exchange of presents. That casket of mine which thou knowest – greener than clover – was wrought from a precious stone, his gift to me. He also gave to serve me as squire one most pure and loyal, his cousin Ither, King of Cumberland. Then we made no long tarrying: we parted, and went each our separate ways, he to aid the Baruch, and I towards Rohas.

'From Cilli I rode towards Rohas; for three Mondays I fought there hard and long. Methought I had fought well there! After that I came riding with all good speed into wide-walled Gandin, whence thy grandsire Gandin had his name, and where Ither was recognised by those who knew him. The site of that place is where the Graian flows into the Trau, a stream with gold in it. There Ither was loved and wooed by thy father's sister, to whom Gandin of Anjoy had given that land to rule. She is called Lammire, the land is Styria. He who plies the service of the shield must roam through many lands!

'But now I am grieved for my red squire, for whose sake she welcomed me with honour. Thou thyself art of Ither's kin; yet thy hand denied the bond of kinship. God, however, has not forgotten it: He can still put it to the test. If thou wouldst live truly in God's sight, thou must pay him the forfeit due. In sorrow I tell thee this: thou art guilty of two great sins. Ither fell by thy hand; thou hast cause also to mourn for thy mother's death. Her deep true love for thee so ordered it that thy last parting from her cut short her life. Now follow my advice, atone for thy sins, and so take thought for thy end that what thou sufferest here may be rewarded yonder, and thy soul find peace.'

The Hermit questioned him further without chiding: 'Nephew, thou hast not told me yet where thy horse came from.' 'Sir, I won it in combat, after I left Sigune. I spoke with her from outside her cell. It was after that I sent a knight flying from his horse and led it thence. He was from Munsalvaesche.'

'If thou art going to rob the Graal's people thus and despite this imagine thou canst gain their love, those are thoughts without reason.' 'Sir, I won it in fair fight. If anyone lays that to my charge, let him first judge how the matter stands. I had lost my own horse before.'

Then Parzival asked a new question. 'Who was the maiden that bore the Graal? They lent me her mantle.' The Hermit said: 'Nephew, if it was hers (she is thy mother's sister), she did not lend it thee to boast of. She thought thou wast to be lord of the Graal and her, and of me too. Thy uncle, he also, gave thee a sword, whereby thou didst cover thyself with sin, since thy fair-spoken mouth, alas, was mute, and did not question. Let that sin be laid with the rest; we will go sleep now to-day is ended.' They went and lay down on a pile of leaves and mould. Neither bed nor quilt was brought them. That couch was little worthy of their high rank.

Parzival stayed there for fifteen days. Roots and herbs were the best fare they had, but he bore that gladly. There was sweet recompense in their talks together; for his uncle freed him from sin, yet gave him counsel which beseemed a knight.

One day, before he left, Parzival asked concerning one other thing. Who the old man was he had seen lying stretched on a couch before the Graal, grey-haired, yet with a fair clear skin? The Hermit answered: 'That was Titurel, thy mother's grandsire. He, first, was chosen to defend the Graal. Now, crippled by a disease called gout, he lies helpless, yet remains fair as of yore, because he has seen the Graal so often that he cannot die. Bed-stricken, he still gives counsel. In his youth he fought many a valiant fight when he rode afield.'

This was the day, when those two parted. Trevrizent spoke and said: 'Leave thy sins with me! I pledge myself to absolve thee in God's sight. And now do as I bade thee: follow that path with dauntless will!' Such was their parting. Consider it as ye may.

Perceval's adventures, from a Parisian ivory casket of c. 1400. Here Perceval arrives at King Arthur's court in his 'fool's garb' or simple rustic clothing, to the amusement of the knights. (Musée du Louvre)

Gawain's adventures in Wolfram von Eschenbach's Parzival. *Gawain is first shown in pursuit of the scornful beauty, Orgeluse, with whom he is in love; he defeats a knight, and (second row) comes to the Castles of Marvels, where he survives the adventure of the perilous bed and kills a lion. In the last row, he overcomes another knight and is reconciled with both Orgeluse and his enemy Gramoflanz. A fourteenth century tapestry from north Germany. (Brunswick, Landesmuseum)*

THE GAWAIN-POET

Sir Gawain and the Green Knight

ARTHUR'S NEPHEW · THE GREATEST OF ENGLISH ROMANCES AN UNKNOWN GENIUS · THEMES AND VARIATIONS & & &

Gawain first appears in Geoffrey of Monmouth's *History of the Kings of Britain* where he is called Walgainus, and in William of Malmesbury's history, written about 1120, where there is a reference to the discovery of his grave at Walwyn's Castle in Pembrokeshire. He resembles the Gwalchmai of Welsh legend and Cuchulainn in the Irish epics. Like the latter, he possesses many of the properties of a sun-hero, such as the increase of his strength until midday and its decline thereafter. He was the real owner of Excalibur, which was originally a dazzling sun-weapon. Of all the knights of the Round Table, he has the longest connections with Arthur, save for Kay and Bedivere; and in Geoffrey of Monmouth he appears as Arthur's nephew. As folk-tale hero, he is the central figure of primitive stories, sometimes scarcely altered from their crude originals, and cuts a less and less imposing figure as the material becomes artificial and literary.

Yet the first of the poems of which he is hero, *Sir Gawain and the Green Knight*, is the most superb literary accomplishment of medieval English Arthurian writing, one of the great masterpieces of the poetry of this period. Both in its treatment of the subject-matter and in the strength of its style and imagery, it represents the climax of English alliterative poetry. The unique manuscript contains in addition three other poems of the same period and probably by the same writer: all are in the West Midland dialect, with a strong Scandinavian influence, which is at its most marked in *Sir Gawain and the Green Knight*. This seems to have been the first of the poems to be written, about 1370 to 1390. It has been suggested that it was commissioned by John of Gaunt, and there is strong evidence for some connection between him and the poet, if not for the actual commission. The identity of the unknown genius now generally known as 'the Gawain-poet' has long been a matter for debate. No suggestion yet put forward has gained more than a handful of supporters; attempts to marshal internal evidence, whether in the form of puns or numerology, all fail to point to a convincing case for the author's identity. All that can be said with certainty about him is that he was well acquainted with courtly life, could read Latin and French, and was probably a scholar of some merit. He might well have been, or become, a clerk in minor orders, since his later poems are distinctly religious in tone.

The story hinges on two distinct themes which has been skilfully welded into one. The Green Knight's challenge to Gawain is an example of a Celtic episode that we may call the Beheading Game. The approaches of his hostess at the castle form the other part, the Temptation. Both incidents are of great age and have a long pedigree. In the case of the Beheading Game, the earliest form of the story is to be found in the Irish epic *Bricriu's Feast*, in which it is part of the contest for the championship of Ulster, with Cuchulainn as its hero. From Ireland it passed to France, perhaps via Wales and Brittany, where three French romances made use of this theme: in two cases Gawain is the hero, in the third Lancelot. The common feature of all versions is a supernatural being who is beheaded without apparent harm and who returns his half of the bargain with a harmless blow.

The Temptation story is also Celtic in origin, the nearest parallel being found in *Pwyll*, one of the stories in the Welsh *Mabinogion*. This offers three major points of resemblance; a noble huntsman who introduces the hero as guest, a temptation scene in which the huntsman's wife is repulsed by the hero, and a year's interval between a challenge incident and its sequel. The huntsman is also the same colour as his horse, grey as opposed to green in the English poem. The same story also appears in varying guises in several French romances, but none are very close to the English version; yet there seems to have been a French story of this type which was known to the Gawain poet.

Just when these two themes were combined has long been disputed. One school of thought favours a lost French original containing both; against this, a poet of the stature of the author of *Sir Gawain and the Green Knight* would be perfectly capable of making such a fusion. Let us for the moment accept the latter view, while remembering that the poem's merit in no way depends on it. Whoever did make the two stories one was a brilliant sculptor of poetic form: for the outcome of one part is made to depend on the other with great subtlety. The crux is the exchange of spoils during the three day's hunting, which provides a motive for the slight blow given to Gawain by the Green Knight. Gawain conceals the girdle out of fear of his encounter on the following day, which would have passed off without incident otherwise. Thus, while the Temptation arises naturally enough out of the Challenge, this addition makes the issue of the Challenge depend on the outcome of the Temptation. But such a plot is as nothing unless matched by verse and language. In the hands of the unknown poet, the alliterative verse is a mirror of mood and imagination. The least description is turned into a jewel of language, whether it be the details of Gawain's arming before his departure or the loving portrayal of the Green Knight's magical axe.

But the greatest passages are those in which the poet depicts Nature and her ways, a theme which underlies the poem in several aspects. Two stanzas at the opening of the second part describe the changing seasons between Christmas and Michaelmas, and surpass all conventional poetry of this kind. They are followed by the harsh weather which Gawain encounters on his journey northwards, where in the sound of the words and in the rugged rhythms the very spirit of winter re-echoes. The northern countryside in which the poet lived rises up before us in its more severe and impressive beauty. Across this background sweeps past the three days' hunting, in which the essence of the chase is exactly caught: days of exhilaration, danger, triumph and noble ritual, at the end of each a homecoming to a warm welcome and a blazing fire when the last horn has been blown. On the day of the tryst at the Green Chapel, the countryside grows grim once more; the hills are mist-mantled, there is a hoar-frost in the oakwoods, snow in the valleys outside.

The people of this harsh, real world are equally alive; their feasts and merry-making, gaiety and good cheer are far from the delicate but artificial world of the French romances, and their conversations are as unforced and natural as those of the heroes and heroines of Chrétien de Troyes are studied and literary.

But just as Nature dominates the real world, so natural magic dominates the spiritual plane of the poem. The Green Knight is a superhuman being with strange powers, who moves in an aura of mystery, the shadow of his ancient role as the incarnation of spring who must be slain in winter in order to renew life for the next year. In the Temptation, he becomes a gay, friendly lord, owner of a fair castle; but this is only a disguise, even if the poet, uneasy at the pagan implications of his subject-matter, blames the whole mystery on Morgan le Fay. The strange legendary world of Norse and Saxon literature is never far from the poet's mind; Gawain encounters dragons, trolls and giants on his journey northward. The contrast between the Green Knight's two shapes is cunningly exploited, to heighten the climax of the poem.

The poet handles what was once no more than a romance with such high intent that it becomes in his treatment a moral and didactic example. Gawain, the model of knighthood, only escapes the fatal return blow because he holds out against the lady's adulterous temptations. This is a far cry from the French writers' easy acceptance, indeed exaltation, of the immorality of courtly love. They would probably have admired such sin, even though it contravened the strictest conception of this code. Yet they would have agreed with his punishment, for by breaking his word in concealing the girdle, he had dishonoured the order of knighthood. The English poet takes even these worldly ideals onto a higher plain: Gawain's device, the pentangle, borne on his shield, is a religious rather than armorial symbol, and he is frequently called 'Mary's knight'. There is an idealism throughout that raises the poem far above the level of the other English romances, and reminds one of Wolfram von Eschenbach. Gawain is an idealised hero who makes one error that cannot be redeemed, although not fatal: Parzival, on the other hand, although he almost fails in the Grail quest when he does not ask the question at his first visit to the Grail castle, gains a second opportunity by long years of atonement. The common subject of Wolfram and the Gawain poet is the search for perfection; for Wolfram it is typified by the achievement of the mysterious Grail, and in the other by the more realistic preservation as eventually attainable; here the hero's reputation is contrasted with reality. Some writers have seen *Sir Gawain and the Green Knight* as a poem with a didactic moral; but it is rather a moral reflection on human weakness.

In this poem, the Arthurian legend leaves its realms of isolated fantasy to become natural and human; the result has the same power and pathos as the closing pages of Malory. Here language, style and a subtle framework combine into a magnificent achievement, and beside it all but a handful of Arthurian poems pale into literary insignificance. Of this handful, only Wolfram can offer the same high idealism and sustained exaltation of chivalry.

The poem opens with an account of the founding of Britain, and tells us that Arthur was the greatest and most honoured of Britain's kings. The story proper then begins. Arthur is at Camelot one Christmastide, and on New Year's Day, in accordance with his custom, does not eat until some adventure has taken place; and soon a gigantic knight duly appears, entirely clad in green, and riding a green horse. He demands to see Arthur, who asks him what he wants. The knight proposes a bargain: any one of Arthur's knights who is bold enough to strike off his head with the axe he had brought, may do so – provided he will accept a return blow in a year's time. The knights, awed by the visitor's appearance, hesitate, and the Green Knight taunts them with cowardice. Arthur angrily leaps forward to take up the challenge himself, but Gawain restrains him, and asks permission to undertake the adventure himself. Arthur agrees, and Gawain beheads the Green Knight. To the astonishment of the onlookers, the latter picks up his head, which admonishes Gawain to meet him at the Green Chapel in a year's time, and gallops away with it under his arm.

Next All Hallows Day, Gawain is armed in preparation for his departure in search of the mysterious trysting place. He rides through the kingdom of Logrees to north Wales, and eventually reaches the wilderness of Wirral, by way of Angelsey, Holyhead and the coast. By now it is Christmas, and he finds himself in a vast dreary forest. He kneels and prays, and shortly afterwards, a splendid castle appears. Here he finds shelter for the night, and learns that the Green Chapel is but a few miles distant. The lord of the castle invites him to remain until the New Year, now only three days away, and proposes a bargain; he will go hunting each day, and Gawain shall remain at the castle with his wife. At the end of each day they will exchange their spoils.

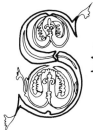

Sir Gawain and the Green Knight

Part Three

I

In the faint light before dawn folk were stirring;
Guests who had to go gave orders to their grooms,
Who busied themselves briskly with the beasts, saddling,
Trimming their tackle and tying on their luggage.
Arrayed for riding in the richest style,
Guests leaped on their mounts lightly, laid hold of their
bridles,
And each rider rode out on his own chosen way.
The beloved lord of the land was not the last up,
Being arrayed for riding with his retinue in force.
He ate a sop hastily when he had heard mass,
And hurried with horn to the hunting field;
Before the sun's first rays fell on the earth,
On their high steeds were he and his knights.
Then these cunning hunters came to couple their hounds,
Cast open the kennel doors and called them out,
And blew on their bugles three bold notes.
The hounds broke out barking, baying fiercely,
And when they went chasing, they were whipped back.
There were a hundred choice huntsmen there, whose fame
Resounds.
To their stations keepers strode;
Huntsmen unleashed hounds:
The forest overflowed
With the strident bugle sounds.

II

At the first cry wild creatures quivered with dread.
The deer in distraction darted down to the dales
Or up to the high ground, but eagerly they were
Driven back by the beaters, who bellowed lustily.
They let the harts with high-branching heads have their
freedom,
And the brave bucks, too, with their broad antlers,
For the noble prince had expressly prohibited
Meddling with male deer in the months of close season.
But the hinds were held back with a 'Hey!' and a 'Whoa!'
And does driven with much din to the deep valleys.
Lo! the arrows' slanting flight as they were loosed!
A shaft flew forth at every forest turning,
The broad head biting on the brown flank.
They screamed as the blood streamed out, sank dead on the
sward,
Always harried by hounds hard on their heels,
And the hurrying hunters' high horn notes.
Like the rending of ramped hills roared the din.
If one of the wild beasts slipped away from the archers
It was dragged down and met death at the dog-bases
After being hunted from the high ground and harried to
the water,
So skilled were the hunt-servants at stations lower down,
So gigantic the greyhounds that grabbed them in a flash,

Seizing them savagely, as swift, I swear,
As sight.
The lord, in humour high,
Would spur, then stop and alight.
In bliss the day went by
Till dark drew on, and night.

III

Thus by the forest borders the brave lord sported,
And the good man Gawain, on his gay bed lying,
Lay hidden till the light of day gleamed on the walls,
Covered with fair canopy, the curtains closed.
And as in slumber he slept on, there slipped into his mind
A slight, suspicious sound, and the door stealthily opened.
He raised up his head out of the bedclothes,
Caught up the corner of the curtain a little
And watched warily towards it, to see what it was.
It was the lady, loveliest to look upon,
Who secretly and silently secured the door,
Then bore towards his bed: the brave knight, embarrassed,
Lay flat with fine adroitness and feigned sleep.
Silently she stepped on, stole to his bed,
Caught up the curtain, crept within,
And seated herself softly on the side of the bed.
There she watched a long while, waiting for him to wake.
Slyly close this long while lay the knight,
Considering in his soul this circumstance,
Its sense and likely sequel, for it seemed marvellous.
'Still, it would be more circumspect,' he said to himself,
'To speak and discover her desire in due course.'
So he stirred and stretched himself, twisting towards her,
Opened his eyes and acted as if astounded;
And, to seem the safer by such service, crossed himself
In dread.
With chin and cheek so fair,
White ranged with rosy red,
With laughing lips, and air
Of love, she lightly said:

IV

'Good morning, Sir Gawain,' the gay one murmured,
'How unsafely you sleep, that one may slip in here!
Now you are taken in a trice. Unless a truce come between us:
I shall bind you to your bed – of that be sure.'
The lady uttered laughingly those playful words.
'Good morning, gay lady,' Gawain blithely greeted her.
'Do with me as you will: that well pleases me.
For I surrender speedily and sue for grace,
Which, to my mind, since I must, is much the best course.'
And thus he repaid her with repartee and ready laughter.
'But if, lovely lady, your leave were forthcoming,
And you were pleased to free your prisoner and pray him to rise,
I would abandon my bed for a better habiliment,
And have more happiness in our honey talk.'
'Nay, verily, fine sir,' urged the voice of that sweet one,
'You shall not budge from your bed. I have a better idea.
I shall hold you fast here on this other side as well
And so chat on with the chevalier my chains have caught.
For I know well, my knight, that your name is Sir Gawain,
Whom all the world worships, wherever he ride;
For lords and their ladies, and all living folk,
Hold your honour in high esteem, and your courtesy.
And now – here you are truly, and we are utterly alone;
My lord and his liegemen are a long way off;
Others still bide in their beds, my bower-maidens too;
Shut fast and firmly with a fine hasp is the door;
And since I have in this house him who pleases all,
As long as my time lasts I shall lingering in talk take
My fill.
My young body is yours,
Do with it what you will;
My strong necessities force
Me to be your servant still.'

V

'In good truth,' said Gawain, 'that is a gain indeed,
Though I am hardly the hero of whom you speak.
To be held in such honour as you here suggest,
I am altogether unworthy, I own it freely,
By God, I should be glad, if you granted it right
For me to essay by speech or some other service,
To pleasure such a perfect lady – pure joy it would be.'
'In good truth, Sir Gawain,' the gay lady replied,
'If I slighted or set at naught your spotless fame
And your all-pleasing prowess, it would show poor breeding.
But there is no lack of ladies who would love, noble one,
To hold you in their arms, as I have you here,
And linger in the luxury of your delightful discourse,
Which would perfectly pleasure them and appease their woes—
Rather than have riches or the red gold they own.
But as I love that Lord, the Celestial Ruler,

I have wholly in my hand what all desire
 Through His grace.'
 Not loth was she to allure,
 This lady fair of face;
 But the knight with speeches pure
 Answered in each case.

VI

Madam,' said the merry man, 'may Mary requite you!
For in good faith I have found in you free-hearted
 generosity.
Certain men for their deeds receive esteem from others,
But for myself, I do not deserve the respect they show me;
Your honourable mind makes you utter only what is good.'
'Now by Mary,' said the noble lady, 'Not so it seems to me,
For were I worth the whole of womankind,
And all the wealth in the world were in my hand,
And if bargaining I were to bid to bring myself a lord –
With your noble qualities, knight, made known to me now,
Your good looks, gracious manner and great courtesy,
All of which I have heard of before, but here prove true –
No lord that is living could be allowed to excel you.'
'Indeed, dear lady, you did better,' said the knight,
'But I am proud of the precious price you put on me,
And solemnly as your servant say you are my sovereign.
May Christ requite it you: I have become your knight.'
Then of many matters they talked till mid-morning and
 after,
And all the time she behaved as if she adored him;
But Sir Gawain was on guard in a gracious manner.
Though she was the winsomest woman the warrior had
 known,
He was less love-laden because of the loss he must
 Now face –
 His destruction by the stroke,
 For come it must was the case.
 The lady of leaving then spoke;
 He assented with speedy grace.

VII

Then she gave him good-bye, glinting with laughter,
And standing up, astounded him with these strong words:
'May He who prospers every speech for this pleasure
 reward you!
I cannot bring myself to believe that you could be Gawain.'
'How so?' said the knight, speaking urgently,
For he feared he had failed to observe the forms of
 courtesy.
But the beauteous one blessed him and brought out this
 argument:
'Such a great man as Gawain is granted to be,
The very vessel of virtue and fine courtesy,
Could scarcely have stayed such a sojourn with a lady
Without craving a kiss out of courtesy,
Touched by some trifling hint at the tail-end of a speech.'
'So be it, as you say,' then said Gawain,
'I shall kiss at your command, as becomes a knight
Who fears to offend you; no further plea is needed.'
Whereupon she approached him, and penned him in her
 arms,
Leaned over him lovingly and gave the lord a kiss.
Then they commended each other to Christ in comely
 style,
And without more words she went out by the door.
He made ready to rise with rapid haste,
Summoned his servant, selected his garb,
And walked down, when he was dressed, debonairly to
 mass.
Then he went to the well-served meal which awaited him,
And made merry sport till the moon rose
 At night.
 Never was baron bold
 So taken by ladies bright,
 That young one and the old:
 They throve all three in delight.

VIII

And still at his sport spurred the castellan,
Hunting the barren hinds in holt and on heath.
So many had he slain, by the setting of the sun,
Of does and other deer, that it was downright wonderful.
Then at the finish the folk flocked in eagerly,
And quickly collected the killed deer in a heap.
Those highest in rank came up with hosts of attendants,
Picked out what appeared to be the plumpest beasts
And, according to custom, had them cut open with finesse.
Some who ceremoniously assessed them there
Found two fingers' breadth of fat on the worst.
Then they slit open the slot, seized the first stomach,
Scraped it with a keen knife and tied up the tripes.
Next they hacked off all the legs, the hide was stripped,
The belly broken open and the bowels removed,
Carefully, lest they loosen the ligature of the knot.
They they gripped the gullet, disengaged deftly

The wezand from the windpipe and whipped out the guts.
Then their sharp knives shore through the shoulder-bones,
Which they slid out of a small hole, leaving the sides intact.
Then they cleft the chest clean through, cutting it in two.
Then again at the gullet a man began to work
And straight away rived it, right to the fork,
Flicked out the shoulder-fillets, and faithfully then
He rapidly ripped free the rib-fillets.
Similarly, as is seemly, the spine was cleared
All the way to the haunch, which hung from it;
And they heaved up the whole haunch and hewed it off;
And that is called, according to its kind, the numbles,
        I find.
    At the thigh-forks then they strain
    And free the folds behind,
    Hurrying to hack all in twain,
    The backbone to unbind.

IX

Then they hewed off the head and also the neck,
And after sundered the sides swiftly from the chine,
And into the foliage they flung the fee of the raven.
Then each fellow, for his fee, as it fell to him to have,
Skewered through the stout flanks beside the ribs,
And then by the hocks of the haunches they hung up their
        booty.
On one of the finest fells they fed their hounds,
And let them have the lights, the liver and the tripes,
With bread well imbrued with blood mixed with them.
Boldly they blew the kill amid the baying of hounds.
Then off they went homewards, holding their meat,
Stalwartly sounding many stout horn-calls.
As dark was descending, they were drawing near
To the comely castle where quietly our knight stayed.
        Fires roared,
    And blithely hearts were beating
    As into hall came the lord.
    When Gawain gave him greeting,
    Joy abounded at the board.

X

Then the master commanded everyone to meet in the hall,
Called the ladies to come down with their company of
        maidens.
Before all the folk on the floor, he bid men
Fetch the venison and place it before him.
Then gaily and in good humour to Gawain he called,
Told over the tally of the sturdy beasts,
And showed him the fine fat flesh flayed from the ribs.
'How does the sport please you? Do you praise me for it?
Am I thoroughly thanked for thriving as a huntsman?'
'Certainly,' said the other. 'Such splendid spoils
Have I not seen for seven years in the season of winter.'
'And I give you all, Gawain,' said the good man then,
'For according to our covenant you may claim it as your
        own.'
'Certes, that is so, and I say the same to you,'
Said Gawain, 'for my true gains in this great house,
I am not loth to allow, must belong to you.'
And he put his arms round his handsome neck, hugging
        him,
And kissed him in the comeliest way he could think of.
'Accept my takings, sir, for I received no more;
Gladly would I grant them, however great they were.'
'And therefore I thank you,' the thane said. 'Good!
Yours may be the better gift, if you would break it to me
Where your wisdom won you wealth of that kind.'
'No such clause in our contract! Request nothing else!'
Said the other. 'You have your due: ask more,
        None should.'
    They laughed in blithe assent
    With worthy words and good;
    Then to supper they swiftly went,
    To fresh delicious food.

XI

And sitting afterwards by the hearth of an audience
        chamber,
Where retainers repeatedly brought them rare wines,
In their jolly jesting they jointly agreed
On a settlement similar to the preceding one;
To exchange the chance achievements of the morrow,
No matter how novel they were, at night when they met.
They accorded on this compact, the whole court
        observing,
And the bumper was brought forth in banter to seal it.
And at last they lovingly took leave of each other,
Each man hastened thereafter to his bed.
The cock having crowed and called only thrice,
The lord leaped from bed, and his liegemen too,
So that mass and a meal were meetly dealt with,
And by first light the folk to the forest were bound
        For the chase.
    Proudly the hunt with horns
    Soon drove through a desert place:

Uncoupled through the thorns
The great hounds pressed apace.

XII

By a quagmire they quickly scented quarry and gave tongue,
And the chief huntsman urged on the first hounds up,
Spurring them on with a splendid spate of words.
The hounds, hearing it, hurried there at once,
Fell on the trail furiously, forty together,
And made such echoing uproar, all howling at once,
That the rocky banks round about rang with the din.
Hunters inspirited them with sound of speech and horn.
Then together in a group, across the ground they surged
At speed between a pool and a spiteful crag.
On a stony knoll by a steep cliff at the side of a bog,
Where rugged rocks had roughly tumbled down,
They careered on the quest, the cry following,
Then surrounded the crag and the rocky knoll as well,
Certain their prey skulked inside their ring,
For the baying of the bloodhounds meant the beast was there.
Then they beat upon the bushes and bade him come out,
And he swung out savagely aslant the line of men,
A baneful boar of unbelievable size,
A solitary long since sundered from the herd,
Being old and brawny, the biggest of them all,
And grim and ghastly when he grunted: great was the grief
When he thrust through the hounds, hurling three to earth,
And sped on scot-free, swift and unscathed.
They hallooed, yelled, 'Look out!' cried, 'Hey, we have him!'
And blew horns boldly, to bring the bloodhounds together;
Many were the merry cries from men and dogs
As they hurried clamouring after their quarry to kill him on The track.
Many times he turns at bay
And tears the dogs which attack.
He hurts the hounds, and they
Moan in a piteous pack.

XIII

Then men shoved forward, shaped to shoot at him,
Loosed arrows at him, hitting him often,
But the points, for all their power, could not pierce his flanks,
Nor would the barbs bite on his bristling brow.
Though the smooth-shaven shaft shattered in pieces;
Wherever it hit, the head rebounded.
But when the boar was battered by blows unceasing,
Goaded and driven demented, he dashed at the men,
Striking them savagely as he assailed them in rushes,
So that some lacking stomach stood back in fear.
But the lord on a lithe horse lunged after him,
Blew his bugle like a bold knight in battle,
Rallied the hounds as he rode through the rank thickets,
Pursuing this savage boar till the sun set.
And so they disported themselves this day
While our lovable lord lay in his bed.
At home the gracious Gawain in gorgeous clothes Reclined:
The gay one did not forget
To come with welcome kind,
And early him beset
To make him change his mind.

XIV

She came to the curtain and cast her eye
On Sir Gawain, who at once gave her gracious welcome,
And she answered him eagerly, with ardent words,
Sat at his side softly, and with a spurt of laughter
And a loving look, delivered these words:
'It seems to me strange if, sir, you are Gawain,
A person so powerfully disposed to good,
Yet nevertheless know nothing of noble conventions,
And when made aware of them, wave them away!
Quickly you have cast away what I schooled you in yesterday
By the truest of all tokens of talk I know of.'
'What?' said the wondering knight, 'I am not aware of one.
But if it be true what you tell, I am entirely to blame.'
'I counselled you then about kissing,' the comely one said;
'When a favour is conferred, it must be forthwith accepted:
That is becoming for a courtly knight who keeps the rules.'
'Sweet one, unsay that speech,' said the brave man,
'For I dared not do that lest I be denied.
If I were forward and were refused, the fault would be mine.'
'But none,' said the noblewoman, 'could deny you, by my faith!
You are strong enough to constrain with your strength if you wish,
If any were so ill-bred as to offer you resistance.'
'Yes, good guidance you give me, by God,' replied Gawain,

'But threateners are ill thought of and do not thrive in my
country,
Nor do gifts thrive when given without good will.
I am here at your behest, to offer a kiss to when you like;
You may do it whenever you deem fit, or desist,
In this place.'
The beautiful lady bent
And fairly kissed his face:
Much speech the two then spent
On love, its grief and grace.

XV

'I would know of you, knight,' the noble lady said,
'If it did not anger you, what argument you use,
Being so hale and hearty as you are at this time,
So generous a gentleman as you are justly famed to be;
Since the choicest thing in Chivalry, the chief thing
praised,
Is the loyal sport of love, the very lore of arms?
For the tale of the contentions of true knights
Is told by the title and text of their feats,
How lords for their true loves put their lives at hazard,
Endured dreadful trials for their dear loves' sakes,
And with valour avenged and made void their woes,
Bringing home abundant bliss by their virtues.
You are the gentlest and most just of your generation:
Everywhere your honour and high fame are known.
Yet I have sat at your side two separate times here
Without hearing you utter in any way
A single syllable of the saga of love.
Being so polished and so punctilious a pledge-fulfiller,
You ought to be eager to lay open to a young thing
Your discoveries in the craft of courtly love.
What! Are you ignorant, with all your renown?
Or do you deem me too dull to drink in your dalliance?
For shame!
I sit here unchaperoned, and stay
To acquire some courtly game;
So while my lord is away,
Teach me your true wit's fame.'

XVI

'In good faith,' said Gawain, 'may God requite you!
It gives me great happiness, and is good sport to me,
That so fine a fair one as you should find her way here
And take pains with so poor a man, make pastime with her
knight,
With any kind of clemency – it comforts me greatly.
But for me to take on the travail of interpreting true love
And construing the subject of the stories of arms
To you who, I hold, have more skill
In that art, by half, than a hundred of such
As I am or ever shall be on the earth I inhabit.
Would in faith would be a manifold folly, noble lady,
To please you I would press with all the power in my soul,
For I am highly beholden to you, and evermore shall be
True servant to your bounteous self, so save me God!'
So the stately lady tempted him and tried him with
questions
To win him to wickedness, whatever else she thought.
But he defended himself so firmly that no fault appeared,
Nor was there any evil apparent on either side,
But bliss:
For long they laughed and played
Till she gave him a gracious kiss.
A fond farewell she bade,
And went her way on this.

XVII

Sir Gawain bestirred himself and went to mass:
Then dinner was dressed and with due honour served.
All day long the lord and the ladies disported,
But the castellan coursed across the country time and
again,
Hunted his hapless boar as it hurtled over the hills,
Then bit the backs of his best hounds asunder
Standing at bay, till the bowmen obliged him to break free
Out into the open for all he could do,
So fast the arrows flew when the folk there concentrated.
Even the strongest he sometimes made start back,
But in time he became so tired he could tear away no more,
And with the speed he still possessed, he spurted to a hole
On a rise by a rock with a running stream beside.
He got the bank at his back, and began to abrade the
ground.
The froth was foaming foully at his mouth,
And he whetted his white tusks; a weary time it was
For the bold men about, who were bound to harass him
From a distance, for none dared to draw near him
For dread.
He had hurt so many men
That it entered no one's head
To be torn by his tusks again
And he raging and seeing red.

XVIII

Till the castellan came himself, encouraging his horse,
And saw the boar at bay with his band of men around.
He alighted in lively fashion, left his courser,
Drew and brandished his bright sword and boldly strode
forward,
Striding at speed through the stream to where the savage
beast was.
The wild thing was aware of the weapon and its wielder,
And so bridled with its bristles in a burst of fierce snorts
That all were anxious for the lord, lest he have the worst
of it.
Straight away the savage brute sprang at the man,
And baron and boar were both in a heap
In the swirling water: the worst went to the beast,
For the man had marked him well at the moment of impact,
Had put the point precisely at the pit of his chest,
And drove it in to the hilt, so that the heart was shattered,
And the spent beast sank snarling and was swept
downstream,
Teeth bare.
A hundred hounds and more
Attack and seize and tear;
Men tug him to the shore
And the dogs destroy him there.

XIX

Bugles blew the triumph, horns blared loud.
There was hallooing in high pride by all present;
Braches bayed at the beast, as bidden by their masters,
The chief huntsmen in charge of the chase so hard.
Then one who was wise in wood-crafts
Started in style to slash open the boar.
First he hewed off the head and hoisted it on high,
Then rent him roughly along the ridge of his back,
Brought out the bowels and broiled them on coals
For blending with bread as the braches' reward.
Then he broke out the brawn from the bright broad flanks,
Took out the offal, as is fit,
Attached the two halves entirely together,
And on a strong stake stoutly hung them.
Then home they hurried with the huge beast,
With the boar's head borne before the baron himself.
Who had destroyed him in the stream by the strength of
his arm,
Above all:
It seemed to him an age
Till he greeted Gawain in hall.
To reap his rightful wage
The latter came at his call.

XX

The lord exclaimed loudly, laughing merrily
When he saw Sir Gawain, and spoke joyously.
The sweet ladies were sent for, and the servants assembled.
Then he showed them the shields, and surely described
The large size and length, and the malignity
Of the fierce boar's fighting when he fled in the woods;
So that Gawain congratulated him on his great deed,
Commended it as a merit he had manifested well,
For a beast with so much brawn, the bold man said,
A boar of such breadth, he had not before seen.
When they handled the huge head the upright man praised it,
Expressed horror thereat for the ear of the lord.
'Now Gawain,' said the good man, 'this game is your own
By our contracted treaty, in truth, you know.'
'It is so,' said the knight, 'and as certainly
I shall give you all my gains as guerdon, in faith.'
He clasped the castellan's neck and kissed him kindly,
And then served him a second time in the same style.
'In all our transactions since I came to sojourn,' asserted
Gawain,
'Up to tonight, as of now, there's nothing that
I owe.'
'By Saint Giles,' the castellan quipped,
'You're the finest fellow I know:
Your wealth will have us all whipped
If your trade continues so!'

XXI

Then the trestles and tables were trimly set out,
Complete with cloths, and clearly-flaming cressets
And waxen torches were placed in the wall-brackets
By retainers, who then tended the entire hall-gathering.
Much gladness and glee then gushed forth there
By the fire on the floor: and in multifarious ways
They sang noble songs at supper and afterwards,
A concert of Christmas carols and new dance songs,
With the most mannerly mirth a man could tell of,
And our courteous knight kept constant company with the
lady.
In a bewitchingly well-mannered way she made up to him,
Secretly soliciting the stalwart knight
So that he was astounded, and upset in himself.

But his upbringing forbade him to rebuff her utterly,
So he behaved towards her honourably, whatever
aspersions might
Be cast.
They revelled in the hall
As long as their pleasure might last
And then at the castellan's call
To the chamber hearth they passed.

XXII

There they drank and discoursed and decided to enjoy
Similar solace and sport on New Year's Eve.
But the princely knight asked permission to depart in the
morning,
For his appointed time was approaching, and perforce he
must go.
But the lord would not let him and implored him to linger,
Saying, 'I swear to you, as a staunch true knight,
You shall gain the Green Chapel to give your dues,
My lord, in the light of New Year, long before sunrise.
Therefore remain in your room and rest in comfort,
While I fare hunting in the forest; in fulfilment of our oath
Exchanging what we achieve when the chase is over.
For twice I have tested you, and twice found you true.
Now "Third time, throw best!" Think of that tomorrow!
Let us make merry while we may, set our minds on joy,
For hard fate can hit man whenever it likes.'
This was graciously granted and Gawain stayed.
Blithely drink was brought, then to bed with lights
They pressed.
All night Sir Gawain sleeps
Softly and still at rest;
But the lord his custom keeps
And is early up and dressed.

XXIII

After mass, he and his men made a small meal.
Merry was the morning; he demanded his horse.
The men were ready mounted before the main gate,
A host of knightly horsemen to follow after him.
Wonderfully fair was the forest-land, for the frost
remained,
And the rising sun shone ruddily on the ragged clouds,
In its beauty brushing their blackness off the heavens.
The huntsmen unleashed the hounds by a holt-side,
And the rocks and surrounding bushes rang with their
horn-calls.
Some found and followed the fox's tracks,
And wove various ways in their wily fashion.
A small hound cried the scent, the senior huntsman called
His fellow foxhounds to him and, feverishly sniffing,
The rout of dogs rushed forward on the right path.
The fox hurried fast, for they found him soon
And, seeing him distinctly, pursued him at speed,
Unmistakably giving tongue with tumultuous din.
Deviously in difficult country he doubled on his tracks,
Swerved and wheeled away, often waited listening,
Till at last by a little ditch he leaped a quickset hedge,
And stole out stealthily at the side of a valley,
Considering his stratagem had given the slip to the hounds.
But he stumbled on a tracking-dogs' tryst-place
unawares,
And there in a cleft three hounds threatened him at once,
All grey.
He swiftly started back
And, full of deep dismay,
He dashed on a different track;
To the woods he went away.

XXIV

Then came the lively delight of listening to hounds
When they had all met in a muster, mingling together,
For, catching sight of him, they cried such curses on him
That the clustering cliffs seemed to be crashing down.
Here he was halloed when the hunters met him,
There savagely snarled at by intercepting hounds;
Then he was called thief and threatened often;
With the tracking dogs on his tail, no tarrying was possible.
When out in the open he was often run at,
So he often swerved in again, that artful Reynard.
Yes, he led the lord and his liegemen a dance
In this manner among the mountains till mid-afternoon,
While harmoniously at home the honoured knight slept
Between the comely curtains in the cold morning.
But the lady's longing to woo would not let her sleep,
Nor would she impair the purpose pitched in her heart,
But rose up rapidly and ran to him
In a ravishing robe that reached to the ground,
Trimmed with finest fur from pure pelts;
Not coifed as to custom, but with costly jewels
Strung in scores on her splendid hairnet.
Her fine-featured face and fair throat were unveiled,
Her breast was bare and her back as well.
She came in by the chamber door and closed it after her,
Cast open a casement and called on the knight,

And briskly thus rebuked him with bountiful words
Of good cheer.
'Ah sir! What, sound asleep?
The morning's crisp and clear.'
He had been drowsing deep,
But now he had to hear.

XXV

The noble sighed ceaselessly in unsettled slumber
As threatening thoughts thronged in the dawn light
About destiny, which the day after would deal him his fate
At the Green Chapel where Gawain was to greet his man,
And be bound to bear his buffet unresisting.
But having recovered consciousness in comely fashion,
He heaved himself out of dreams and answered hurriedly.
The lovely lady advanced, laughing adorably,
Swooped over his splendid face and sweetly kissed him.
He welcomed her worthily with noble cheer
And, gazing on her gay and glorious attire,
Her features so faultless and fine of complexion,
He felt a flush of rapture suffuse his heart.
Sweet and genial smiling slid them into joy
Till bliss burst forth between them, beaming gay
And bright;
With joy the two contended
In talk of true delight,
And peril would have impended
Had Mary not minded her knight.

XXVI

For that peerless princess pressed him so hotly,
So invited him to the very verge, that he felt forced
Either to allow her love or blackguardly rebuff her.
He was concerned for his courtesy, lest he be called caitiff,
But more especially for his evil plight if he should plunge into sin,
And dishonour the owner of the house treacherously.
'God shield me! That shall not happen, for sure,' said the knight.
So with laughing love-talk he deflected gently
The downright declarations that dropped from her lips.
Said the beauty to the bold man, 'Blame will be yours
If you love not the living body lying close to you
More than all wooers in the world who are wounded in heart;
Unless you have a lover more beloved, who delights you more,
A maiden to whom you are committed, so immutably bound
That you do not seek to sever from her – which I see is so.
Tell me the truth of it, I entreat you now;
By all the loves there are, do not hide the truth
With guile.'
Then gently, 'By Saint John,'
Said the knight with a smile,
'I owe my oath to none,
Nor wish to yet a while.'

XXVII

'Those words,' said the fair woman, 'are the worst there could be,
But I am truly answered, to my utter anguish.
Give me now a gracious kiss, and I shall go from here
As a maid that loves much, mourning on this earth.'
Then, sighing, she stooped, and seemlily kissed him,
And, severing herself from him, stood up and said,
'At this adieu, my dear one, do me this pleasure:
Give me something as gift, your glove if no more,
To mitigate my mourning when I remember you.'
'Now certainly, for your sake,' said the knight,
'I wish I had here the handsomest thing I own,
For you have deserved, forsooth, superabundantly
And rightfully, a richer reward than I could give.
But as tokens of true love, trifles mean little.
It is not to your honour to have at this time
A mere glove as Gawain's gift to treasure.
For I am here on an errand in unknown regions,
And have no bondsmen, no baggages with dear-bought things in them.
This afflicts me now, fair lady, for your sake.
Man must do as he must; neither lament it
Nor repine.'
'No, highly honoured one,'
Replied that lady fine,
'Though gift you give me none,
You must have something of mine.'

XXVIII

She proffered him a rich ring wrought in red gold,
With a sparkling stone set conspicuously in it,
Which beamed as brilliantly as the bright sun;
You may well believe its worth was wonderfully great.
But the courteous man declined it and quickly said,
'Before God, gracious lady, no giving just now!

Not having anything to offer, I shall accept nothing.'
She offered it him urgently and he refused again,
Fast affirming his refusal on his faith as a knight.
Put out by this repulse, she presently said,
'If you reject my ring as too rich in value,
Doubtless you would be less deeply indebted to me
If I gave you my girdle, a less gainful gift.'
She swiftly slipped off the cincture of her gown
Which went round her waist under the wonderful mantle,
A girdle of green silk with a golden hem
Embroidered only at the edges, with hand-stitched
ornament.
And she pleaded with the prince in a pleasant manner,
To take it notwithstanding its trifling worth;
But he told her that he could touch no treasure at all,
Not gold nor any gift, till God gave him grace
To pursue to success the search he was bound on.
'And therefore I beg you not to be displeased:
Press no more your purpose, for I promise it never
Can be.
I owe you a hundredfold
For grace you have granted me;
And ever through hot and cold
I shall stay your devotee.'

XXIX

'Do you say "no" to this silk?' then said the beauty;
'Because it is simple in itself? And so it seems.
Lo! It is little indeed, and so less worth your esteem.
But one who was aware of the worth twined in it
Would appraise its properties as more precious perhaps,
For the man that binds his body with this belt of green,
As long as he laps it closely about him,
No hero under heaven can hack him to pieces,
For he cannot be killed by any cunning on earth.'
Then the prince pondered, and it appeared to him
A precious gem to protect him in the peril appointed him
When he gained the Green Chapel to be given checkmate:
It would be a splendid stratagem to escape being slain.
Then he allowed her to solicit him and let her speak.
She pressed the belt upon him with potent words
And having got his agreement, she gave it him gladly,
Beseeching him for her sake to conceal it always,
And hide it from her husband with all diligence.
That never should another know of it, the noble swore
Outright.
Then often his thanks gave he
With all his heart and might,
And thrice by then had she
Kissed the constant knight.

XXX

Then with a word of farewell she went away,
For she could not force further satisfaction from him.
Directly she withdrew, Sir Gawain dressed himself,
Rose and arrayed himself in rich garments,
But laid aside the love-lace the lady had given him,
Secreted it carefully where he could discover it later.
Then he went his way at once to the chapel,
Privily approached a priest and prayed him there
To listen to his life's sins and enlighten him
On how he might have salvation in the hereafter.
Then, confessing his faults, he fairly shrove himself,
Begging mercy for both major and minor sins.
He asked the holy man for absolution
And was absolved with certainty and sent out so pure
That Doomsday should have been declared the day after.
Then he made merrier among the noble ladies,
With comely carolling and all kinds of pleasure,
Than ever he had done, with ecstasy, till came
Dark night.
Such honour he did to all,
They said, 'Never has this knight
Since coming into hall
Expressed such pure delight.'

XXXI

Now long may he linger there, love sheltering him!
The prince was still on the plain, pleasuring in the chase,
Having finished off the fox he had followed so far.
As he leaped over a hedge looking out for the quarry,
Where he heard the hounds that were harrying the fox,
Reynard came running through a rough thicket,
With the pack all pell-mell, panting at his heels.
The lord, aware of the wild beast, waited craftily,
Then drew his dazzling sword and drove at the fox.
The beast baulked at the blade to break sideways,
But a dog bounded at him before he could,
And right in front of the horse's feet they fell on him,
All worrying their wily prey with a wild uproar.
The lord quickly alighted and lifted him up,
Wrenched him beyond reach of the ravening fangs,
Held him high over his head and hallooed lustily,
While the angry hounds in hordes bayed at him.
Thither hurried the huntsmen with horns in plenty,

Sounding the rally splendidly till they saw their lord.
When the company of his court had come up to the kill,
All who bore bugles blew at once,
And the others without horns hallooed loudly.
The requiem that was raised for Reynard's soul
And the commotion made it the merriest meet ever,
Men said.
The hounds must have their fee:
They pat them on the head,
Then hold the fox; and he
Is reft of his skin of red.

XXXII

Then they set off for home, it being almost night,
Blowing their big horns bravely as they went.
At last the lord alighted at his beloved castle
And found upon the floor a fire, and beside it
The good Sir Gawain in glad humour
By reason of the rich friendship he had reaped from the ladies.
He wore a turquoise tunic extending to the ground;
His softly-furred surcoat suited him well,
And his hood of the same hue hung from his shoulder.
All trimmed with ermine were hood and surcoat.
Meeting the master in the middle of the floor,
Gawain went forward gladly and greeted him thus:
'Forthwith, I shall be the first to fulfil the contract
We settled so suitably without sparing the wine.'
Then he clasped the castellan and kissed him thrice
As sweetly and steadily as a strong knight could.
'By Christ!' quoth the other. 'You will carve yourself a fortune
By traffic in this trade when the terms suit you!'
'Do not chop logic about the exchange,' chipped in Gawain,
'As I have properly paid over the profit I made.'
'Marry,' said the other man, 'mine is inferior,
For I have hunted all day and have only taken
This ill-favoured fox's skin, may the Fiend take it!
And that is a poor price to pay for such precious things
As you have pressed upon me here, three pure kisses
So good.'
'Enough!' acknowledged Gawain,
'I thank you, by the Rood.'
And how the fox was slain
The lord told him as they stood.

XXXIII

With mirth and minstrelsy, and meals when they liked,
They made as merry then as ever men could;
With the laughter of ladies and delightful jesting,
Gawain and his good host were very gay together,
Save when excess or sottishness seemed likely.
Master and men made many a witty sally,
Until presently, at the appointed parting-time,
The brave men were bidden to bed at last.
Then of his host the hero humbly took leave,
The first to bid farewell, fairly thanking him:
'May the High King requite you for your courtesy at this feast,
And the wonderful week of my dwelling here!
I would offer to be one of your own men if you liked,
But that I must move on tomorrow, as you know,
If you will give me the guide you granted me,
To show me the Green Chapel where my share of doom
Will be dealt on New Year's Day, as God deems for me.'
'With all my heart!' said the host. 'In good faith,
All that I ever promised you, I shall perform.'
He assigned him a servant to set him on his way,
And lead him in the hills without any delay,
Faring through forest and thicket by the most straightforward route
They might.
With every honour due
Gawain then thanked the knight,
And having bid him adieu,
Took leave of the ladies bright.

XXXIV

So he spoke to them sadly, sorrowing as he kissed,
And urged on them heartily his endless thanks,
And they gave to Sir Gawain words of grace in return,
Commending him to Christ with cries of chill sadness.
Then from the whole household he honourably took his leave,
Making all the men that he met amends
For their several services and solicitous care,
For they had been busily attendant, bustling about him;
And every soul was as sad to say farewell
As if they had always had the hero in their house.
Then the lords led him with lights to his chamber,
And blithely brought him to bed to rest.
If he slept – I dare not assert it – less soundly than usual,

There was much on his mind for the morrow, if he meant to
give
It thought.
Let him lie there still,
He almost has what he sought;
So tarry a while until
The process I report.

Part Four

I

Now the New Year neared, the night passed,
Daylight fought darkness as the Deity ordained.
But wild was the weather the world awoke to;
Bitterly the clouds cast down cold on the earth,
Inflicting on the flesh flails from the north.
Bleakly the snow blustered, and beasts were frozen;
The whistling wind wailed from the heights,
Driving great drifts deep in the dales.
Keenly the lord listened as he lay in his bed;
Though his lids were closed, he was sleeping little.
Every cock that crew recalled to him his tryst.
Before the day had dawned, he had dressed himself,
For the light from a lamp illuminated his chamber.
He summoned his servant, who swiftly answered,
Commanded that his mail-coat and mount's saddle be
brought.
The man fared forth and fetched him his armour,
And set Sir Gawain's array in splendid style.
First he clad him in his clothes to counter the cold,
Then in his other armour which had been well kept;
His breast- and belly-armour had been burnished bright,
And the rusty rings of his rich mail-coat rolled clean,
And all being as fresh as at first, he was fain to give thanks
Indeed.
Each wiped and polished piece
He donned with due heed.
The gayest from here to Greece,
The strong man sent for his steed.

II

While he was putting on apparel of the most princely kind –
His surcoat, with its symbol of spotless deeds
Environed on velvet with virtuous gems,
Was embellished and bound with embroidered seams,
And finely fur-lined with the fairest skins –
He did not leave the lace belt, the lady's gift:
For his own good, Gawain did not forget that!
When he had strapped the sword on his swelling hips,
The knight lapped his loins with his love-token twice,
Quickly wrapped it with relish round his waist.
The green silken girdle suited the gallant well,
Backed by the royal red cloth that richly showed.
But Gawain wore the girdle not for its great value,
Nor through pride in the pendants, in spite of their polish,
Nor for the gleaming gold which glinted on the ends,
But to save himself when of necessity he must
Stand an evil stroke, not resisting it with knife
Or sword.
When ready and robed aright,
Out came the comely lord;
To the men of name and might
His thanks in plenty poured.

III

Then was Gringolet got ready, that great huge horse.
Having been assiduously stabled in seemly quarters,
The fiery steed was fit and fretting for a gallop.
Sir Gawain stepped to him and, inspecting his coat,
Said earnestly to himself, asserting with truth,
'Here in this castle is a company whose conduct is
honourable.
The man who maintains them, may he have joy!
The delightful lady, love befall her while she lives!
Thus for charity they cherish a chance guest
Honourably and open-handedly; may He on high,
The King of Heaven, requite you and your company too!
And if I could live any longer in lands on earth,
Some rich recompense, if I could, I should readily give
you.'
Then he stepped into the stirrup and swung aloft.
His man showed him his shield; on his shoulder he put it,
And gave the spur to Gringolet with his gold-spiked heels.
The horse sprang forward from the paving, pausing no
more
To prance.
His man was mounted and fit,
Laden with spear and lance.
'This castle to Christ I commit:
May He its fortune enhance!'

IV

The drawbridge was let down and the broad double gates
Were unbarred and borne open on both sides.
Passing over the planks, the prince blessed himself

And praised the kneeling porter, who proffered him
'Good day',
Praying God to grant that Gawain would be saved.
And Gawain went on his way with the one man
To put him on the right path for that perilous place
Where the sad assault must be received by him.
By bluffs where boughs were bare they passed,
Climbed by cliffs where the cold clung:
Under the high clouds, ugly mists
Merged damply with the moors and melted on the
mountains;
Each hill had a hat, a huge mantle of mist.
Brooks burst forth above them, boiling over their banks
And showering down sharply in shimmering cascades.
Wonderfully wild was their way through the woods;
Till soon the sun in the sway of that season
Brought day.
They were on a lofty hill
Where snow beside them lay,
When the servant stopped still
And told his master to stay.

V

'For I have guided you to this ground, Sir Gawain, at this
time,
And now you are not far from the noted place
Which you have searched for and sought with such special
zeal.
But I must say to you, forsooth, since I know you,
And you are a lord whom I love with no little regard:
Take my governance as guide, and it shall go better for you,
For the place is perilous that you are pressing towards.
In that wilderness dwells the worst man in the world,
For he is valiant and fierce and fond of fighting,
And mightier than any man that may be on earth,
And his body is bigger than the best four
In Arthur's house, or Hector, or any other.
At the Green Chapel he gains his great adventures.
No man passes that place, however proud in arms,
Without being dealt a death-blow by his dreadful hand.
For he is an immoderate man, to mercy a stranger;
For whether churl or chaplain by the chapel rides,
Monk or mass-priest or man of other kind,
He thinks it as convenient to kill him as keep alive himself.
Therefore I say, as certainly as you sit in your saddle,
If you come there you'll be killed, I caution you, knight,
Take my troth for it, though you had twenty lives
And more.
He has lived here since long ago
And filled the field with gore.
You cannot counter his blow,
It strikes so sudden and sore.

VI

'Therefore, good Sir Gawain, leave the grim man alone!
Ride by another route, to some region remote!
Go in the name of God, and Christ grace your fortune!
And I shall go home again and undertake
To swear solemnly by God and his saints as well
(By my halidom, so help me God, and every other oath)
Stoutly to keep your secret, not saying to a soul
That ever you tried to turn tail from any man I knew.'
'Great thanks,' replied Gawain, somewhat galled, and said,
'It is worthy of you to wish for my well-being, man,
And I believe you would loyally lock it in your heart.
But however quiet you kept it, if I quit this place,
Fled from the fellow in the fashion you propose,
I should become a cowardly knight with no excuse
whatever,
For I will go to the Green Chapel, to get what Fate sends,
And have whatever words I wish with that worthy,
Whether weal or woe is what Fate
Demands.
Fierce though that fellow be,
Clutching his club where he stands,
Our Lord can certainly see
That his own are in safe hands.'

VII

'By Mary!' said the other man. 'If you mean what you say,
You are determined to take all your trouble on yourself.
If you wish to lose your life, I'll no longer hinder you.
Here's your lance for your hand, your helmet for your
head.
Ride down this rough track round yonder cliff
Till you arrive in a rugged ravine at the bottom,
Then look about on the flat, on your left hand,
And you will view there in the vale that very chapel,
And the grim gallant who guards it always.
Now, noble Gawain, good-bye in God's name.
For all the gold on God's earth I would not go with you,
Nor foot it an inch further through this forest as your
fellow.'

Whereupon he wrenched at his reins, that rider in the
woods,
Hit the horse with his heels as hard as he could,
Sent him leaping along, and left the knight there
Alone.
'By God!' said Gawain, 'I swear
I will not weep or groan:
Being given to God's good care,
My trust in Him shall be shown.'

VIII

Then he gave the spur to Gringolet and galloped down
the path,
Thrust through a thicket there by a bank,
And rode down the rough slope right into the ravine.
Then he searched about, but it seemed savage and wild,
And no sign did he see of any sort of dwelling;
But on both sides banks, beetling and steep,
And great crooked crags, cruelly jagged;
The bristling barbs of rock seemed to brush the sky.
Then he held in his horse, halted there,
Scanned on every side in search of the chapel.
He saw no such thing anywhere, which seemed remarkable,
Save, hard by in the open, a hillock of sorts,
A smooth-surfaced barrow on a slope beside a stream
Which flowed forth fast there in its course,
Foaming and frothing as if feverishly boiling.
The knight, urging his horse, pressed onwards to the
mound,
Dismounted manfully and made fast to a lime-tree
The reins, hooking them round a rough branch;
Then he went to the barrow, which he walked round,
inspecting,
Wondering what in the world it might be.
It had a hole in each end and on either side,
And was overgrown with grass in great patches.
All hollow it was within, only an old cavern
Or the crevice of an ancient crag: he could not explain it
Aright.
'O God, is the Chapel Green
This mound?' said the noble knight.
'At such might Satan be seen
Saying matins at midnight.'

IX

'Now certainly the place is deserted,' said Gawain,
'It is a hideous oratory, all overgrown,
And well graced for the gallant garbed in green
To deal out his devotions in the Devil's fashion.
Now I feel in my five wits, it is the Fiend himself
That has tricked me into this tryst, to destroy me here.
This is a chapel of mischance – checkmate to it!
It is the most evil holy place I ever entered.'
With his high helmet on his head, and holding his lance,
He roamed up to the roof of that rough dwelling.
Then from that height he heard, from a hard rock
On the bank beyond the brook, a barbarous noise.
What! It clattered amid the cliffs fit to cleave them apart,
As if a great scythe were being ground on a grindstone
there.
What! It whirred and it whetted, like water in a mill.
What! It made a rushing, ringing din, rueful to hear.
'By God!' then said Gawain, 'that is going on,
I suppose, as a salute to myself, to greet me
Hard by.
God's will be warranted:
"Alas!" is a craven cry.
No din shall make me dread
Although today I die.'

X

Then the courteous knight called out clamorously,
'Who holds sway here and has an assignation with me?
For the good knight Gawain is on the ground here.
If anyone there wants anything, wend your way hither fast,
And further your needs either now, or not at all.'
'Bide there!' said one on the bank above his head,
'And you shall swiftly receive what I once swore to give
you.'
Yet for a time he continued his tumult of scraping,
Turning away as he whetted, before he would descend.
Then he thrust himself round a thick crag through a hole,
Whirling round a wedge of rock with a frightful weapon,
A Danish axe duly honed for dealing the blow,
With a broad biting edge, bow-bent along the handle,
Ground on a grindstone, a great four-foot blade –
No less, by that love-lace gleaming so brightly!
And the gallant in green was garbed as at first,
His looks and limbs the same, his locks and beard;
Save that steadily on his feet he strode on the ground,
Setting the handle to the stony earth and stalking beside it.
He would not wade through the water when he came to it,
But vaulted over on his axe, then with huge strides
Advanced violently and fiercely along the field's width
On the snow.

Sir Gawain went to greet
The knight, not bowing low.
The man said, 'Sir so sweet,
You honour the trysts you owe.'

XI

'Gawain,' said the green knight, 'may God guard you!
You are welcome to my dwelling, I warrant you,
And you have timed your travel here as a true man ought.
You know plainly the pact we pledged between us:
This time a twelvemonth ago you took your portion,
And now at this New Year I should nimbly requite you.
And we are on our own here in this valley
With no seconds to sunder us, spar as we will.
Take your helmet off your head, and have your payment
here.
And offer no more argument or action than I did
When you whipped off my head with one stroke.'
'No,' said Gawain, 'by God who gave me a soul,
The grievous gash to come I grudge you not at all;
Strike but the one stroke and I shall stand still
And offer you no hindrance: you may act freely,
I swear.'
Head bent, Sir Gawain bowed,
And showed the bright flesh bare.
He behaved as if uncowed,
Being loth to display his care.

XII

Then the gallant in green quickly got ready,
Heaved his horrid weapon on high to hit Gawain,
With all the brute force in his body bearing it aloft,
Swinging savagely enough to strike him dead.
Had it driven down as direly as he aimed,
The daring dauntless man would have died with the blow.
But Gawain glanced up at the grim axe beside him
As it came shooting through the shivering air to shatter
him,
And his shoulders shrank slightly from the sharp edge.
The other suddenly stayed the descending axe,
And then reproved the prince with many proud words:
'You are not Gawain,' said the gallant, 'whose greatness is
such
That by hill or hollow no army ever frightened him;
For now you flinch for fear before you feel harm.
I never did know that knight to be a coward.
I neither flinched nor fled when you let fly your blow,
Nor offered any quibble in the house of King Arthur.
My head flew to my feet, but flee I did not.
Yet you quail cravenly though unscathed so far.
So I am bound to be called the better man
Therefore.'
Said Gawain, 'Not again
Shall I flinch as I did before;
But if my head pitch to the plain,
It's off for evermore.

XIII

'But be brisk, man, by your faith, and bring me to the
point;
Deal me my destiny and do it out of hand,
For I shall stand your stroke, not starting at all
Till your axe has hit me. Here is my oath on it.'
'Have at you then,' said the other, heaving up his axe,
Behaving as angrily as if he were mad.
He menaced him mightily, but made no contact,
Smartly withholding his hand without hurting him.
Gawain waited unswerving, with not a wavering limb,
But stood still as a stone or the stump of a tree
Gripping the rocky ground with a hundred grappling roots.
Then again the green knight began to gird:
'So now you have a whole heart I must hit you.
May the high knighthood which Arthur conferred
Preserve you and save your neck, if so it avail you!'
Then said Gawain, storming with sudden rage,
'Thrash on, you thrustful fellow, you threaten too much.
It seems your spirit is struck with self-dread.'
'Forsooth,' the other said, 'You speak so fiercely
I will no longer lengthen matters by delaying your
business,
I vow.'
He stood astride to smite,
Lips pouting, puckered brow.
No wonder he lacked delight
Who expected no help now.

XIV

Up went the axe at once and hurtled down straight
At the naked neck with its knife-like edge.
Though it swung down savagely, slight was the wound,
A mere snick on the side, so that the skin was broken.
Through the fair fat to the flesh fell the blade,
And over his shoulders the shimmering blood shot to
the ground.

When Sir Gawain saw his gore glinting on the snow,
He leapt feet close together a spear's length away,
Hurriedly heaved his helmet on to his head,
And shrugging his shoulders, shot his shield to the front,
Swung out his bright sword and said fiercely
(For never had the knight since being nursed by his mother
Been so buoyantly happy, so blithe in this world),
'Cease your blows, sir, strike me no more.
I have sustained a stroke here unresistingly,
And if you offer any more I shall earnestly reply,
Resisting, rest assured, with the most rancorous
Despite.
The single stroke is wrought
To which we pledged our plight
In high King Arthur's court:
Enough now, therefore, knight!'

XV

The bold man stood back and bent over his axe,
Putting the haft to earth, and leaning on the head.
He gazed at Sir Gawain on the ground before him,
Considering the spirited and stout way he stood,
Audacious in arms; his heart warmed to him.
Then he gave utterance gladly in his great voice,
With resounding speech saying to the knight,
'Bold man, do not be so bloodily resolute.
No one here has offered you evil discourteously,
Contrary to the covenant made at King Arthur's court.
I promised a stroke, which you received: consider yourself
paid.
I cancel all other obligations of whatever kind.
If I had been more active, perhaps I could
Have made you suffer by striking a savager stroke.
First in foolery I made a feint at striking,
Not rending you with a riving cut – and right I was,
On account of the first night's covenant we accorded;
For you truthfully kept your trust in troth with me,
Giving me your gains, as a good man should.
The further feinted blow was for the following day,
When you kissed my comely wife, and the kisses came to
me:
For those two things, harmlessly I thrust twice at you
Feinted blows.
Truth for truth's the word;
No need for dread, God knows.
From your failure at the third
The tap you took arose.

XVI

'For that braided belt you wear belongs to me.
I am well aware that my own wife gave it you.
Your conduct and your kissings are completely known to
me,
And the wooing of my wife – my work set it on.
I instructed her to try you, and you truly seem
To be the most perfect paladin ever to pace the earth.
As the pearl to the white pea in precious worth,
So in good faith is Gawain to other gay knights.
But here your faith failed you, you flagged somewhat, sir,
Yet it was not for a well-wrought thing, nor for wooing
either,
But for love of your life, which is less blameworthy.'
The other strong man stood considering this a while,
So filled with fury that his flesh trembled,
And the blood from his breast burst forth in his face
As he shrank for shame at what the chevalier spoke of.
The first words the fair knight could frame were:
'Curses on both cowardice and covetousness!
Their vice and villainy are virtue's undoing.'
Then he took the knot, with a twist twitched it loose,
And fiercely flung the fair girdle to the knight.
'Lo! There is the false thing, foul fortune befall it!
I was craven about our encounter, and cowardice taught me
To accord with covetousness and corrupt my nature
And the liberality and loyalty belonging to chivalry.
Now I am faulty and false and found fearful always.
In the train of treachery and untruth go woe
And shame.
I acknowledge, knight, how ill
I behaved, and take the blame.
Award what penance you will:
Henceforth I'll shun ill-fame.'

XVII

Then the other lord laughed and politely said,
'In my view you have made amends for your
misdemeanour;
You have confessed your faults fully with fair
acknowledgement,
And plainly done penance at the point of my axe.
You are absolved of your sin and as stainless now
As if you had never fallen in fault since first you were born.
As for the gold-hemmed girdle, I give it you, sir.
Seeing it is as green as my gown, Sir Gawain, you may
Think about this trial when you throng in company
With paragons of princes, for it is a perfect token,

At knightly gatherings, of the great adventure at the
Green Chapel.
You shall come back to my castle this cold New Year,
And we shall revel away the rest of this rich feast;
Let us go.'
Thus urging him, the lord
Said, 'You and my wife, I know
We shall bring to clear accord,
Though she was your fierce foe.'

XVIII

'No, forsooth,' said the knight, seizing his helmet,
And doffing it with dignity as he delivered his thanks,
'My stay has sufficed me. Still, luck go with you!
May He who bestows all good, honour you with it!
And commend me to the courteous lady, your comely wife;
Indeed, my due regards to both dear ladies,
Who with their wanton wiles have thus waylaid their
knight.
But it is no marvel for a foolish man to be maddened thus
And saddled with sorrow by the sleights of women.
For here on earth was Adam taken in by one,
And Solomon by many such, and Samson likewise;
Delilah dealt him his doom; and David, later still,
Was blinded by Bathsheba, and badly suffered for it.
Since these were troubled by their tricks, it would be true
joy
To love them but not believe them, if a lord could,
For these were the finest of former times, most favoured by
fortune
Of all under the heavenly kingdom whose hearts were
Abused;
These four all fell to schemes
Of women whom they used.
If I am snared, it seems
I ought to be excused.

XIX

'But your girdle,' said Gawain, 'God requite you for it!
Not for the glorious gold shall I gladly wear it,
Nor for the stuff nor the silk nor the swaying pendants,
Nor for its worth, fine workmanship or wonderful honour;
But as a sign of my sin I shall see it often,
Remembering with remorse, when I am mounted in glory,
The fault and faintheartedness of the perverse flesh,
How it tends to attract tarnishing sin.
So when pride shall prick me for my prowess in arms,
One look at this love-lace will make lowly my heart.
But one demand I make of you, may it not incommode
you:
Since you are master of the demesne I have remained in a
while,
Make known, by your knighthood, – and now may He
above,
Who sits on high and holds up heaven, requite you! –
How you pronounce your true name; and no more
requests.'
'Truly,' the other told him, 'I shall tell you my title.
Bertilak of the High Desert I am called here in this land.
Through the might of Morgan the Fay, who remains in
my house.
Through the wiles of her witchcraft, a lore well learned –
Many of the magical arts of Merlin has she acquired,
For she lavished fervent love long ago
On that susceptible sage: certainly your knights know
Of their fame.
So "Morgan the goddess"
She accordingly became;
The proudest she can oppress
And to her purpose tame –

XX

'She sent me forth in this form to your famous hall
To put to the proof the great pride of the house,
The reputation for high renown of the Round Table;
She bewitched me in this weird way to bewilder your wits,
And to grieve Guinevere and goad her to death
With ghastly fear of that ghost's ghoulish speaking
With his head in his hand before the high table.
That is the aged beldame who is at home:
She is indeed your own aunt, Arthur's half-sister,
Daughter of the Duchess of Tintagel who in due course,
By Uther, was mother of Arthur, who now holds sway.
Therefore I beg you, bold sir, come back to your aunt,
Make merry in my house, for my men love you,
And by my faith, brave sir, I bear you as much good will
As I grant any man under God, for your great honesty.'
But Gawain firmly refused with a final negative.
They clasped and kissed, commending each other
To the Prince of Paradise, and parted on the cold ground
Right there.
Gawain on steed serene
Spurred to court with courage fair,
And the gallant garbed in green
To wherever he would elsewhere.

XXI

Now Gawain goes riding on Gringolet
In lonely lands, his life saved by grace.
Often he stayed at a house, and often in the open,
And often overcame hazards in the valleys,
Which at this time I do not intend to tell you about.
The hurt he had had in his neck was healed,
And the glittering girdle that girt him round
Obliquely, like a baldric, was bound by his side
And laced under the left arm with a lasting knot,
In token that he was taken in a tarnishing sin;
And so he came to court, quite unscathed.
When the great became aware of Gawain's arrival,
There was general jubilation at the joyful news.
The King kissed the knight, and the Queen likewise,
And so did many a staunch noble who sought to salute him.
They all asked him about his expedition,
And he truthfully told them of his tribulations –
What chanced at the chapel, the good cheer of the knight,
The lady's love-making, and lastly, the girdle.
He displayed the scar of the snick on his neck
Where the bold man's blow had bit, his bad faith to
Proclaim;
He groaned at his disgrace,
Unfolding his ill-fame,
And blood suffused his face
When he showed his mark of shame.

XXII

'Look, my lord,' said Gawain, the lace in his hand.
'This belt confirms the blame I bear on my neck,
My bane and debasement, the burden I bear
For being caught by cowardice and covetousness.
This is the figure of the faithlessness found in me,
Which I must needs wear while I live.
For man can conceal sin but not dissever from it,
So, when it is once fixed, it will never be worked loose.'
First the King, then all the court, comforted the knight,
And all the lords and ladies belonging to the Table
Laughed at it loudly, and concluded amiably
That each brave man of the brotherhood should bear a
baldric,
A band, obliquely about him, of a bright green,
Of the same hue as Sir Gawain's, and for his sake wear it.
So it ranked as renown to the Round Table,
And an everlasting honour to him who had it,
As is rendered in Romance's rarest book.
Thus in the days of Arthur this exploit was achieved,
To which the books of Brutus bear witness;
After the bold baron, Brutus, came here,
The siege and the assault being ceased at Troy
Before.
Such exploits, I'll be sworn,
Have happened here of yore.
Now Christ with his crown of thorn
Bring us his bliss evermore! AMEN

HONY SOYT QUI MAL PENCE

SIR THOMAS MALORY

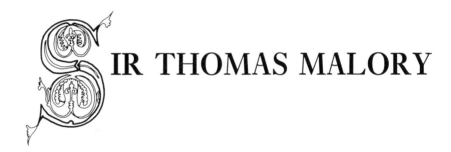

The most piteous tale of the Morte Arthur Saunz Guerdon

The Round Table at the feast of Pentecost (Whitsun), from a North Italian manuscript of the late fourteenth century (Paris, Bibliothèque Nationale MS Fr. 343 f.3)

THE FRENCH CYCLE OF ROMANCES · MALORY AND HIS WORK · LANCELOT AS HERO · MALORY'S ACHIEVEMENT & & &

From single romances with individual heroes, French writers moved on to an attempt to tell the whole history of Arthur and his knights, beginning with the earliest events in the story of the Holy Grail and ending with the dissolution of the Round Table. The cycle of linked romances that resulted exists in varying versions, but generally speaking they fall into five parts: *The History of the Holy Grail*, dealing with the story of how Joseph of Arimathea brought the Grail to Britain; *Merlin*, describing the birth and early adventures of the magician, up to the birth and coronation of Arthur; *Lancelot*, a huge compilation of all the secular adventures of Arthur's knights; *The Quest for the Holy Grail*, which was derived from Chrétien's work but with strong spiritual overtones; and finally *The Death of Arthur*, describing the end of the Round Table. This vast body of material could be added to at will, as the story did not follow a rigid outline, but consisted of interwoven episodes, different adventures which the story-teller picked up and left at will: extra adventures could easily be introduced. But in the fifteenth century, there was a general demand for an abbreviated, more coherent version, and two or three Continental examples of attempts at this have survived.

The greatest of all these new versions, however, was that made by Sir Thomas Malory, 'knight-prisoner', in the 1460s, translating it into English. Much has been written about Malory's identity, and whether he wrote a single work or eight separate tales. Both questions are still open: there are three possible Thomas Malorys who might be the author, and the argument as to the nature of his work depends on whether you prefer William Caxton's description of it as a 'whole book', or the one surviving manuscript which divides it into eight separate tales. Personally, I think that Caxton's description underlines the change from manuscripts to books: a manuscript was made up slowly and piecemeal, and the binding might unite, by chance or otherwise, more than one item, or might impose an arbitrary division. A book, on the other hand, was always an entity, a single unit. Malory's work, on the internal evidence, is somewhere between the two: it is a cycle of stories which combine to form a unit, and Malory certainly intended to make a complete and whole cycle, though not a single unity, from his material.

Malory's sources were not entirely French. He seems to have begun translating into prose the alliterative poem *Morte Arthure* (see p. 11 above), and he may have returned to another English poem in his closing pages. But the bulk of *Le Morte Darthur* is taken from 'the French book' which he often quotes as an authority. He does not follow it slavishly, however, and differs notably in his technique of storytelling. As already mentioned, in the French a number of themes were interwoven in an almost inextricable mesh, giving a tapestry-like effect to the whole. Quite frequently, the themes or their sequels extended between separate romances, thus giving the cycle its unity. Malory succeeded in both isolating many of the incidents, often told in passages many pages apart in the French, and in strengthening such links as remained, especially if they offered a point of contact between his own tales. This process is well illustrated by *The Tale*

The knights depart from Arthur's court in quest of the Holy Grail. North Italian, late fourteenth century.
(Paris, Bibliothèque Nationale, MS Fr. 343 f.8ᵛ)

of Balin and Balan, where Malory has added to the original story the incident of the Dolorous Blow, by which an entire country is laid waste. The latter forms a quite separate incident in the original, but by adding it, Malory heightens the portrayal of Balin as a fated knight, who is destined to do harm. It is chiefly changes of this kind that distinguish *The Tale of King Arthur* from a mere translation, and which enable Malory to reduce the prominence of Morgan le Fay and Merlin, concentrating instead on Arthur himself.

Because Malory began with the *Morte Arthure*, Lancelot's early career is given a totally different emphasis from that in the French romances. He now rises to fame by his military exploits in Arthur's Roman wars, and goes on to become first knight of the Round Table in deeds of chivalry thereafter, whereas the reverse was true in the French cycle. His position as Guinevere's lover, the role in which his character first became of importance, is given less emphasis by Malory, who did not entirely sympathise with the point of view of the French writers on this.

When Malory came to *The Tale of Sir Lancelot du Lake* he selected parts only of the French *Lancelot*. He began with the third section and reduced it by about a half, while retaining the outline of the original. He then moved to the next reference to the Lancelot-Lionel theme, separated by many pages of material on other themes in the French version, which he omits *en bloc*. The third section has no known source, but it is probable that Malory followed with the same degree of closeness a version of the romance now lost. The conclusion, as so often, is Malory's own, and probably cuts short his source well before the end.

The Tale of Sir Gareth is the shortest unit of Malory's works, really a single episode or theme from a larger romance, the *Prose Tristan*, which was not part of the main French cycle. *The Book of Sir Tristram de Lyones* which follows represents over one-third of his entire output, and is drawn from the same source. The introduction dealing with Tristram's parentage has been omitted, and the whole is divided into sections.

Malory has not altered the literary style of the French so much as its character. The Tristram story is not presented here as a tragedy; we only learn of the death of the lovers – in a version very different from the earliest and most familiar one – by chance remark in the last part of *Lancelot and Guinevere*. The tragic undertones disappear with the blackening of Mark's character, thus representing Iseult as in great measure justified in turning to Tristram. Tristram becomes above all a knight-errant; his love for Iseult seems to be less the prime motive of his existence than an adjunct of his chivalry. The return of the lovers to Joyous Gard is invented by Malory to replace the ending of the original, and we leave them in domestic bliss there. This replacement of earlier attitudes by his own brand of chivalry is typical of Malory; yet he fails to remove entirely Sir Dinadan, whose mocking counterpoint questions the very ideals he cherishes, in the manner of a privileged jester.

The original of the *Tale of the Sankgreall* was the French Vulgate *Quest for the Holy Grail*, this follows the *Lancelot* section to form the fourth branch of the cycle. No surviving manuscript exactly corresponds to the passages selected by Malory, but there are no substantial differences in the actual material. His skill here has been directed at omissions calculated to alter considerably the character of the Quest. The French work was virtually an exposition of the doctrine of Grace and Salvation, and to emphasise and interpret the lesson of each adventure hermits appear on every other page, moralising or preaching over the unfortunate knights whose injuries they tend. Malory ruthlessly excises most of these, and abbreviates the moralisings of the surviving hermits. In doing so, he manages to make Lancelot, and the chivalry which Lancelot represents, emerge with much greater credit from the Grail adventures. He seems to have been concerned to diminish the distinction between religious and secular chivalry, and to remove the religious atmosphere of purification and repentance as a keynote of the Quest. Lancelot's relative success is emphasised rather than his eventual failure at the vital stage. If the result is not always sound theology, it brings the story more into line with the rest of the cycle.

For the last two of his eight tales, Malory combined English and French romances, but depended less and less on his sources. The two works he used were an early fifteenth-century rhyming poem in English, *Le Mort Arthur*, and the conclusion of the Vulgate Cycle, *La Mort Artu*. In the *Book of Sir Launcelot and Queen Guinevere*, the first two parts are careful selections taken almost directly from the sources. Thereafter he departs from any known version of either French or English. In *The Great Tournament*, for example, the actual description of the tournament is Malory's own work, and *The Knight of the Cart* is very much rewritten: whereas Chrétien long ago had made Lancelot's journey in the cart so shameful that Guinevere seemed almost divine in her power over him, Malory passes it over as merely another adventure. In *The Healing of Sir Urry*, he presents his own contribution to the legend, the apotheosis of Lancelot. After a vast procession of knights, whose names read like a roll-call of Malory's by now extensive reading, have failed to heal the stricken Sir Urry, Lancelot succeeds, and, movingly, weeps 'as he had been a child that had been beaten' when this private miracle is granted him.

Until now, in spite of *The Tale of the Sankgreall*, Malory had had relatively little difficulty in making Lancelot his hero. But when he came to the tragic conclusion of the cycle, he found that the French writers had made Lancelot the main agent of Arthur's downfall. Malory could not blame him for this without bringing down the whole carefully-constructed edifice built around the idea of Lancelot as the flower of chivalry; nor did the blunt statement at the end of the previous tale actually resolve the problem: 'and now I go unto the morte Arthur, and that caused sir Aggravayne'. He had to make a major alteration to the emphasis of the old tale, and he effected this by standing back from all moral judgements, thus shifting the focus onto character and situation rather than cause and effect. The feeling throughout this last book is that of a series of accidents, combined with regret and longing for what might have been. By heightening the intimacy of the relationship between Lancelot, Guinevere, Arthur and Gawain, the tragedy is intensified. Loyalty plays an important part: Lancelot's loyalty to Guinevere is brought into implacable opposition to Gawain's loyalty to kith and kin.

The conclusion is the most brilliant part of the work. The author of *La Mort Artu* became over-florid and the English poet insipid when confronted with this problem, but it is here that Malory's prose reaches its majestic climax of greatness and grief. His revision of the incidents of the last stages of the disaster is done with much finesse and feeling, especially where Lancelot's death is concerned. The French version makes him die, rather uncharacteristically, of religious devotion; but Malory gives the cause as his enduring love for Guinevere. A certain premonition of disaster before the great battle between Arthur and Mordred heightens the tension, while the aftermath shows the totality and human intensity of the tragedy.

Within the ponderous elaborations of the Vulgate Cycle, there lay hidden a great epic drama, ranging through every human passion, joy and grief. Malory drew out the noble tragedy of Arthur from the mass of adventures and marvels in which it had become entangled, and gave to it a new unity and clarity. He made its protagonists real people once more, stripped off the moralising to restore the unrelenting onset of the tragedy, and gave to the climax a befitting majesty and grandeur which it had never before attained. It needed Malory's skilful hand and the remarkable clarity of his prose to reveal the full force of the 'noble chyvalrye, curtosye, humanyté, frendlynesse, hardynesse, love, frendshyp, cowardyse, murdre, hate, vertue and synne' which in Caxton's words the epic contained. By doing so he ensured that the Arthurian tradition, at least in England, did not become a mere literary curiosity like the medieval stories of Charlemagne and Alexander but would re-emerge to inspire new masterpieces.

Lancelot arrives just in time to save Guinevere from being burnt at the stake for her adultery with him. In the fray he kills Gawain's brothers, Gareth and Gaheriet, by mistake, and this leads to war between him and Arthur. From a North French manuscript dated 1274.
(*Paris, Bibliothèque Nationale, MS Fr.342, f.186*)

The transcription which follows is modernised in spelling only, with one or two rare words translated. It is based on A. W. Pollard's version of 1911, using Caxton's text but takes into account the readings of the unique manuscript found in 1934.

The most piteous tale of the Morte Arthur Saunz Guerdon

As Sir Mordred was ruler of all England, he let make letters as though that they had come from beyond the sea, and the letters specified that King Arthur was slain in battle with Sir Launcelot. Wherefore Sir Mordred made a parliament, and called the lords together, and there he made them to choose him king; and so was he crowned at Canterbury, and held a feast there fifteen days.

And afterward he drew him unto Winchester, and there he took Queen Guenever, and said plainly that he would wed her which was his uncle's wife and his father's wife. And so he made ready for the feast, and a day prefixed that they should be wedded; wherefore Queen Guenever was passing heavy. But she durst not discover her heart, but spake fair, and agreed to Sir Mordred's will.

And anow she desired of Sir Mordred to go to London, to buy all manner of things that longed to the bridal. And because of her fair speech Sir Mordred trusted her well enough, and gave her leave; and so when she came to London she took the Tower of London, and suddenly in all haste possible she stuffed it with all manner of victual, and well garnished it with men, and so kept it.

And when Sir Mordred wist this, he was passing wroth out of measure. And, short tale to make, he laid a mighty siege about the Tower of London, and made many assaults, and threw engines unto them, and shot great guns. But all might not prevail for Queen Guenever would never, for fair speech nor for foul, never to trust unto Sir Mordred to come in his hands again.

Then came the Bishop of Canterbury, the which was a noble clerk and an holy man, and thus he said to Sir Mordred: Sir, what will ye do? will ye first displease God and sithen shame yourself, and all knighthood? Is not King Arthur your uncle, no farther but your mother's brother, and on her himself King Arthur begat you upon his own sister, therefore how may you wed your father's wife? And therefore Sir, said the Bishop, leave this opinion or I shall curse you with book and bell and candle. Do thy worst, said Sir Mordred, and I defy thee. Sir, said the Bishop, wit you well I shall not fear me to do that me ought to do. Also where ye noise where my lord Arthur is slain, and that is not so, and therefore ye will make a foul work in this land. Peace, thou false priest, said Sir Mordred, for an thou chafe me any more I shall strike off thy head.

So the Bishop departed and did the cursing in the most solemn wise that might be done. And then Sir Mordred sought the Bishop of Canterbury, for to have slain him. Then the Bishop fled, and took part of his goods with him, and went nigh unto Glastonbury; and there he was a priest-hermit in a chapel, and lived in poverty and in holy prayers, for well he understood that mischievous war was at hand.

Then Sir Mordred sought on Queen Guenever by letters and sonds, and by fair means and foul means, for to have her to come out of the Tower of London; but all this availed not, for she answered him shortly, openly and privily, that she had liefer slay herself than to be married with him. Then came word to Sir Mordred that King

Arthur had araised the siege for Sir Launcelot, and he was coming homeward with a great host, to be avenged upon Sir Mordred; wherefore Sir Mordred made writs to all the barony of this land. And much people drew to him; for then was the common voice among them that with Arthur was none other life but war and strife, and with Sir Mordred was great joy and bliss. Thus was King Arthur depraved, and evil said of; and many there were that King Arthur had brought up of nought, and given them lands, might not then say him a good word.

Lo ye all Englishmen, see ye not what a mischief here was! For he that was the most king and noblest knight of the world, and most loved the fellowship of noble knights, and by him they all were upholden, now might not these Englishmen hold them content with him. Lo thus was the old custom and usage of this land; and also men say that we of this land have not yet lost nor forgotten that custom and usage. Alas, this is a great default of us Englishmen, for there may no thing please us for long.

And so fared the people at that time, they were better pleased with Sir Mordred than they were with King Arthur; and much people drew unto Sir Mordred, and said they would abide with him for better and for worse. And so Sir Mordred drew with a great host to Dover, for there he heard say that King Arthur would arrive, and so he thought to beat his own father from his lands; and the most part of all England held with Sir Mordred, the people were so new-fangled.

And so as Sir Mordred was at Dover with his host, there came King Arthur with a great navy of ships, and galleys, and carracks. And there was Sir Mordred ready awaiting upon his landing, to hinder his own father from landing upon the land that he was King over.

Then there was launching of great boats and small, and full of noble men of arms; and there was much slaughter of gentle knights, and many a full bold baron was laid full low, on both parties.

But King Arthur was so courageous that there might no manner of knights let him to land, and his knights fiercely followed him; and so they landed in spite of Sir Mordred and all his power, and put Sir Mordred aback, that he fled and all his people.

So when this battle was done, King Arthur let bury his people that were dead. And then was noble Sir Gawaine found in a great boat, lying more than half dead. When King Arthur knew that he was laid so low, he went unto him and so found him. And there the King made sorrow out of measure, and took Sir Gawaine in his arms, and thrice he there swooned. And then when he was waked, King Arthur said: Alas, Sir Gawaine, my sister's son, here now thou liest, the man in the world that I loved most; and now is my joy gone, for now, my nephew Sir Gawaine, I will discover me unto your person: in Sir Launcelot and you I most had my joy, and mine affiance, and now have I lost my joy of you both; wherefore all mine earthly joy is gone from me.

Ah, my uncle, said Sir Gawaine, now I want you to know that my death-day is come! And all, I may wit, though mine own hastiness and my wilfulness, for through my wilfulness I was causer of my own death; for I was this day hurt and smitten upon mine old wound that Sir Launcelot gave me, and I feel myself that I must needs be dead by the hour of noon. And through me and my pride ye have all this shame and disease, for had that noble knight Sir Launcelot been with you, as he was and would have been, this unhappy war had never been begun; for he, through his noble knighthood and his noble blood, held all your cankered enemies in subjection and danger. And now, said Sir Gawaine, ye shall miss Sir Launcelot. But alas, I would not accord with him, and therefore, fair uncle, I pray you that I may have paper, pen and ink, that I may write unto Sir Launcelot a letter written with mine own hand.

So when paper, pen and ink was brought, then Sir Gawaine was set up weakly by King Arthur, for he was shriven a little to-fore. And then he took his pen and wrote thus, as the French book maketh mention:

Unto thee, Sir Launcelot, flower of all noble knights that ever I heard of or saw by my days, I Sir Gawaine, King Lot's son of Orkney, and sister's son unto the noble King Arthur, send thee greeting, letting thee have knowledge that the tenth day of May I was smitten upon the old wound that thou gavest me afore the city of Benwick, and through that wound I am come to my death-day. And I will that all the world wit, that I, Sir Gawaine, knight of the Table Round, sought my death, and not through thy deserving, but mine own seeking. Wherefore I beseech thee, Sir Launcelot, to return again unto this realm, and see my tomb, and pray some prayer more or less for my soul. And this same day that I wrote the same letter, I was hurt to the death, which wound I had of thy hand, Sir Launcelot; for of a more nobler man might I not be slain.

Also Sir Launcelot, for all the love that ever was betwixt us, make no tarrying, but come over the sea in all the goodly haste that ye may with your noble knights, and rescue that noble King that made thee knight; for he is full straitly bestead with a false traitor, that is my half-brother, Sir Mordred. For he hath crowned himself King, and would have wedded my lady Queen Guenever, and so had he done had she not kept the Tower of London with strong hand. And so the tenth day of May last past, my lord King Arthur and we all landed upon them at Dover; and there he put that false traitor, Sir Mordred, to flight. And so it thus misfortuned me to be smitten upon the stroke that ye gave me of old. And the date of this letter was written but two hours and a half afore my death, written with mine own hand and subscribed with part of my heart's blood. And therefore I require thee, most famous knight of the world, that thou wilt see my tomb.

And then he wept, and King Arthur both; and swooned. And when they were awaked both, the King made Sir Gawaine to receive his sacrament, and then Sir Gawaine prayed the King for to send for Sir Launcelot and to cherish him above all other knights.

And so at the hour of noon Sir Gawaine yielded up the ghost. And then the King let inter him in a chapel within Dover Castle. And there yet all men may see the skull of him, and the same wound is seen that Sir Launcelot gave in battle.

Then was it told the King that Sir Mordred had pitched a new field upon Barham Down. And upon the morn the King rode thither to him, and there was a great battle betwixt them, and much people was slain on both parties. But at the last King Arthur's party stood best, and Sir Mordred and his party fled unto Canterbury.

And then the King let search all the downs for his knights that were slain, and interred them; and salved them with soft salves that full sore were wounded. Then much people drew unto King Arthur, and then they said that Sir Mordred warred upon King Arthur with wrong.

And then King Arthur drew him with his host down by the seaside westward, toward Salisbury. And there was a day assigned betwixt King Arthur and Sir Mordred, that they should meet upon a down beside Salisbury, and not far from the seaside; and this day was assigned on a Monday after Trinity Sunday, whereof King Arthur was passing glad, that he might be avenged upon Sir Mordred.

Then Sir Mordred araised much people about London, for they of Kent, Southsex, and Surrey, Estsex, and of Southfolk, and of Northfolk, held the most part with Sir Mordred and many a full noble knight drew unto Sir Mordred; and to the King: but they that loved Sir Launcelot drew unto Sir Mordred.

So upon Trinity Sunday at night, King Arthur dreamed a wonderful dream, and in his dream him seemed he saw upon a scaffold a chair, and the chair was fast to a wheel, and thereupon sat King Arthur in the richest cloth of gold that might be made. And the King thought there was under him, far from him, an hideous deep black water, and therein were all manner of serpents, and worms, and wild beasts, foul and horrible. And suddenly the King thought the wheel turned up-so-down, and he fell among the serpents, and every beast took him by a limb; and then the King cried as he lay in his bed and slept: Help, help!

And then knights, squires, and yeomen, awaked the King; and then he was so amazed that he wist not where he was; and then he fell a-slumbering again, not sleeping nor thoroughly waking. So the King seemed verily that there came Sir Gawaine unto him with a number of fair ladies with him. So when King Arthur saw him, then he said: Welcome, my sister's son; I weened thou hadst been dead, and now I see thee alive, much am I beholding unto Almighty Jesu. Ah, fair nephew, what be these ladies that hither be come with you? Sir, said Sir Gawaine, all these be ladies for whom I have fought when I was a man living, and all these are those that I did battle for in righteous quarrel; and God hath given them that grace at their great prayer, because I did battle for them for their right, that they should bring me hither unto you. Thus much hath God given me leave for to warn you of your death; for if ye fight tomorrow with Sir Mordred, as ye both have assigned, doubt ye not ye shall be slain, and the most part of your people on both parties. And for the great grace and goodness that Almighty Jesu hath unto you, and for pity of you, and many more other good men there shall be slain, God hath sent me to you of his special grace, to give you warning that in no wise ye do battle as to-morn, but that ye take a treaty for a month day; and proffer you largely, so that to-morn ye put in a delay. For within a month shall come Sir Launcelot with all his noble knights, and rescue you worshipfully, and slay Sir Mordred, and all that ever will hold with him.

Then Sir Gawaine and all the ladies vanished, and anon the King called upon his knights, squires, and yeomen, and charged them wightly to fetch his noble lords and wise bishops unto him. And when they were come, the King told them his vision, what Sir Gawaine had told him, and warned him that if he fought on the morn he should be slain. Then the King commanded Sir Lucan the Butler, and his brother Sir Bedivere the Bold, with two bishops with them, and charged them in any wise to take a treaty for a month day with Sir Mordred. And spare not, proffer him lands and goods as much as ye think best. So then they departed, and came to Sir Mordred, where he had a grim host of an hundred thousand, and there they entreated Sir Mordred long time, and at the last Sir Mordred was agreed for to have Cornwall and Kent, by King Arthur's days; and after that, all England, after the days of King Arthur.

Then were they condescended that King Arthur and Sir Mordred should meet betwixt both their hosts, and everych of them should bring fourteen persons; and they came with this word unto Arthur. Then said he: I am glad that this is done: and so he went into the field.

And when King Arthur should depart, he warned all his host that an they see any sword drawn: Look ye come on fiercely, and slay that traitor Sir Mordred, for I in no wise trust him. In like wise Sir Mordred warned his host that: If ye see any sword drawn, look that ye come on fiercely, and so slay all that ever before you standeth; for in no wise I will not trust for this treaty; for I know well my father will be avenged on me.

And so they met as their appointment was, and so they were agreed and accorded thoroughly. And wine was fetched, and they drank together. Right soon came an adder out of a little heath bush, and it stung a knight on the foot. And when the knight felt him stung, he looked down and saw the adder, and then he drew his sword to slay the adder, and thought of none other harm. And when the host on both parties saw that sword drawn, then they blew beams, trumpets, and horns, and shouted grimly, and so both hosts dressed them together. And King Arthur took his horse, and said: Alas this unhappy day! and so rode to his party. And Sir Mordred in like wise.

And never since was there seen a more dolefuller battle in no Christian land; for there was but rushing and riding, foining and striking, and many a grim word was there spoken either to other, and many a deadly stroke. But ever King Arthur rode throughout the battle of Sir Mordred many times, and did full nobly, as a noble King should do, and at all times he fainted never; and Sir Mordred did his duty that day and put himself in great peril.

And thus they fought all the day long, and never stinted till the noble knights were laid to the cold earth; and ever they fought still till it was near night, and by that time was there an hundred thousand laid dead upon the down. Then was King Arthur wood wroth out of measure, when he saw his people so slain from him.

And so he looked about him and could see no more of all his host and good knights left no more alive but two knights; the one was Sir Lucan the Butler, and his brother Sir Bedivere, and yet they were full sore wounded.

Jesu mercy, said the King, where are all my noble knights become? Alas that ever I should see this doleful day, for now said King Arthur, I am come to mine end. But would to God that I wist now where were that traitor Sir Mordred, that hath caused all this mischief. Then King Arthur looked about and was ware where stood Sir Mordred leaning upon his sword among a great heap of dead men.

Now give me my spear, said Arthur unto Sir Lucan, for yonder I have espied the traitor that all this woe hath wrought. Sir, let him be, said Sir Lucan, for he is unhappy; and if ye pass this unhappy day ye shall be right well revenged upon him. And, good lord, remember ye of your night's dream, and what the spirit of Sir Gawaine told you this night, yet God of his great goodness hath preserved you hitherto. And for God's sake, my lord, leave off this, for blessed be God ye have won the field, for here we be three alive and with Sir Mordred is not one alive. And therefore if ye leave off now this wicked day of destiny is past. Now tide me death, tide me life, saith the King, now I see him yonder alone he shall never escape mine hands, for at a better avail shall I never have him.

God speed you well, said Sir Bedivere.

Then the King gat his spear in both his hands, and ran toward Sir Mordred, crying and saying:

Traitor, now is thy death-day come. And when Sir Mordred saw King Arthur, he ran until him with his sword drawn in his hand, and there King Arthur smote Sir Mordred under the shield, with a foin of his spear, throughout the body, more than a fathom. And when Sir Mordred felt that he had his death wound he thrust himself with the might that he had up to the burr of King Arthur's spear, and right so he smote his father, King Arthur, with his sword holden in both his hands, on the side of the head, that the sword pierced the helmet and the brain-pan. And therewith Mordred dashed down stark dead to the earth.

And the noble King Arthur fell in a swoon to the earth, and there he swooned ofttimes, and Sir Lucan and Sir Bedivere ofttimes heaved him up. And so weakly betwixt them they led him to a little chapel not far from the sea, and when the King was there he thought him reasonably eased.

Then heard they people cry in the field. Now go thou, Sir Lucan, said the King, and do me to wit what betokens that noise in the field. So Sir Lucan departed, for he was grievously wounded in many places. And so as he went, he saw and hearkened by the moonlight, how that pillers and robbers were come into the field, to pill and to rob many

Because the illuminating of manuscripts of the complete cycle of stories was a long and expensive task, few of them were finished. The remaining illustrations in this section are modern artists' views of Malory's story. This is Arthur Rackham's version of the combat between Arthur and Mordred (1917).

a full noble knight of brooches, and beads, of many a good ring, and of many a rich jewel; and who that were not dead all out, there they slew them for their harness and their riches. When Sir Lucan understood this work, he came to the King as soon as he might, and told him all what he had heard and seen. Therefore by my rede, said Sir Lucan, it is best that we bring you to some town.

I would it were so, said the King, but I may not stand, mine head works so. Ah Sir Launcelot, said King Arthur, this day have I sore missed thee: alas, that ever I was against thee! For now have I my death, whereof Sir Gawaine me warned in my dream.

Then Sir Lucan took up the King the one part, and Sir Bedivere the other part, and in the lifting the King swooned; and Sir Lucan fell in a swoon with the lift, that the part of his guts fell out of his body, and therewith the noble knight's heart brast. And when the King awoke, he beheld Sir Lucan, how he lay foaming at the mouth, and part of his guts lay at his feet.

Alas, said the King, this is to me a full heavy sight, to see this noble duke so die for my sake, for he would have holpen me, that had more need of help than I. Alas, he would not complain him, his heart was so set to help me: now Jesu have mercy upon his soul!

Then Sir Bedivere wept for the death of his brother. Now leave this mourning and weeping, gentle knight, said the King, for all this will not avail me. For wit thou well if I might live myself, the death of Sir Lucan would grieve me evermore. But my time passeth on fast, said the King. Therefore, said King Arthur unto Sir Bedivere, take thou here Excalibur, my good sword, and go with it to yonder water side, and when thou comest there I charge thee throw my sword in that water, and come again and tell me what thou seest there. My lord, said Bedivere, your commandment shall be done, and lightly bring you word again.

So Sir Bedivere departed, and by the way he beheld that noble sword, and the pommel and the haft was all of precious stones; and then he said to himself: If I throw this rich sword in the water, thereof shall never come good, but harm and loss. And then Sir Bedivere hid Excalibur under a tree. And so, as soon as he might, he came again unto the King, and said he had been at the water, and had thrown the sword in the water. What saw thou there? said the King. Sir, he said, I saw nothing but waves and winds. That is untruly said of thee, said the King, therefore go thou lightly again, and do my commandment; as thou art to me lief and dear, spare not, but throw it in. Then Sir Bedivere returned again, and took the sword in his hand; and yet him thought sin and shame to throw away that noble sword, and so eft he hid the sword, and returned again, and told to the King that he had been at the water, and done his commandment. What saw thou there? said the King. Sir, he said, I saw nothing but waters wap and waves wan. Ah, traitor unto me and untrue, said King Arthur, now has thou betrayed me twice. Who would have weened that, thou that hast been to me so lief and dear, and also named a noble knight, and would betray me for the richness of the sword? But now go again lightly, for thy long tarrying putteth me in great jeopardy of my life, for I have taken cold. And but if thou do now as I bid thee, if ever I may see thee, I shall slay thee with mine own hands; for thou wouldst for my rich sword see me dead.

The Sir Bedivere departed, and went to the sword, and lightly took it up, and so he went to the water side; and there he bound the girdle about the hilts, and then he threw the sword as far into the water as he might; and there came an arm and an hand above the water and met it, and clasped it, and so shook it thrice and brandished, and then vanished with the sword in the water. So Sir Bedivere came again to the King, and told him what he saw. Alas, said the King, help me hence, for I dread me I have tarried over long.

Then Sir Bedivere took the King upon his back, and so went with him to that water side. And when they were there, even fast by the bank hoved a little barge with many fair ladies in it, and among them all was a queen, and all they had black hoods. And all they wept and shrieked when they saw King Arthur. Now put me into the barge, said the King. And so he did softly; and there received him three queens with great mourning; and so they set them down, and in one of their laps King Arthur laid his head. And then that queen said: Ah, dear brother, why have ye tarried so long from me? alas, this wound on your head hath caught over-much cold. And so then they rowed from the land, and Sir Bedivere beheld all those ladies go from him. Then Sir Bedivere cried: Ah my lord Arthur, what shall become of me, now ye go from me and leave me here alone among mine enemies? Comfort thyself, said the King, and do as well as thou mayst, for in me is no trust for to trust in; for I will into the vale of Avilion to heal me of my grievous wound: and if thou hear never more of me, pray for my soul.

But ever the queens and ladies wept and shrieked, that it was pity to hear. And as soon as Sir Bedivere had lost the sight of the barge, he wept and wailed, and so took the forest, and went all that night.

And in the morning he was ware betwixt two holts hoar, of a chapel and an hermitage. Then was Sir Bedivere glad, and thither he went; and when he came into the chapel, he saw where lay an hermit grovelling on all four, there fast by a tomb was new graven. When the hermit saw Sir Bedivere he knew him well, for he was but little to-fore Bishop of Canterbury, that Sir Mordred banished. Sir, said Sir Bedivere, what man is there interred that ye pray so fast for? Fair son, said the hermit, I wot not verily, but by deeming. But this night, at midnight, here came a number of ladies, and brought hither a dead corpse, and prayed me to inter him; and here they offered an hundred tapers, and they gave me a thousand besants. Alas, said

The death of Arthur; an unfinished picture by F. G. Stephens (c. 1850–5).
(Tate Gallery)

Arthur and the weeping queens, by Dante Gabriel Rossetti.
(Tate Gallery)

Sir Bedivere, that was my lord King Arthur, that here lieth buried in this chapel.

Then Sir Bedivere swooned; and when he awoke he prayed the hermit he might abide with him still there, to live with fasting and prayers. For from hence will I never go, said Sir Bedivere, by my will, but all the days of my life here to pray for my lord Arthur. Sir, ye are welcome to me, said the hermit, for I know ye better than ye ween that I do. Ye are Sir Bedivere the Bold, and the full noble duke, Sir Lucan de Butler was your brother. Then Sir Bedivere told the hermit all as ye have heard to-fore, and so he lived with the hermit that was beforehand Bishop of Canterbury. And there Sir Bedivere put upon him poor clothes, and served the hermit fully lowly in fasting and in prayers.

Thus of Arthur I find never more written in books that be authorised, nor more of the very certainty of his death heard I never read, but thus was he led away in a ship wherein were three queens; that one was King Arthur's sister, Queen Morgan le Fay; the other was the Queen of North Galis; the third was the Queen of the Waste Lands. Also there was dame Nimue, the chief lady of the lake, that had wedded Pelleas the good knight; and this lady had done much for King Arthur. (And this dame Nimue would never suffer Sir Pelleas to be in no place where he should be in danger of his life; and so he lived to the uttermost of his days with her in great rest.) Now more of the death of King Arthur could I never find, but that these ladies brought him to his grave; and such one was interred there, which the hermit bare witness that sometime was Bishop of Canterbury. But yet the hermit knew not in certain that he was verily the body of King Arthur: for this tale Sir Bedivere, a knight of the Table Round, made it to be written.

Yet some men say in many parts of England that King Arthur is not dead, but had by the will of our Lord Jesu into another place; and men say that he shall come again, and he shall win the Holy Cross. Yet I will not say that it shall be so, but rather I would say: here in this world he changed his life. And many men say that there is written upon the tomb this: *Hic jacet Arthurus, Rex quondam, Rexque futurus.*

And thus leave I here Sir Bedivere with the hermit that dwelled that time in a chapel beside Glastonbury, and there was his hermitage. And so they lived in their prayers and fastings, and great abstinence.

And when Queen Guenever understood that King Arthur was slain, and all the noble knights, Sir Mordred and all the remnant, then she stole away, with five ladies with her, and so she went to Almesbury. And there she let make herself a nun, and wore white clothes and black, and great penance she took upon her, as ever did sinful lady in this land. And never creature could make her merry; but lived in fasting, prayers, and alms-deeds, that all manner of people marvelled how virtuously she was changed.

Now leave we the Queen in Almesbury, a nun in white clothes and black – and there she was Abbess and ruler as reason would – and turn we from her, and speak we of Sir Launcelot du Lake, that when he heard in his country that Sir Mordred was crowned King in England, and made war against King Arthur, his own father, and would hinder him from landing in his own land (also it was told him how that Sir Mordred had laid a siege about the Tower of London, because the Queen would not wed him) then was Sir Launcelot wroth out of measure, and said to his kinsmen:

Alas, that double traitor Sir Mordred, now me repenteth that ever he escaped my hands, for much shame hath he done unto my lord Arthur; for all I feel by this doleful letter that Sir Gawaine sent me, on whose soul Jesu have mercy, that my lord Arthur is full hard bestead. Alas, said Sir Launcelot, that ever I should live to hear of that most noble King that made me knight thus to be overset with his subject in his own realm. And this doleful letter that my lord, Sir Gawaine, hath sent me afore his death, praying me to see his tomb, wit you well his doleful words shall never go from mine heart. For he was a full noble knight as ever was born. And in an unhappy hour was I born that ever I should have that unhap to slay first Sir Gawaine, Sir Gaheris the good knight, and mine own friend Sir Gareth, that full noble knight. Now, alas, I may say I am unhappy that ever I should do thus. And yet, alas, might I never have hap to slay that traitor, Sir Mordred.

Now leave your complaints, said Sir Bors, and first revenge you of the death of Sir Gawaine, on whose soul Jesu have mercy. And it will be well done that ye see his tomb, and secondly that ye revenge my lord Arthur, and my lady, Queen Guenever. I thank you, said Sir Launcelot, for ever ye will my worship.

Then they made them ready in all the haste that might be, with ships and galleys, with him and his host to pass into England. And so, at the last, he came to Dover, and there he landed with seven kings, and the number was hideous to behold. Then Sir Launcelot asked of men of Dover where was King Arthur become. Then the people told him how that he was slain, and Sir Mordred too with an hundred thousand that died upon a day; and how Sir Mordred gave King Arthur the first battle there at his landing, and there was good Sir Gawaine slain; and on the morn Sir Mordred fought with the King upon Barham Down, and there the King put Sir Mordred to the worse.

Alas, said Sir Launcelot, this is the heaviest tidings that ever came to me. Now, fair sirs, said Sir Launcelot, shew me the tomb of Sir Gawaine. And anon he was brought into the castle of Dover, and so they shewed him the tomb. Then Sir Launcelot kneeled down by the tomb and wept, and prayed heartily for his soul.

And that night he made a dole, and all they that would come had as much flesh, and fish and wine and ale, and every man and woman he dealt to twelve pence, come who so would. Thus with his own hand dealt he this money, in a mourning gown; and ever he wept, and prayed the people to pray for the soul of Sir Gawaine.

And on the morn all the priests and clerks that might be gotten in the country and in the town were there, and sang masses of Requiem. And there offered first Sir Launcelot, and he offered an hundred pound; and then the seven kings offered and every of them offered forty pound. Also there was a thousand knights, and every of them offered a pound; and the offering dured from morn till night. And there Sir Launcelot lay two nights upon his tomb, in prayers and doleful weeping. Then on the third day Sir Launcelot called the kings, dukes, earls, with the barons, and all his noble knights, and said thus: My fair lords, I thank you all of your coming into this country with me. But wit you well all, we are come too late, and that shall repent me while I live, but against death may no man rebel. But sithen it is so, said Sir Launcelot, I will myself ride and seek my lady, Queen Guenever, for as I hear say she hath had great pain and much disease; and I hear say that she is fled into the west. And therefore ye all shall abide me here, and but if I come again within fifteen days, then take your ships and your fellowship, and depart into your country, for I will do as I say you.

Then came Sir Bors de Ganis, and said: My lord Sir Launcelot, what think ye for to do, now to ride in this realm? wit ye well ye shall find few friends. Be as be may for that, said Sir Launcelot, keep you still here, for I will forth on my journey, and no man nor child shall go with me.

So it was no boot to strive, but he departed and rode westerly, and there he sought a seven or eight days; and at last he came to a nunnery, and then was Queen Guenever ware of Sir Launcelot as she walked in the cloister. And when she saw him there she swooned thrice, that all the ladies and gentlewomen had work enough to hold the Queen from the earth. So when she might speak, she called ladies and gentlewomen to her, and said: Ye marvel, fair ladies, why I make this fare. Truly, she said, it is for the sight of yonder knight that yonder standeth; wherefore I pray you call him hither to me.

Then Sir Launcelot was brought to her; then the Queen said to all the ladies: Through this same man and me hath all this war been wrought, and the death of the most noblest knights of the world; for through our love that we have loved together is my most noble lord slain. Therefore, Sir Launcelot, wit thou well I am set in such a plight to get my soul-heal; and yet I trust through God's grace and through His Passion of his wide wounds that after my death I may have a sight of the blessed face of Christ Jesu, and at domesday to sit on his right side, for as sinful as ever I was, now are saints in heaven. And therefore, Sir Launcelot, I require thee and beseech thee heartily, for all the love that ever was betwixt us, that thou never see me more in the visage. And I command thee, on God's behalf, that thou forsake my company. And to thy kingdom thou turn again, and keep well thy realm from war and wrack; for as well as I have loved thee heretofor, mine heart will not serve now to see thee, for through thee and me is the flower of kings and knights destroyed. And therefore go thou to thy realm, and there take ye a wife, and live with her with joy and bliss. And I pray thee heartily to pray for me to the Everlasting Lord that I may amend my misliving.

Now, my sweet madam, said Sir Launcelot, would ye that I should now return again unto my country, and there to wed a lady? Nay, madam, wit you well that shall I never do, for I shall never be so false to you of that I have promised. But the same destiny that ye have taken you to, I will take me unto, for the pleasure of Jesu, and ever for you I cast me specially to pray.

Ah, Sir Launcelot, if you will do so and hold thy promise, but I may never believe you, said the Queen, but that ye will turn to the world again.

Well, madam, said he, ye say as it pleaseth you, yet wist you me never false of my promise. And God defend but I should forsake the world as ye have done! For in the quest of the Sangreal I had forsaken the vanities of the world had not your love been. And if I had done so at that time, with my heart, will, and thought, I had passed all the knights that were in the Sangreal except Sir Galahad, my son. And therefore, lady, sithen ye have taken you to perfection, I must needs take me to perfection, of right. For I take record of God, in you I have had mine earthly joy; and if I had found you now so disposed, I had cast me to have had you into mine own realm.

But sithen I find you thus disposed, I ensure you faithfully, I will ever take me to penance, and pray while my

Lancelot and Guinevere at Arthur's tomb, by Dante Gabriel Rossetti. Rossetti has transposed the scene of the lovers' last meeting.

life lasteth, if I may find any hermit, either gray or white, that will receive me. Wherefore, madam, I pray you kiss me and never do no more. Nay, said the Queen, that shall I never do, but abstain you from such works: and they departed. But there was never so hard an hearted man but he would have wept to see the dolour that they made; for there was lamentation as they had been stung with spears; and many times they swooned, and the ladies bare the Queen to her chamber.

And Sir Launcelot awoke, and went and took his horse, and rode all that day and all night in a forest, weeping. And at the last he was ware of an hermitage and a chapel stood betwixt two cliffs; and then he heard a little bell ring to mass, and thither he rode and alighted, and tied his horse to the gate, and heard mass. And he that sang mass was the Bishop of Canterbury. Both the Bishop and Sir Bedivere knew Sir Launcelot, and they spake together after mass. But when Sir Bedivere had told his tale all whole, Sir Launcelot's heart almost brast for sorrow, and Sir Launcelot threw his arms abroad, and said: Alas, who may trust this world. And then he kneeled down on his knee, and prayed the Bishop to shrive him and assoil him. And then he besought the Bishop that he might be his brother. Then the Bishop said: I will gladly; and there he put an habit upon Sir Launcelot, and there he served God day and night with prayers and fastings.

Thus the great host abode at Dover. And then Sir Lionel took fifteen lords with him, and rode to London to seek Sir Launcelot; and there Sir Lionel was slain and many of his lords. Then Sir Bors de Ganis made the great host for to go home again; and Sir Bors, Sir Ector de Maris, Sir Blamore, Sir Bleoberis, with more other of Sir Launcelot's kin, took on them to ride all England overthwart and endlong, to seek Sir Launcelot. So Sir Bors by fortune rode so long till he came to the same chapel where Sir Launcelot was; and so Sir Bors heard a little bell knell, that rang to mass; and there he alighted and heard mass. And when mass was done, the Bishop, Sir Launcelot, and Sir Bedivere, came to Sir Bors. And when Sir Bors saw Sir Launcelot in that manner clothing, then he prayed the Bishop that he might be in the same suit. And so there was an habit put upon him, and there he lived in prayers and fasting. And within half a year, there was come Sir Galihud, Sir Galihodin, Sir Blamore, Sir Bleoberis, Sir Villiars, Sir Clarras, and Sir Gahalantine. So all these seven noble knights there abode still. And when they saw Sir Launcelot had taken him to such perfection, they had no lust to depart, but took such an habit as he had.

Thus they endured in great penance six year; and then Sir Launcelot took the habit of priesthood of the Bishop, and a twelvemonth he sang mass. And there was none of these other knights but they read in books, and help for to sing mass, and rang bells, and did bodily all manner of service. And so their horses went where they would, for they took no regard of no worldly riches. For when they saw Sir Launcelot endure such penance, in prayers, and fastings, they took no force what pain they endured, for to see the noblest knight of the world take such abstinence that he waxed full lean.

And thus upon a night, there came a vision to Sir Launcelot, and charged him, in remission of his sins, to haste him unto Almesbury: And by then thou come there, thou shalt find Queen Guenever dead. And therefore take thy fellows with thee, and purvey them of an horse bier, and fetch thou the corpse of her, and bury her by her husband, the noble King Arthur. So this avision came to Sir Launcelot thrice in one night.

Then Sir Launcelot rose up or day, and told the hermit. It were well done, said the hermit, that ye made you ready, and that you disobey not the avision. Then Sir Launcelot took his eight fellows with him, and on foot they yede from Glastonbury to Almesbury, the which is little more than thirty mile. And thither they came within two days, for they were weak and feeble to go. And when Sir Launcelot was come to Almesbury within the nunnery, Queen Guenever died but half an hour afore. And the ladies told Sir Launcelot that Queen Guenever told them all or she passed, that Sir Launcelot had been priest near a twelvemonth, And hither he cometh as fast as he may to fetch my corpse; and beside my lord, King Arthur, he shall bury me. Wherefore the Queen said in hearing of them all: I beseech Almighty God that I may never have power to see Sir Launcelot with my worldly eyen; and thus, said all the ladies, was ever her prayer these two days, till she was dead. Then Sir Launcelot saw her visage, but he wept not greatly, but sighed. And so he did all the observance of the service himself, both the dirige, and on the morn he sang mass. And there was ordained an horse bier; and so with an hundred torches ever brenning about the corpse of the Queen, and ever Sir Launcelot with his eight fellows went about the horse bier, singing and reading many an holy orison, and frankincense upon the corpse incensed. Thus Sir Launcelot and his eight fellows went on foot from Almesbury unto Glastonbury.

And when they were come to the chapel and the hermitage, there she had a dirge, with great devotion. And on the morn the hermit that sometime was Bishop of Canterbury sang the mass of Requiem with great devotion. And Sir Launcelot was the first that offered, and then also his eight fellows. And then she was wrapped in cered cloth of Raines, from the top to the toe, in thirtyfold; and after she was put in a web of lead, and then in a coffin of marble. And when she was put in the earth Sir Launcelot swooned, and lay long still, while the hermit came and awaked him, and said: Ye be to blame, for ye displease God with such manner of sorrow-making. Truly, said Sir Launcelot, I trust I do not displease God, for He knoweth mine intent. For my sorrow was not, nor is not, for any rejoicing of sin, but my sorrow may never have end. For when I remember of her beauty, and of her noblesse, that was both with her king and with her, so when I saw his corpse and her corpse so lie together, truly mine heart would not serve to sustain my careful body. Also when I remember me how by my default, mine orgule and my pride, that they were both laid full low, that were peerless that ever was living of Christian people, wit you well, said Sir Launcelot, this remembered, of their kindness and mine unkindness, sank so to mine heart, that I might not sustain myself. So the French book maketh mention.

Then Sir Launcelot never after ate but little meat, ne drank, till he was dead. For then he sickened more and more, and dried, and dwined away. For the Bishop nor

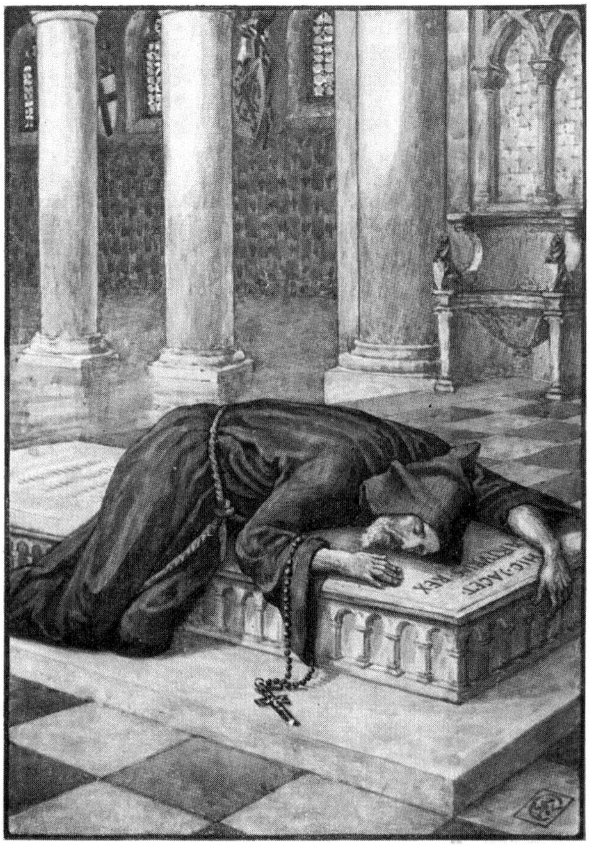

The death of Sir Lancelot; a book illustration by Walter Crane (1904).

none of his fellows might not make him to eat, and little he drank, that he was waxen by a cubit shorter than he was, that the people could not know him. For evermore, day and night, he prayed, but sometime he slumbered a broken sleep; ever he was lying grovelling on the tomb of King Arthur and Queen Guenever. And there was no comfort that the Bishop, nor Sir Bors, nor none of his fellows, could make him, it availed not. So within six weeks after, Sir Launcelot fell sick, and lay in his bed; and then he sent for the Bishop that there was hermit, and all his true fellows. Then Sir Launcelot said with dreary steven: Sir Bishop, I pray you give to me all my rites that longeth to a Christian man. It shall not need you, said the hermit and all his fellows, it is but heaviness of your blood, ye shall be well mended by the grace of God to-morn. My fair lords, said Sir Launcelot, wit you well my careful body will into the earth, I have warning more than now I will say; therefore give me my rites. So when he was houseled and anealed, and had all that a Christian man ought to have, he prayed the Bishop that his fellows might bear his body to Joyous Gard. Some men say it was Alnwick, and some men say it was Bamborough. Howbeit, said Sir Launcelot, me repenteth sore, but I made mine avow sometime, that in Joyous Gard I would be buried. And because of breaking of mine avow, I pray you all, lead me thither. Then there was weeping and wringing of hands among his fellows.

So at a season of the night they all went to their beds, for they all lay in one chamber. And so after midnight, against day, the Bishop that then was hermit, as he lay in his bed asleep, he fell upon a great laughter. And therewith all the fellowship awoke, and came to the Bishop, and asked him what he ailed. Ah Jesu mercy, said the Bishop, why did ye awake me? I was never in all my life so merry and so well at ease. Wherefore? said Sir Bors. Truly, said the Bishop, here was Sir Launcelot with me with mo angels than ever I saw men in one day. And I saw the angels heave up Sir Launcelot unto heaven, and the gates of heaven opened against him. It is but dretching of swevens, said Sir Bors, for I doubt not Sir Launcelot aileth nothing but good. It may well be, said the Bishop; go ye to his bed, and then shall ye prove the sooth. So when Sir Bors and his fellows came to his bed they found him stark dead, and he lay as he had smiled, and the sweetest savour about him that ever they felt.

Then was there weeping and wringing of hands, and the greatest dole they made that ever made men. And on the morn the Bishop did his mass of Requiem; and after, the Bishop and all the nine knights put Sir Launcelot in the same horse bier that Queen Guenever was laid in to-fore that she was buried. And so the Bishop and they all together went with the body of Sir Launcelot daily, till they came to Joyous Gard; and ever they had an hundred torches brenning about him. And so within fifteen days they came to Joyous Gard. And there they laid his corpse in the body of the quire, and sang and read many psalters and prayers over him and about him. And ever his visage was laid open and naked, that all folks might behold him. For such was the custom in those days, that all men of worship should so lie with open visage till that they were buried. And right thus as they were at their service, there came Sir Ector de Maris, that had seven years sought all England, Scotland, and Wales seeking his brother, Sir Launcelot.

And when Sir Ector heard such noise and light in the quire of Joyous Gard, he alighted and put his horse from him, and came into the quire, and there he saw men sing and weep. And all they knew Sir Ector, but he knew not them. Then went Sir Bors unto Sir Ector, and told him how there lay his brother, Sir Launcelot, dead; and then Sir Ector threw his shield, sword, and helm from him. And when he beheld Sir Launcelot's visage, he fell down in a swoon. And when he waked it were hard any tongue to tell the doleful complaints that he made for his brother. Ah Launcelot, he said, thou were head of all Christian knights, and now I dare say, said Sir Ector, thou Sir Launcelot, there thou liest, that thou were never matched of earthly knight's hand. And thou were the courteoust knight that ever bare shield. And thou were the truest friend to thy lover that ever bestrad horse. And thou were the truest lover of a sinful man that ever loved woman. And thou were the kindest man that ever struck with sword. And thou were the goodliest person that ever came among press of knights. And thou was the meekest man and the gentlest that ever ate in hall among ladies. And thou were the sternest knight to thy mortal foe that ever put spear in the rest. Then there was weeping and dolour out of measure.

Thus they kept Sir Launcelot's corpse aloft fifteen days, and then they buried it with great devotion. And then at leisure they went all with the Bishop of Canterbury to his hermitage, and there they were together more than a month. Then Sir Constantine, that was Sir Cador's son of Cornwall, was chosen King of England. And he was a full noble knight, and worshipfully he ruled this realm. And then this King Constantine sent for the Bishop of Canterbury, for he heard say where he was. And so he was restored unto his Bishopric, and left that hermitage. And Sir Bedivere was there ever still hermit to his life's end. Then Sir Bors de Ganis, Sir Ector de Maris, Sir Gahalantine, Sir Galihud, Sir Galihodin, Sir Blamore, Sir Bleoberis, Sir Villiars le Valiant, Sir Clarrus of Clermont, all these knights drew them to their countries. Howbeit King Constantine would have had them with him, but they would not abide in this realm. And there they all lived in their countries as holy men. And some English books make mention that they went never out of England after the death of Sir Launcelot, but that was but favour of makers. For the French book maketh mention, and is authorised, that Sir Bors, Sir Ector, Sir Blamore, and Sir Bleoberis, went into the Holy Land thereas Jesu Christ was quick and dead, and anon as they had stablished their lands. For the book saith, so Sir Launcelot commanded them for to do, or ever he passed out of this world. And these four knights did many battles upon the miscreants or

Turks. And there they died upon a Good Friday for God's sake.

Here is the end of the book of King Arthur, and of his noble knights of the Round Table, that when they were whole together there was ever an hundred and forty. And here is the end of the death of Arthur. I pray you all, gentlemen and gentlewomen that readeth this book of Arthur and his knights, from the beginning to the ending, pray for me while I am alive, that God send me good deliverance, and when I am dead, I pray you all pray for my soul. For this book was ended the ninth year of the reign of King Edward the fourth, by Sir Thomas Maleore, knight, as Jesu help him for his great might, as he is the servant of Jesu both day and night.

THE TUDOR HISTORIANS

THE ROMANCES UNDER ATTACK · ARTHUR'S EXISTENCE QUESTIONED · LELAND'S COUNTER-ATTACK · ARTHUR AND THE ANTIQUARIES · SEVENTEENTH CENTURY EPICS & & &

The new classical learning of the Renaissance and the more extreme advocates of the Reformation were both hostile to the medieval splendours of the Arthurian legends. The romances themselves appeared in edition after edition throughout Europe; the new printing presses poured out endless copies of these once rare works, and Arthur and his court were more popular than they had ever been before. Popular, that is, in terms of being more widely read; for with intellectuals and reforming clergy they were quite the reverse. Roger Ascham, who taught Elizabeth I, wrote in his book *The Schoolmaster*:

> In our forefather's time, when Papistry, like a standing pool, covered and overflowed all England, few books were read in our tongue, saving certain books of chivalry, as they said, for pastime and pleasure, which, as some say, were made in monasteries by idle monks, or wanton canons: as one, for example, *Morte Arthure*: the whole pleasure of which book stands in two special points, in open manslaughter and bold bawdiness: in which book those be counted the noblest knights that do kill most men without any quarrel, and commit foulest adulteries by subtlest shifts: as Sir Lancelot with the wife of King Arthur his master: Sir Tristram with the wife of King Mark his uncle: Sir Lamerok with the wife of King Lot, that was his own aunt. This is good stuff for wise men to laugh at, or honest men to take pleasure at. Yet I know [of a time] when God's Bible was banished the Court and *Morte Arthure* received into the prince's chamber.

The romances were an easy enough target, however. The historians of Tudor England went further, and some questioned the truth of Geoffrey of Monmouth's *History of the Kings of Britain*, by now generally accepted as a valuable historical source. Robert Fabyan, writing in the 1490s, rejected much of Geoffrey's material, but it was left to an Italian, the learned humanist Polydore Vergil, who spent some years in England and wrote a large history of England from the best sources, to attack Arthur as almost entirely fabulous. His efforts, first published in 1534, caused a storm of protest, and the antiquary John Leland replied with an elaborate defence in Latin ten years later. Yet Polydore Vergil's criticism had had some effect: *Elyot's Dictionary* in 1548 contained the following entry:

> Arthurus, a King of England when it was called Britannia, a man of excellent prowess in fifteen great battles against the Saxons, vanquished them, and finally drove the most part of them out of this realm. He subdued Scotland and Ireland, at that time being well inhabited and in culture. And afterwards he kept an honourable house of valiant and noble personages, wherein was such magnificence, that it gave occasion to Frenchmen and Spaniards to exercise their wits in advancing Arthur's majesty with incredible fables, which is no more to be marvelled at than the similar inventions and fantasies of the Greeks. Albeit this Arthur was a very noble and famous prince, yet by them who wrote histories about his time he was unremembered.

But during the rest of the century the tide slowly turned. The London historian Stow followed Fabyan in the 1565 edition of his Chronicle; by 1580 he had put back most of Geoffrey of Monmouth, and believed that Arthur had conquered thirty kingdoms. William Camden, the greatest of the Tudor antiquaries, believed firmly in Arthur's famous deeds, with only minor doubts.

Poets attempting to produce modern versions of the great classical epics, which were in ways no more than the Renaissance equivalents of the romances, were still attracted to Arthur as a possible hero. Edmund Spenser's *The Faerie Queene* has Prince Arthur as its central character; but Spenser was not concerned with the traditional story of *King* Arthur. He wrote in his preface to Sir Walter Raleigh:

> I labour to pourtraict in Arthure, before he was king, the image of a brave knight, perfected in the twelve morall virtues, as Aristotle has devised . . . In the persone of prince Arthure I sette forth magnificence in particular, which vertue, for that (according to Aristotle and the rest) it is the perfection of all the rest, and conteineth in it them all, therefore in the whole course I mention the deedes of Arthure applyable to that vertue which I write of in that booke.

By deliberately using the one blank period in Arthur's career, between his birth and his accession to the throne, Spencer is free to invent as he pleases, but the result is a hero with a traditional name yet without his traditional character. This image of Arthur as a possible epic hero could go hand in hand with attacks on the romances; in Ben Jonson's words, they were

Abortives of the fabulous dark cloister
Sent out to poison courts, and infest manners.

Milton, considering a possible Arthurian epic in the years 1639–41, was more polite; preferring the epic form as having the virtue of 'high argument', he dismissed the romances as merely trivial, fit only

. . . to describe Races and Games
Or tilting Furniture, emblazon'd Shields,
Impresses quaint, Caparisons and Steeds;
Bases and tinsel Trappings, gorgeous Knights
At Joust and Tournament . . .

Nothing came of Milton's plans, and Dryden, who also had ambitions in the same direction, managed to produce only the libretto of Purcell's *King Arthur*, much altered for political reasons between its writing in 1684 and first performances in 1691. It is no more than a masque, and an indifferent one at that. The only Arthurian epic that actually graced – if that is the right word – a seventeenth century library would have been Richard Blackmore's two works on Arthur, written 'as my Recreation and the Entertainment of my idle hours', in an attempt 'to write an Epick poem . . . a work of that Difficulty that no-one for near seventeen hundred years has succeeded in it.' Blackmore was more successful as physician than as amateur author; Pope made him a central figure in the *Dunciad* and Dryden commented:

At leisure hours, in epic song he deals,
Writes to the rumbling of his coaches wheels,
Prescribes in haste, and seldom kills by rule,
But rides triumphant between stool and stool.

POLYDORE VERGIL · ENGLISH HISTORY · BOOK III & & &

About the same time Uther departed this life; whom his son Arthur succeeded, a man of such accomplishment that if he had lived longer, he might have gradually somewhat restored the almost lost cause of his Britons. For this, on account of the great strength of his body and the virtues of his mind, posterity generally praised him, just as in the case of Roland, Charlemagne's sister's son, who was the topic of Italian poems within our own memory, and who like him perished in the flower of his youth. The common people praise Arthur to the skies in a marvellous fashion, as one who in fact overcame three Saxon leaders in war, who brought Scotland and its neighbouring islands under his power, who annihilated the Romans in the fields outside Paris together with their leader, a certain Lucius, who laid waste France, and who indeed killed gigantic and powerful men in battle. In the end, they say, this victor of so many battles, when he wished to take the city of Rome by storm, was recalled from his expedition by domestic strife: he slew Mordred, his nephew, who had occupied the realm as a usurper during his absence, and was in the same battle wounded and killed. Likewise, a few years later, Arthur was buried at Glastonbury Abbey, in a magnificently wrought tomb; which later generations felt to be worthy of all kinds of ornaments, when in fact the monastery had not yet been founded in Arthur's time.

A LEARNED AND TRUE ASSERTION OF THE ORIGINAL LIFE, ACTS AND DEATH OF THE MOST NOBLE, VALIANT, AND RENOWNED PRINCE ARTHURE, KING OF GREAT BRITAIN · COLLECTED AND WRITTEN OF LATE YEARS IN LATIN BY THE LEARNED ENGLISH ANTIQUARY OF WORTHY MEMORY JOHN LEYLAND · NEWLY TRANSLATED INTO ENGLISH BY RICHARD ROBINSON & & &

Chapter X. King Arthur's commendation

Arthur is now dead (if so he may be said to have died well) whose fame, memory and praise fully and wholly live, and shine forth in the world.

Our ancestors, both poets and also historiographers were so friendly, honest, and thankful towards Arthur that they ennobled his fame and facts, and also adorned them with eternal memory and commendation. Taliesin, Mailgwn, who is also called Mevinus, Ambrosius Maridunensis and Merlin of Caledonia, the most excellent stars of Britain, have performed no less memory, bestowing their stately styles of commendations accordingly. Touching whom, and others also, we have before fitly spoken in their places, trusting in the authority of Geoffrey of Monmouth, Alfred of Beverley, Henry of Huntingdon, John (termed the Golden Historiographer), William of Malmesbury, Sir John Gray and Boccaccio.

But if it now avail any man to know anything as yet more in matter and larger discourse, I will not refuse (with the best diligence that I can) to restore to light a few words taken up out of the most approved authors . . .

The memory also of Arthur the noble King of Britain ought not to be buried or utterly trodden under foot, whom the histories of the monastery of Glastonbury (whose chief patron, benefactor and mighty supporter he also was in his days) do much advance. John Annevillanus, no doubt a witty poet of his time, and no less elegant, solemnizes Arthur's praise in these verses, which even at this day appear in his book *Architrenio*

Another Achilles Arthur was, whose first grown grace,
throughout his Table Round,
Him Phrygius made, as of a branch with fruits which
doth abound,
For liberal hand; not river he, but a main sea y-found.

But here if, over and besides this, I should endeavour largely to adorn Arthur with praise as the multitude of authors do most truly write and agree upon him, sooner should copy of eloquence fail me than magnificence of lightsome testimony howsoever. Be it sufficient, then, that we use at this present the most famous commendations, though of few writers. I pray you, what is the cause that Johann Trittheim in his brief chronicle makes such excellent mention of Arthur? Doubtless the cause is plain enough. For because he learned the same of others in plain truth, therefore he did as thankfully commit it to posterity; which thing doubtless he would never have done, had he doubted of the verity of the cause. But now let Trittheim himself speak in our presence:

Which Arthur, excellent in great humanity, wisdom, clemency and manhood, studied by all endeavour to show himself beloved and reverenced of all, and to excel all: because he also abounded in valour of mind, with wonderful liberality towards all men, and specially towards churchmen, unto whom for zeal towards God, he gave very many benefits, and rewards as well. He drove out of Britain both Saxons and Picts. He mightily subdued the Scots, Irishmen and Orkneymen into his kingdom.

Volterra in his third book of geography honours the fame of Arthur and diligently celebrates his valiant acts.

Furthermore also Jacobus Philippus of Bergamo, in his ninth book of Chronicles, advances Arthur's valour, even with most condign commendations. And neither does Nauclerus in his history make any less relation of him. These testimonies doubtless men most learned and most exercised in antiquity would never have set down, if they had not first been fully persuaded that Arthur in times past was abundantly notable by all ornaments of valour. But such is the lewdness of many men, and their disdainful mind, that they, being altogether seduced with ignorance – and very rude ignorance at that, to not manifestly see in full, but blindly neglect, despise and altogether reject the truth. Censors or judges in ancient histories let such men go in God's name, and let them enjoy their foolishness, (I will not say madness) to the full. What if I should bring forth amongst the rest that notable testimony of Hector Boece, a writer in our time, touching the immortal glory of Arthur? Surely through this account nothing shall fall from his dignity, but very much shall be added thereto, because the Scots in old times (I know not by what instinct of nature) hated the Britons . . . Whereupon to be praised of an adversary, enemy, and even a deadly foe, stands in place of a reward for victory. These are then his words:

King Arthur was no less famous in glory for notable exploits and for majesty, than the kings of Britain which lived before his days: whereupon the Britons during his reign very much increased in riches and power.

Thus far says Boece. What just occasion I would like Polydore Vergil the Italian to give me now, so that, by some memorable testimony of his, I might also lift up Arthur's countenance and make him look aloft? Polydore does indeed handle Arthur's cause, but in doing so he is so faint-hearted, lukewarm and negligent that he makes me not only laugh, but also angers me (for example when he is contrary to truth and filled with Italian bitterness). I know not whether he is smiling or in anger. For he struggles wretchedly to compile his history, and yet so that he might somehow manage it, he must willy-nilly come to terms with Geoffrey of Monmouth, whom beforehand (as it seemed unto him) he had in many words (proceeding mightily from a bitter stomach rather than from good digestion) corrected by his own standards. Geoffrey of Monmouth I have defended as an interpreter, only once or twice where the cause was clearly justified, for great danger might indeed redound upon my head if I should pass beyond the bounds of equity. I will take heed therefore and, trusting only in the verity of the cause, I will continually bear the same about me for a bulwark and sure defence. Though Polydore holds his peace, it is not needful by and by for the whole world to be mute. Although Italy in times past so esteemed Arthur and still does, when books printed both about his prowess and victories are read in the Italian tongue, in the Spanish and also in the French tongue (whereupon also the English collection of Thomas Malory's work is published abroad), an adversary will say, I know, that many lies have crept into those books. But to say this is nothing else but teaching him who is fully taught. As I despise fables, so I reverence and embrace the truth of the history. Neither will I suffer this to be taken away from me at any time, but with loss of life. I utterly eschew unthankful persons and betake me to those rocks and monuments, the true witnesses of Arthur's renown and majesty.

Arthur underwent an artistic eclipse between the last manuscript miniatures and the pre-Raphaelites in the mid-nineteenth century. The 'history painters' of the early nineteenth century preferred scenes from real history or from the classics, and only Spenser came within their range. This is William Etty's Britomart redeems fair Amoret.
(*Tate Gallery*)

THE GOTHICK REVIVAL

THOMAS WARTON · ARTHUR AND THE ROMANTIC POETS · ARTHURIAN COMEDY ⅋ ⅋ ⅋

The general revival of interest in things medieval which took place in the second half of the eighteenth century was surprisingly slow to come to terms with medieval literature. 'Gothick' might be the fashion with Horace Walpole at Strawberry Hill, but the taste for poetry was more for the Elizabethans, who had also been neglected in favour of classical models: 'old poetry but not too old'. Though Pope knew of and admired Chaucer, it was not until the 1770s, when Tyrwhitt edited his works, that the greatest of the medieval poets was appreciated again. Part of the problem was the 'discovery' of the poems of Ossian, supposedly a Scottish bard of the Dark Ages, but in fact the nicely-judged work of James Macpherson. These showed the medieval world as his readers expected it to be, and when the real poems of the period were examined by scholars, they found them difficult and unappealing beside the forgeries put out under Ossian's name.

Nevertheless, the world of medieval romance was gradually opened up. One of the pioneers was Thomas Warton, who in preparing his history of English literature had read widely in medieval literature. He wrote an important essay on Spenser's *Faerie Queene*, drawing attention to the poem, which had been largely forgotten. In his own collection of poems, published in 1777, he included one on *The Grave of King Arthur*; it is by no means a great work, but it is included here to show what an eighteenth century writer made of the Arthurian legend: the chosen episode is drawn from Gerald of Wales' account of the discoveries at Glastonbury in 1191, and is therefore based on history rather than romance.

It was not until Sir Walter Scott edited *Sir Tristrem*, a medieval English version of the Tristan legend, in 1804, supplying the missing ending in his own imitation of the original, that English readers had access to one of the great Arthurian romances in something approaching its first form. Scott himself, despite his enthusiasm for things medieval, produced only one Arthurian poem of his own, and that rather dull: *The Bridal of Triermain* is a curious mixture of fairytale and high gothic, which Scott originally published anonymously. Likewise Wordsworth, who expressed interest in the Arthurian romance, produced only the curious poem *The Egyptian Maid*, in which Galahad, the 'virgin knight' of the Grail adventures, is married!

Wordsworth was of course entitled to change the character of Galahad as he pleased, but it could no longer be from ignorance of the originals. Between the publication of *The Bridal of Triermain* in 1813 and that of *The Egyptian Maid* in 1835, no less than three editions of Sir Thomas Malory had appeared, as well as the first scholarly survey of Arthur and his legends, Joseph Ritson's *The Life of King Arthur* (1825). Furthermore, one of the rising poets of the young generation, Alfred Tennyson, had published an Arthurian poem in 1832.

On the lighter side, by contrast to all this earnest scholarship and high-minded literature, Arthurian romance was also proving a useful vehicle for satire. Cervantes had long ago pointed out the innate absurdity of much of the later romances, in *Don Quixote*; as the Canon of Toledo says of the Spanish books of chivalry:

> What beauty can there be, or what harmony between the parts and the whole, or between the whole and its parts, in a book or story in which a sixteen-year-old lad deals a giant as tall as a steeple one blow with his sword and cuts him in two as if he were made of marzipan? And when they want to describe a battle, first they tell us that there are a million fighting men on the enemy's side. But if the hero of the book is against them, inevitably, whether we like it or not, we have to believe that such and such a knight gained the victory by the valour of his strong arm alone. Then what are we to say of the ease with which a hereditary Queen or Empress throws herself into the arms of an unknown and wandering knight?

Such material was a natural target for burlesque: Henry Fielding had used it in *The Tragedy of Tragedies or the Life and Death of Tom Thumb the Great* a hundred years earlier, a send-up of the extravagant melodramas of his day. In 1829 Thomas Love Peacock, already well-established as a writer of humorous novels, published *The Misfortunes of Elphin*, a highly entertaining mixture of satire, genuine learning about early Welsh poetry, and sheer burlesque. The plot is slight, and the humour has dated with the course of time: but the scene where Elphin encounters Seithenyn, the drunken guardian of the great embankment, is an excellent piece of comedy. Peacock's satire is directed against the Tories who opposed the movement to reform the Parliamentary system, which aimed at abolishing the rotten boroughs where a handful of electors returned a member of parliament. This was finally achieved three years later, with the Reform Bill of 1832.

The Grave of King Arthur

THOMAS WARTON

King Henry the Second, having undertaken an expedition into Ireland, to suppress a rebellion raised by Roderick King of Connaught, commonly called O'Connor Dun, or 'the brown Monarch of Ireland', was entertained, in his passage through Wales, with the songs of the Welsh Bards. The subject of their poetry was King Arthur, whose history had been so disguised by fabulous inventions, that the place of his burial was in general scarcely known or remembered. But in one of these Welsh poems, sung before Henry, it was recited, that King Arthur, after the battle of Camlan, in Cornwall, was interred at Glastonbury Abbey, before the high altar, yet without any external mark or memorial. Afterwards Henry visited the abbey, and commanded the spot, described by the Bard, to be opened: when digging near twenty feet deep, they found the body, deposited under a large stone, inscribed with Arthur's name. This is the ground-work of the following Ode: but, for the better accommodation of the story to our present purpose, it is told with some slight variations from the Chronicle of Glastonbury. The castle of Cilgarran, where this discovery is supposed to have been made, now a romantic ruin, stands on a rock descending to the River Teivi, in Pembrokeshire; and was built by Roger Montgomery, who led the van of the Normans at Hastings. W.

Stately the feast, and high the cheer:
Girt with many an armed peer,
And canopied with golden pall,
Amid Cilgarran's castle hall,
Sublime in formidable state,
And warlike splendour, Henry sate;
Prepar'd to stain the briny flood
Of Shannon's lakes with rebel blood.

Illumining the vaulted roof,
A thousand torches flam'd aloof:
From massy cups, with golden gleam
Sparkled the red metheglin's stream:
To grace the gorgeous festival,
Along the lofty-window'd hall,
The storied tapestry was hung:
With minstrelsy the rafters rung
Of harps, that with reflected light
From the proud gallery glitter'd bright:
While gifted bards, a rival throng,
(From distant Mona, nurse of song,
From Teivi, fring'd with umbrage brown,
From Elvy's vale, and Cader's crown,
From many a shaggy precipice
That shades Ierne's hoarse abyss,
And many a sunless solitude
Of Radnor's inmost mountains rude,)
To crown the banquet's solemn close,
Themes of British glory chose;
And to the strings of various chime
Attemper'd thus the fabling rhyme:

'O'er Cornwall's cliffs the tempest roar'd,
High the screaming sea-mew soar'd;
On Tintagel's topmost tower
Darksome fell the sleety shower;
Round the rough castle shrilly sung
The whirling blast, and wildly flung
On each tall rampart's thundering side
The surges of the tumbling tide:
When Arthur rang'd his red-cross ranks
On conscious Camlan's crimson'd banks:
By Mordred's faithless guile decreed
Beneath a Saxon spear to bleed!
Yet in vain a paynim foe
Arm'd with fate the mighty blow;
For when he fell, an elfin queen,
All in secret, and unseen,
O'er the fainting hero threw
Her mantle of ambrosial blue;
And bade her spirits bear him far,
In Merlin's agate-axled car,
To her green isle's enamell'd steep,
Far in the navel of the deep.
O'er his wounds she sprinkled dew
From flowers that in Arabia grew:
On a rich inchanted bed
She pillow'd his majestic head;
O'er his brow, with whispers bland,
Thrice she wav'd on opiate wand;
And to soft music's airy sound,
Her magic curtains clos'd around.
There, renew'd the vital spring,
Again he reigns a mighty king;
And many a fair and fragrant clime,
Blooming in immortal prime,
By gales of Eden ever fann'd,
Owns the monarch's high command:
Thence to Britain shall return,
(If right prophetic rolls I learn)
Borne on Victory's spreading plume,
His ancient sceptre to resume;
Once more, in old heroic pride,
His barbed courser to bestride;
His knightly table to restore,
And brave the tournaments of yore.'

They ceas'd; when on the tuneful stage
Advanc'd a bard, of aspect sage;
His silver tresses, thin besprent,
To age a graceful reverence lent;
His beard, all white as spangles frore
That clothe Plinlimmon's forests hoar,
Down to his harp descending flow'd;
With Time's faint rose his features glow'd;
His eyes diffus'd a soften'd fire,
And thus he wak'd the warbling wire:

'Listen, Henry, to my rede!
Not from fairy realms I lead
Bright-rob'd Tradition, to relate
In forged colours Arthur's fate;
Though much of old romantic lore
On the high theme I keep in store:
But boastful Fiction should be dumb,
Where Truth the strain might best become.
If thine ear may still be won
With songs of Uther's glorious son,

Henry, I a tale unfold,
Never yet in rhyme enroll'd,
Nor sung nor harp'd in hall or bower;
Which in my youth's full early flower,
A minstrel, sprung of Cornish line,
Who spoke of kings from old Locrine,
Taught me to chant, one vernal dawn,
Deep in a cliff-encircled lawn,
What time the glistening vapours fled
From cloud-envelop'd Clyder's head;
And on its sides the torrents gray
Shone to the morning's orient ray.

'When Arthur bow'd his haughty crest,
No princess, veil'd in azure vest,
Snatch'd him, by Merlin's potent spell,
In groves of golden bliss to dwell;
Where, crown'd with wreaths of misletoe,
Slaughter'd kings in glory go:
But when he fell, with winged speed,
His champions, on a milk-white steed,
From the battle's hurricane,
Bore him to Joseph's towered fane,
In the fair vale of Avalon;
There, with chanted orison,
And the long blaze of tapers clear,
The stoled fathers met the bier:
Through the dim aisles, in order dread
Of martial woe, the chief they led,
And deep intomb'd in holy ground,
Before the altar's solemn bound.
Around no dusky banners wave,
No mouldering trophies mark the grave:
Away the ruthless Dane has torn
Each trace that Time's slow touch had worn;
And long, o'er the neglected stone,
Oblivion's veil its shade has thrown:
The faded tomb, with honour due,
'Tis thine, O Henry, to renew!
Thither, when Conquest has restor'd
Yon recreant isle, and sheath'd the sword,
When Peace with palm has crown'd thy brows,
Haste thee, to pay thy pilgrim vows,
There, observant of my lore,
The pavement's hallow'd depth explore;
And thrice a fathom underneath
Dive into the vaults of death.
There shall thine eye, with wild amaze,
On his gigantic stature gaze;
There shalt thou find the monarch laid,
All in warrior-weeds array'd;
Wearing in death his helmet-crown,
And weapons huge of old renown.
Martial prince, 'tis thine to save
From dark oblivion Arthur's grave!
So may thy ships securely stem
The western frith: thy diadem
Shine victorious in the van,
Nor heed the slings of Ulster's clan:
Thy Norman pike-men win their way
Up the dun rocks of Harald's bay:
And from the steeps of rough Kildare
Thy prancing hoofs the falcon scare:
So may thy bow's unerring yew
Its shafts in Roderic's heart imbrew.'

Amid the pealing symphony
The spiced goblets mantled high;
With passions new the song impress'd
The listening king's impatient breast:
Flash the keen lightnings from his eyes;
He scorns awhile his bold emprise;
Ev'n now he seems, with eager pace,
The consecrated floor to trace,
And ope, from its tremendous gloom,
The treasure of the wondrous tomb:
Ev'n now he burns in thought to rear,
From its dark bed, the ponderous spear,
Rough with the gore of Pictish kings:
Ev'n now fond hope his fancy wings,
To poise the monarch's massy blade,
Of magic-temper'd metal made;
And drag to day the dinted shield
That felt the storm of Camlan's field.
O'er the sepulchre profound
Ev'n now, with arching sculpture crown'd,
He plans the chantry's choral shrine,
The daily dirge, and rites divine.

The Misfortunes of Elphin

THOMAS LOVE PEACOCK

The three immortal drunkards of the isle of Britain: Ceraint of Essyllwg; Gwrtheyrn Gwrthenau; and Seithenyn ap Seithyn Saidi. *Triads of the Isles of Britain.*

The sun had sunk beneath the waves when they reached the castle of Seithenyn. The sound of the harp and the song saluted them as they approached it. As they entered the great hall, which was already blazing with torchlight, they found his highness, and his highness's household, convincing themselves and each other with wine and wassail, of the excellence of their system of virtual superintendence; and the following jovial chorus broke on the ears of the visitors:

THE CIRCLING OF THE MEAD HORNS

Fill the blue horn, the blue buffalo horn:
Natural is mead in the buffalo horn:
As the cuckoo in spring, as the lark in the morn,
So natural is mead in the buffalo horn.

As the cup of the flower to the bee when he sips,
Is the full cup of mead to the true Briton's lips:
From the flower-cups of summer, on field and on tree,
Our mead cups are filled by the vintager bee.

Seithenyn ap Seithyn, the generous, the bold,
Drinks the wine of the stranger from vessels of gold;
But we from the horn, the blue silver-rimmed horn,
Drink the ale and the mead in our fields that were born.

The ale-froth is white, and the mead sparkles bright;
They both smile apart, and with smiles they unite:
The mead from the flower, and the ale from the corn,
Smile, sparkle, and sing in the buffalo horn.

The horn, the blue horn, cannot stand on its tip;
Its path is right on from the hand to the lip:
Though the bowl and the wine-cup our tables adorn,
More natural the draught from the buffalo horn.

But Seithenyn ap Seithyn, the generous, the bold,
Drinks the bright-flowing wine from the far-gleaming gold:
The wine, in the bowl by his lip that is worn,
Shall be glorious as mead in the buffalo horn.

The horns circle fast, but their fountains will last,
As the stream passes over, and never is past:
Exhausted so quickly, replenished so soon,
They wax and they wane like the horns of the moon.

Fill high the blue horn, the blue buffalo horn;
Fill high the long silver-rimmed buffalo horn:
While the roof of the hall by our chorus is torn,
Fill, fill to the brim, the deep silver-rimmed horn.

Elphin and Teithrin stood some time on the floor of the hall before they attracted the attention of Seithenyn, who, during the chorus was tossing and flourishing his golden goblet. The chorus had scarcely ended when he noticed them, and immediately roared aloud, 'You are welcome all four.'

Elphin answered, 'We thank you: we are but two.'

'Two or four,' said Seithenyn, 'all is one. You are welcome all. When a stranger enters, the custom in other places is to begin by washing his feet. My custom is, to begin by washing his throat. Seithenyn ap Seithyn Saidi bids you welcome.'

Elphin, taking the wine-cup, answered, 'Elphin ap Gwythno Garanhir thanks you.'

Seithenyn started up. He endeavoured to straighten himself into perpendicularity, and to stand steadily on his legs. He accomplished half his object by stiffening all his joints but those of his ankles, and from these the rest of his body vibrated upwards with the inflexibility of a bar. After thus oscillating for a time, like an inverted pendulum, finding that the attention requisite to preserve his rigidity absorbed all he could collect of his dissipated energies, and that he required a portion of them for the management of his voice, which he felt a dizzy desire to wield with peculiar steadiness in the presence of the son of the king, he suddenly relaxed the muscles that performed the operation of sitting, and dropped into his chair like a plummet. He then, with a gracious gesticulation, invited Prince Elphin to take his seat on his right hand, and proceeded to compose himself into a dignified attitude, throwing his body back into the left corner of his chair, resting his left elbow on its arm and his left cheekbone on the middle of the back of his left hand, placing his left foot on a footstool, and stretching out his right leg as straight and as far as his position allowed. He had thus his right hand at liberty, for the ornament of his eloquence and the conduct of his liquor.

Elphin seated himself at the right hand of Seithenyn. Teithrin remained at the end of the hall: on which Seithenyn exclaimed, 'Come on, man, come on. What, if you be not the son of a king, you are the guest of Seithenyn ap Seithyn Saidi. The most honourable place to the most honourable guest, and the next most honourable place to the next most honourable guest; the least honourable guest above the most honourable inmate; and, where there are but two guests, be the most honourable who he may, the least honourable of the two is next in honour to the most honourable of the two, because they are no more but two; and, where there are only two, there can be nothing between. Therefore sit, and drink. GWIN O EUR: wine from gold.'

Elphin motioned Teithrin to approach, and sit next to him.

Prince Seithenyn, whose liquor was 'his eating and his drinking solely', seemed to measure the gastronomy of his guests by his own; but his groom of the pantry thought the strangers might be disposed to eat, and placed before them a choice of provision, on which Teithrin ap Tathral did vigorous execution.

'I pray your excuses,' said Seithenyn, 'my stomach is weak, and I am subject to dizziness in the head, and my memory is not so good as it was, and my faculties of attention are somewhat impaired, and I would dilate more upon the topic, whereby you should hold me excused, but I am troubled with a feverishness and parching of the mouth, that very much injures my speech, and impedes my saying all I would say, and will say before I have done, in token of my loyalty and fealty to your highness and your highness's house. I must just moisten my lips, and I will then proceed with my observations. Cupbearer, fill.'

'Prince Seithenyn,' said Elphin, 'I have visited you on a subject of deep moment. Reports have been brought to me, that the embankment, which has been so long intrusted to your care, is in a state of dangerous decay.'

'Decay,' said Seithenyn, 'is one thing, and danger is another. Every thing that is old must decay. That the embankment is old, I am free to confess; that it is somewhat rotten in parts, I will not altogether deny; that it is any the worse for that, I do most sturdily gainsay. It does its business well: it works well: it keeps out the water from the land, and it lets in the wine upon the High Commission of Embankment. Cupbearer, fill. Our ancestors were wiser than we: they built it in their wisdom; and, if we should be so rash as to try to mend it, we should only mar it.'

'The stonework,' said Teithrin, 'is sapped and mined: the piles are rotten, broken, and dislocated: the floodgates and sluices are leaky and creaky.'

'That is the beauty of it,' said Seithenyn. 'Some parts of it are rotten, and some parts of it are sound.'

'It is well,' said Elphin, 'that some parts are sound: it were better that all were so.'

'So I have heard some people say before,' said Seithenyn; 'perverse people, blind to venerable antiquity: that very unamiable sort of people, who are in the habit of indulging their reason. But I say, the parts that are rotten give elasticity to those that are sound: they give them elasticity, elasticity, elasticity. If it were all sound, it would break by its own obstinate stiffness: the soundness is checked by the rottenness, and the stiffness is balanced by the elasticity. There is nothing so dangerous as innovation. See the waves in the equinoctial storms, dashing and clashing, roaring and pouring, spattering and battering, rattling and battling against it. I would not be so presumptuous as to say, I could build any thing that would stand against them half an hour; and here this immortal old work, which God forbid the finger of modern mason should bring into jeopardy, this immortal work has stood for centuries, and will stand for centuries more, if we let it alone. Cupbearer, fill. It was half rotten when I was born, and that is a conclusive reason why it should be three parts rotten when I die.'

The whole body of the High Commission roared approbation.

'And after all,' said Seithenyn, 'the worst that could happen would be the overflow of a spring tide, for that was the worst that happened before the embankment was thought of; and, if the high water should come in, as it did before, the low water would go out again, as it did before. We should be no deeper in it than our ancestors were, and we could mend as easily as they could make.'

'The level of the sea,' said Teithrin, 'is materially altered.'

'The level of the sea!' exclaimed Seithenyn. 'Who ever heard of such a thing as altering the level of the sea? Alter the level of that bowl of wine before you, in which, as I sit here, I see a very ugly reflection of your very goodlooking face. Alter the level of that: drink up the reflection: let me see the face without the reflection, and leave the sea to level itself.'

'Not to level the embankment,' said Teithrin.

'Good, very good,' said Seithenyn. 'I love a smart saying, though it hits at me. But, whether yours is a smart saying or no, I do not very clearly see; and, whether it hits at me or no, I do not very sensibly feel. But all is one. Cupbearer, fill.

'I think,' pursued Seithenyn, looking as intently as he could at Teithrin ap Tathral, 'I have seen something very like you before. There was a fellow here the other day very like you: he stayed here some time: he would not talk: he did nothing but drink: he used to drink till he could not stand, and then he went walking about the embankment. I suppose he thought it wanted mending; but he did not say any thing. If he had, I should have told him to embank his own throat, to keep the liquor out of that. That would have posed him: he could not have answered that: he would not have had a word to say for himself after that.'

'He must have been a miraculous person,' said Teithrin, 'to walk when he could not stand.'

'All is one for that,' said Seithenyn. 'Cupbearer, fill.'

'Prince Seithenyn,' said Elphin, 'if I were not aware that wine speaks in the silence of reason, I should be astonished at your strange vindication of your neglect of duty, which I take shame to myself for not having sooner known and remedied. The wise bard has well observed, "Nothing is done without the eye of the king." '

'I am very sorry,' said Seithenyn, 'that you see things in a wrong light: but we will not quarrel for three reasons: first, because you are the son of the king, and may do and say what you please, without any one having a right to be displeased: second, because I never quarrel with a guest, even if he grows riotous in his cups: third, because there is nothing to quarrel about; and perhaps that is the best reason of the three; or rather the first is the best, because you are the son of the king; and the third is the second, that is, the second best, because there is nothing to quarrel about; and the second is nothing to the purpose, because, though guests will grow riotous in their cups, in spite of my good orderly example, God forbid I should say, that is the case with you. And I completely agree in the truth of your remark, that reason speaks in the silence of wine.'

Seithenyn accompanied his speech with a vehement swinging of his right hand: in so doing, at this point, he dropped his cup: a sudden impulse of rash volition, to pick it dexterously up before he resumed his discourse, ruined all his devices for maintaining dignity; in stooping forward from his chair, he lost his balance, and fell prostrate on the floor.

The whole body of the High Commission arose in simultaneous confusion, each zealous to be the foremost in uplifting his fallen chief. In the vehemence of their uprise, they hurled the benches backward and the tables forward; the crash of cups and bowls accompanied their overthrow; and rivulets of liquor ran gurgling through the hall. The household wished to redeem the credit of their leader in the eyes of the Prince; but the only service they could render him was to participate in his discomfiture; for Seithenyn, as he was first in dignity, was also, as was fitting, hardest in skull; and that which had impaired his equilibrium had utterly destroyed theirs. Some fell in the first impulse, with the tables and benches; others were tripped up by the rolling bowls; and the remainder fell at different points of progression, by jostling against each other, or stumbling over those who had fallen before them.

THE VICTORIAN IMAGE OF THE LEGENDS

Arthur and Lancelot, from a stained glass window designed by William Morris for Morris and Co. (Bradford City Art Gallery)

TENNYSON AND VICTORIAN ATTITUDES · MATTHEW ARNOLD WILLIAM MORRIS AND THE PRE-RAPHAELITES · ALGERNON SWINBURNE & & &

'The power of romance is that it fits itself anew to every period. Each one takes up again the undying legend of Arthur, and more or less deludes itself with the notion that the latest version is the truest. But every century must still read its own emotion and its own colours into the past.' This was written in 1905, when the revival of interest in the Arthurian stories was an established fact. Yet without the work of one man, the 'undying legend of Arthur' might well have been more dead than alive. Alfred Tennyson's *Idylls of the King* are the greatest of the modern versions of the legend, and after Malory, are the reason for its vitality. They are still controversial: the extreme reactions against Victorian values among the literary critics of the 1920s and 1930s has almost, but not quite, worn off, and Harold Nicholson's condemnation of the poems as 'for the most part intellectually insincere', or W. H. Auden's comment that Tennyson 'had the finest ear, perhaps, of any English poet; he was also undoubtedly the stupidest' still influence modern attitudes to the *Idylls*. In reality, if we shed the prejudices of the last half century, these are complex, subtle and very rich poems, mirroring not only the Victorians' immense self-confidence, but also the darker side of doubt and despair.

Although he published his first Arthurian poems in 1832, and what was to be the last poem of the cycle in 1842, Tennyson did not decide finally on even the general shape of the cycle until some ten years later, in about 1855. Once he embarked on the project, work progressed rapidly and the outline of the cycle was completed in 1869.

Tennyson's reading in preparation for the work included much early Arthurian literature, though he depended heavily on Malory. There had been three editions of the *Morte Darthur* in 1816 and 1817, and it was now firmly entrenched as a classic work. He had read the *Mabinogion*, which Lady Guest translated in 1838, Layamon's *Brut* in Sir Frederick Madden's edition, and some of the French romances. He seems also to have made some study of the early Welsh material. He introduced few variations of his own, preferring to simplify Malory's many details.

As the work progressed, Tennyson's concepts of the ideals underlying his stories seem to have changed and shifted somewhat, unlike Malory's resolute admiration for his chosen hero Lancelot. The symbolic element, too, occupied a less prominent place than originally intended, and was not intended to be interpreted as literally as the drafts might suggest. Tennyson said on one occasion: 'I hate to be tied down to say, "This means that", because the thought within the image is much more than any one interpretation.' Yet, on another occasion he provides a seemingly contradictory indication: 'Of course Camelot for instance . . . is everywhere symbolic of the gradual growth of human beliefs and institutions, and of the spiritual development of man. Yet there is no single fact in the *Idylls*, however seemingly mystical, which cannot be explained without any mystery or allegory whatsoever.' His final judgement seems to have been this: 'Poetry is like shot-silk, with many glancing colours. Every reader must find his own interpretation according to his ability, and according to his sympathy with the poet.'

With these warnings in mind, there is nonetheless a broad general symbolism for us to discern. Arthur stands for the ideal soul. The whole epic is that of man's Utopian dreams coming into contact with practical life and the warring elements of the flesh, and how such high aspirations can be ruined by a single sin. Arthur's birth is a mystery, as is his death; 'from the great deep to the great deep he goes'. Between the two lies life with its conflict of flesh and spirit. He attempts to realise himself in the sensual world, represented by Guinevere, and to control and elevate human passion and capacity by 'liberal institutions', represented here, as in the earlier draft, by the Round Table. Thus Sir Galahad, who might at first seem to be the hero of the poems, is not in fact Tennyson's ideal; he is the figure of spiritual life divorced from this earth, who negates man's dual nature by withdrawing into purely spiritual realms. Merlin stands for the intellect, and his disastrous affair with Vivien is symbolic of the corruption of the intellectual by the sensual.

The keystone of Tennyson's cycle is therefore Arthur and the Table. Arthur himself appears as little short of perfect: warrior, statesman, the uniting force of the Round Table. Ambrosius says of Arthur's knights:

Good ye are and bad, and like to coins,
Some true, some light, but every one of you
Stamp'd with the image of the King.

To follow and obey Arthur is the foremost law of the Round Table; and the high demands he makes are learnt by Gareth before he rides out to seek Camelot and Arthur's company:

Guenevere *by William Morris.*
(Tate Gallery : Photo John Webb)

The Damosel of the Sanct Grael *by Dante Gabriel Rossetti.*
(*Tate Gallery : Photo John Webb*)

The Lady of Shalott *by J. W. Waterhouse (1883).*
(Tate Gallery : Photo John Webb)

Down she came and found a boat
Beneath a willow left afloat . . .
And at the closing of the day
She loosed the chain and down she lay;
The broad stream bore her far away,
The Lady of Shalott. – Tennyson

The Vision of the Holy Grail : tapestry designed by Sir Edward Burne-Jones and made by Morris & Co. The three knights are Perceval, Bors and Galahad.
(City of Birmingham Museums and Art Gallery)

The Lady of Shalott *by W. Holman Hunt.*
(Wadsworth Atheneum, Hartford, Connecticut; the Ella Gallup Sumner and Mary Catlin Summer Collection)

But in her web she still delights
To weave the mirror's magic sights. – Tennyson

Morgan le Fay *by Frederick Sandys. Morgan le Fay, Arthur's half-sister, was an enchantress who used her spells to try to destroy the Round Table and its knights, as in* Sir Gawain and the Green Knight.
(*City of Birmingham Museums and Art Gallery*)

La Mort d'Arthur *by James G. Archer. Arthur is shown with the three queens who have come to take him to Avalon.*
(City of Manchester Art Gallery)

'But hither shall I never come again,
Never lie by thy side; see thee no more –
Farewell!'

Arthur says farewell to Guinevere; book illustration by Gustave Doré (1867).

The King
Will bind thee by such vows, as is a shame
A man should be bound by, yet the which
No man can keep . . .

The vows that the King demands are clear and restrained, lacking the fire which knightly ardour might well desire; they accord well with Guinevere's first assessment of him as 'cold, high, self-contain'd, and passionless', though the description of the founding of the Order shows how Arthur himself could breathe enthusiasm into his warriors. Tennyson's code is dutiful rather than inspiring:

To reverence the King, as if he were
Their conscience, and their conscience as their King,
To break the heathen and uphold the Christ,
To ride abroad redressing human wrongs,
To speak no slander, no, nor listen to it,
To honour his own word as if his God's,
To lead sweet lives in purest chastity,
To love one maiden only, cleave to her,
And worship her by years of noble deeds,
Until they won her.

It is in his match with Guinevere that Arthur fails. He misjudges Lancelot, misjudges Guinevere, failing to see the other side of the coin, the carnal passions which move him not at all. He chooses Guinevere partly because only the most beautiful bride can match his position and spiritual attainment, forgetting that earthly and heavenly beauty are not one and the same thing. And from the high hopes of the early poems, a steady progress towards the abyss of failure develops. The sin of Lancelot and Guinevere permeates the Court. Balin is unable to save himself because of the false ideals they have spread; Pelleas and Etarre imitate their sin; the Holy Grail is misunderstood and misused by the knights imbued with this worldly ideal, of whom Lancelot is the chief, and they approach it with superstition instead of reverence. *The Last Tournament* shows the final stage of the process, cynicism; this poem was originally entitled *The True and the False* and contrasts the decay caused by the false ideal with the original truth. Lancelot the bold has become slothful, Tristram the courteous has forgotten his courtesy.

The cycle of poems is set at intervals throughout the natural year; *The Coming of Arthur* on New Year's Day, his wedding 'when the world is white with may', the appearance of the Grail at Camelot on a summer's night. *The Last Tournament* is in the dead time of the year, autumn, while the final battle in midwinter looks forward from present disaster to the hope of the future rebirth and spring, through Lancelot and Guinevere's repentance, and the forgiveness offered them by Arthur.

Lancelot and Elaine is taken fairly directly from Malory, and in many places follows the original closely. (I have not included Tennyson's version of Arthur's death, arguably the finest poem in the whole of the *Idylls*, because its subject matter duplicates that of the extract from Sir Thomas Malory).

Tristan and Iseult clearly did not attract Tennyson's sympathies: their love is free of the redeeming guilt which characterises that of Lancelot and Guinevere, and he portrays their passion as 'peculiarly modern and joyless', in the words of a recent writer. But other Victorian poets found their story an attractive one. Matthew Arnold wrote the first new version for over five hundred years in 1852, handling his material very freely, and telling the story in a mood of recollection in tranquility; Iseult of Ireland reaches Tristan on his deathbed, and they look back at their past together before he dies. The second part describes Iseult of Brittany after Tristan's death, in a rather charming kind of domestic medievalism. It is a quiet, understated version of a passionate subject, but nonetheless attractive in its very different approach.

A more passionate attitude – almost a riposte to Tennyson, one feels – is struck by William Morris in *The Defence of Guinevere* which belongs to the world of the Pre-Raphaelites. And indeed it is in painting that the most rewarding approach to the Victorian view of the Arthurian legend is often to be found, through the work of the Pre-Raphaelite painters and their successors. Tennyson and Malory were their chief inspiration, and the two most important painters to use Arthurian subjects were Sir Edward Burne-Jones and Dante Gabriel Rossetti, though Holman Hunt, Beardsley, Gustav Doré, and many lesser artists, such as James Archer and Henry Ryland, also contributed their visions of the medieval world. Sadly, the most important series of Arthurian paintings to be undertaken, the Oxford Union frescoes of the 1850s, was undertaken with an inadequate knowledge of the techniques of tempera painting and many of the frescoes decayed very rapidly. It is chiefly in Burne-Jones' and Rossetti's water-colours that the freshness of the original inspiration survives and several of their pictures are based on Morris's poems, whose strength lies in the powerful evocation of a single event or image; the briefer the poem, the surer his handling of it. His object was the realisation of a tragic event or situation, 'the perception and experience of tragic truth, of subtle and noble, terrible and piteous things', and at his best he achieves almost visionary sight in the mood and setting of these rich pictures.

Morris's Arthurian poems are marginal to his fame: but the opposite is true of Algernon Swinburne. *Tristram of Lyonesse* was always intended to be his *magnum opus*, and is indeed the finest of the English versions of the subject. It covers most of the events of the traditional legend, though Swinburne overweights his material by attempting a sustained richness which the texture of the story will not always bear. Much reading preceded the composition of the poem; he studied the romances of Thomas and Beroul, insofar as they were published, as well as Scott's version of *Sir Tristrem* and Malory's excerpts from the French.

Where Tennyson had debased Tristram and Iseult, fiercely condemning their love, Swinburne as fiercely glorifies them and their passion, exalting both while aware of the sinfulness inherent in the tale. His view is similar to, if more lenient than, that of Dante, who places them among the lesser sinners of the *Inferno*; their sin involves mutual sacrifice, but acknowledges no loyalty outside itself and thus leads the participants to betray others. Swinburne, like other writers, diminishes their guilt in this last respect by portraying Mark as mean and cold, until such time as he learns the truth and offers them noble forgiveness in death.

Swinburne obscures the story with psychological excursions, protracted similes and extended descriptions, as he attempts a continuous evocation of their feelings at each stage of the tragedy, from the amazement of their first fiery kiss through the woes of separation and joys of reunion, to the last moving scene where the lovers, who have seemed too young, are revealed as grown old and subject to death.

Through the poem run recurrent themes and motifs; the first and last embraces are connected by variations on the same words, and the ship that bears Tristram on the first fateful voyage is named *Swallow*, while that which takes Iseult on her last journey is called *Swan*. One theme runs throughout the whole poem, pervading it and occasionally dominating the verse; the sea itself. Both for the unknown author of the *Prose Tristan* and for Malory, Tristram had been a knight of the greenwood, a hunter skilled in venery. But for the earliest romancers who had formed and shaped the heart of the legend, Tristram was essentially a man of the sea. Swinburne harks back to this, and the theme provides a powerful and closely connected background against which to set his poem. *Iseult at Tintagel*, which shows Iseult in separation thinking of her distant lover, is continually underlined by the mood of the sea:

And all their past came wailing in the wind,
And all their future thundered in the sea.

The sea sets off and heightens the great moments of the tragedy. The famous love-potion is drunk against a background of storm; Tristram and Iseult both look seawards for comfort when they are parted; the lovelessness of Tristram's marriage to Iseult of the White Hands is emphasised by the sea's absence, and the one calm moment of their tempestuous relationship, at Joyous Gard, is mirrored in the sea's quietness.

Throughout the poem, there is more than an echo of Chrétien de Troyes and Gottfried von Strassburg, the two great medieval exponents of the literature of feeling. The psychological detail, the life-like portraits, as well as the secondary regard for narrative, all bring Swinburne's poem into the same class as the medieval writers, but, fine though it is, the verse sometimes seems to be more important than what is being said.

Idylls of the King

ALFRED TENNYSON

LANCELOT AND ELAINE

Elaine the fair, Elaine the loveable,
Elaine, the lily maid of Astolat,
High in her chamber up a tower to the east
Guarded the sacred shield of Lancelot;
Which first she placed where morning's earliest ray
Might strike it, and awake her with the gleam;
Then fearing rust or soilure fashion'd for it
A case of silk, and braided thereupon
All the devices blazon'd on the shield
In their own tinct, and added, of her wit,
A border fantasy of branch and flower,
And yellow-throated nestling in the nest.
Nor rested thus content, but day by day,
Leaving her household and good father, climb'd
That eastern tower, and entering barr'd her door,
Stript off the case, and read the naked shield,
Now guess'd a hidden meaning in his arms,
Now made a pretty history to herself
Of every dint a sword had beaten in it,
And every scratch a lance had made upon it,
Conjecturing when and where: this cut is fresh;
That ten years back; this dealt him at Caerlyle;
That at Caerleon; this at Camelot:
And ah God's mercy, what a stroke was there!
And here a thrust that might have kill'd, but God
Broke the strong lance, and roll'd his enemy down,
And saved him: so she lived in fantasy.
  How came the lily maid by that good shield
Of Lancelot, she that knew not ev'n his name?
He left it with her, when he rode to tilt
For the great diamond in the diamond jousts,
Which Arthur had ordain'd, and by that name
Had named them, since a diamond was the prize.
  For Arthur, long before they crown'd him King,
Roving the trackless realm of Lyonnesse,
Had found a glen, gray boulder and black tarn.
A horror lived about the tarn, and clave
Like its own mists to all the mountain side:
For here two brothers, one a king, had met
And fought together; but their names were lost;
And each had slain his brother at a blow;
And down they fell and made the glen abhorr'd:
And there they lay till all their bones were bleach'd,
And lichen'd into colour with the crags:
And he, that once was king, had on a crown
Of diamonds, one in front, and four aside,
And Arthur came, and labouring up the pass,
All in a misty moonshine, unawares
Had trodden that crown'd skeleton, and the skull
Brake from the nape, and from the skull the crown
Roll'd into light, and turning on its rims
Fled like a glittering rivulet to the tarn:
And down the shingly scaur he plunged, and caught,
And set it on his head, and in his heart
Heard murmurs, 'Lo, thou likewise shalt be King.'
  Thereafter, when a King, he had the gems
Pluck'd from the crown, and show'd them to his knights,
Saying, 'These jewels, whereupon I chanced

Divinely, are the kingdom's, not the King's –
For public use: henceforward let there be,
Once every year, a joust for one of these:
For so by nine years' proof we needs must learn
Which is our mightiest, and ourselves shall grow
In use of arms and manhood, till we drive
The heathen, who, some say, shall rule the land
Hereafter, which God hinder.' Thus he spoke:
And eight years past, eight jousts had been, and still
Had Lancelot won the diamond of the year,
With purpose to present them to the Queen,
When all were won: but meaning all at once
To snare her royal fancy with a boon
Worth half her realm, had never spoken word.
Now for the central diamond and the last
And largest, Arthur, holding then his court
Hard on the river nigh the place which now
Is this world's hugest, let proclaim a joust
At Camelot, and when the time drew nigh
Spake (for she had been sick) to Guinevere,
'Are you so sick, my Queen, you cannot move
To these fair jousts?' 'Yea, lord,' she said, 'ye know it.'
'Then will ye miss,' he answer'd, 'the great deeds
Of Lancelot, and his prowess in the lists,
A sight ye love to look on.' And the Queen
Lifted her eyes, and they dwelt languidly
On Lancelot, where he stood beside the King.
He thinking that he read her meaning there,
'Stay with me, I am sick; my love is more
Than many diamonds,' yielded; and a heart
Love-loyal to the least wish of the Queen
(However much he yearn'd to make complete
The tale of diamonds for his destined boon)
Urged him to speak against the truth, and say,
'Sir King, mine ancient wound is hardly whole,
And lets me from the saddle;' and the King
Glanced first at him, then her, and went his way.
No sooner gone than suddenly she began:
'To blame, my lord Sir Lancelot, much to blame!
Why go ye not to these fair jousts? the knights
Are half of them our enemies, and the crowd
Will murmur, 'Lo the shameless ones, who take
Their pastime now the trustful King is gone!'
Then Lancelot vext at having lied in vain:
'Are ye so wise? ye were not once so wise,
My Queen, that summer, when ye loved me first.
Then of the crowd ye took no more account
Than of the myriad cricket of the mead,
When its own voice clings to each blade of grass,

Sir Launcelot in the Queen's chamber, by Dante Gabriel Rossetti. Rossetti shows the moment when Agravaine, Mordred and their followers surprise the lovers together; Lancelot kills all of them except Mordred.
(City of Birmingham Art Gallery)

And every voice is nothing. As to knights,
Them surely can I silence with all ease.
But now my loyal worship is allow'd
Of all men: many a bard, without offence,
Has link'd our names together in his lay,
Lancelot, the flower of bravery, Guinevere,
The pearl of beauty: and our knights at feast
Have pledged us in this union, while the King
Would listen smiling. How then? is there more?
Has Arthur spoken aught? or would yourself
Now weary of my service and devoir,
Hencefort be truer to your faultless lord?'
She broke into a little scornful laugh:
'Arthur, my lord, Arthur, the faultless King,
That passionate perfection, my good lord –
But who can gaze upon the Sun in heaven?
He never spake word of reproach to me,
He never had a glimpse of mine untruth,
He cares not for me: only here to-day
There gleam'd a vague suspicion in his eyes:
Some meddling rogue has tamper'd with him – else
Rapt in this fancy of his Table Round,
And swearing men to vows impossible,
To make them like himself: but, friend, to me
He is all fault who hath no fault at all:
For who loves me must have a touch of earth;
The low sun makes the colour: I am yours,

Not Arthur's, as ye know, save by the bond.
And therefore hear my words: go to the jousts:
The tiny-trumpeting gnat can break our dream
When sweetest; and the vermin voices here
May buzz so loud – we scorn them, but they sting.'
Then answer'd Lancelot, the chief of knights:
'And with what face, after my pretext made,
Shall I appear, O Queen, at Camelot, I
Before a King who honours his own word,
As if it were his God's?'
'Yea,' said the Queen,
'A moral child without the craft to rule,
Else had he not lost me: but listen to me,
If I must find you wit: we hear it said
That men go down before your spear at a touch,
But knowing you are Lancelot; your great name,
This conquers: hide it therefore; go unknown:
Win! by this kiss you will: and our true King
Will then allow your pretext, O my knight,
As all for glory; for to speak him true,
Ye know right well, how meek soe'er he seem,
No keener hunter after glory breathes.
He loves it in his knights more than himself:
They prove to him his work: win and return.'
Then got Sir Lancelot suddenly to horse,
Wroth at himself. Not willing to be known,
He left the barren-beaten thoroughfare,
Chose the green path that show'd the rarer foot,
And there among the solitary downs,
Full often lost in fancy, lost his way;
Till as he traced a faintly-shadow'd track,
That all in loops and links among the dales
Ran to the Castle of Astolat, he saw
Fired from the west, far on a hill, the towers.
Thither he made, and blew the gateway horn.
Then came an old, dumb, myriad-wrinkled man,
Who let him into lodging and disarm'd.
And Lancelot marvell'd at the wordless man;
And issuing found the Lord of Astolat
With two strong sons, Sir Torre and Sir Lavaine,
Moving to meet him in the castle court;
And close behind them stept the lily maid
Elaine, his daughter: mother of the house
There was not: some light jest among them rose
With laughter dying down as the great knight
Approach'd them: then the Lord of Astolat:
'Whence comest thou, my guest, and by what name
Livest between the lips? for by thy state
And presence I might guess thee chief of those,
After the King, who eat in Arthur's halls.
Him have I seen: the rest, his Table Round,
Known as they are, to me they are unknown.'
Then answer'd Lancelot, the chief of knights:
'Known am I, and of Arthur's hall, and known,
What I by mere mischance have brought, my shield.
But since I go to joust as one unknown
At Camelot for the diamond, ask me not,
Hereafter ye shall know me – and the shield –
I pray you lend me one, if such you have,
Blank, or at least with some device not mine.'
Then said the Lord of Astolat, 'Here is Torre's:
Hurt in his first tilt was my son, Sir Torre.
And so, God wot, his shield is blank enough.
His ye can have.' Then added plain Sir Torre,
'Yea, since I cannot use it, ye may have it.'
Here laugh'd the father saying, 'Fie, Sir Churl,
Is that an answer for a noble knight?
Allow him! but Lavaine, my younger here,
He is so full of lustihood, he will ride,
Joust for it, and win, and bring it in an hour,
And set it in this damsel's golden hair,
To make her thrice as wilful as before.'
'Nay, father, nay, good father, shame me not
Before this noble knight,' said young Lavaine,
'For nothing. Surely I but play'd on Torre:
He seem'd so sullen, vext he could not go:
A jest, no more! for, knight, the maiden dreamt
That some one put this diamond in her hand,
And that it was too slippery to be held,
And slipt and fell into some pool or stream,
The castle-well, belike; and then I said
That *if* I went and *if* I fought and won it
(But all was jest and joke among ourselves)
Then must she keep it safelier. All was jest.
But, father, give me leave, an if he will,
To ride to Camelot with this noble knight:
Win shall I not, but do my best to win:
Young as I am, yet would I do my best.'
'So ye will grace me,' answer'd Lancelot,
Smiling a moment, 'with your fellowship
O'er these waste downs whereon I lost myself,
Then were I glad of you as guide and friend:
And you shall win this diamond, – as I hear
It is a fair large diamond, – if ye may,
And yield it to this maiden, if ye will.'
'A fair large diamond,' added plain Sir Torre,
'Such be for queens, and not for simple maids.'
Then she, who held her eyes upon the ground,

Guinevere and Elaine, cartoon for stained glass by William Morris.
(Tate Gallery)

Elaine, and heard her name so tost about,
Flush'd slightly at the slight disparagement
Before the stranger knight, who, looking at her,
Full courtly, yet not falsely, thus return'd:
'If what is fair be but for what is fair,
And only queens are to be counted so,
Rash were my judgment then, who deem this maid
Might wear as fair a jewel as is on earth,
Not violating the bond of like to like.'
He spoke and ceased: the lily maid Elaine,
Won by the mellow voice before she look'd,
Lifted her eyes, and read his lineaments.
The great and guilty love he bare the Queen,
In battle with the love he bare his lord,
Had marr'd his face, and mark'd it ere his time.
Another sinning on such heights with one,
The flower of all the west and all the world,
Had been the sleeker for it: but in him
His mood was often like a fiend, and rose
And drove him into wastes and solitudes
For agony, who was yet a living soul.
Marr'd as he was, he seem'd the goodliest man
That ever among ladies ate in hall,
And noblest, when she lifted up her eyes.
However marr'd, of more than twice her years,
Seam'd with an ancient swordcut on the cheek,
And bruised and bronzed, she lifted up her eyes
And loved him, with that love which was her doom.
Then the great knight, the darling of the court,
Loved of the loveliest, into that rude hall
Stept with all grace, and not with half disdain
Hid under grace, as in a smaller time,
But kindly man moving among his kind:
Whom they with meats and vintage of their best
And talk and minstrel melody entertain'd.
And much they ask'd of court and Table Round,
And ever well and readily answer'd he:
But Lancelot, when they glanced at Guinevere,
Suddenly speaking of the wordless man,
Heard from the Baron that, ten years before,
The heathen caught and reft him of his tongue.
'He learnt and warn'd me of their fierce design
Against my house, and him they caught and maim'd;
But I, my sons, and little daughter fled
From bonds or death, and dwelt among the woods
By the great river in a boatman's hut.
Dull days were those, till our good Arthur broke
The Pagan yet once more on Badon hill.'
'O there, great lord, doubtless,' Lavaine said, rapt
By all the sweet and sudden passion of youth
Toward greatness in its elder, 'you have fought.
O tell us – for we live apart – you know
Of Arthur's glorious wars.' And Lancelot spoke
And answer'd him at full, as having been
With Arthur in the fight which all day long
Rang by the white mouth of the violent Glem;
And in the four loud battles by the shore
Of Duglas; that on Bassa; then the war
That thunder'd in and out the gloomy skirts
Of Celidon the forest; and again
By castle Gurnion, where the glorious King
Had on his cuirass worn our Lady's Head,
Carved of one emerald center'd in a sun
Of silver rays, that lighten'd as he breathed;
And at Caerleon had he help'd his lord,
When the strong neighings of the wild white Horse
Set every gilded parapet shuddering;
And up in Agned-Cathregonion too,
And down the waste sand-shores of Trath Treroit,
Where many a heathen fell; 'and on the mount
Of Badon I myself beheld the King
Charge at the head of all his Table Round,
And all his legions crying Christ to him,
And break them; and I saw him, after, stand

High on a heap of slain, from spur to plume
Red as the rising sun with heathen blood,
And seeing me, with a great voice he cried,
"They are broken, they are broken!" for the King,
However mild he seems at home, nor cares
For triumph in our mimic wars, the jousts –
For if his own knight cast him down, he laughs
Saying, his knights are better men than he –
Yet in this heathen war the fire of God
Fills him: I never saw his like: there lives
No greater leader.'
While he utter'd this,
Low to her own heart said the lily maid,
'Save your great self, fair lord;' and when he fell
From talk of war to traits of pleasantry –
Being mirthful he, but in a stately kind –
She still took note that when the living smile
Died from his lips, across him came a cloud
Of melancholy severe, from which again,
Whenever in her hovering to and fro
The lily maid had striven to make him cheer,
There brake a sudden-beaming tenderness
Of manners and of nature: and she thought
That all was nature, all, perchance, for her.
And all night long his face before her lived,
As when a painter, poring on a face,
Divinely thro' all hindrance finds the man
Behind it, and so paints him that his face,
The shape and colour of a mind and life,
Lives for his children, ever at its best
And fullest; so the face before her lived,
Dark-splendid, speaking in the silence, full
Of noble things, and held her from her sleep.
Till rathe she rose, half-cheated in the thought
She needs must bid farewell to sweet Lavaine.
First as in fear, step after step, she stole
Down the long tower-stairs, hesitating:
Anon, she heard Sir Lancelot cry in the court,
'This shield, my friend, where is it?' and Lavaine
Past inward, as she came from out the tower.
There to his proud horse Lancelot turn'd, and smooth'd
The glossy shoulder, humming to himself.
Half-envious of the flattering hand, she drew
Nearer and stood. He look'd, and more amazed
Than if seven men had set upon him, saw
The maiden standing in the dewy light.
He had not dream'd she was so beautiful.
Then came on him a sort of sacred fear,
For silent, tho' he greeted her, she stood
Rapt on his face as if it were a God's.
Suddenly flashed on her a wild desire,
That he should wear her favour at the tilt.
She braved a riotous heart in asking for it:
'Fair lord, whose name I know not – noble it is,
I well believe, the noblest – will you wear
My favour at this tourney?' 'Nay,' said he,
'Fair lady, since I never yet have worn
Favour of any lady in the lists.
Such is my wont, as those, who know me, know.'
'Yea so,' she answer'd; 'then in wearing mine
Needs must be lesser likelihood, noble lord,
That those who know should know you.' And he turn'd
Her counsel up and down within his mind,
And found it true, and answer'd, 'True, my child,
Well, I will wear it: fetch it out to me:
What is it?' and she told him 'A red sleeve
Broider'd with pearls,' and brought it: then he bound
Her token on his helmet, with a smile
Saying, 'I never yet have done so much
For any maiden living,' and the blood
Sprang to her face and fill'd her with delight;
But left her all the paler, when Lavaine
Returning brought the yet-unblazon'd shield,
His brother's; which he gave to Lancelot,
Who parted with his own to fair Elaine:
'Do me this grace, my child, to have my shield
In keeping till I come.' 'A grace to me,'
She answer'd, 'twice to-day. I am your squire!'
Whereat Lavaine said, laughing, 'Lily maid,
For fear our people call you lily maid
In earnest, let me bring your colour back;
Once, twice, and thrice: now get you hence to bed:'
So kiss'd her, and Sir Lancelot his own hand,
And thus they moved away: she stay'd a minute,
Then made a sudden step to the gate, and there –
Her bright hair blown about the serious face
Yet rosy-kindled with her brother's kiss –
Paused by the gateway, standing near the shield
In silence, while she watch'd their arms far-off
Sparkle, until they dipt below the downs.
Then to her tower she climb'd, and took the shield
There kept it, and so lived in fantasy.
Meanwhile the new companions past away
Far o'er the long backs of the bushless downs,
To where Sir Lancelot knew there lived a knight
Not far from Camelot, now for forty years
A hermit, who had pray'd, labour'd and pray'd,
And ever labouring had scoop'd himself

'Then to her tower she climb'd, and took the shield,
There kept it, and so lived in fantasy.'
Book illustration by Eleanor Fortescue-Brickdale for Idylls of the King, *c. 1910.*

In the white rock a chapel and a hall
On massive columns, like a shorecliff cave,
And cells and chambers: all were fair and dry;
The green light from the meadows underneath
Struck up and lived along the milky roofs;
And in the meadows tremulous aspen-trees
And poplars made a noise of falling showers.
And thither wending there that night they bode.
But when the next day broke from underground,
And shot red fire and shadows thro' the cave,
They rose, heard mass, broke fast, and rode away:
Then Lancelot saying, 'Hear, but hold my name
Hidden, ye ride with Lancelot of the Lake,'
Abash'd Lavaine, whose instant reverence,
Dearer to true young hearts than their own praise,
But left him leave to stammer, 'Is it indeed?'
And after muttering 'The great Lancelot,'
At last he got his breath and answer'd, 'One,
One have I seen – that other, our liege lord,
The dread Pendragon, Britain's King of kings,
Of whom the people talk mysteriously,
He will be there – then were I stricken blind
That minute, I might say that I had seen.'
So spake Lavaine, and when they reach'd the lists
By Camelot in the meadow, let his eyes
Run thro' the peopled gallery which half round
Lay like a rainbow fall'n upon the grass,
Until they found the clear-faced King, who sat
Robed in red samite, easily to be known,
Since to his crown the golden dragon clung,
And down his robe the dragon writhed in gold,
And from the carven-work behind him crept
Two dragons gilded, sloping down to make
Arms for his chair, while all the rest of them
Thro' knots and loops and folds innumerable
Fled ever thro' the woodwork, till they found
The new design wherein they lost themselves,
Yet with all ease, so tender was the work:
And, in the costly canopy o'er him set,
Blazed the last diamond of the nameless king.
Then Lancelot answer'd young Lavaine and said,
'Me you call great: mine is the firmer seat,
The truer lance: but there is many a youth
Now crescent, who will come to all I am
And overcome it; and in me there dwells
No greatness, save it be some far-off touch
Of greatness to know well I am not great:
There is the man.' And Lavaine gaped upon him
As on a thing miraculous, and anon
The trumpets blew; and then did either side,
They that assail'd, and they that held the lists,
Set lance in rest, strike spur, suddenly move,
Meet in the midst, and there so furiously
Shock, that a man far-off might well perceive
If any man that day were left afield,
The hard earth shake, and a low thunder of arms.
And Lancelot bode a little, till he saw
Which were the weaker; then he hurl'd into it
Against the stronger: little need to speak
Of Lancelot in his glory! King, duke, earl,
Count, baron – whom he smote, he overthrew.
But in the field were Lancelot's kith and kin,
Ranged with the Table Round that held the lists,
Strong men, and wrathful that a stranger knight
Should do and almost overdo the deeds
Of Lancelot: and one said to the other, 'Lo!

What is he? I do not mean the force alone –
The grace and versatility of the man?
Is it not Lancelot?' 'When had Lancelot worn
Favour of any lady in the lists?
Not such his wont, as we, that know him, know.'
'How then? who then?' a fury seized them all,
A fiery family passion for the name
Of Lancelot, and a glory one with theirs.
They couch'd their spears and prick'd their steeds, and thus,
Their plumes driv'n backward by the wind they made
In moving, all together down upon him
Bare, as a wild wave in the wide North-sea,
Green-glimmering toward the summit, bears, with all
Its stormy crests that smoke against the skies,
Down on a bark, and overbears the bark,
And him that helms it, so they overbore
Sir Lancelot and his charger, and a spear
Down-glancing lamed the charger, and a spear
Prick'd sharply his own cuirass, and the head
Pierced thro' his side, and there snapt, and remain'd.
Then Sir Lavaine did well and worshipfully;
He bore a knight of old repute to the earth,
And brought his horse to Lancelot where he lay.
He up the side, sweating with agony, got,
But thought to do while he might yet endure,
And being lustily holpen by the rest,
His party, – tho' it seem'd half-miracle
To those he fought with, – drave his kith and kin,
And all the Table Round that held the lists,
Back to the barrier: then the trumpets blew
Proclaiming his the prize, who wore the sleeve
Of scarlet, and the pearls; and all the knights,
His party, cried 'Advance and take thy prize
The diamond;' but he answer'd, 'Diamond me
No diamonds! for God's love, a little air!
Prize me no prizes, for my prize is death!
Hence will I, and I charge you, follow me not.'
He spoke, and vanish'd suddenly from the field
With young Lavaine into the poplar grove.
There from his charger down he slid, and sat,
Gasping to Sir Lavaine, 'Draw the lance-head:'
'Ah, my sweet lord, Sir Lancelot,' said Lavaine,
'I dread me, if I draw it, you will die.'
But he, 'I die already with it: draw –
Draw,' – and Lavaine drew, and Sir Lancelot gave
A marvellous great shriek and ghastly groan,
And half his blood burst forth, and down he sank
For the pure pain, and wholly swoon'd away.
Then came the hermit out and bare him in,
There stanch'd his wound; and there, in daily doubt
Whether to live or die, for many a week
Hid from the wide world's rumour by the grove
Of poplars with their noise of falling showers,
And ever-tremulous aspen-trees, he lay.
But on that day when Lancelot fled the lists,
His party, knights of utmost North and West,
Lords of waste marches, kings of desolate isles,
Came round their great Pendragon, saying to him,
'Lo, Sire, our knight, thro' whom we won the day
Hath gone sore wounded, and hath left his prize
Untaken, crying that his prize is death.'
'Heaven hinder,' said the King, 'that such an one
So great a knight as we have seen to-day –
He seem'd to me another Lancelot –
Yea, twenty times I thought him Lancelot –
He must not pass uncared for. Wherefore, rise,
O Gawain, and ride forth and find the knight.
Wounded and wearied needs must he be near.
I charge you that you get at once to horse.
And, knights and kings, there breathes not one of you
Will deem this prize of ours is rashly given:
His prowess was too wondrous. We will do him
No customary honour: since the knight
Came not to us, of us to claim the prize,
Ourselves will send it after. Rise and take
This diamond, and deliver it, and return,
And bring us where he is, and how he fares,
And cease not from your quest until ye find.'
So saying, from the carven flower above,
To which it made a restless heart, he took,
And gave, the diamond: then from where he sat
At Arthur's right, with smiling face arose,
With smiling face and frowning heart, a Prince
In the mid might and flourish of his May,
Gawain, surnamed The Courteous, fair and strong,
And after Lancelot, Tristram, and Geraint
And Gareth, a good knight, but therewithal
Sir Modred's brother, and the child of Lot,
Nor often loyal to his word, and now
Wroth that the King's command to sally forth
In quest of whom he knew not, made him leave
The banquet, and concourse of knights and kings.
So all in wrath he got to horse and went;
While Arthur to the banquet, dark in mood,
Past, thinking 'Is it Lancelot who hath come
Despite the wound he spake of, all for gain
Of glory, and hath added wound to wound,

And ridd'n away to die?' So fear'd the King,
And, after two days' tarriance there, return'd.
Then when he saw the Queen, embracing ask'd,
'Love, are you yet so sick?' 'Nay, lord,' she said.
'And where is Lancelot?' Then the Queen amazed
'Was he not with you? won he not your prize?'
'Nay, but one like him.' 'Why that like was he.'
And when the King demanded how she knew,
Said, 'Lord, no sooner had ye parted from us,
Than Lancelot told me of a common talk
That men went down before his spear at a touch,
But knowing he was Lancelot; his great name
Conquer'd; and therefore would he hide his name
For all men, ev'n the King, and to this end
Had made the pretext of a hindering wound,
That he might joust unknown of all, and learn
If his old prowess were in aught decay'd;
And added, "Our true Arthur, when he learns,
Will well allow my pretext, as for gain
Of purer glory." '
Then replied the King:
'Far lovelier in our Lancelot had it been,
In lieu of idly dallying with the truth,
To have trusted me as he hath trusted thee.
Surely his King and most familiar friend
Might well have kept his secret. True, indeed,
Albeit I know my knights fantastical,
So fine a fear in our large Lancelot
Must needs have moved my laughter: now remains
But little cause for laughter: his own kin –
Ill news, my Queen, for all who love him, this! –
His kith and kin, not knowing, set upon him;
So that he went sore wounded from the field:
Yet good news too: for goodly hopes are mine
That Lancelot is no more a lonely heart.
He wore, against his wont, upon his helm
A sleeve of scarlet, broider'd with great pearls,
Some gentle maiden's gift.'
'Yea, lord,' she said,
'Thy hopes are mine,' and saying that, she choked,
And sharply turn'd about to hide her face,
Past to her chamber, and there flung herself
Down on the great King's couch, and writhed upon it,
And clench'd her fingers till they bit the palm,
And shriek'd out 'Traitor' to the unhearing wall,
Then flash'd into wild tears, and rose again,
And moved about her palace, proud and pale.
Gawain the while thro' all the region round
Rode with his diamond, wearied of the quest,
Touch'd at all points, except the poplar grove,
And came at last, tho' late, to Astolat:
Whom glittering in enamell'd arms the maid
Glanced at, and cried, 'What news from Camelot, lord?
What of the knight with the red sleeve?' 'He won.'
'I knew it,' she said. 'But parted from the jousts
Hurt in the side,' whereat she caught her breath;
Thro' her own side she felt the sharp lance go;
Thereon she smote her hand: wellnigh she swoon'd:
And, while he gazed wonderingly at her, came
The Lord of Astolat out, to whom the Prince
Reported who he was, and on what quest
Sent, that he bore the prize and could not find
The victor, but had ridd'n a random round
To seek him, and had wearied of the search.
To whom the Lord of Astolat, 'Bide with us,
And ride no more at random, noble Prince!
Here was the knight, and here he left a shield;
This will he send or come for: furthermore
Our son is with him; we shall hear anon,
Needs must we hear.' To this the courteous Prince
Accorded with his wonted courtesy,
Courtesy with a touch of traitor in it,
And stay'd; and cast his eyes on fair Elaine:
Where could be found face daintier? then her shape
From forehead down to foot, perfect – again
From foot to forehead exquisitely turn'd:
'Well – if I bide, lo! this wild flower for me!'
And oft they met among the garden yews,
And there he set himself to play upon her
With sallying wit, free flashes from a height
Above her, graces of the court, and songs,
Sighs, and slow smiles, and golden eloquence
And amorous adulation, till the maid
Rebell'd against it, saying to him, 'Prince,
O loyal nephew of our noble King,
Why ask you not to see the shield he left,
Whence you might learn his name? Why slight your King,
And lose the quest he sent you on, and prove
No surer than our falcon yesterday,
Who lost the hern we slipt her at, and went
To all the winds?' 'Nay, by mine head,' said he,
'I lose it, as we lose the lark in heaven,
O damsel, in the light of your blue eyes;
But an ye will it let me see the shield.'
And when the shield was brought, and Gawain saw
Sir Lancelot's azure lions, crown'd with gold,
Ramp in the field, he smote his thigh, and mock'd:
'Right was the King! our Lancelot! that true man!'

'And right was I,' she answer'd merrily, 'I
Who dream'd my knight the greatest knight of all.'
'And if *I* dream'd,' said Gawain, 'that you love
This greatest knight, your pardon! lo, ye know it!
Speak therefore: shall I waste myself in vain?'
Full simple was her answer, 'What know I?
My brethren have been all my fellowship;
And I, when often they have talk'd of love,
Wish'd it had been my mother, for they talk'd,
Meseem'd, of what they knew not; so myself –
I know not if I know what true love is,
But if I know, then, if I love not him,
I know there is none other I can love.'
'Yea, by God's death,' said he, 'ye love him well,
But would not, knew ye what all others know,
And whom he loves.' 'So be it,' cried Elaine,
And lifted her fair face and moved away:
But he pursued her, calling, 'Stay a little!
One golden minute's grace! he wore your sleeve:
Would he break faith with one I may not name?
Must our true man change like a leaf at last?
Nay – like enow: why then, far be it from me
To cross our mighty Lancelot in his loves!
And, damsel, for I deem you know full well
Where your great knight is hidden, let me leave
My quest with you; the diamond also: here!
For if you love, it will be sweet to give it;
And if he love, it will be sweet to have it
From your own hand; and whether he love or not,
A diamond is a diamond. Fare you well
A thousand times! – a thousand times farewell!
Yet if he love, and his love hold, we two
May meet at court hereafter: there, I think,
So ye will learn the courtesies of the court,
We two shall know each other.'
Then he gave,
And slightly kiss'd the hand to which he gave,
The diamond, and all wearied of the quest
Leapt on his horse, and carolling as he went
A true-love ballad, lightly rode away.
Thence to the court he past; there told the King
What the King knew, 'Sir Lancelot is the knight.'
And added, 'Sire, my liege, so much I learnt;
But fail'd to find him, tho' I rode all round
The region: but I lighted on the maid
Whose sleeve he wore; she loves him; and to her,
Deeming our courtesy is the truest law,
I gave the diamond: she will render it;
For by mine head she knows his hiding-place.'
The seldom-frowning King frown'd, and replied,
'Too courteous truly! ye shall go no more
On quest of mine, seeing that ye forget
Obedience is the courtesy due to kings.'
He spake and parted. Wroth, but all in awe,
For twenty strokes of the blood, without a word,
Linger'd that other, staring after him;
Then shook his hair, strode off, and buzz'd abroad
About the maid of Astolat, and her love.
All ears were prick'd at once, all tongues were loosed:
'The maid of Astolat loves Sir Lancelot,
Sir Lancelot loves the maid of Astolat.'
Some read the King's face, some the Queen's, and all
Had marvel what the maid might be, but most
Predoom'd her as unworthy. One old dame
Came suddenly on the Queen with the sharp news.
She, that had heard the noise of it before,
But sorrowing Lancelot should have stoop'd so low,
Marr'd her friend's aim with pale tranquility.
So ran the tale like fire about the court,
Fire in dry stubble a nine-days' wonder flared:
Till ev'n the knights at banquet twice or thrice
Forgot to drink to Lancelot and the Queen,
And pledging Lancelot and the lily maid
Smiled at each other, while the Queen, who sat
With lips severely placid, felt the knot
Climb in her throat, and with her feet unseen
Crush'd the wild passion out against the floor
Beneath the banquet, where the meats became
As wormwood, and she hated all who pledged.
But far away the maid in Astolat,
Her guiltless rival, she that ever kept
The one-day-seen Sir Lancelot in her heart,
Crept to her father, while he mused alone,
Sat on his knee, stroked his gray face and said,
'Father, you call me wilful, and the fault
Is yours, who let me have my will, and now,
Sweet father, will you let me lose my wits?'
'Nay,' said he, 'surely.' 'Wherefore, let me hence,'
She answer'd, 'and find out our dear Lavaine.'
'Ye will not lose your wits for dear Lavaine:
Bide,' answer'd he: 'we needs must hear anon
Of him and of that other.' 'Ay,' she said,
'And of that other, for I needs must hence
And find that other, wheresoe'er he be,
And with mine own hand give his diamond to him,
Lest I be found as faithless in the quest
As yon proud Prince who left the quest to me.
Sweet father, I behold him in my dreams

Gaunt as it were the skeleton of himself,
Death-pale, for lack of gentle maiden's aid.
The gentler-born the maiden, the more bound,
My father, to be sweet and serviceable
To noble knights in sickness, as ye know
When these have worn their tokens: let me hence
I pray you.' Then her father nodding said,
'Ay, ay, the diamond: wit ye well, my child,
Right fain were I to learn this knight were whole,
Being our greatest: yea, and you must give it –
And sure I think this fruit is hung too high
For any mouth to gape for save a queen's –
Nay, I mean nothing: so then, get you gone,
Being so very wilful you must go.'
   Lightly, her suit allow'd, she slipt away,
And while she made her ready for her ride,
Her father's latest word humm'd in her ear,
'Being so very wilful you must go,'
And changed itself and echo'd in her heart,
'Being so very wilful you must die.'
But she was happy enough and shook it off,
As we shake off the bee that buzzes at us;
And in her heart she answer'd it and said,
'What matter, so I help him back to life?'
Then far away with good Sir Torre for guide
Rode o'er the long backs of the bushless downs
To Camelot, and before the city-gates
Came on her brother with a happy face
Making a roan horse caper and curvet
For pleasure all about a field of flowers:
Whom when she saw, 'Lavaine,' she cried, 'Lavaine,
How fares my lord Sir Lancelot?' He amazed,
'Torre and Elaine! why here? Sir Lancelot!
How know ye my lord's name is Lancelot?'
But when the maid had told him all her tale,
Then turned Sir Torre, and being in his moods
Left them, and under the strange-statued gate,
Where Arthur's wars were render'd mystically,
Past up the still rich city to his kin,
His own far blood, which dwelt at Camelot;
And her, Lavaine across the poplar grove
Led to the caves: there first she saw the casque
Of Lancelot on the wall: her scarlet sleeve,
Tho' carved and cut, and half the pearls away,
Stream'd from it still; and in her heart she laugh'd,
Because he had not loosed it from his helm,
But meant once more perchance to tourney in it.
And when they gained the cell wherein he slept,
His battle-writhen arms and mighty hands
Lay naked on the wolfskin, and a dream
Of dragging down his enemy made them move.
Then she that saw him lying unsleek, unshorn,
Gaunt as it were the skeleton of himself,
Utter'd a little tender dolorous cry.
The sound not wonted in a place so still
Woke the sick knight, and while he roll'd his eyes
Yet blank from sleep, she started to him, saying,
'Your prize the diamond sent you by the King:'
His eyes glisten'd: she fancied 'Is it for me?'
And when the maid had told him all the tale
Of King and Prince, the diamond sent, the quest
Assign'd to her not worthy of it, she knelt
Full lowly by the corners of his bed,
And laid the diamond in his open hand.
Her face was near, and as we kiss the child
That does the task assign'd, he kiss'd her face.
At once she slipt like water to the floor.
'Alas,' he said, 'your ride hath wearied you.
Rest must you have.' 'No rest for me,' she said;
'Nay, for near you, fair lord, I am at rest.'
What might she mean by that? his large black eyes,
Yet larger thro' his leanness, dwelt upon her,
Till all her heart's sad secret blazed itself
In the heart's colours on her simple face;
And Lancelot look'd and was perplext in mind,
And being weak in body said no more;
But did not love the colour; woman's love,
Save one, he not regarded, and so turn'd
Sighing, and feign'd a sleep, until he slept.
   Then rose Elaine and glided thro' the fields,
And past beneath the weirdly-sculptured gates
Far up the dim rich city to her kin;
There bode the night: but woke with dawn, and past
Down thro' the dim rich city to the fields,
Thence to the cave: so day by day she past
In either twilight ghost-like to and fro
Gliding, and every day she tended him,
And likewise many a night: and Lancelot
Would, tho' he call'd his wound a little hurt
Whereof he should be quickly whole, at times
Brain-feverous in his heat and agony, seem
Uncourteous, even he: but the meek maid
Sweetly forbore him ever, being to him
Meeker than any child to a rough nurse,
Milder than any mother to a sick child,
And never woman yet, since man's first fall,
Did kindlier unto man, but her deep love
Upbore her; till the hermit, skill'd in all

Lancelot and Elaine, by Sidney E. Paget (1891).
(Bristol City Art Gallery)

The simples and the sciences of that time,
Told him that her fine care had saved his life.
And the sick man forgot her simple blush,
Would call her friend and sister, sweet Elaine,
Would listen for her coming and regret
Her parting step, and held her tenderly,
And loved her with all love except the love
Of man and woman when they love their best,
Closest and sweetest, and had died the death
In any knightly fashion for her sake.
And peradventure had he seen her first
She might have made this and that other world
Another world for the sick man; but now
The shackles of an old love straiten'd him,
His honour rooted in dishonour stood,
And faith unfaithful kept him falsely true.
Yet the great knight in his mid-sickness made
Full many a holy vow and pure resolve.
These, as but born of sickness, could not live:
For when the blood ran lustier in him again,
Full often the bright image of one face,
Making a treacherous quiet in his heart,
Dispersed his resolution like a cloud.
Then if the maiden, while that ghostly grace
Beam'd on his fancy, spoke, he answer'd not,
Or short and coldly, and she knew right well
What the rough sickness meant, but what this meant
She knew not, and the sorrow dimm'd her sight,
And drave her ere her time across the fields
Far into the rich city, where alone
She murmur'd, 'Vain, in vain: it cannot be.
He will not love me: how then? must I die?'
Then as a little helpless innocent bird,
That has but one plain passage of few notes,
Will sing the simple passage o'er and o'er
For all an April morning, till the ear
Wearies to hear it, so the simple maid
Went half the night repeating, 'Must I die?'
And now to right she turn'd; and now to left,
And found no ease in turning or in rest;
And 'Him or death,' she mutter'd, 'death or him.'
Again and like a burthen, 'Him or death.'
But when Sir Lancelot's deadly hurt was whole,
To Astolat returning rode the three.
There morn by morn, arraying her sweet self
In that wherein she deem'd she look'd her best,
She came before Sir Lancelot, for she thought
'If I be loved, these are my festal robes,
If not, the victim's flowers before he fall.'
And Lancelot ever prest upon the maid
That she should ask some goodly gift of him
For her own self or hers; 'and do not shun
To speak the wish most near to your true heart;
Such service have ye done me, that I make
My will of yours, and Prince and Lord am I
In mine own land, and what I will I can.'
Then like a ghost she lifted up her face,
But like a ghost without the power to speak.
And Lancelot saw that she withheld her wish,
And bode among them yet a little space
Till he should learn it; and one morn it chanced
He found her in among the garden yews,
And said, 'Delay no longer, speak your wish,
Seeing I go to-day:' then out she brake:
'Going? and we shall never see you more.
And I must die for want of one bold word.'
'Speak: that I live to hear,' he said, 'is yours.'
Then suddenly and passionately she spoke:
'I have gone mad. I love you: let me die.'
'Ah, sister,' answer'd Lancelot, 'what is this?'
And innocently extending her white arms,
'Your love,' she said, 'your love – to be your wife.'
And Lancelot answer'd, 'Had I chosen to wed,
I had been wedded earlier, sweet Elaine:
But now there never will be wife of mine.'
'No, no,' she cried, 'I care not to be wife,
But to be with you still, to see your face,
To serve you, and to follow you thro' the world.'
And Lancelot answer'd, 'Nay, the world, the world,
All ear and eye, with such a stupid heart

To interpret ear and eye, and such a tongue
To blare its own interpretation – nay,
Full ill then should I quit your brother's love,
And your good father's kindness.' And she said,
'Not to be with you, not to see your face –
Alas for me then, my good days are done.'
'Nay, noble maid,' he answer'd, 'ten times nay!
This is not love: but love's first flash in youth,
Most common: yea, I know it of mine own self:
And you yourself will smile at your own self
Hereafter, when you yield your flower of life
To one more fitly yours, not thrice your age:
And then will I, for true you are and sweet
Beyond mine old belief in womanhood,
More specially should your good knight be poor,
Endow you with broad land and territory
Even to the half my realm beyond the seas,
So that would make you happy: furthermore,
Ev'n to the death, as tho' ye were my blood,
In all your quarrels will I be your knight.
This will I do, dear damsel, for your sake,
And more than this I cannot.'
While he spoke
She neither blush'd nor shook, but deathly-pale
Stood grasping what was nearest, then replied:
'Of all this will I nothing;' and so fell,
And thus they bore her swooning to her tower.
Then spake, to whom thro' those black walls of yew
Their talk had pierced, her father: 'Ay, a flash,
I fear me, that will strike my blossom dead.
Too courteous are ye, fair Lord Lancelot.
I pray you, use some rough discourtesy
To blunt or break her passion.'
Lancelot said,
'That were against me: what I can I will;'
And there that day remain'd, and toward even
Sent for his shield: full meekly rose the maid,
Stript off the case, and gave the naked shield;
Then, when she heard his horse upon the stones,
Unclasping flung the casement back, and look'd
Down on his helm, from which her sleeve had gone.
And Lancelot knew the little clinking sound;
And she by tact of love was well aware
That Lancelot knew that she was looking at him.
And yet he glanced not up, nor waved his hand,
Nor bad farewell, but sadly rode away.
This was the one discourtesy that he used.
So in her tower alone the maiden sat:
His very shield was gone: only the case,
Her own poor work, her empty labour, left.
But still she heard him, still his picture form'd
And grew between her and the pictured wall.
Then came her father, saying in low tones,
'Have comfort,' whom she greeted quietly.
Then came her brethren saying, 'Peace to thee,
Sweet sister,' whom she answer'd with all calm.
But when they left her to herself again,
Death, like a friend's voice from a distant field
Approaching thro' the darkness, call'd; the owls
Wailing had power upon her, and she mixt
Her fancies with the sallow-rifted glooms
Of evening, and the moaning of the wind.
And in those days she made a little song,
And call'd her song 'The Song of Love and Death,'
And sang it: sweetly could she make and sing.

'Sweet is true love tho' given in vain, in vain;
And sweet is death who puts an end to pain:
I know not which is sweeter, no, not I.
'Love, art thou sweet? then bitter death must be:
Love, thou art bitter; sweet is death to me.
O Love, if death be sweeter, let me die.
'Sweet love, that seems not made to fade away,
Sweet death, that seems to make us loveless clay,
I know not which is sweeter, no, not I.
'I fain would follow love, if that could be;
I needs must follow death, who calls for me;
Call and I follow, I follow! let me die.'

High with the last line scaled her voice, and this,
All in a fiery dawning wild with wind
That shook her tower, the brothers heard, and thought
With shuddering, 'Hark the Phantom of the house
That ever shrieks before a death,' and call'd
The father, and all three in hurry and fear
Ran to her, and lo! the blood-red light of dawn
Flared on her face, she shrilling, 'Let me die!'
As when we dwell upon a word we know,
Repeating, till the word we know so well
Becomes a wonder, and we know not why,
So dwelt the father on her face, and thought
'Is this Elaine?' till back the maiden fell,
Then gave a languid hand to each, and lay,
Speaking a still good-morrow with her eyes.
At last she said, 'Sweet brothers, yesternight
I seem'd a curious little maid again,
As happy as when we dwelt among the woods,
And when ye used to take me with the flood
Up the great river in the boatman's boat.

Only ye would not pass beyond the cape
That has the poplar on it: there ye fixt
Your limit, oft returning with the tide.
And yet I cried because ye would not pass
Beyond it, and far up the shining flood
Until we found the palace of the King.
And yet he would not; but this night I dream'd
That I was all alone upon the flood,
And then I said, "Now shall I have my will:"
And there I woke, but still the wish remain'd.
So let me hence that I may pass at last
Beyond the poplar and far up the flood,
Until I find the palace of the King.
There will I enter in among them all,
And no man there will dare to mock at me;
But there the fine Gawain will wonder at me,
And there the great Sir Lancelot muse at me;
Gawain, who bad a thousand farewells to me,
Lancelot, who coldly went, nor bad me one:
And there the King will know me and my love,
And there the Queen herself will pity me,
And all the gentle court will welcome me,
And after my long voyage I shall rest!'
  'Peace,' said her father, 'O my child, ye seem
Light-headed, for what force is yours to go
So far, being sick? and wherefore would ye look
On this proud fellow again, who scorns us all?'
  Then the rough Torre began to heave and move,
And bluster into stormy sobs and say,
'I never loved him: an I meet with him,
I care not howsoever great he be,
Then will I strike at him and strike him down,
Give me good fortune, I will strike him dead,
For this discomfort he hath done the house.'
  To whom the gentle sister made reply,
'Fret not yourself, dear brother, nor be wroth,
Seeing it is no more Sir Lancelot's fault
Not to love me, than it is mine to love
Him of all men who seems to me the highest.'
  'Highest?' the father answer'd, echoing 'highest?'
(He meant to break the passion in her) 'nay,
Daughter, I know not what you call the highest;
But this I know, for all the people know it,
He loves the Queen, and in an open shame;
And she returns his love in open shame;
If this be high, what is it to be low?'
  Then spake the lily maid of Astolat:
'Sweet father, all too faint and sick am I
For anger: these are slanders: never yet
Was noble man but made ignoble talk.
He makes no friend who never made a foe.
But now it is my glory to have loved
One peerless, without stain: so let me pass,
My father, howsoe'er I seem to you,
Not all unhappy, having loved God's best
And greatest, tho' my love had no return:
Yet, seeing you desire your child to live,
Thanks, but you work against your own desire;
For if I could believe the things you say
I should but die the sooner; wherefore cease,
Sweet father, and bid call the ghostly man
Hither, and let me shrive me clean, and die.'
  So when the ghostly man had come and gone,
She with a face, bright as for sin forgiven,
Besought Lavaine to write as she devised
A letter, word for word; and when he ask'd
'Is it for Lancelot, is it for my dear lord?
Then will I bear it gladly;' she replied,
'For Lancelot and the Queen and all the world,
But I myself must bear it.' Then he wrote
The letter she devised; which being writ
And folded, 'O sweet father, tender and true,
Deny me not,' she said – 'ye never yet
Denied my fancies – this, however strange,
My latest: lay the letter in my hand
A little ere I die, and close the hand
Upon it; I shall guard it even in death.
And when the heat is gone from out my heart,
Then take the little bed on which I died
For Lancelot's love, and deck it like the Queen's
For richness, and me also like the Queen
In all I have of rich, and lay me on it.
And let there be prepared a chariot-bier
To take me to the river, and a barge
Be ready on the river, clothed in black.
I go in state to court, to meet the Queen.
There surely I shall speak for mine own self,
And none of you can speak for me so well.
And therefore let our dumb old man alone
Go with me, he can steer and row, and he
Will guide me to that palace, to the doors.'
  She ceased: her father promised: whereupon
She grew so cheerful that they deem'd her death
Was rather in the fantasy than the blood.
But ten slow mornings past, and on the eleventh
Her father laid the letter in her hand,
And closed the hand upon it, and she died.
So that day there was dole in Astolat.

But when the next sun brake from underground,
Then, those two brethren slowly with bent brows
Accompanying, the sad chariot-bier
Past like a shadow thro' the field, that shone
Full-summer, to that stream whereon the barge,
Pall'd all its length in blackest samite, lay.
There sat the lifelong creature of the house,
Loyal, the dumb old servitor, on deck,
Winking his eyes, and twisted all his face.
So those two brethren from the chariot took
And on the back decks laid her in her bed
Set in her hand a lily, o'er her hung
The silken case with braided blazonings,
And kiss'd her quiet brows, and saying to her
'Sister, farewell for ever,' and again
'Farewell, sweet sister,' parted all in tears.
Then rose the dumb old servitor, and the dead,
Oar'd by the dumb, went upward with the flood –
In her right hand the lily, in her left
The letter – all her bright hair streaming down –
And all the coverlid was cloth of gold
Drawn to her waist, and she herself in white
All but her face, and that clear-featured face
Was lovely, for she did not seem as dead,
But fast asleep, and lay as tho' she smiled.
That day Sir Lancelot at the palace craved
Audience of Guinevere, to give at last
The price of half a realm, his costly gift,
Hard-won and hardly won with bruise and blow,
With deaths of others and almost his own,
The nine-years-fought-for diamonds: for he saw
One of her house, and sent him to the Queen
Bearing his wish, whereto the Queen agreed
With such and so unmoved a majesty
She might have seem'd her statue, but that he,
Low-drooping till he wellnigh kiss'd her feet
For loyal awe, saw with a sidelong eye
The shadow of some piece of pointed lace,
In the Queen's shadow, vibrate on the walls,
And parted, laughing in his courtly heart.
All in an oriel on the summer side,
Vine-clad, of Arthur's palace toward the stream,
They met, and Lancelot kneeling utter'd, 'Queen,
Lady, my liege, in whom I have my joy,
Take, what I had not won except for you,
These jewels, and make me happy, making them
An armlet for the roundest arm on earth,
Or necklace for a neck to which the swan's
Is tawnier than her cygnet's: these are words:
Your beauty is your beauty, and I sin
In speaking, yet O grant my worship of it
Words, as we grant grief tears. Such sin in words
Perchance, we both can pardon: but, my Queen,
I hear of rumours flying thro' your court.
Our bond, as not the bond of man and wife,
Should have in it an absoluter trust
To make up that defect: let rumours be:
When did not rumours fly? these, as I trust
That you trust me in your own nobleness,
I may not well believe that you believe.'
While thus he spoke, half turn'd away, the Queen
Brake from the vast oriel-embowering vine
Leaf after leaf, and tore, and cast them off,
Till all the place whereon she stood was green;
Then, when he ceased, in one cold passive hand
Received at once and laid aside the gems
There on a table near her, and replied:
'It may be, I am quicker of belief
Than you believe me, Lancelot of the Lake.
Our bond is not the bond of man and wife.
This good is in it, whatsoe'er of ill,
It can be broken easier. I for you
This many a year have done despite and wrong
To one whom ever in my heart of hearts
I did acknowledge nobler. What are these?
Diamonds for me! they had been thrice their worth
Being your gift, had you not lost your own.
To loyal hearts the value of all gifts
Must vary as the giver's. Not for me!
For her! for your new fancy. Only this
Grant me, I pray you: have your joys apart.
I doubt not that however changed, you keep
So much of what is graceful: and myself
Would shun to break those bounds of courtesy
In which as Arthur's Queen I move and rule:
So cannot speak my mind. An end to this!
A strange one! yet I take it with Amen.
So pray you, add my diamonds to her pearls;
Deck her with these; tell her, she shines me down:
An armlet for an arm to which the Queen's
Is haggard, or a necklace for a neck
O as much fairer – as a faith once fair
Was richer than these diamonds – hers not mine –
Nay, by the mother of our Lord himself,
Or hers or mine, mine now to work my will –
She shall not have them.'
Saying which she seized,
And thro' the casement standing wide for heat,

Flung them, and down they flash'd, and smote the stream.
Then from the smitten surface flash'd, as it were,
Diamonds to meet them, and they past away.
Then while Sir Lancelot leant, in half disdain
At love, life, all things, on the window ledge,
Close underneath his eyes, and right across
Where these had fallen, slowly past the barge
Whereon the lily maid of Astolat
Lay smiling, like a star in blackest night.
  But the wild Queen, who saw not, burst away
To weep and wail in secret; and the barge,
On to the palace-doorway sliding, paused.
There two stood arm'd, and kept the door; to whom,
All up the marble stair, tier over tier,
Were added mouths that gaped, and eyes that ask'd
'What is it?' but that oarsman's haggard face,
As hard and still as is the face that men
Shape to their fancy's eye from broken rocks
On some cliff-side, appal'd them, and they said,
'He is enchanted, cannot speak – and she,
Look how she sleeps – the Fairy Queen, so fair!
Yea, but how pale! what are they? flesh and blood?
Or come to take the King to Fairyland?
For some do hold our Arthur cannot die,
But that he passes into Fairyland.'
  While thus they babbled of the King, the King
Came girt with knights: then turned the tongueless man
From the half-face to the full eye, and rose
And pointed to the damsel, and the doors.
So Arthur bad the meek Sir Percivale
And pure Sir Galahad to uplift the maid;
And reverently they bore her into hall.
Then came the fine Gawain and wonder'd at her,
And Lancelot later came and mused at her,
And last the Queen herself, and pitied her:
But Arthur spied the letter in her hand,
Stoopt, took, brake seal, and read it; this was all:

  '*Most noble lord, Sir Lancelot of the Lake*
I, sometime call'd the maid of Astolat,
Come, for you left me taking no farewell,
Hither, to take my last farewell of you.
I loved you, and my love had no return,
And therefore my true love has been my death.
And therefore to our Lady Guinevere,
And to all other ladies, I make moan.
Pray for my soul, and yield me burial.
Pray for my soul thou too, Sir Lancelot,
As thou art a knight peerless.'

                    Thus he read;
And ever in the reading, lords and dames
Wept, looking often from his face who read
To hers which lay so silent, and at times,
So touch'd were they, half-thinking that her lips,
Who had devised the letter, moved again.
  Then freely spoke Sir Lancelot to them all:
'My lord liege Arthur, and all ye that hear,
Know that for this most gentle maiden's death
Right heavy am I; for good she was and true,
But loved me with a love beyond all love
In women, whomsoever I have known.
Yet to be loved makes not to love again;
Not at my years, however it hold in youth.
I swear by truth and knighthood that I gave
No cause, not willingly, for such a love:
To this I call my friends in testimony,
Her brethren, and her father, who himself
Besought me to be plain and blunt, and use,
To break her passion, some discourtesy
Against my nature: what I could, I did.
I left her and I bad her no farewell;
Tho', had I dreamt the damsel would have died,
I might have put my wits to some rough use,
And help'd her from herself.'
                    Then said the Queen
(Sea was her wrath, yet working after storm)
'Ye might at least have done her so much grace,
Fair lord, as would have help'd her from her death.'
He raised his head, their eyes met and hers fell,
He adding,
          'Queen, she would not be content
Save that I wedded her, which could not be.
Then might she follow me thro' the world, she ask'd;
It could not be. I told her that her love
Was but the flash of youth, would darken down
To rise hereafter in a stiller flame
Toward one more worthy of her – then would I,
More specially were he, she wedded, poor,
Estate them with large land and territory
In mine own realm beyond the narrow seas,
To keep them in all joyance: more than this
I could not; this she would not, and she died.'
  He pausing, Arthur answer'd, 'O my knight,
It will be to thy worship, as my knight,
And mine, as head of all our Table Round,
To see that she be buried worshipfully.'
  So toward that shrine which then in all the realm
Was richest, Arthur leading, slowly went

The marshall'd Order of their Table Round,
And Lancelot sad beyond his wont, to see
The maiden buried, not as one unknown,
Nor meanly, but with gorgeous obsequies,
And mass, and rolling music, like a queen.
And when the knights had laid her comely head
Low in the dust of half-forgotten kings,
Then Arthur spake among them, 'Let her tomb
Be costly, and her image thereupon,
And let the shield of Lancelot at her feet
Be carven, and her lily in her hand.
And let the story of her dolorous voyage
For all true hearts be blazon'd on her tomb
In letters gold and azure!' which was wrought
Thereafter; but when now the lords and dames
And people, from the high door streaming, brake
Disorderly, as homeward each, the Queen,
Who mark'd Sir Lancelot where he moved apart,
Drew near, and sigh'd in passing, 'Lancelot,
Forgive me; mine was jealousy in love.'
He answer'd with his eyes upon the ground,
'That is love's curse; pass on, my Queen, forgiven.'
But Arthur, who beheld his cloudy brows,
Approach'd him, and with full affection said,
'Lancelot, my Lancelot, thou in whom I have
Most joy and most affiance, for I know
What thou hast been in battle by my side,
And many a time have watch'd thee at the tilt
Strike down the lusty and long practised knight,
And let the younger and unskill'd go by
To win his honour and to make his name,
And loved thy courtesies and thee, a man
Made to be loved; but now I would to God,
Seeing the homeless trouble in thine eyes,
Thou couldst have loved this maiden, shaped, it seems,
By God for thee alone, and from her face,
If one may judge the living by the dead,
Delicately pure and marvellously fair,
Who might have brought thee, now a lonely man
Wifeless and heirless, noble issue, sons
Born to the glory of they name and fame,
My knight, the great Sir Lancelot of the Lake.'
Then answer'd Lancelot, 'Fair she was, my King,
Pure, as you ever wish your knights to be.
To doubt her fairness were to want an eye,
To doubt her pureness were to want a heart –
Yea, to be loved, if what is worthy love
Could bind him, but free love will not be bound.'
'Free love, so bound, were freest,' said the King.
'Let love be free; free love is for the best:
And, after heaven, on our dull side of death,
What should be best, if not so pure a love
Clothed in so pure a loveliness? yet thee
She fail'd to bind, tho' being, as I think,
Unbound as yet, and gentle, as I know.'
And Lancelot answer'd nothing, but he went,
And at the inrunning of a little brook
Sat by the river in a cove, and watch'd
The high reed wave, and lifted up his eyes
And saw the barge that brought her moving down,
Far-off, a blot upon the stream, and said
Low in himself, 'Ah simple heart and sweet,
Ye loved me, damsel, surely with a love
Far tenderer than my Queen's. Pray for thy soul?
Ay, that will I. Farewell too – now at last –
Farewell, fair lily. "Jealousy in love"?
Not rather dead love's harsh heir, jealous pride?
Queen, if I grant the jealousy as of love,
May not your crescent fear for name and fame
Speak, as it waxes, of a love that wanes?
Why did the King dwell on my name to me?
Mine own name shames me, seeming a reproach,
Lancelot, whom the Lady of the Lake
Caught from his mother's arms – the wondrous one
Who passes thro' the vision of the night –
She chanted snatches of mysterious hymns
Heard on the winding waters, eve and morn
She kiss'd me saying, "Thou art fair, my child,
As a king's son," and often in her arms
She bare me, pacing on the dusky mere.
Would she had drown'd me in it, where'er it be!
For what am I? what profits me my name
Of greatest knight? I fought for it, and have it:
Pleasure to have it, none; to lose it, pain;
Now grown a part of me: but what use in it?
To make men worse by making my sin known?
Our sin seem less, the sinner seeming great?
Alas for Arthur's greatest knight, a man
Not after Arthur's heart! I needs must break
These bonds that so defame me: not without
She will it: would I, if she will'd it? nay,
Who knows? but if I would not, then may God,
I pray him, send a sudden Angel down
To seize me by the hair and bear me far,
And fling me deep in that forgotten mere,
Among the tumbled fragments of the hills.'
So groan'd Sir Lancelot in remorseful pain,
Not knowing he should die a holy man.

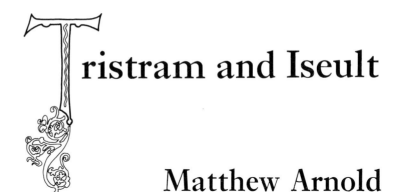

Tristram and Iseult

Matthew Arnold

Tristram

Is she not come? The messenger was sure.
Prop me upon the pillows once again –
Raise me, my page! this cannot long endure.
– Christ, what a night! how the sleet whips the pane!
What lights will those out to the northward be?

The Page

The lanterns of the fishing-boats at sea.

Tristram

Soft – who is that, stands by the dying fire?

The Page

Iseult.

Tristram

Ah! not the Iseult I desire.

* * * * *

What Knight is this so weak and pale,
Though the locks are yet brown on his noble head,
Propt on pillows in his bed,
Gazing seaward for the light
Of some ship that fights the gale
On this wild December night?
Over the sick man's feet is spread
A dark green forest-dress;
A gold harp leans against the bed,
Ruddy in the fire's light.
I know him by his harp of gold,
Famous in Arthur's court of old;
I know him by his forest-dress –
The peerless hunter, harper, knight,
Tristram of Lyoness.
What Lady is this, whose silk attire
Gleams so rich in the light of the fire?
The ringlets on her shoulders lying
In their flitting lustre vying
With the clasp of burnish'd gold
Which her heavy robe doth hold.
Her looks are sweet, her fingers slight
As the driven snow are white;
But her cheeks are sunk and pale.
Is it that the bleak sea-gale
Beating from the Atlantic sea
On this coast of Brittany,
Nips too keenly the sweet flower?
Is it that a deep fatigue
Hath come on her, chilly fear
Passing all her youthful hour
Spinning with her maidens here,
Listlessly through the window-bars
Gazing seawards many a league
From her lonely shore-built tower,
While the knights are at the wars?
Or, perhaps, has her young heart
Felt already some deeper smart
Of those that in secret the heart-strings rive,

Leaving her sunk and pale, though fair?
Who is this snowdrop by the sea? –
I know her by her mildness rare,
Her snow-white hands, her golden hair;
I know her by her rich silk dress,
And her fragile loveliness –
The sweetest Christian soul alive,
Iseult of Brittany.
Iseult of Brittany? – but where
Is that other Iseult fair,
That proud, first Iseult, Cornwall's queen?
She, whom Tristram's ship of yore
From Ireland to Cornwall bore,
To Tyntagel, to the side
Of King Marc, to be his bride?
She who, as they voyaged, quaff'd
With Tristram that spiced magic draught,
Which since then for ever rolls
Through their blood, and binds their souls,
Working love, but working teen? –
There were two Iseults who did sway
Each her hour of Tristram's day;
But one possess'd his waning time,
The other his resplendent prime.
Behold her here, the patient flower,
Who possess'd his darker hour!
Iseult of the Snow-White Hand
Watches pale by Tristram's bed.
She is here who had his gloom,
Where art thou who hadst his bloom?
One such kiss as those of yore
Might thy dying knight restore!
Does the love-draught work no more?
Art thou cold, or false, or dead,
Iseult of Ireland?

* * * * *

Loud howls the wind, sharp patters the rain,
And the knight sinks back on his pillows again.
He is weak with fever and pain,
And his spirit is not clear;
Hark! he mutters in his sleep,
As he wanders far from here.
Changes place and time of year,
And his closéd eye doth sweep
O'er some fair unwintry sea,
Not this fierce Atlantic deep,
While he mutters brokenly:–

Tristram

The calm sea shines, loose hang the vessel's sails.
Before us are the sweet green fields of Wales,
And overhead the cloudless sky of May. –
'*Ah, would I were in those green fields at play,*
Not pent on ship-board this delicious day!
Tristram, I pray thee, of thy courtesy,
Reach me my golden cup that stands by thee,
But pledge me in it first for courtesy. –'
Ha! dost thou start? are thy lips blanch'd like mine?
Child, 'tis no true draught this, 'tis poison'd wine!
Iseult! . . .

* * * * *

Ah, sweet angels, let him dream!
Keep his eyelids! let him seem
Not this fever-wasted wight
Thinn'd and paled before his time,
But the brilliant youthful knight
In the glory of his prime,
Sitting in the gilded barge,
At thy side, thou lovely charge,
Bending gaily o'er thy hand.
Iseult of Ireland!
And she too, that princess fair,
If her bloom be now less rare,
Let her have her youth again –
Let her be as she was then!
Let her have her proud dark eyes
And her petulant quick replies –
Let her sweep her dazzling hand
With its gesture of command,
And shake back her raven hair
With the old imperious air!
As of old, so let her be,
That first Iseult, princess bright,
Chatting with her youthful knight
As he steers her o'er the sea,
Quitting at her father's will
The green isle where she was bred,
And her bower in Ireland,
For the surge-beat Cornish strand;
Where the prince whom she must wed
Dwells on loud Tyntagel's hill,
High above the sounding sea.
And that phial rare her mother
Gave her, that her future lord,
Gave her, that King Marc and she
Might drink it on their marriage-day,

And for ever love each other –
Let her, as she sits on board,
Ah, sweet saints, unwittingly!
See it shine, and take it up,
And to Tristram laughing say:
'Sir Tristram, of thy courtesy,
Pledge me in my golden cup!'
Let them drink it – let their hands
Tremble, and their cheeks be flame,
As they feel the fatal bands
Of a love they dare not name,
With a wild delicious pain,
Twine about their hearts again!
Let the early summer be
Once more round them, and the sea
Blue, and o'er its mirror kind
Let the breath of the May-wind,
Wandering through their drooping sails,
Die on the green fields of Wales!
Let a dream like this restore
What his eye must see no more!

Tristram

Chill blows the wind, the pleasaunce-walks are drear –
Madcap, what jest was this, to meet me here?
Were feet like those made for so wild a way?
The southern winter-parlour, by my fay,
Had been the likeliest trysting-place to-day! –
'*Tristram! – nay, nay – thou must not take my hand! –*
Tristram! – sweet love! – we are betrayed – out-plann'd.
Fly – save thyself – save me! – I dare not stay.' –
One last kiss first! – ' '*Tis vain – to horse – away!*'

* * * * *

Ah! sweet saints, his dream doth move
Faster surely than it should,
From the fever in his blood!
All the spring-time of his love
Is already gone and past,
And instead thereof is seen
Its winter, which endureth still –
Tyntagel on its surge-beat hill,
The pleasaunce-walks, the weeping queen,
The flying leaves, the straining blast,
And that long, wild kiss – their last.
And this rough December-night,
And his burning fever-pain,
Mingle with his hurrying dream,
Till they rule it, till he seem
The press'd fugitive again,
The love-desperate banish'd knight
With a fire in his brain
Flying o'er the stormy main.
– Whither does he wander now?
Haply in his dreams the wind
Wafts him here, and lets him find
The lovely orphan child again
In her castle by the coast;
The youngest, fairest chatelaine,
That this realm of France can boast
Our snowdrop by the Atlantic sea,
Iseult of Brittany.
And – for through the haggard air,
The stain'd arms, the matted hair
Of that stranger-knight ill-starr'd,
There gleam'd something, which recall'd
The Tristram who in better days
Was Launcelot's guest at Joyous Gard –
Welcomed here, and here install'd,
Tended of his fever here,
Haply he seems again to move
His young guardian's heart with love;
In his exiled loneliness,
In his stately, deep distress,
Without a word, without a tear.
– Ah! 'tis well he should retrace
His tranquil life in this lone place;
His gentle bearing at the side
Of his timid youthful bride,
His long rambles by the shore
On winter-evenings, when the roar
Of the near waves came, sadly grand,
Through the dark, up the drown'd sand;
Or his endless reveries
In the woods, where the gleams play
On the grass under the trees,
Passing the long summer's day
Idle as a mossy stone
In the forest-depths alone,
The chase neglected, and his hound
Couch'd beside him on the ground.
– Ah! what trouble's on his brow?
Hither let him wander now;
Hither, to the quiet hours
Pass'd among these heaths of ours
By the grey Atlantic sea;
Hours, if not of ecstasy,
From violent anguish surely free!

Tristram

All red with blood the whirling river flows,
The wide plain rings, the dazed air throbs with blows.
Upon us are the chivalry of Rome!
Their spears are down, their steeds are bathed in foam.
'Up, Tristram, up,' men cry, 'thou moonstruck knight!
What foul fiend rides thee? On into the fight!'
– Above the din her voice is in my ears;
I see her form glide through the crossing spears. –
Iseult! . . .

* * * * *

Ah! he wanders forth again;
We cannot keep him; now, as then,
There's a secret in his breast
Which will never let him rest.
These musing fits in the green wood,
They cloud the brain, they dull the blood!
– His sword is sharp, his horse is good;
Beyond the mountains will he see
The famous towns of Italy,
And label with the blessed sign
The heathen Saxons on the Rhine.
At Arthur's side he fights once more
With the Roman Emperor.
There's many a gay knight where he goes
Will help him to forget his care;
The march, the leaguer, Heaven's blithe air,
The neighing steeds, the ringing blows –
Sick pining comes not where these are.
– Ah! what boots it, that the jest
Lightens every other brow,
What, that every other breast
Dances as the trumpets blow.
If one's own heart beats not light
On the waves of the toss'd fight,
If oneself cannot get free
From the clog of misery?
Thy lovely youthful wife grows pale
Watching by the salt sea-tide
With her children at her side
For the gleam of thy white sail.
Home, Tristram, to thy halls again!
To our lonely sea complain,
To our forests tell thy pain!

Tristram

All round the forest sweeps off, black in shade;
But it is moonlight in the open glade.
And in the bottom of the glade shine clear
The forest-chapel and the fountain near.
– I think, I have a fever in my blood;
Come, let me leave the shadow of this wood,
Ride down, and bathe my hot brow in the flood.
– Mild shines the cold spring in the moon's clear light.
God! 'tis *her* face plays in the waters bright.
'Fair love,' she says, 'canst thou forget so soon,
At this soft hour, under this sweet moon?'
Iseult! . . .

* * * * *

Ah, poor soul! if this be so,
Only death can balm thy woe.
The solitudes of the green wood
Had no medicine for thy mood;
The rushing battle clear'd thy blood
As little as did solitude.
– Ah! his eyelids slowly break
Their hot seals, and let him wake;
What new change shall we now see?
A happier? Worse it cannot be.

Tristram

Is my page here? Come, turn me to the fire!
Upon the window-panes the moon shines bright;
The wind is down – but she'll not come to-night.
Ah no! she is asleep in Cornwall now,
Far hence; her dreams are fair – smooth is her brow.
Of me she recks not, nor my vain desire.
– I have had dreams, I have had dreams, my page,
Would take a score years from a strong man's age;
And with a blood like mine, will leave, I fear,
Scant leisure for a second messenger.
– My princess, art thou there? Sweet, 'tis too late!
To bed, and sleep! my fever is gone by;
To-night my page shall keep me company.
Where do the children sleep? kiss them for me!
Poor child, thou art almost as pale as I;
This comes of nursing long and watching late.
To bed – good-night!

* * * * *

She left the gleam-lit fire-place,
She came to the bed-side;
She took his hands in hers – her tears
Down on her slender fingers rain'd.
She raised her eyes upon his face –
Not with a look of wounded pride,
A look as if the heart complain'd –
Her look was like a sad embrace;
The gaze of one who can divine

A grief, and sympathise.
Sweet flower! thy children's eyes
Are not more innocent than thine.
But they sleep in shelter'd rest,
Like helpless birds in the warm nest,
On the castle's southern side;
Where feebly comes the mournful roar
Of buffeting wind and surging tide
Through many a room and corridor.
– Full on their window the moon's ray
Makes their chamber as bright as day.
It shines upon the blank white walls,
And on the snowy pillow falls,
And on two angel-heads doth play
Turn'd to each other – the eyes closed,
The lashes on the cheeks reposed.
Round each sweet brow the cap close-set
Hardly lets peep the golden hair;
Through the soft-open'd lips the air
Scarcely moves the coverlet.
One little wandering arm is thrown
At random on the counterpane,
And often the fingers close in haste
As if their baby-owner chased
The butterflies again.
This stir they have, and this alone;
But else they are so still!
– Ah, tired madcaps! you lie still;
But were you at the window now,
To look forth on the fairy sight
Of your illumined haunts by night,
To see the park-glades where you play
Far lovelier than they are by day,
To see the sparkle on the eaves,
And upon every giant-bough
Of these old oaks, whose wet red leaves
Are jewell'd with bright drops of rain –
How would your voices run again!
And far beyond the sparkling trees
Of the castle-park one sees
The bare heaths spreading, clear as day,
Moor behind moor, far, far away,
Into the heart of Brittany.
And here and there, lock'd by the land,
Long inlets of smooth glittering sea
And many a stretch of watery sand
All shining in the white moon-beams –
But you see fairer in your dreams!
What voices are these on the clear night air?
What lights in the court – what steps on the stair?

The Defence of Guenevere

WILLIAM MORRIS

But, knowing now that they would have her speak,
She threw her wet hair backward from her brow,
Her hand close to her mouth touching her cheek,

As though she had had there a shameful blow,
And feeling it shameful to feel ought but shame
All through her heart, yet felt her cheek burned so,

She must a little touch it; like one lame
She walked away from Gauwaine, with her head
Still lifted up; and on her cheek of flame

The tears dried quick; she stopped at last and said:
O knights and lords, it seems but little skill
To talk of well-known things past now and dead.

God wot I ought to say, I have done ill,
And pray you all forgiveness heartily!
Because you must be right, such great lords; still

Listen, suppose your time were come to die,
And you were quite alone and very weak;
Yea, laid a dying while very mightily

The wind was ruffling up the narrow streak
Of river through your broad lands running well:
Suppose a hush should come, then some one speak:

'One of these cloths is heaven, and one is hell,
Now choose one cloth for ever; which they be,
I will not tell you, you must somehow tell

Of your own strength and mightiness; here, see!'
Yea, yea, my lord, and you to ope your eyes,
At foot of your familiar bed to see

A great God's angel standing, with such dyes,
Not known on earth, on his great wings, and hands,
Held out two ways, light from the inner skies

Showing him well, and making his commands
Seem to be God's commands, moreover, too,
Holding within his hands the cloths on wands;

And one of these strange choosing cloths was blue
Wavy and long, and one cut short and red;
No man could tell the better of the two.

After a shivering half-hour you said:
'God help! heaven's colour, the blue;' and he said, 'hell.'
Perhaps you then would roll upon your bed,

And cry to all good men that loved you well,
'Ah Christ! if only I had known, known, known;'
Launcelot went away, then I could tell,

Like wisest man how all things would be, moan,
And roll and hurt myself, and long to die,
And yet fear much to die for what was sown.

Nevertheless you, O Sir Gauwaine, lie,
Whatever may have happened through these years,
God knows I speak truth, saying that you lie.

Her voice was low at first, being full of tears,
But as it cleared, it grew full loud and shrill,
Growing a windy shriek in all men's ears,

A ringing in their startled brains, until
She said that Gauwaine lied, then her voice sunk,
And her great eyes began again to fill,

Guenevere, by William Morris.
(Tate Gallery)

Though still she stood right up, and never shrunk,
But spoke on bravely, glorious lady fair!
Whatever tears her full lips may have drunk,

She stood, and seemed to think, and wrung her hair,
Spoke out at last with no more trace of shame,
With passionate twisting of her body there:

It chanced upon a day that Launcelot came
To dwell at Arthur's court: at Christmas-time
This happened; when the heralds sung his name,

Son of King Ban of Benwick, seemed to chime
Along with all the bells that rang that day,
O'er the white roofs, with little change of rhyme.

Christmas and whitened winter passed away,
And over me the April sunshine came,
Made very awful with black hail-clouds, yea

And in the Summer I grew white with flame,
And bowed my head down: Autumn, and the sick
Sure knowledge things would never be the same,

However often Spring might be most thick
Of blossoms and buds, smote on me, and I grew
Careless of most things, let the clock tick, tick,

To my unhappy pulse, that beat right through
My eager body; while I laughed out loud,
And let my lips curl up at false or true,

Seemed cold and shallow without any cloud.
Behold my judges, then the cloths were brought;
While I was dizzied thus, old thoughts would crowd,

Belonging to the time ere I was bought
By Arthur's great name and his little love;
Must I give up for ever then, I thought,

That which I deemed would ever round me move
Glorifying all things; for a little word,
Scarce ever meant at all, must I now prove

Stone-cold for ever? Pray you, does the Lord
Will that all folks should be quite happy and good?
I love God now a little, if this cord

Were broken, once for all what striving could
Make me love anything in earth or heaven?
So day by day it grew, as if one should

Slip slowly down some path worn smooth and even,
Down to a cool sea on a summer day;
Yet still in slipping there was some small leaven

Of stretched hands catching small stones by the way,
Until one surely reached the sea at last,
And felt strange new joy as the worn head lay

Back, with the hair like sea-weed; yea all past
Sweat of the forehead, dryness of the lips,
Washed utterly out by the dear waves o'ercast,

In the lone sea, far off from any ships!
Do I not know now of a day in Spring?
No minute of that wild day ever slips

From out my memory; I hear thrushes sing,
And wheresoever I may be, straightway
Thoughts of it all come up with most fresh sting:

I was half mad with beauty on that day,
And went without my ladies all alone,
In a quiet garden walled round every way;

I was right joyful of that wall of stone,
That shut the flowers and trees up with the sky,
And trebled all the beauty: to the bone,

Yea right through to my heart, grown very shy
With weary thoughts, it pierced, and made me glad;
Exceedingly glad, and I knew verily,

A little thing just then had made me mad;
I dared not think, as I was wont to do,
Sometimes, upon my beauty; If I had

Held out my long hand up against the blue,
And, looking on the tenderly darken'd fingers,
Thought that by rights one ought to see quite through,

There, see you, where the soft still light yet lingers,
Round by the edges; what should I have done,
If this had joined with yellow spotted singers,

And startling green drawn upward by the sun?
But shouting, loosed out, see now! all my hair,
And trancedly stood watching the west wind run

With faintest half-heard breathing sound: why there
I lose my head e'en now in doing this;
But shortly listen: In that garden fair

Came Launcelot walking; this is true, the kiss
Wherewith we kissed in meeting that spring day,
I scarce dare talk of the remember'd bliss,

When both our mouths went wandering in one way,
And aching sorely, met among the leaves;
Our hands being left behind strained far away.

Never within a yard of my bright sleeves
Had Launcelot come before: and now, so nigh!
After that day why is it Guenevere grieves?

Nevertheless you, O Sir Gauwaine, lie,
Whatever happened on through all those years,
God knows I speak truth, saying that you lie.

Being such a lady could I weep these tears
If this were true? A great queen such as I
Having sinn'd this way, straight her conscience sears;

And afterwards she liveth hatefully,
Slaying and poisoning, certes never weeps:
Gauwaine be friends now, speak me lovingly.

Do I not see how God's dear pity creeps
All through your frame, and trembles in your mouth?
Remember in what grave your mother sleeps,

Buried in some place far down in the south,
Men are forgetting as I speak to you;
By her head sever'd in that awful drouth

Of pity that drew Agravaine's fell blow,
I pray your pity! let me not scream out
For ever after, when the shrill winds blow

Through half your castle-locks! let me not shout
For ever after in the winter night
When you ride out alone! in battle-rout

Let not my rusting tears make your sword light!
Ah! God of mercy, how he turns away!
So, ever must I dress me to the fight,

So: let God's justice work! Gauwaine, I say,
See me hew down your proofs: yea all men know
Even as you said how Mellyagraunce one day,

One bitter day in *la Fausse Garde*, for so
All good knights held it after, saw:
Yea, sirs, by cursed unknightly outrage; though

You, Gauwaine, held his word without a flaw,
This Mellyagraunce saw blood upon my bed:
Whose blood then pray you? is there any law

To make a queen say why some spots of red
Lie on her coverlet? or will you say:
Your hands are white, lady, as when you wed,

Where did you bleed? and must I stammer out, Nay,
I blush indeed, fair lord, only to rend
My sleeve up to my shoulder, where there lay

A knife-point last night: so must I defend
The honour of the Lady Guenevere?
Not so, fair lords, even if the world should end

This very day, and you were judges here
Instead of God. Did you see Mellyagraunce
When Launcelot stood by him? what white fear

Curdled his blood, and how his teeth did dance,
His side sink in? as my knight cried and said:
Slayer of unarm'd men, here is a chance!

Setter of traps, I pray you guard your head,
By God I am so glad to fight with you,
Stripper of ladies, that my hand feels lead

For driving weight; hurrah now! draw and do,
For all my wounds are moving in my breast,
And I am getting mad with waiting so.

He struck his hands together o'er the beast,
Who fell down flat, and grovell'd at his feet,
And groan'd at being slain so young: At least,

My knight said, rise you, sir, who are so fleet
At catching ladies, half-arm'd will I fight,
My left side all uncovered! then I weet,

Up sprang Sir Mellyagraunce with great delight
Upon his knave's face; not until just then
Did I quite hate him, as I saw my knight

Along the lists look to my stake and pen
With such a joyous smile, it made me sigh
From agony beneath my waist-chain, when

The fight began, and to me they drew nigh;
Ever Sir Launcelot kept him on the right,
And traversed warily, and ever high

And fast leapt caitiff's sword, until my knight
Sudden threw up his sword to his left hand,
Caught it, and swung it; that was all the fight,

Except a spout of blood on the hot land;
For it was hottest summer; and I know
I wonder'd how the fire, while I should stand,

And burn, against the heat, would quiver so,
Yards above my head; thus these matters went;
Which things were only warnings of the woe

That fell on me. Yet Mellyagraunce was shent,
For Mellyagraunce had fought against the Lord;
Therefore, my lords, take heed lest you be blent

With all this wickedness; say no rash word
Against me, being so beautiful; my eyes,
Wept all away to grey, may bring some sword

To drown you in your blood; see my breast rise,
Like waves of purple sea, as here I stand;
And how my arms are moved in wonderful wise,

Yea also at my full heart's strong command,
See through my long throat how the words go up
In ripples to my mouth; how in my hand

The shadow lies like wine within a cup
Of marvellously colour'd gold; yea now
This little wind is rising, look you up,

And wonder how the light is falling so
Within my moving tresses: will you dare,
When you have looked a little on my brow,

To say this thing is vile? or will you care
For any plausible lies of cunning woof,
When you can see my face with no lie there

For ever? am I not a gracious proof:
But in your chamber Launcelot was found:
Is there a good knight then would stand aloof,

When a queen says with gentle queenly sound:
O true as steel come now and talk with me,
I love to see your step upon the ground

Unwavering, also well I love to see
That gracious smile light up your face, and hear
Your wonderful words, that all mean verily

The thing they seem to mean: good friend, so dear
To me in everything, come here to-night,
Or else the hours will pass most dull and drear;

If you come not, I fear this time I might
Get thinking over much of times gone by,
When I was young, and green hope was in sight:

For no man cares now to know why I sigh;
And no man comes to sing me pleasant songs,
Nor any brings me the sweet flowers that lie

So thick in the gardens; therefore one so longs
To see you, Launcelot; that we may be
Like children once again, free from all wrongs

Just for one night. Did he not come to me?
What thing could keep true Launcelot away
If I said, Come? there was one less than three

In my quiet room that night, and we were gay;
Till sudden I rose up, weak, pale, and sick,
Because a bawling broke our dream up, yea

I looked at Launcelot's face and could not speak,
For he looked helpless too, for a little while;
Then I remember how I tried to shriek,

And could not, but fell down; from tile to tile
The stones they threw up rattled o'er my head
And made me dizzier; till within a while

My maids were all about me, and my head
On Launcelot's breast was being soothed away
From its white chattering, until Launcelot said:

By God! I will not tell you more to-day,
Judge any way you will: what matters it?
You know quite well the story of that fray,

How Launcelot still'd their bawling, the mad fit
That caught up Gauwaine: all, all, verily,
But just that which would save me; these things flit.

Nevertheless you, O Sir Gauwaine, lie,
Whatever may have happen'd these long years,
God knows I speak truth, saying that you lie!

All I have said is truth, by Christ's dear tears.
She would not speak another word, but stood
Turn'd sideways; listening, like a man who hears

His brother's trumpet sounding through the wood
Of his foes' lances. She lean'd eagerly,
And gave a slight spring sometimes, as she could

At last hear something really; joyfully
Her cheek grew crimson, as the headlong speed
Of the roan charger drew all men to see,
The knight who came was Launcelot at good need.

Tristram of Lyonesse

ALGERNON SWINBURNE

THE SAILING OF THE SWALLOW

About the middle music of the spring
Came from the castled shore of Ireland's king
A fair ship stoutly sailing, eastward bound
And south by Wales and all its wonders round
To the loud rocks and ringing reaches home
That take the wild wrath of the Cornish foam,
Past Lyonesse unswallowed of the tides
And high Carlion that now the steep sea hides
To the wind-hollowed heights and gusty bays
Of sheer Tintagel, fair with famous days.
Above the stem a gilded swallow shone,
Wrought with straight wings and eyes of glittering stone
As flying sunward oversea, to bear
Green summer with it through the singing air.
And on the deck between the rowers at dawn,
As the bright sail with brightening wind was drawn,
Sat with full face against the strengthening light
Iseult, more fair than foam or dawn was white.
Her gaze was glad past love's own singing of,
And her face lovely past desire of love.
Past thought and speech her maiden motions were,
And a more golden sunrise was her hair.
The very veil of her bright flesh was made
As of light woven and moonbeam-coloured shade
More fine than moonbeams; white her eyelids shone
As snow sun-stricken that endures the sun,
And through their curled and coloured clouds of deep
Luminous lashes thick as dreams in sleep
Shone as the sea's depth swallowing up the sky's
The springs of unimaginable eyes.
As the wave's subtler emerald is pierced through
With the utmost heaven's inextricable blue,
And both are woven and molten in one sleight
Of amorous colour and implicated light
Under the golden guard and gaze of noon,
So glowed their awless amorous plenilune,
Azure and gold and ardent grey, made strange
With fiery difference and deep interchange
Inexplicable of glories multiform;
Now as the sullen sapphire swells toward storm
Foamless, their bitter beauty grew acold,
And now afire with ardour of fine gold.
Her flower-soft lips were meek and passionate,
For love upon them like a shadow sate
Patient, a foreseen vision of sweet things,
A dream with eyes fast shut and plumeless wings
That knew not what man's love or life should be,
Nor had it sight nor heart to hope or see
What thing should come, but childlike satisfied
Watched out its virgin vigil in soft pride
And unkissed expectation; and the glad
Clear cheeks and throat and tender temples had
Such maiden heat as if a rose's blood
Beat in the live heart of a lily-bud.
Between the small round breasts a white way led
Heavenward, and from slight foot to slender head
The whole fair body flower-like swayed and shone
Moving, and what her light hand leant upon

Grew blossom-scented: her warm arms began
To round and ripen for delight of man
That they should clasp and circle: her fresh hands,
Like regent lilies of reflowering lands
Whose vassal firstlings, crown and star and plume,
Bow down to the empire of that sovereign bloom,
Shone sceptreless, and from her face there went
A silent light as of a God content;
Save when, more swift and keen than love or shame,
Some flash of blood, light as the laugh of flame,
Broke it with sudden beam and shining speech,
As dream by dream shot through her eyes, and each
Outshone the last that lightened, and not one
Showed her such things as should be borne and done.
Though hard against her shone the sunlike face
That in all change and wreck of time and place
Should be the star of her sweet living soul.
Nor had love made it as his written scroll
For evil will and good to read in yet;
But smooth and mighty, without scar or fret,
Fresh and high-lifted was the helmless brow
As the oak-tree flower that tops the topmost bough,
Ere it drop off before the perfect leaf;
And nothing save his name he had of grief,
The name his mother, dying as he was born,
Made out of sorrow in very sorrow's scorn,
And set it on him smiling in her sight,
Tristram; who now, clothed with sweet youth and might,
As a glad witness wore that bitter name,
The second symbol of the world for fame.
Famous and full of fortune was his youth
Ere the beard's bloom had left his cheek unsmooth,
And in his face a lordship of strong joy
And height of heart no chance could curb or cloy
Lightened, and all that warmed them at his eyes
Loved them as larks that kindle as they rise
Toward light they turn to music love the blue strong skies.
So like the morning through the morning moved
Tristram, a light to look on and be loved.
Song sprang between his lips and hands, and shone
Singing, and strengthened and sank down thereon
As a bird settles to the second flight,
Then from beneath his harping hands with might
Leapt, and made way and had its fill and died,
And all whose hearts were fed upon it sighed
Silent, and in them all the fire of tears
Burned as wine drunken not with lips but ears.
And gazing on his fervent hands that made
The might of music all their souls obeyed
With trembling strong subservience of delight
Full many a maid that had him once in sight
Thought in the secret rapture of her heart
In how dark onset had these hands borne part
How oft, and were so young and sweet of skill;
And those red lips whereon the song burned still,
What words and cries of battle had they flung
Athwart the swing and shriek of swords, so young;
And eyes as glad as summer, what strange youth
Fed them so full of happy heart and truth,
That had seen sway from side to sundering side
The steel flow of that terrible springtide
That the moon rules not, but the fire and light
Of men's hearts mixed in the mid mirth of fight.
Therefore the joy and love of him they had
Made thought more amorous in them and more glad
For his fame's sake remembered, and his youth
Gave his fame flowerlike fragrance and soft growth
As of a rose requickening, when he stood
Fair in their eye, a flower of faultless blood.
And that sad queen to whom his life was death,
A rose plucked forth of summer in mid breath,
A star fall'n out of season in mid throe
Of that life's joy that makes the star's life glow,
Made their love sadder toward him and more strong.
And in mid change of time and fight and song
Chance cast him westward on the low sweet strand
Where songs are sung of the old green Irish land,
And the sky loves it, and the sea loves best,
And as a bird is taken to man's breast
The sweet-souled land where sorrow sweetest sings
Is wrapt round with them as with hands and wings
And taken to the sea's heart as a flower.
There in the luck and light of his good hour
Came to the king's court like a noteless man
Tristram, and while some half a season ran
Abode before him harping in his hall,
And taught sweet craft of new things musical
To the dear maiden mouth and innocent hands
That for his sake are famous in all lands.
Yet was not love between them, for their fate
Lay wrapt in its appointed hour at wait,
And had no flower to show yet, and no sting.
But once being vexed with some past wound the king
Bade give him comfort of sweet baths, and then
Should Iseult watch him as his handmaiden,
For his more honour in men's sight, and ease
The hurts he had with holy remedies
Made by her mother's magic in strange hours

Out of live roots and life-compelling flowers.
And finding by the wound's shape in his side
This was the knight by whom their strength had died
And all their might in one man overthrown
Had left their shame in sight of all men shown,
She would have slain him swordless with his sword;
Yet seemed he to her so great and fair a lord
She heaved up hand and smote not; then said he,
Laughing – 'What comfort shall this dead man be,
Damsel? what hurt is for my blood to heal?
But set your hand not near the toothed steel
Lest the fang strike it.' – 'Yea, the fang,' she said,
'Should it not sting the very serpent dead
That stung mine uncle? for his slayer art thou,
And half my mother's heart is bloodless now
Through thee, that mad'st the veins of all her kin
Bleed in his wounds whose veins through thee ran thin.'
Yet thought she how their hot chief's violent heart
Had flung the fierce word forth upon their part
Which bade to battle the best knight that stood
On Arthur's, and so dying of his wild mood
Had set upon his conqueror's flesh the seal
Of his mishallowed and anointed steel,
Whereof the venom and enchanted might
Made the sign burn here branded in her sight.
These things she stood recasting, and her soul
Subsiding till its wound of wrath were whole
Grew smooth again, as thought still softening stole
Through all its tempered passion; nor might hate
Keep high the fire against him lit of late;
But softly from his smiling sight she passed.
And peace thereafter made between them fast
Made peace between two kingdoms, when he went
Home with hands reconciled and heart content,
To bring fair truce 'twixt Cornwall's wild bright strand
And the long wrangling wars of that loud land.
And when full peace was struck betwixt them twain
Forth must he fare by those green straits again,
And bring back Iseult for a plighted bride
And set to reign at Mark his uncle's side.
So now with feast made and all triumphs done
They sailed between the noonfall and the sun
Under the spent stars eastward; but the queen
Out of wise heart and subtle love had seen
Such things as might be, dark as in a glass,
And lest some doom of these should come to pass
Bethought her with her secret soul alone
To work some charm for marriage unison
And strike the heart of Iseult to her lord
With power compulsive more than stroke of sword.
Therefore with marvellous herbs and spells she wrought
To win the very wonder of her thought,
And brewed it with her secret hands and blest
And drew and gave out of her secret breast
To one her chosen and Iseult's handmaiden,
Brangwain, and bade her hide from sight of men
This marvel covered in a golden cup,
So covering in her heart the counsel up
As in the gold the wondrous wine lay close;
And when the last shout with the last cup rose
About the bride and bridegroom bound to bed,
Then should this one word of her will be said
To her new-married maiden child, that she
Should drink with Mark this draught in unity,
And no lip touch it for her sake but theirs:
For with long love and consecrating prayers
The wine was hallowed for their mouths to pledge;
And if a drop fell from the beaker's edge
That drop should Iseult hold as dear as blood
Shed from her mother's heart to do her good.
And having drunk they twain should be one heart
Who were one flesh till fleshly death should part –
Death, who parts all. So Brangwain swore, and kept
The hid thing by her while she waked or slept.
And now they sat to see the sun again
Whose light of eye had looked on no such twain
Since Galahault in the rose-time of the year
Brought Launcelot first to sight of Guenevere.
  And Tristram caught her changing eyes and said:
'As this day raises daylight from the dead
Might not this face the life of a dead man?'
  And Iseult, gazing where the sea was wan
Out of the sun's way, said: 'I pray you not
Praise me, but tell me there in Camelot,
Saving the queen, who hath most name of fair?
I would I were a man and dwelling there,
That I might win me better praise than yours,
Even such as you have; for your praise endures,
That with great deeds ye wring from mouths of men,
But ours – for shame, where is it? Tell me then,
Since woman may not wear a better here,
Who of this praise hath most save Guenevere?'
  And Tristram, lightening with a laugh held in –
'Surely a little praise is this to win,
A poor praise and a little! but of these
Hapless, whom love serves only with bowed knees,
Of such poor women fairer face hath none
That lifts her eyes alive against the sun

Than Arthur's sister, whom the north seas call
Mistress of isles; so yet majestical
Above the crowns on younger heads she moves,
Outlightening with her eyes our late-born loves.'
'Ah,' said Iseult, 'is she more tall than I?
Look, I am tall;' and struck the mast hard by,
With utmost upward reach of her bright hand;
'And look, fair lord, now, when I rise and stand,
How high with feet unlifted I can touch
Standing straight up; could this queen do thus much?
Nay, over tall she must be then, like me;
Less fair than lesser women. May this be,
That still she stands the second stateliest there,
So more than many so much younger fair,
She, born when yet the king your lord was not,
And has the third knight after Launcelot
And after you to serve her? nay, sir, then
God made her for a godlike sign to men.'
'Ay,' Tristram answered, 'for a sign, a sign –
Would God it were not! for no planets shine
With half such fearful forecast of men's fate
As a fair face so more unfortunate.'
Then with a smile that lit not on her brows
But moved upon her red mouth tremulous
Light as a sea-bird's motion oversea,
'Yea,' quoth Iseult, 'the happier hap for me,
With no such face to bring men no such fate.
Yet her might all we women born too late
Praise for good hap, who so enskied above
Not more in age excels us than man's love.'
There came a glooming light on Tristram's face
Answering: 'God keep you better in his grace
Than to sit down beside her in men's sight,
For if men be not blind whom God gives light
And lie not in whose lips he bids truth live,
Great grief shall she be given, and greater give.
For Merlin witnessed of her years ago
That she should work woe and should suffer woe
Beyond the race of women: and in truth
Her face, a spell that knows nor age nor youth,
Like youth being soft, and subtler-eyed than age,
With lips that mock the doom her eyes presage,
Hath on it such a light of cloud and fire,
With charm and change of keen or dim desire,
And over all a fearless look of fear
Hung like a veil across its changing cheer,
Made up of fierce foreknowledge and sharp scorn,
That it were better she had not been born.
For not love's self can help a face which hath
Such insubmissive anguish of wan wrath,
Blind prescience and self-contemptuous hate
Of her own soul and heavy-footed fate,
Writ broad upon its beauty: none the less
Its fire of bright and burning bitterness
Takes with as quick a flame the sense of men
As any sunbeam, nor is quenched again
With any drop of dewfall; yea, I think
No herb of force or blood-compelling drink
Would heal a heart that ever it made hot.
Ay, and men too that greatly love her not,
Seeing the great love of her and Lamoracke,
Make no great marvel, nor look strangely back
When with his gaze about her she goes by
Pale as a breathless and star-quickening sky
Between moonrise and sunset, and moves out
Clothed with the passion of his eyes about
As night with all her stars, yet night is black;
And she, clothed warm with love of Lamoracke,
Girt with his worship as with girdling gold,
Seems all at heart anhungered and acold,
Seems sad at heart and loveless of the light,
As night, star-clothed or naked, is but night.'
And with her sweet eyes sunken, and the mirth
Dead in their look as earth lies dead in earth
That reigned on earth and triumphed, Iseult said:
'Is it her shame of something done and dead
Or fear of something to be born and done
That so in her soul's eye puts out the sun?'
And Tristram answered: 'Surely, as I think,
This gives her soul such bitterness to drink,
The sin born blind, the sightless sin unknown,
Wrought when the summer in her blood was blown
But scarce aflower, and spring first flushed her will
With bloom of dreams no fruitage should fulfil,
When out of vision and desire was wrought
The sudden sin that from the living thought
Leaps a live deed and dies not: then there came
On that blind sin swift eyesight like a flame
Touching the dark to death, and made her mad
With helpless knowledge that too late forbade
What was before the bidding: and she knew
How sore a life dead love should lead her through
To what sure end how fearful; and though yet
Nor with her blood nor tears her way be wet
And she look bravely with set face on fate,
Yet she knows well the serpent hour at wait
Somewhere to sting and spare not; ay, and he,
Arthur' –

'The king,' quoth Iseult suddenly,
'Doth the king too live so in sight of fear?
They say sin touches not a man so near
As shame a woman; yet he too should be
Part of the penance, being more deep than she
Set in the sin.'
'Nay,' Tristram said, 'for thus
It fell by wicked hap and hazardous,
That wittingly he sinned no more than youth
May sin and be assoiled of God and truth,
Repenting; since in his first year of reign
As he stood splendid with his foemen slain
And light of new-blown battles, flushed and hot
With hope and life, came greeting from King Lot
Out of his wind-worn islands overseas,
And homage to my king and fealty
Of those north seas wherein the strange shapes swim
As from his man; and Arthur greeted him
As his good lord and courteously, and bade
To his high feast; who coming with him had
This Queen Morgause of Orkney, his fair wife,
In the green middle Maytime of her life,
And scarce in April was our king's as then,
And goodliest was he of all flowering men,
And of what graft as yet himself knew not;
But cold as rains in autumn was King Lot
And grey-grown out of season: so there sprang
Swift love between them, and all spring through sang
Light in their joyous hearing; for none knew
The bitter bond of blood between them two,
Twain fathers but one mother, till too late
The sacred mouth of Merlin set forth fate
And brake the secret seal on Arthur's birth,
And showed his ruin and his rule on earth
Inextricable, and light on lives to be.
For surely, though time slay us, yet shall we
Have such high name and lordship of good days
As shall sustain us living, and men's praise
Shall burn a beacon lit above us dead.
And of the king how shall not this be said
When any of us from any mouth has praise,
That such were men in only this king's days,
In Arthur's? yea, come shine or shade, no less
His name shall be one name with knightliness,
His fame one light with sunlight. Yet in sooth
His age shall bear the burdens of his youth
And bleed from his own bloodshed; for indeed
Blind to him blind his sister brought forth seed,
And of the child between them shall be born
Destruction: so shall God not suffer scorn,
Nor in men's souls and lives his law lie dead.'
And as one moved and marvelling Iseult said:
'Great pity it is and strange it seems to me
God could not do them so much right as we,
Who slay not men for witless evil done;
And these the noblest under God's glad sun
For sin they knew not he that knew shall slay,
And smite blind men for stumbling in fair day.
What good is it to God that such should die?
Shall the sun's light grow sunnier in the sky
Because their light of spirit is clean put out?'
And sighing, she looked from wave to cloud about,
And even with that the full-grown feet of day
Sprang upright on the quivering water-way,
And his face burned against her meeting face
Most like a lover's thrilled with great love's grace
Whose glance takes fire and gives; the quick sea shone
And shivered like spread wings of angels blown
By the sun's breath before him; and a low
Sweet gale shook all the foam-flowers of thin snow
As into rainfall of sea-roses shed
Leaf by wild leaf on that green garden-bed
Which tempests till and sea-winds turn and plough
For rosy and fiery round the running prow
Fluttered the flakes and feathers of the spray,
And bloomed like blossoms cast by God away
To waste on the ardent water; swift the moon
Withered to westward as a face in swoon
Death-stricken by glad tidings: and the height
Throbbed and the centre quivered with delight
And the depth quailed with passion as of love,
Till like the heart of some new-mated dove
Air, light, and wave seemed full of burning rest,
With motion as of one God's beating breast.
And her heart sprang in Iseult, and she drew
With all her spirit and life the sunrise through,
And through her lips the keen triumphant air
Sea-scented, sweeter than land-roses were,
And through her eyes the whole rejoicing east
Sun-satisfied, and all the heaven at feast
Spread for the morning; and the imperious mirth
Of wind and light that moved upon the earth,
Making the spring, and all the fruitful might
And strong regeneration of delight
That swells the seedling leaf and sapling man,
Since the first life in the first world began
To burn and burgeon through void limbs and veins,
And the first love with sharp sweet procreant pains

To pierce and bring forth roses; yea, she felt
Through her own soul the sovereign morning melt,
And all the sacred passion of the sun;
And as the young clouds flamed and were undone
About him coming, touched and burnt away
In rosy ruin and yellow spoil of day,
The sweet veil of her body and corporal sense
Felt the dawn also cleave it, and incense
With light from inward and with effluent heat
The kindling soul through fleshly hands and feet.
And as the august great blossom of the dawn
Burst, and the full sun scarce from sea withdrawn
Seemed on the fiery water a flower afloat,
So as a fire the mighty morning smote
Throughout her, and incensed with the influent hour
Her whole soul's one great mystical red flower
Burst, and the bud of her sweet spirit broke
Rose-fashion, and the strong spring at a stroke
Thrilled, and was cloven, and from the full sheath came
The whole rose of the woman red as flame:
And all her Mayday blood as from a swoon
Flushed, and May rose up in her and was June.
So for a space her heart as heavenward burned:
Then with half summer in her eyes she turned,
And on her lips was April yet, and smiled,
As though the spirit and sense unreconciled
Shrank laughing back, and would not ere its hour
Let life put forth the irrevocable flower.
And the soft speech between them grew again
With questionings and records of what men
Rose mightiest, and what names for love or fight
Shone starriest overhead of queen or knight.
There Tristram spake of many a noble thing,
High feast and storm of tournay round the king,
Strange quest by perilous lands of marsh and brake
And circling woods branch-knotted like a snake
And places pale with sins that they had seen,
Where was no life of red fruit or of green
But all was as a dead face wan and dun;
And bowers of evil builders whence the sun
Turns silent, and the moon holds hardly light
Above them through the sick and star-crossed night;
And of their hands through whom such holds lay waste,
And all their strengths dishevelled and defaced
Fell ruinous, and were not from north to south:
And of the might of Merlin's ancient mouth,
The son of no man's loins, begot by doom
In speechless sleep out of a spotless womb;
For sleeping among graves where none had rest

Tristram fights his rival Palomides; book illustration by W. Russell Flint, 1911.

And ominous houses of dead bones unblest
Among the grey grass rough as old rent hair
And wicked herbage whitening like despair
And blown upon with blasts of dolorous breath
From gaunt rare gaps and hollow doors of death,
A maid unspotted, senseless of the spell,
Felt not about her breathe some thing of hell
Whose child and hers was Merlin; and to him
Great light from God gave sight of all things dim
And wisdom of all wondrous things, to say
What root should bear what fruit of night or day,
And sovereign speech and counsel higher than man;
Wherefore his youth like age was wise and wan,
And his age sorrowful and fain to sleep;
Yet should sleep never, neither laugh nor weep,
Till in some depth of deep sweet land or sea
The heavenly hands of holier Nimue,
That was the nurse of Launcelot, and most sweet
Of all that move with magical soft feet

Among us, being of lovelier blood and breath,
Should shut him in with sleep as kind as death:
For she could pass between the quick and dead:
And of her love toward Pelleas, for whose head
Love-wounded and world-wearied she had won
A place beyond all pain in Avalon;
And of the fire that wasted afterward
The loveless eyes and bosom of Ettarde,
In whose false love his faultless heart had burned;
And now being rapt from her, her lost heart yearned
To seek him, and passed hungering out of life:
And after all the thunder-hours of strife
That roared between King Claudas and King Ban
How Nimue's mighty nursling waxed to man,
And how from his first field such grace he got
That all men's hearts bowed down to Launcelot,
And how the high prince Galahault held him dear
And led him even to love of Guenevere
And to that kiss which made break forth as fire
The laugh that was the flower of his desire,
The laugh that lightened at her lips for bliss
To win from Love so great a lover's kiss:
And of the toil of Balen all his days
To reap but thorns for fruit and tears for praise,
Whose hap was evil as his heart was good,
And all his works and ways by wold and wood
Led through much pain to one last labouring day
When blood for tears washed grief with life away:
And of the kin of Arthur, and their might;
The misborn head of Mordred, sad as night,
With cold waste cheeks and eyes as keen as pain,
And the close angry lips of Agravaine;
And gracious Gawain, scattering words as flowers,
The kindliest head of worldly paramours;
And the fair hand of Gareth, found in fight
Strong as a sea-beast's tushes and as white;
And of the king's self, glorious yet and glad
For all the toil and doubt of doom he had,
Clothed with men's loves and full of kingly days.
  Then Iseult said: 'Let each knight have his praise
And each good man good witness of his worth;
But when men laud the second name on earth,
Whom would they praise to have no worldly peer
Save him whose love makes glorious Guenevere?'
  'Nay,' Tristram said, 'such man as he is none.'
  'What,' said she, 'there is none such under sun
Of all the large earth's living? yet I deemed
Men spake of one – but maybe men that dreamed,
Fools and tongue-stricken, witless, babbler's breed –
That for all high things was his peer indeed
Save this one highest, to be so loved and love.'
  And Tristram: 'Little wit had these thereof;
For there is none such in the world as this.'
  'Ay, upon land,' quoth Iseult, 'none such is,
I doubt not, nor where fighting folk may be;
But were there none such between sky and sea,
The world's whole worth were poorer than I wist.'
  And Tristram took her flower-white hand and kissed,
Laughing; and through his fair face as in shame
The light blood lightened. 'Hear they no such name?'
She said; and he, 'If there be such a word,
I wot the queen's poor harper hath not heard.'
Then, as the fuller-feathered hours grew long,
He help to speed their warm slow feet with song.

'Love, is it morning risen or night deceased
That makes the mirth of this triumphant east?
  Is it bliss given or bitterness put by
That makes most glad men's hearts at love's high feast?
  Grief smiles, joy weeps, that day should live and die.

'Is it with soul's thirst or with body's drouth
That summer yearns out sunward to the south,
  With all the flowers that when thy birth drew nigh
Were molten in one rose to make thy mouth?
  O love, what care though day should live and die?

'Is the sun glad of all the love on earth,
The spirit and sense and work of things and worth?
  Is the moon sad because the month must fly
And bring her death that can but bring back birth?
  For all these things as day must live and die.

'Love, is it day that makes thee thy delight
Or thou that seest day made out of thy light?
  Love, as the sun and sea are thou and I,
Sea without sun dark, sun without sea bright;
  The sun is one though day should live and die.

'O which is elder, night or light, who knows?
And life or love, which first of these twain grows?
  For life is born of love to wail and cry,
And love is born of life to heal his woes,
  And light of night, that day should live and die.

'O sun of heaven above the worldly sea,
O very love, what light is this of thee!
  My sea of soul is deep as thou art high,
But all thy light is shed through all of me,
  As love's through love, while day shall live and die.

'Nay,' said Iseult, 'your song is hard to read.'
'Ay?' said he: 'or too light a song to heed,
Too slight to follow, it may be? Who shall sing
Of love but as a churl before a king
If by love's worth men rate his worthiness?
Yet as the poor churl's worth to sing is less,
Surely the more shall be the great king's grace
To show for churlish love a kindlier face.'
'No churl,' she said, 'but one in soothsayer's wise
Who tells but truths that help no more than lies.
I have heard men sing of love a simpler way
Than these wrought riddles made of night and day,
Like jewelled reins whereon the rhyme-bells hang.'

And Tristram smiled and changed his song and sang.

'The breath between my lips of lips not mine,
Like spirit in sense that makes pure sense divine,
Is as life in them from the living sky
That entering fills my heart with blood of thine
And thee with me, while day shall live and die.

'Thy soul is shed into me with thy breath,
And in my heart each heartbeat of thee saith
How in thy life the lifesprings of me lie,
Even one life to be gathered of one death
In me and thee, though day may live and die.

'Ah, who knows now if in my veins it be
My blood that feels life sweet, or blood of thee,
And this thine eyesight kindled in mine eye
That shows me in thy flesh the soul of me,
For thine made mine, while day may live and die?

'Ah, who knows yet if one be twain or one,
And sunlight separable again from sun,
And I from thee with all my lifesprings dry,
And thou from me with all thine heartbeats done,
Dead separate souls while day shall live and die?

'I see my soul within thine eyes, and hear
My spirit in all thy pulses thrill with fear,
And in my lips the passion of thee sigh,
And music of me made in mine own ear;
Am I not thou while day shall live and die?

'Art thou not I as I thy love am thou?
So let all things pass from us; we are now,
For all that was and will be, who knows why?
And all that is and is not, who knows how?
Who knows? God knows why day should live and die.'

And Iseult mused and spake no word, but sought
Through all the hushed ways of her tongueless thought
What face or covered likeness of a face
In what veiled hour or dream-determined place
She seeing might take for love's face, and believe
This was the spirit to whom all spirits cleave.
For that sweet wonder of the twain made one
And each one twain, incorporate sun with sun,
Star with star molten, soul with soul imbued,
And all the soul's works, all their multitude,
Made one thought and one vision and one song,
Love – this thing, this, laid hand on her so strong
She could not choose but yearn till she should see.
So went she musing down her thoughts; but he,
Sweet-hearted as a bird that takes the sun
With clear strong eyes and feels the glad god run
Bright through his blood and wide rejoicing wings,
And opens all himself to heaven and sings,
Made her mind light and full of noble mirth
With words and songs the gladdest grown on earth,
Till she was blithe and high of heart as he.
So swam the Swallow through the springing sea.
And while they sat at speech as at a feast,
Came a light wind fast hardening forth of the east
And blackening till its might had marred the skies;
And the sea thrilled as with heart-sundering sighs
One after one drawn, with each breath it drew,
And the green hardened into iron blue,
And the soft light went out of all its face.
Then Tristram girt him for an oarsman's place
And took his oar and smote, and toiled with might
In the east wind's full face and the strong sea's spite
Labouring; and all the rowers rowed hard, but he
More mightily than any wearier three.
And Iseult watched him rowing with sinless eyes
That loved him but in holy girlish wise
For noble joy in his fair manliness
And trust and tender wonder; none the less
She thought if God had given her grace to be
Man, and make war on danger of earth and sea,
Even such a man she would be; for his stroke
Was mightiest as the mightier water broke,
And in sheer measure like strong music drave
Clean through the wet weight of the wallowing wave;
And as a tune before a great king played
For triumph was the tune their strong strokes made,
And sped the ship through with smooth strife of oars
Over the mid sea's grey foam-paven floors,
For all the loud breach of the waves at will.

So for an hour they fought the storm out still,
And the shorn foam spun from the blades, and high
The keel sprang from the wave-ridge, and the sky
Glared at them for a breath's space through the rain;
Then the bows with a sharp shock plunged again
Down, and the sea clashed on them, and so rose
The bright stem like one panting from swift blows,
And as a swimmer's joyous beaten head
Rears itself laughing, so in that sharp stead
The light ship lifted her long quivering bows
As might the man his buffeted strong brows
Out of the wave-breach; for with one stroke yet
Went all men's oars together, strongly set
As to loud music, and with hearts uplift
They smote their strong way through the drench and drift:
Till the keen hour had chafed itself to death
And the east wind fell fitfully, breath by breath,
Tired; and across the thin and slackening rain
Sprang the face southward of the sun again.
Then all they rested and were eased at heart;
And Iseult rose up where she sat apart,
And with her sweet soul deepening her deep eyes
Cast the furs from her and subtle embroideries
That wrapped her from the storming rain and spray,
And shining like all April in one day,
Hair, face, and throat dashed with the straying showers,
She stood the first of all the whole world's flowers,
And laughed on Tristram with her eyes, and said,
'I too have heart then, I was not afraid.'
And answering some light courteous word of grace
He saw her clear face lighten on his face
Unwittingly, with unenamoured eyes,
For the last time. A live man in such wise
Looks in the deadly face of his fixed hour
And laughs with lips wherein he hath no power
To keep the life yet some five minutes' space.
So Tristram looked on Iseult face to face
And knew not, and she knew not. The last time –
The last that should be told in any rhyme
Heard anywhere on mouths of singing men
That ever should sing praise of them again;
The last hour of their hurtless hearts at rest,
The last that peace should touch them, breast to breast,
The last that sorrow far from them should sit,
This last was with them, and they knew not it.
  For Tristram being athirst with toil now spake,
Saying, 'Iseult, for all dear love's labour's sake
Give me to drink, and give me for a pledge
The touch of four lips on the beaker's edge.'
And Iseult sought and would not wake Brangwain
Who slept as one half dead with fear and pain,
Being tender-natured; so with hushed light feet
Went Iseult round her, with soft looks and sweet
Pitying her pain; so sweet a spirited thing
She was, and daughter of a kindly king.
And spying what strange bright secret charge was kept
Fast in that maid's white bosom while she slept,
She sought and drew the gold cup forth and smiled
Marvelling, with such light wonder as a child
That hears of glad sad life in magic lands;
And bare it back to Tristram with pure hands
Holding the love-draught that should be for flame
To burn out of them fear and faith and shame,
And lighten all their life up in men's sight,
And make them sad for ever. Then the knight
Bowed toward her and craved whence had she this strange thing
That might be spoil of some dim Asian king,
By starlight stolen from some waste place of sands,
And a maid bore it here in harmless hands.
And Iseult, laughing – 'Other lords that be
Feast, and their men feast after them; but we,
Our men must keep the best wine back to feast
Till they be full and we of all men least
Feed after them and fain to fare so well:
So with mine handmaid and your squire it fell
That hid this bright thing from us in a wile:'
And with light lips yet full of their swift smile,
And hands that wist not though they dug a grave,
Undid the hasps of gold, and drank, and gave,
And he drank after, a deep glad kingly draught:
And all their life changed in them, for they quaffed
Death; if it be death so to drink, and fare
As men who change and are what these twain were.
And shuddering with eyes full of fear and fire
And heart-stung with a serpentine desire
He turned and saw the terror in her eyes
That yearned upon him shining in such wise
As a star midway in the midnight fixed.
  Their Galahault was the cup, and she that mixed;
Nor other hand there needed, nor sweet speech
To lure their lips together; each on each
Hung with strange eyes and hovered as a bird
Wounded, and each mouth trembled for a word;
Their heads neared, and their hands were drawn in one,
And they saw dark, though still the unsunken sun
Far through fine rain shot fire into the south;
And their four lips became one burning mouth.

Tristan and Iseult, by Dante Gabriel Rossetti (1867)
(Cecil Higgins Museum, Bedford)

THE TWENTIETH CENTURY

HARDY AND THE MUMMERS' PLAY · MASEFIELD'S BALLADS · A MYSTIC VIEW OF ARTHUR · THE ONCE AND FUTURE KING & &

After Tennyson's enormous success, a host of lesser writers seized eagerly on the Arthurian stories, and poems and plays poured forth in an unending stream until the First World War. Little of merit emerged: the occasional flash of insight here, a haunting line or two there; and even when the flood had died down and greater writers took over, success was far from being ready to hand. Thomas Hardy wrote *The Famous Tragedy of the Queen of Cornwall* in 1923, in an experimental style designed for mummers. Hardy declared that he had 'tried to avoid turning the rude personages of, say, the fifth century into respectable Victorians, as was done by Tennyson, Swinburne, Arnold etc.'. He chose an archaic vocabulary, and believed that by underplaying the dramatic side of the acting the play could achieve a 'curiously hypnotising' effect. On the page, it offers nothing more than a certain strangeness: a conscious attempt at a medieval play every bit as anachronistic as the Victorian works he so decried. The characters have a rough-hewn quality but belong to Hardy's Wessex rather than a Court in whatever age. It is a minor, curious work from a master's hand, with rare flashes of greater illumination.

Yet another version of the Tristram legend comes from the pen of an American writer, E. A. Robinson's poem *Tristram* (1927), awarded the Pulitzer Prize for that year, is more in the tradition of Arnold than Swinburne; the love potion is entirely absent, and the lovers die by Andret's hand. Robinson observes not the ecstasy of passionate love, but the resulting torment:

And for a time nothing was to he heard
Except the pounding of two hearts in prison,
The torture of a doom-begotten music
Above them, and the wash of a cold foam
Below them on those cold eternal rocks
Where Tristram and Iseult had yesterday
Come to be wrecked together. When her eyes
Opened again, he saw there, watching him,
An aching light of memory; and his heart beat
Beat harder for remembering the same light
That he had seen before in the same eyes.

Here is no serene security in requited love, but an anguished, doubting passion full of deeps and shadows. This clear-sighted and tender poem is the best American contribution to the legend yet.

John Masefield's *Midsummer Night and Other Tales in Verse* (1927) presents us with a series of linked pictures and incidents that cover the main events of the life of Arthur. He draws on a wide range of sources, both classical and medieval, sometimes going back to early Welsh material, sometimes offering his own alternative versions of the legend.

Masefield's work is in an unfashionable medium, a series of historical ballads, in ballad metre; and it is difficult to estimate their true worth. His handling of plot and character is strong, but the ballad form itself has a comfortable homeliness about it that ill consorts with the high romanticism of the story. For this is still an idealised treatment; for all its would-be realism, Masefield has a vivid way of lighting up a figure: Mordred's outburst of hatred – 'Thirty years' anguish made by your idle lust' – strikes home, as does Arthur's helpless and equivocal relationship with his son, and Guinevere looking at Lancelot in death:

'I had not thought of him as old'. Yet in the end it is not the great version of the legend that it promises at moments to become, because Masefield has not really come to terms with his theme. The inner spiritual power that the subject demands is never present.

Charles Williams, a very different poet from Masefield, provides that spiritual element in his two volumes *Taliessin through Logres* and *The Region of the Summer Stars*. In essence, he adopts Tennyson's vision of Arthur as ideal man, for in Williams' poems Arthur's kingdom of Logres is to be the perfect union between earth and heaven. The symbolism is involved to the point of being at moments laboured, as the image at the centre of the spiritual and physical geography of the poems shows. Williams' central theme, the Empire of Rome and Byzantium from which spiritual power derives, is seen as a reclining female figure. The 'skull-stone' is the rocky outer edge of Britain/Logres which stands as the Empire's soul and brain. The breasts are in Gaul, where the schools of Paris, famous in the Middle Ages, provide the nourishing milk of learning. On Rome the hands lie clasped: here the Pope says Mass with its 'heart-breaking manual acts'. Jerusalem is the womb, from which Adam, fallen man, came. Lastly there is Byzantium, the navel, in which all the 'dialects' arise and re-echo. These are the 'themes' of the Empire, which are related in the same way as the body.

There is an antithesis to the Empire, on the other side of the world, in P'o-Lu, where the headless Emperor of the Antipodes walks. This is the consequence of the Fall: bodies become shameful instead of a glory of creation, and so here the 'feet of creation' walk backwards. For in P'o-Lu are the feet of the Empire, and they are feet of clay. It is from here that the failure of Arthur's mission springs.

At the opposite extreme, beyond Logres, lies the Wood of Broceliande – a sea-wood, Williams calls it – and beyond a certain part of it, Carbonek, the castle in which the Grail is kept. Beyond this and a stretch of open sea is Sarras, the home of the Grail. Through Broceliande lies the way from earth to heaven – as witness the Grail city and castle. But Williams insists that these last lie beyond only a certain part of it. If one goes far enough the Antipodes may be reached through these same regions. C. S. Lewis in his commentary on the poems explains this apparent contradiction as follows:

> In a writer whose philosophy was Pantheistic or whose poetry was merely romantic, this formidable wood . . . would undoubtedly figure as the Absolute itself. . . . All journeys away from the solid earth are equally, at the outset journeys into the abyss. Saint, sorcerer, lunatic and romantic lover, all alike are drawn to Broceliande, but Carbonek is beyond a certain part of it only. It is by no means the Absolute. It is rather what the Greeks called the Apeiron – the unlimited, the formless origin of forms.

Such then is the geography, physical and spiritual, of Williams' world. Against this background Arthur, Taliessin and Merlin work out their mission. Nimue, lady of Broceliande, sends her children, Merlin and Brisen, to perform the great task of perfect union. They meet Taliessin, the pagan poet of Wales, as they go to create the holy kingdom of Carbonek, in which the Empire and Broceliande, the physical, the intellectual and the spiritual shall meet. Arthur is to be their instrument; they depart for Logres, and Taliessin for Byzantium, where he is converted.

Taliessin's part in the mission is not immediately clear, but we learn that on his return from Byzantium he bears with him the vision of the Empire, standing for order, which he must impose on the as yet chaotic Logres; this must be accomplished before the Grail can come to dwell there. He is also the type of poet which is bound up in his personal task. The poet, in Williams' view, cannot inspire love for himself, yet can inspire others to it; this is illustrated in *Taliessin's Song of the Unicorn*, where the poet is likened to the legendary unicorn, attracted to a virgin; she will not love him, and her lover will come and kill the creature out of jealousy.

Taliessin's mission is a success, and the Golden Age of Logres ensues. The lyric pieces which describe this involve various philosophical concepts, but centre on the nature of love.

But the plan as a whole is doomed to failure: the actual deeds which prevent Logres from becoming the kingdom of the Grail are Arthur's unwitting incest with Morgause, and Balin's equally unconscious slaying of his brother and giving of the Dolorous Blow. Both pairs act blindly; it is not their individual fault that these things are done, but the fault of human nature, of fallen men, operating deep below the surfact of Logres.

Yet out of this failure springs a measure of success. The Grail cannot come to Logres; but the uncorrupted part of Logres may reach the Grail. It is again Taliessin's task to prepare the way. The company of his household are his instrument; at the base of their efforts lies salvation worked through poetry and the senses, Taliessin's own special task. None save three will succeed, and reach Carbonek; the rest will sink into Britain.

The climax and simultaneously the anti-climax are now

reached. The Grail is achieved at the expense of the Round Table. So triumph on the one hand, in *Percivale at Carbonek* and *The Last Voyage* are balanced by the implied disaster of *The Meditation of Mordred* and *The Prayers of the Pope*. As the Grail is achieved, and withdrawn to Sarras, Logres sinks into the chaos out of which it had risen. Taliessin dissolves his company, but they gather for the last time, in flesh or in spirit, at the Mass performed by Lancelot. The mission has reached its end; all that could or can ever be achieved has been achieved. Lancelot's voice singing '*Ite; missa est*' is the signal for the irrevocable dispersal, and 'that which was once Taliessin' rides slowly away.

The poems are symbolic and sometimes obscure in concept; the poet in Williams struggles, sometimes unsuccessfully, with the philosopher. But the verse itself is brilliant in its incantation, and the words flow in a rich music. The final impact of the poems depends on an acceptance of Williams' particular brand of religious mysticism, a mysticism that is expressed in symbols that are at best evocative and at worst confusing.

T. H. White's *The Once and Future King* is also a very individual work, but of a totally different kind. It is a modern retelling of Malory in which 'all characters are the same, save that Pellinore has a love-affair, and the fact that Lancelot is ugly'. But there is one further very important difference: White has tempered the story with comedy without destroying the impact of its ultimate tragedy. His exposition of Malory is often worth a dozen essays on the subject, and White takes his story as an 'Aristotelian tragedy', in which the crux is the political and spiritual question so well put by Charles Williams:

The king made for the kingdom, or the kingdom made for the king?

In Williams, Arthur offers the wrong solution, and this is partly why he fails. In *The Once and Future King* Merlin directs Arthur's education with the sole aim of making him a king for the kingdom. Only Mordred, born of human weakness, can bring about his downfall by exploiting the love of Lancelot and Guinevere.

White succeeds best in two aspects of the story. His characters are convincing, and Arthur emerges as a real human being rather than a symbol; where Malory glosses over his feelings, White uses the techniques of the modern novelist to draw them for us, as when, despite his insistence on doing his duty as King, he nonetheless hopes that Lancelot will rescue Guinevere from the stake. Gawain and his brothers are strongly depicted: the sullen Agravaine, gentle, loyal Gareth and Gaheris, and Mordred, their bitter, tortured half-brother. Only Lancelot and Guinevere lose a little of their aura in the retelling.

The evocation of England in the Middle Ages is masterly, and here White's delightful and wide funds of knowledge come into their own, whether it be on his own favourite subject of hawking, practice for a tournament, a siege, or merely the details of everyday life in a medieval castle, all of which he conveys deftly and entertainingly, without letting the reader suspect that he is being given an expert lesson. Indeed, it is White rather than Williams who, in reworking the great legend, has read 'its own emotion and its own colours into the past' for us in the twentieth century.

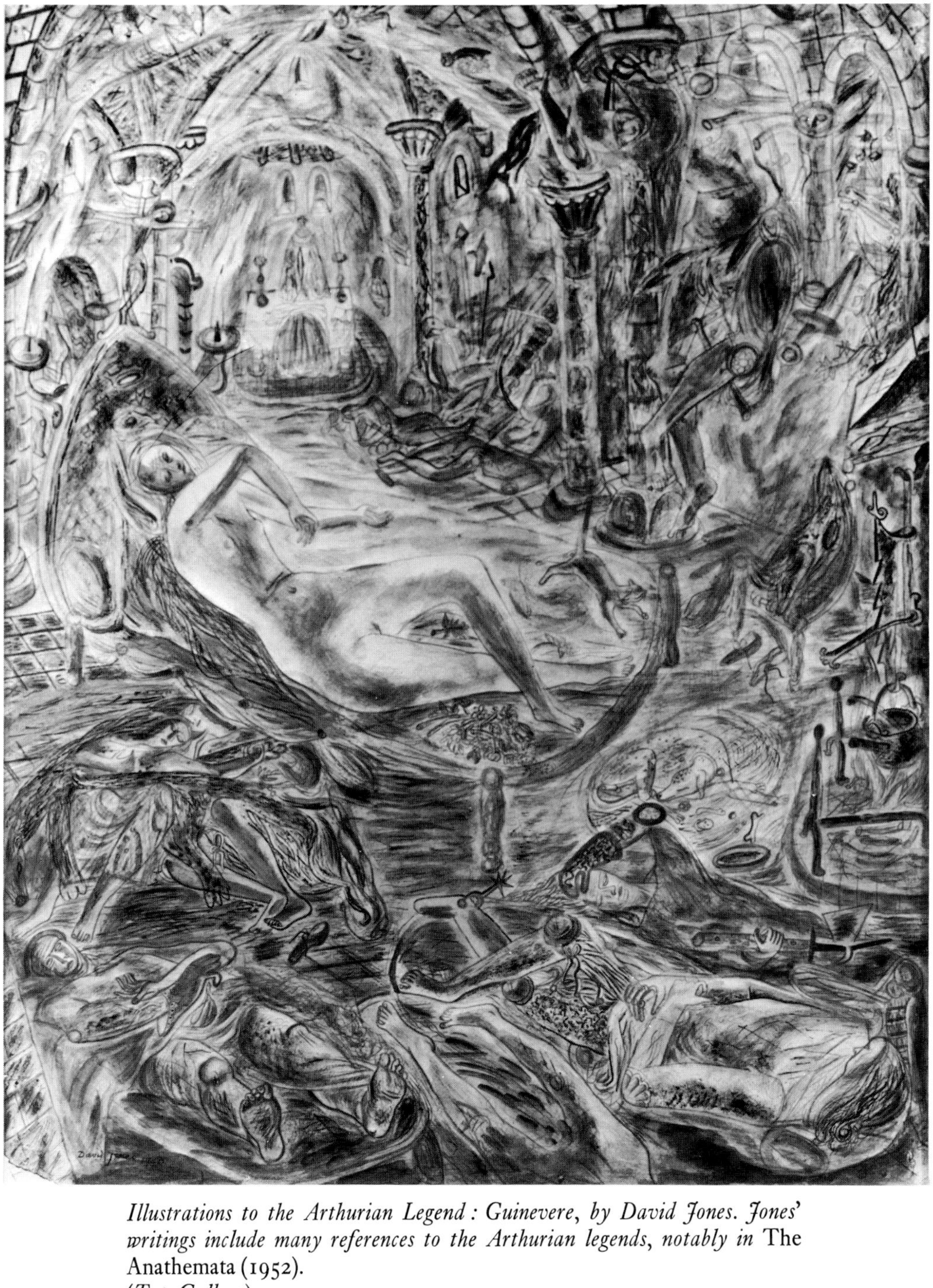

Illustrations to the Arthurian Legend: Guinevere, by David Jones. Jones' writings include many references to the Arthurian legends, notably in The Anathemata (1952).
(*Tate Gallery*)

Taliessin through Logres

CHARLES WILLIAMS

THE CROWNING OF ARTHUR

The king stood crowned; around in the gate,
midnight striking, torches and fires
massing the colour, casting the metal,
furnace of jubilee, through time and town,
Logres heraldically flaunted the king's state.

The lords sheathed their swords; they camped
by Camelot's wall; thick-tossed torches,
tall candles flared, opened, deployed;
between them rose the beasts of the banners;
flaring over all the king's dragon ramped.

Wars were at end; the king's friend stood
at the king's side; Lancelot's lion
had roared in the pattern the king's mind cherished,
in charges completing the strategy of Arthur;
the king's brain working in Lancelot's blood.

Presaging intelligence of time climbed,
Merlin climbed, through the dome of Stephen,
over chimneys and churches; from the point of Camelot
he looked through the depth to the dome of Sophia;
the kingdom and the power and the glory chimed.

He turned where the fires, amid burning mail,
poured, tributaried by torches and candles,
to a point in a massive of colour, one
aureole flame; the first shield's deep azure,
sidereally pointed, the lord Percivale.

Driving back that azure a sea rose black;
on a fess of argent rode a red moon.
The Queen Morgause leaned from a casement;
her forehead's moon swallowed the fires,
it was crimson on the bright-banded sable of Lamorack.

The tincture changed; ranged the craft
of the king's new champion in a crimson field;
mockery in mockery, a dolphin naiant;
a silver fish under bloody waters,
conquered or conquering, Dinadan laughed.

A pelican in golden piety struck well
the triple bloody drops from its wound;
in strong nurture of instinct, it smote
for its young its breast; the shield of Bors
bore its rich fervours, to itself most fell.

Shouldering shapes through the skies rise and run,
through town and time; Merlin beheld
the beasts of Broceliande, the fish of Nimue,
hierarchic, republican, the glory of Logres,
patterns of the Logos in the depth of the sun.

Taliessin in the crowd beheld the compelled brutes,
wildness formalized, images of mathematics,
star and moon, dolphin and pelican,
lion and leopard, changing their measure.
Over the mob's noise rose gushing the sound of the flutes.

Gawaine's thistle, Bedivere's rose, drew near:
flutes infiltrating the light of candles.
Through the magical sound of the fire-strewn air,
spirit, burning to sweetness of body,
exposed in the midst of its bloom the young queen
   Guinevere.

Lancelot moved to descend; the king's friend kneeled,
the king's organic motion, the king's mind's blood,
the lion in the blood roaring through the mouth of creation
as the lions roar that stand in the Byzantine glory.
Guinevere's chalice flew red on an argent field.

So, in Lancelot's hand, she came through the glow,
into the king's mind, who stood to look on his city:
the king made for the kingdom, or the kingdom made for
   the king?
Thwart drove his current against the current of Merlin:
in beleaguered Sophia they sang of the dolorous blow.

Doom in shocks sprinkled the burning gloom,
molten metals and kindling colours pouring
into the pyre; at the zenith lion and dragon
rose, clawed, twisted, screamed;
Taliessin beheld a god lie in his tomb.

At the door of the gloom sparks die and revive;
the spark of Logres fades, glows, fades.
It is the first watch; the Pope says Matins in Lateran;
the hollow call is beaten on the board in Sophia;
the ledge of souls shudders, whether they die or live.

TALIESSIN AT LANCELOT'S MASS

I came to his altar when dew was bright on the grass;
he – he was not sworn of the priesthood – began the Mass.
The altar was an ancient stone laid upon stones;
Carbonek's arch, Camelot's wall, frame of Bors' bones.

In armour before the earthen footpace he stood;
on his surcoat the lions of his house, dappled with blood,
rampant, regardant; but he wore no helm or sword,
and his hands were bare as Lateran's to the work of our Lord.

In the ritual before the altar Lancelot began to pass;
all the dead lords of the Table were drawn from their graves to the Mass;
they stood, inward turned, as shields on a white rushing deck,
between Nimue of Broceliande and Helayne of Carbonek.

In Blanchefleur's cell at Almesbury the queen Guinevere
felt the past exposed; and the detail, sharp and dear,
drew at the pang in the breast till, rich and reconciled,
the mystical milk rose in the mother of Logres' child.

Out of the queen's substitution the wounded and dead king
entered into salvation to serve the holy Thing;
singly seen in the Mass, owning the double Crown,
going to the altar Pelles, and Arthur moving down.

Lancelot and Arthur wove the web; the sky
opened on moon and sun; between them, light-traced on high,
the unseen knight of terror stood as a friend;
invisible things and visible waited the end.

Lancelot came to the Canon; my household stood
around me, bearers of the banners, bounteous in blood;
each at the earthen footpace ordained to be blessed and to bless,
each than I and than all lordlier and less.

Then at the altar We sang in Our office the cycle of names
of their great attributed virtues; the festival of flames
fell from new sky to new earth; the light in bands
of bitter glory renewed the imperial lands.

Then the Byzantine ritual, the Epiclesis, began;
then their voices in Ours invoked the making of man;
petal on petal floated out of the blossom of the Host,
and all ways the Theotokos conceived by the Holy Ghost.

We exposed, We exalted the Unity; prismed shone
web, paths, points; as it was done
the antipodean zones were retrieved round a white rushing deck,
and the Acts of the Emperor took zenith from Caucasia to Carbonek.

Over the altar, flame of anatomized fire,
the High Prince stood, gyre in burning gyre;
day level before him, night massed behind;
the Table ascended; the glories intertwined.

The Table ascended; each in turn lordliest and least –
slave and squire, woman and wizard, poet and priest;
interchanged adoration, interdispersed prayer,
the ruddy pillar of the Infant was the passage of the porphyry stair.

That which had been Taliessin rose in the rood;
in the house of Galahad over the altar he stood,
manacled by the web, in the web made free;
there was no capable song for the joy in me:

joy to new joy piercing from paths foregone;
that which had been Taliessin made joy to a Joy unknown;
manifest Joy speeding in a Joy unmanifest.
Lancelot's voice below sang: *Ite; missa est.*

Fast to the Byzantine harbour gather the salvaged sails;
that which was once Taliessin rides to the barrows of Wales
up the vales of the Wye; if skill be of work or of will
in the dispersed homes of the household, let the Company pray for it still.

The Once and Future King

T. H. WHITE

Tilting and horsemanship had two afternoons a week, because they were the most important branches of a gentleman's education in those days. Merlyn grumbled about athletics, saying that nowadays people seemed to think that you were an educated man if you could knock another man off a horse and that the craze for games was the ruin of scholarship – nobody got scholarships like they used to do when he was a boy, and all the public schools had been forced to lower their standards – but Sir Ector, who was an old tilting blue, said that the battle of Crécy had been won upon the playing fields of Camelot. This made Merlyn so furious that he gave Sir Ector rheumatism two nights running before he relented.

Tilting was a great art and needed practice. When two knights jousted they held their lances in their right hands, but they directed their horses at one another so that each man had his opponent on his near side. The base of the lance, in fact, was held on the opposite side of the body to the side at which the enemy was charging. This seems rather inside out to anybody who is in the habit, say, of opening gates with a hunting-crop, but it had its reasons. For one thing, it meant that the shield was on the left arm, so that the opponents charged shield to shield, fully covered. It also meant that a man could be unhorsed with the side or edge of the lance, in a kind of horizontal swipe, if you did not feel sure of hitting him with your point. This was the humblest or least skilful blow in jousting.

A good jouster, like Lancelot or Tristram, always used the blow of the point, because, although it was liable to miss in unskilful hands, it made contact sooner. If one knight charged with his lance held rigidly sideways, to sweep his opponent out of the saddle, the other knight with his lance held directly forward would knock him down a lance length before the sweep came into effect.

Then there was how to hold the lance for the point stroke. It was no good crouching in the saddle and clutching it in a rigid grip preparatory to the great shock, for if you held it inflexibly like this its point bucked up and down to every movement of your thundering mount and you were practically certain to miss the aim. On the contrary, you had to sit loosely in the saddle with the lance easy and balanced against the horse's motion. It was not until the actual moment of striking that you clamped your knees into the horse's sides, threw your weight forward in your seat, clutched the lance with the whole hand instead of with the finger and thumb, and hugged your right elbow to your side to support the butt.

There was the size of the spear. Obviously a man with a spear one hundred yards long would strike down an opponent with a spear of ten or twelve feet before the latter came anywhere near him. But it would have been impossible to make a spear one hundred yards long and, if made, impossible to carry it. The jouster had to find out the greatest length which he could manage with the greatest speed, and he had to stick to that. Sir Lancelot, who came some time after this part of the story, had several sizes of spear and would call for his Great Spear or his Lesser Spear as occasion demanded.

There were the places on which the enemy should be hit. In the armoury of The Castle of the Forest Sauvage there was a big picture of a knight in armour with circles round his vulnerable points. These varied with the style of armour, so that you had to study your opponent before the charge and select a point. The good armourers – the best lived at Warrington, and still live near there – were careful to make all the forward or entering sides of their suits convex, so that the spear point glanced off them. Curiously enough, the shields of Gothic suits were more inclined to be concave. It was better that a spear point should stay on the shield, rather than glance off upward or downward, and perhaps hit a more vulnerable point of the body armour. The best place of all for hitting people was on the very crest of the tilting helm, that is, if the person in question were vain enough to have a large metal crest in whose folds and ornaments the point would find a ready lodging. Many were vain enough to have these armorial crests, with bears and dragons or even ships or castles on them, but Sir Lancelot always contented himself with a bare helmet, or a bunch of feathers which would not hold spears, or, on one occasion, a soft lady's sleeve.

It would take too long to go into all the interesting details of proper tilting which the boys had to learn, for in those days you had to be a master of your craft from the bottom upward. You had to know what wood was best for spears, and why, and even how to turn them so that they would not splinter or warp. There were a thousand disputed questions about arms and armour, all of which had to be understood.

Just outside Sir Ector's castle there was a jousting field for tournaments, although there had been no tournaments in it since Kay was born. It was a green meadow, kept short, with a broad grassy bank raised round it on which pavilions could be erected. There was an old wooden grandstand at one side, lifted on stilts for the ladies. At present the field was only used as a practice-ground for tilting, so a quintain had been erected at one end and a ring at the other. The quintain was a wooden saracen on a pole. He was painted with a bright blue face and red beard and glaring eyes. He had a shield in his left hand and a flat wooden sword in his right. If you hit him in the middle of his forehead all was well, but if your lance struck him on the shield or on any part to left or right of the middle line, then he spun round with great rapidity, and usually caught you a wallop with his sword as you galloped by, ducking. His paint was somewhat scratched and the wood picked up over his right eye. The ring was just an ordinary iron ring tied to a kind of gallows by a thread. If you managed to put your point through the ring, the thread broke, and you could canter off proudly with the ring round your spear.

The day was cooler than it had been for some time, for the autumn was almost within sight, and the two boys were in the tilting yard with the master armourer and Merlyn. The master armourer, or sergeant-at-arms, was a stiff, pale, bouncy gentleman with waxed moustaches. He always marched about with his chest stuck out like a pouter pigeon, and he called out 'On the word One –' on every possible occasion. He took great pains to keep his stomach in, and often tripped over his feet because he could not see them over his chest. He was generally making his muscles ripple, which annoyed Merlyn.

Wart lay beside Merlyn in the shade of the grandstand and scratched himself for harvest bugs. The saw-like sickles had only lately been put away, and the wheat stood in stooks of eight among the tall stubble of those times. The Wart still itched. He was also sore about the shoulders and had a burning ear, from making bosh shots at the quintain – for, of course, practice tilting was done without armour. Wart was pleased that it was Kay's turn to go through it now and he lay drowsily in the shade, snoozing, scratching, twitching like a dog and partly attending to the fun.

Merlyn, sitting with his back to all the athleticism, was practising a spell which he had forgotten. It was a spell to make the sergeant's moustaches uncurl, but at present it only uncurled one of them, and the sergeant had not noticed it. He absent-mindedly curled it up again every time Merlyn did the spell, and Merlyn said, 'Drat it!' and began again. Once he made the sergeant's ears flap by mistake, and the latter gave a startled look at the sky.

From far off at the other side of the tilting ground the sergeant's voice came floating on the still air.

'Nah, Nah, Master Kay, that ain't it at all. Has you were. Has you were. The spear should be 'eld between the thumb and forefinger of the right 'and, with the shield in line with the seam of the trahser leg . . .'

The Wart rubbed his sore ear and sighed.

'What are you grieving about?'

'I was not grieving; I was thinking.'

'What were you thinking?'

'Oh, it was not anything. I was thinking about Kay learning to be a knight.'

'And well you may grieve,' exclaimed Merlyn hotly. 'A lot of brainless unicorns swaggering about and calling themselves educated just because they can push each other off a horse with a bit of stick! It makes me tired. Why, I believe Sir Ector would have been gladder to get a by-our-

*T. H. White's nickname for Arthur as a boy.

lady tilting blue for your tutor, that swings himself along on his knuckles like an anthropoid ape, rather than a magician of known probity and international reputation with first-class honours from every European university. The trouble with the Norman Aristocracy is that they are games-mad, that is what it is, games-mad.'

He broke off indignantly and deliberately made the sergeant's ears flap slowly twice, in unison.

'I was not thinking quite about that,' said the Wart. 'As a matter of fact, I was thinking how nice it would be to be a knight, like Kay.'

'Well, you will be one soon enough, won't you?' asked the old man, impatiently.

Wart did not answer.

'Won't you?'

Merlyn turned round and looked closely at the boy through his spectacles.

'What is the matter now?' he enquired nastily. His inspection had shown him that his pupil was trying not to cry, and if he spoke in a kind voice he would break down and do it.

'I shall not be a knight,' replied the Wart coldly. Merlyn's trick had worked and he no longer wanted to weep: he wanted to kick Merlyn. 'I shall not be a knight because I am not a proper son of Sir Ector's. They will knight Kay, and I shall be his squire.'

Merlyn's back was turned again, but his eyes were bright behind his spectacles. 'Too bad,' he said, without commiseration.

The Wart burst out with all his thoughts aloud. 'Oh,' he cried, 'but I should have liked to be born with a proper father and mother, so that I could be a knight errant.'

'What would you have done?'

'I should have had a splendid suit of armour and dozens of spears and a black horse standing eighteen hands, and I should have called myself The Black Knight. And I should have hoved at a well or a ford or something and made all true knights that came that way to joust with me for the honour of their ladies, and I should have spared them all after I had given them a great fall. And I should live out of doors all the year round in a pavilion, and never do anything but joust and go on quests and bear away the prize at tournaments, and I should not ever tell anybody my name.'

'Your wife will scarcely enjoy the life.'

'Oh, I am not going to have a wife. I think they are stupid.

'I shall have to have a lady-love, though,' added the future knight uncomfortably, 'so that I can wear her favour in my helm, and do deeds in her honour.'

A bumblebee came zooming between them, under the grandstand and out into the sunlight.

'Would you like to see some real knights errant?' asked the magician slowly. 'Now, for the sake of your education?'

'Oh, I would! We have never even had a tournament since I was here.'

'I suppose it could be managed.'

'Oh, please do. You could take me to some like you did to the fish.'

'I suppose it is educational, in a way.'

'It is very educational,' said the Wart. 'I can't think of anything more educational than to see some real knights fighting. Oh, won't you please do it?'

'Do you prefer any particular knight?'

'King Pellinore,' he said immediately. He had a weakness for this gentleman since their strange encounter in the Forest.

Merlyn said, 'That will do very well. Put your hands to your sides and relax your muscles. *Cabricias arci thuram*, *catalamus*, *singulariter*, *nominativa*, *haec musa*. Shut your eyes and keep them shut. *Bonus*, *Bona*, *Bonum*. Here we go. *Deus Sanctus*, *est-ne oratio Latinas? Etiam*, *oui*, *quare? Pourquoi? Quai substantivo et adjectivum concordat in generi*, *numerum et casus*. Here we are.'

While this incantation was going on, the patient felt some queer sensations. First he could hear the sergeant calling out to Kay, 'Nah, then, nah then, keep the 'eels dahn and swing the body from the 'ips.' Then the words got smaller and smaller, as if he were looking at his feet through the wrong end of a telescope, and began to swirl round in a cone, as if they were at the pointed bottom end of a whirlpool which was sucking him into the air. Then there was nothing but a loud rotating roaring and hissing noise which rose to such a tornado that he felt that he could not stand it any more. Finally there was utter silence and Merlyn saying, 'Here we are.' All this happened in about the time that it would take a sixpenny rocket to start off with its fiery swish, bend down from its climax and disperse itself in thunder and coloured stars. He opened his eyes just at the moment when one would have heard the invisible stick hitting the ground.

They were lying under a beech tree in the Forest Sauvage.

'Here we are,' said Merlyn. 'Get up and dust your clothes.

'And there, I think,' continued the magician, in a tone of satisfaction because his spells had worked for once without a hitch, 'is your friend, King Pellinore, pricking toward us o'er the plain.'

'Hallo, hallo,' cried King Pellinore, popping his visor up and down. 'It's the young boy with the feather bed, isn't it, I say, what?'

'Yes, it is,' said the Wart. 'And I am very glad to see you. Did you manage to catch the Beast?'

'No,' said King Pellinore. 'Didn't catch the beast. Oh, do come here, you brachet, and leave that bush alone. Tcha! Tcha! Naughty, naughty! She runs riot, you know, what. Very keen on rabbits. I tell you there's nothing in it, you beastly dog. Tcha! Tcha! Leave it, leave it! Oh, do come to heel, like I tell you.

'She never does come to heel,' he added.

At this the dog put a cock pheasant out of the bush, which rocketed off with a tremendous clatter, and the dog became so excited that it ran round its master three or four times at the end of its rope, panting hoarsely as if it had asthma. King Pellinore's horse stood patiently while the rope was wound round its legs, and Merlyn and the Wart had to catch the brachet and unwind it before the conversation could go on.

'I say,' said King Pellinore. 'Thank you very much, I must say. Won't you introduce me to your friend, what?'

'This is my tutor Merlyn, a great magician.'

'How-de-do,' said the King. 'Always like to meet magicians. In fact I always like to meet anybody. It passes the time away, what, on a quest.'

'Hail,' said Merlyn, in his most mysterious manner.

'Hail,' replied the King, anxious to make a good impression.

They shook hands.

'Did you say Hail?' inquired the King, looking about him nervously. 'I thought it was going to be fine, myself.'

'He meant How-do-you-do,' explained the Wart.

'Ah, yes, How-de-do?'

They shook hands again.

'Good afternoon,' said King Pellinore. 'What do you think the weather looks like now?'

'I think it looks like an anti-cyclone.'

'Ah, yes,' said the King. 'An anti-cyclone. Well, I suppose I ought to be getting along.'

At this the King trembled very much, opened and shut his visor several times, coughed, wove his reins into a knot, exclaimed, 'I beg your pardon?' and showed signs of cantering away.

'He is a white magician,' said the Wart. 'You need not be afraid of him. He is my best friend, your majesty, and in any case he generally gets his spells muddled up.'

'Ah, yes,' said King Pellinore. 'A white magician, what? How small the world is, is it not? How-de-do?'

'Hail,' said Merlyn.

'Hail,' said King Pellinore.

They shook hands for the third time.

'I should not go away,' said the wizard, 'if I were you. Sir Grummore Grummursum is on the way to challenge you to a joust.'

'No, you don't say? Sir What-you-may-call-it coming here to challenge me to a joust?'

'Assuredly.'

'Good handicap man?'

'I should think it would be an even match.'

'Well, I must say,' exclaimed the King, 'it never hails but it pours.'

'Hail,' said Merlyn.

'Hail,' said King Pellinore.

'Hail,' said the Wart.

'Now I really won't shake hands with anybody else,' announced the monarch. 'We must assume that we have all met before.'

'Is Sir Grummore really coming,' inquired the Wart, hastily changing the subject, 'to challenge King Pellinore to a battle?'

'Look yonder,' said Merlyn, and both of them looked in the direction of his outstretched finger.

Sir Grummore Grummursum was cantering up the clearing in full panoply of war. Instead of his ordinary helmet with a visor he was wearing the proper tilting-helm, which looked like a large coal-scuttle, and as he cantered he clanged.

He was singing his old school song:

'We'll tilt together
Steady from crupper to poll,
And nothin' in life shall sever
Our love for the dear old coll.
Follow-up, follow-up, follow-up, follow-up, follow-up
Till the shield ring again and again
With the clanks of the clanky true men.'

'Goodness,' exclaimed King Pellinore. 'It's about two months since I had a proper tilt, and last winter they put me up to eighteen. That was when they had the new handicaps.'

Sir Grummore had arrived while he was speaking, and had recognised the Wart.

'Mornin',' said Sir Grummore. 'You're Sir Ector's boy, ain't you? And who's that chap in the comic hat?'

'That is my tutor,' said the Wart hurriedly. 'Merlyn, the magician.'

Sir Grummore looked at Merlyn – magicians were considered rather middle-class by the true jousting set in those days – and said distantly, 'Ah, a magician. How-de-do?'

'And this is King Pellinore,' said the Wart. 'Sir Grummore Grummursum – King Pellinore.'

'How-de-do?' inquired Sir Grummore.

'Hail,' said King Pellinore. 'No, I mean it won't hail, will it?'

'Nice day,' said Sir Grummore.

'Yes, it is nice, isn't it, what?'

'Been questin' today?'

'Oh, yes, thank you. Always am questing, you know. After the Questing Beast.'

'Interestin' job, that, very.'

'Yes, it is interesting. Would you like to see some fewmets?'

'By Jove, yes. Like to see some fewmets.'

'I have some better ones at home, but these are quite good, really.'

'Bless my soul. So these are her fewmets.'

'Yes, these are her fewmets.'

'Interestin' fewmets.'

'Yes, they are interesting, aren't they? Only you get tired of them,' added King Pellinore.

'Well, well. It's a fine day, isn't it?'

'Yes, it is rather fine.'

'Suppose we'd better have a joust, eh, what?'

'Yes, I suppose we had better,' said King Pellinore, 'really.'

'What shall we have it for?'

'Oh, the usual thing, I suppose. Would one of you kindly help me on with my helm?'

They all three had to help him on eventually, for, what with the unscrewing of screws and the easing of nuts and bolts which the King had clumsily set on the wrong thread when getting up in a hurry that morning, it was quite a feat of engineering to get him out of his helmet and into his helm. The helm was an enormous thing like an oil drum, padded inside with two thicknesses of leather and three inches of straw.

As soon as they were ready, the two knights stationed themselves at each end of the clearing and then advanced to meet in the middle.

'Fair knight,' said King Pellinore, 'I pray thee tell me thy name.'

'That me regards,' replied Sir Grummore, using the proper formula.

'That is uncourteously said,' said King Pellinore, 'what? For no knight ne dreadeth for to speak his name openly, but for some reason of shame.'

'Be that as it may, I choose that thou shalt not know my name as at this time, for no askin'.'

'Then you must stay and joust with me, false knight.'

'Haven't you got that wrong, Pellinore?' inquired Sir Grummore. 'I believe it ought to be "thou shalt".'

'Oh, I'm sorry, Sir Grummore. Yes, so it should, of course. Then thou shalt stay and joust with me, false knight.'

Without further words, the two gentlemen retreated to the opposite ends of the clearing, fewtered their spears, and prepared to hurtle together in the preliminary charge.

'I think we had better climb this tree,' said Merlyn. 'You never know what will happen in a joust like this.'

They climbed up the big beech, which had easy branches sticking out in all directions, and the Wart stationed himself toward the end of a smooth bough about fifteen feet up, where he could get a good view. Nothing is so comfortable to sit in as a beech.

To be able to picture the terrible battle which now took place, there is one thing which ought to be known. A knight in his full armour of those days, or at any rate during the heaviest days of armour, was generally carrying as much or more than his own weight in metal. He often weighed no less than twenty-two stone, and sometimes as much as twenty-five. This meant that his horse had to be a slow and enormous weight-carrier, like the farm horse of today, and that his own movements were so hampered by his burden of iron and padding that they were toned down into slow motion, as on the cinema.

'They're off!' cried the Wart, holding his breath with excitement.

Slowly and majestically, the ponderous horses lumbered into a walk. The spears, which had been pointing in the air, bowed to a horizontal line and pointed at each other. King Pellinore and Sir Grummore could be seen to be thumping their horses' sides with their heels for all they were worth, and in a few minutes the splendid animals had shambled into an earth-shaking imitation of a trot. Clank, rumble, thump-thump went the horses, and now the two knights were flapping their elbows and legs in unison, showing a good deal of daylight at their seats. There was a change in tempo, and Sir Grummore's horse could be definitely seen to be cantering. In another minute King Pellinore's was doing so too. It was a terrible spectacle.

'Oh, dear!' exclaimed the Wart, feeling ashamed that his blood-thirstiness had been responsible for making these two knights joust before him. 'Do you think they will kill each other?'

'Dangerous sport,' said Merlyn, shaking his head.

'Now!' cried the Wart.

With a blood-curdling beat of iron hoofs the mighty

equestrians came together. Their spears wavered for a moment within a few inches of each other's helms – each had chosen the difficult point-stroke – and then they were galloping off in opposite directions. Sir Grummore drove his spear deep into the beech tree where they were sitting, and stopped dead. King Pellinore, who had been run away with, vanished altogether behind his back.

'Is it safe to look?' inquired the Wart, who had shut his eyes at the critical moment.

'Quite safe,' said Merlyn. 'It will take them some time to get back in position.'

'Whoa, whoa, I say!' cried King Pellinore in muffled and distant tones, far away among the gorse bushes.

'Hi, Pellinore, hi!' shouted Sir Grummore. 'Come back, my dear fellah, I'm over here.'

There was a long pause, while the complicated stations of the two knights readjusted themselves, and then King Pellinore was at the opposite end from that at which he had started, while Sir Grummore faced him from his original position.

'Traitor knight!' cried Sir Grummore.

'Yield, recreant, what?' cried King Pellinore.

They fewtered their spears again, and thundered into the charge.

'Oh,' said the Wart, 'I hope they don't hurt themselves.'

But the two mounts were patiently blundering together, and the two knights had simultaneously decided on the sweeping stroke. Each held his spear at right angles toward the left, and, before the Wart could say anything further, there was a terrific yet melodious thump. Clang! went the armour, like a motor omnibus in collision with a smithy, and the jousters were sitting side by side on the green sward, while their horses cantered off in opposite directions.

'A splendid fall,' said Merlyn.

The two horses pulled themselves up, their duty done, and began resignedly to eat the sward. King Pellinore and Sir Grummore sat looking straight before them, each with the other's spear clasped hopefully under his arm.

'Well!' said the Wart. 'What a bump! They both seem to be all right, so far.'

Sir Grummore and King Pellinore laboriously got up.

'Defend thee,' cried King Pellinore.

'God save thee,' cried Sir Grummore.

With this they drew their swords and rushed together with such ferocity that each, after dealing the other a dint on the helm, sat down suddenly backwards.

'Bah!' cried King Pellinore.

'Booh!' cried Sir Grummore, also sitting down.

'Mercy,' exclaimed the Wart. 'What a combat!'

The knights had now lost their tempers and the battle was joined in earnest. It did not matter much, however, for they were so encased in metal that they could not do each other much damage. It took them so long to get up, and the dealing of a blow when you weighed the eighth part of a ton was such a cumbrous business, that every stage of the contest could be marked and pondered.

In the first stage King Pellinore and Sir Grummore stood opposite each other for about half an hour, and walloped each other on the helm. There was only opportunity for one blow at a time, so they more or less took it in turns, King Pellinore striking while Sir Grummore was recovering, and vice versa. At first, if either of them dropped his sword or got it stuck in the ground, the other put in two or three extra blows while he was patiently fumbling for it or trying to tug it out. Later, they fell into the rhythm of the thing more perfectly, like the toy mechanical people who saw wood on Christmas trees. Eventually the exercise and the monotony restored their good humour and they began to get bored.

The second stage was introduced as a change, by common consent. Sir Grummore stumped off to one end of the clearing, while King Pellinore plodded off to the other. Then they turned round and swayed backward and forward once or twice, in order to get their weight on their toes. When they leaned forward they had to run forward, to keep up with their weight, and if they leaned too far backward they fell down. So even walking was complicated. When they had got their weight properly distributed in front of them, so that they were just off their balance, each broke into a trot to keep up with himself. They hurtled together as it had been two boars.

They met in the middle, breast to breast, with a noise of shipwreck and great bells tolling, and both, bouncing off, fell breathless on their backs. They lay thus for a few minutes, panting. Then they slowly began to heave themselves to their feet, and it was obvious that they had lost their tempers once again.

King Pellinore had not only lost his temper but he seemed to have been a bit astonished by the impact. He got up facing the wrong way, and could not find Sir Grummore. There was some excuse for this, since he had only a slit to peep through – and that was three inches away from his eye owing to the padding of straw – but he looked muddled as well. Perhaps he had broken his spectacles. Sir Grummore was quick to seize his advantage.

'Take that!' cried Sir Grummore, giving the unfortunate monarch a two-handed swipe on the nob as he was slowly turning his head from side to side, peering in the opposite direction.

King Pellinore turned round morosely, but his opponent had been too quick for him. He had ambled round so that he was still behind the King, and now gave him another terrific blow in the same place.

'Where are you?' asked King Pellinore.

'Here,' cried Sir Grummore, giving him another.

The poor King turned himself round as nimbly as possible, but Sir Grummore had given him the slip again.

'Tally-ho back!' shouted Sir Grummore, with another wallop.

'I think you're a *cad*,' said the King.

'Wallop!' replied Sir Grummore, doing it.

What with the preliminary crash, the repeated blows on the back of his head, and the puzzling nature of his opponent, King Pellinore could now be seen to be visibly troubled in his brains. He swayed backward and forward under the hail of blows which were administered, and feebly wagged his arms.

'Poor King,' said the Wart. 'I wish he would not hit him so.'

As if in answer to his wish, Sir Grummore paused in his labours.

'Do you want Pax?' asked Sir Grummore.

King Pellinore made no answer.

Sir Grummore favoured him with another whack and said, 'If you don't say Pax, I shall cut your head off.'

'I won't,' said the King.

Whang! went the sword on the top of his head.

Whang! it went again.

Whang! for the third time.

'Pax,' said King Pellinore, mumbling rather.

Then, just as Sir Grummore was relaxing with the fruits of victory, he swung round upon him, shouted 'Non!' at the top of his voice, and gave him a good push in the middle of the chest.

Sir Grummore fell over backwards.

'Well!' exclaimed the Wart. 'What a cheat! I would not have thought it of him.'

King Pellinore hurriedly sat on his victim's chest, thus increasing the weight upon him to a quarter of a ton and making it quite impossible for him to move, and began to undo Sir Grummore's helm.

'You said Pax!'

'I said Pax Non under my breath.'

'It's a swindle.'

'It's not.'

'You're a cad.'

'No, I'm not.'

'Yes, you are.'

'No, I'm not.'

'Yes, you are.'

'I said Pax Non.'

'You said Pax.'

'No, I didn't.'

'Yes, you did.'

'No, I didn't.'

'Yes, you did.'

By this time Sir Grummore's helm was unlaced and they could see his bare head glaring at King Pellinore, quite purple in the face.

'Yield thee, recreant,' said the King.

'Shan't,' said Sir Grummore.

'You have got to yield, or I shall cut off your head.'

'Cut it off then.'

'Oh, come on,' said the King. 'You know you have to yield when your helm is off.'

'Feign I,' said Sir Grummore.

'Well, I shall just cut your head off.'

'I don't care.'

The King waved his sword menacingly in the air.

'Go on,' said Sir Grummore. 'I dare you to.'

The King lowered his sword and said, 'Oh, I say, do yield, please.'

'You yield,' said Sir Grummore.

'But I can't yield, I am on top of you after all, am I not, what?'

'Well, I have feigned yieldin'.'

'Oh, come on, Grummore. I do think you are a cad not to yield. You know very well I can't cut your head off.'

'I would not yield to a cheat who started fightin' after he said Pax.'

'I am not a cheat.'

'You are a cheat.'

'No, I'm not.'

'Yes, you are.'

'No, I'm not.'

'Yes, you are.'

'Very well,' said King Pellinore. 'You can jolly well get up and put on your helm and we will have a fight. I won't be called a cheat for anybody.'

'Cheat!' said Sir Grummore.

They stood up and fumbled together with the helm, hissing, 'No, I'm not' – 'Yes, you are,' until it was safely on. Then they retreated to opposite ends of the clearing, got their weight upon their toes, and came rumbling and thundering together like two runaway trams.

Unfortunately they were now so cross that they had both ceased to be vigilant, and in the fury of the moment they missed each other altogether. The momentum of their armour was too great for them to stop till they had passed each other handsomely, and then they manoeuvred about in such a manner that neither happened to come within the other's range of vision. It was funny watching them, because King Pellinore, having already been caught from behind once, was continually spinning round to look behind him, and Sir Grummore, having used the stratagem himself, was doing the same thing. Thus they wandered for some five minutes, standing still, listening, clanking, crouching, creeping, peering, walking on tiptoe, and occasionally making a chance swipe behind their backs. Once they were standing within a few feet of each other, back to back, only to stalk off in opposite directions with infinite precaution, and once King Pellinore did hit Sir Grummore with one of his back strokes, but they both immediately spun round so often that they became giddy and mislaid each other afresh.

After five minutes Sir Grummore said, 'All right, Pellinore. It is no use hidin'. I can see where you are.'

'I am not hiding,' exclaimed King Pellinore indignantly. 'Where am I?'

They discovered each other and went up close together, face to face.

'Cad,' said Sir Grummore.

'Yah,' said King Pellinore.

They turned round and marched off to their corners, seething with indignation.

'Swindler,' shouted Sir Grummore.

'Beastly bully,' shouted King Pellinore.

With this they summoned all their energies together for one decisive encounter, leaned forward, lowered their heads like two billy-goats, and positively sprinted together for the final blow. Alas, their aim was poor. They missed each other by about five yards, passed at full steam doing at least eight knots, like ships that pass in the night but speak not to each other in passing, and hurtled onward to their doom. Both knights began waving their arms like windmills, anti-clockwise, in the vain effort to slow up. Both continued with undiminished speed. Then Sir Grummore rammed his head against the beech in which the Wart was sitting, and King Pellinore collided with a chestnut at the other side of the clearing. The trees shook, the forest rang. Blackbirds and squirrels cursed and wood-pigeons flew out of their leafy perches half a mile away. The two knights stood to attention while one could count three. Then, with a last unanimous melodious clang, they both fell prostrate on the fatal sward.

'Stunned,' said Merlyn, 'I should think.'

'Oh, dear,' said the Wart. 'Ought we to get down and help them?'

'We could pour water on their heads,' said Merlyn reflectively, 'if there was any water. But I don't suppose they would thank us for making their armour rusty. They will be all right. Besides, it is time that we were home.'

'But they might be dead!'

'They are not dead, I know. In a minute or two they will come round and go off home to dinner.'

'Poor King Pellinore has not got a home.'

'Then Sir Grummore will invite him to stay the night. They will be the best of friends when they come to. They always are.'

'Do you think so?'

'My dear boy, I know so. Shut your eyes and we will be off.'

The Wart gave in to Merlyn's superior knowledge. 'Do you think,' he asked with his eyes shut, 'that Sir Grummore has a feather bed?'

'Probably.'

'Good,' said the Wart. 'That will be nice for King Pellinore, even if he was stunned.'

The Latin words were spoken, and the secret passes made. The funnel of whistling noise and space received them. In two seconds they were lying under the grand-stand, and the sergeant's voice was calling from the opposite side of the tilting ground, 'Nah, then, Master Art, nah then. You've been a-snoozing there long enough. Come aht into the sunlight 'ere with Master Kay, one-two, one-two, and see some real tilting.'

Bibliography

1 Translations

The Mabinogion tr. Gwyn and Thomas Jones (Everyman 1947)

Geoffrey of Monmouth, *The History of the Kings of Britain*, tr. Lewis Thorpe (Penguin 1966)

Wace and Layamon, *Arthurian Chronicles represented by Wace and Layamon*, tr. L. A. Paton (Everyman 1912, 1970)

Marie de France, *Lais* tr. Eugene Mason (Everyman 1911)

Chrétien de Troyes, *Arthurian Romances* (excludes *Perceval*), tr. W. W. Comfort (Everyman 1914)

Gottfried von Strassburg, *Tristan* (with *Tristan* of Thomas), tr. A. T. Hatto (Penguin 1960)

Wolfram von Eschenbach, *Parzival*, tr. Helen M. Mustard and Charles E. Passage (Vintage 1961)

The Quest of the Holy Grail tr. Pauline Matrasso (Penguin 1969)

The Death of King Arthur tr. James Cable (Penguin 1971)

Sir Gawain and the Green Knight tr. Brian Stone (Penguin 1974)

Sir Thomas Malory, *Works*, ed. E. Vinaver (Oxford 1967)

2 Modern Critical Works

R. S. Loomis, *Arthurian Literature in the Middle Ages* (Oxford 1959)

Richard Barber, *King Arthur in Legend and History* (Boydell/Rowman and Littlefield 1974)

J. D. Merriman, *The Flower of Kings* (University of Kansas 1973)

N. C. Starr, *King Arthur Today* (University of Florida 1954)

Illustrations

The source of each illustration is acknowledged below the picture. Full references are as follows:

Colour

Bodleian Library, Oxford: *Guiron le Courtois*, MS Douce 282, f.16 and f.17; *Queste del Saint Graal*, MS Douce 215, f.14

Chetham's Library, Manchester: *Flores Historiarum*, MS 6712, col. 185

City of Birmingham Museums and Art Gallery: Sir Edward Burne-Jones, *The Vision of the Holy Grail*, tapestry by Morris and Co.; Frederick Sandys, *Morgan le Fay*

City of Manchester Art Gallery: James G. Archer, *La Mort d'Arthur*

John Rylands University Library of Manchester: *Lancelot*, MS Fr 1, f.212

Photo Giraudon, Paris: Bibliothèque nationale, Paris: *Lancelot*, MS Arsenal 3479, f.1; Chantilly, Musée Conde: *Tristan*, MS 315–317, f.59 and 234

Tate Gallery, London (photos John Webb): J. W. Waterhouse, *The Lady of Shalott*; William Morris, *Guenevere*; Dante Gabriel Rossetti, *The Damsel of the Sanct Grael*

Wadsworth Atheneum, Hartford, Connecticut (Ella Gallup Sumner and Mary Catlin Sumner Collection): W. Holman Hunt, *The Lady of Shalott*

Illustrations

Black and white

Augustinermuseum, Freiburg im Breisgau (photo Herder): Malterer tapestry

Bibliothèque nationale, Paris: Chrétien de Troyes, *Yvain*, MS Fr 1433, f.67^{v}; *Tristan*, MS Fr 100, f.50; *Queste del Saint Graal*, MS Fr 342, f.84^{v}; *Mort Artu*, MS Fr 342, f.186; Chrétien de Troyes, *Perceval*, MS Fr 12577, f.84^{v}; *Queste del Saint Graal*, MS Fr 343, f.3, 8^{v}

Bibliothèque royale Albert Ier, Brussels: *Chroniques de Hainaut*, MS 9243, f.36^{v}, 39^{v}, 45, 55^{v}

Bradford City Art Gallery: *Arthur and Lancelot*, stained glass window designed by William Morris for Morris & Co.

Bristol City Art Gallery: Sidney E. Paget, *Lancelot and Elaine* (1891)

British Museum, Department of Medieval Antiquities: Tristan and Mark, from Chertsey Abbey tiles (Reproduced by courtesy of the Trustees of the British Museum)

British Tourist Authority: Round Table at Winchester Castle

Cecil Higgins Museum, Bradford: Dante Gabriel Rossetti, *Tristan and Iseult*

City of Birmingham Museums and Art Gallery: Arthur Gaskin, *Kilhwych, the king's son* (1901); Dante Gabriel Rossetti, *Sir Launcelot in the queen's chamber*

Herzog Anton Ulrich Museum, Brunswick: *Gawain* embroidery, fourteenth century

Lambeth Palace Library: *St Albans Chronicle*, MS 6, f.54^{v}, 66^{v}

Metropolitan Museum, New York: *Nine worthies* tapestry (Cloisters Collection); Ivory casket showing adventures of Gawain and Lancelot

Musée du Louvre (photo Musées nationaux, Paris): Ivory casket showing adventures of Perceval

National Monuments Record: Lincoln Cathedral, misericord showing Yvain trapped by portcullis

Soprintendenza Provinciale Beni Culturali, Bolzano (photo H. Walder): Iwein fresco from Schloss Rodeneck, South Tirol

Staatsbibliothek, Munich: Gottfried von Strassburg, *Tristan*, MS Germ. 51, f.15^{v}, 82, 90; Wolfram von Eschenbach, *Parzival*, MS Germ. 19, f.49, 49^{v}, 50, 50^{v}

Tate Gallery, London: F. G. Stephens, *The death of Arthur* (*c.* 1850–5); Dante Gabriel Rossetti, *Arthur and the weeping queens*; William Etty, *Britomart redeems fair Amoret*; William Morris, *Guinevere and Elaine* (cartoon for stained glass); William Morris, *Guenevere*; David Jones: *Illustrations to the Arthurian Legends: Guinevere*

Book Illustrations

Arthur Rackham, illustration to Sir Thomas Malory, *The Death of King Arthur* (Macmillan 1917); facing p. 486, *Arthur slays Mordred*

Walter Crane, illustration to Henry Gilbert, *Stories of the Knights of the Round Table* (T. C. and E. C. Jack, 1914): facing p. 163, *The Death of Sir Lancelot*

Gustave Doré, illustration to Alfred Lord Tennyson, *The Idylls of the King* (1867); facing p. 338, *Arthur says farewell to Guinevere*

Eleanor Fortescue-Brickdale, illustration to Alfred Lord Tennyson, *The Idylls of the King* (Hutchinson, n.d., *c.* 1910); facing p. 110, *Elaine*

W. Russell Flint, illustration to Sir Thomas Malory, *Le Morte Darthur*, (Grant Richards 1911); facing p. 328, *Tristram fights his rival Palomides*

Other photographs are from the author's collection.

Endpapers

Illustrations by Aubrey Beardsley to *Le Morte Darthur*, first published 1893. The originals are in one colour; the pagination is that of the third edition (1927).

Front: Bedivere casts Excalibur in the Lake (p. 525)

Back: 'How Sir Lancelot was known by Dame Elaine': Elaine, daughter of king Pelles, finds Lancelot in madness (pp. 364–5).

I am most grateful to all those who have supplied photographs, and should like to thank in particular Professor Hans Sklenar of Göttingen and Dr Karl Wolfsgruber of the Soprintendenza provinciale ai beni Culturali, Bolzano, for help in obtaining photos of the Schloss Rodeneck frescoes, and Miss Christine Stenstrom of the Pierpont Morgan Library for providing a microfilm and the photographs of the Pierpont Morgan MSS 805–6.

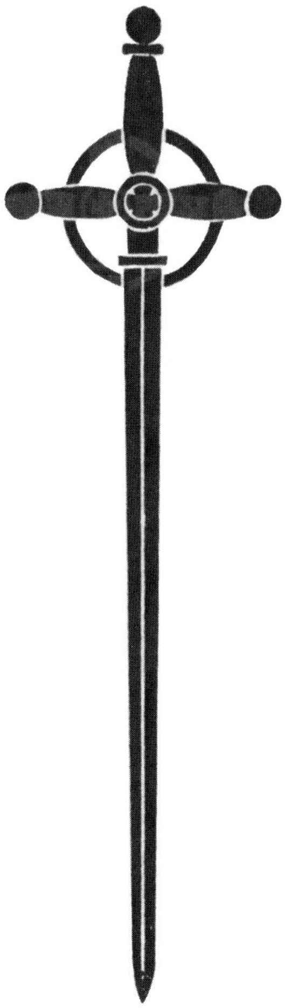